SELECTED LETTERS OF CHARLES DICKENS

Also edited by David Paroissien

CHARLES DICKENS: *Pictures from Italy*

SELECTED LETTERS
OF CHARLES DICKENS

Edited and arranged by
David Paroissien

Twayne Publishers
Boston
1985

Published by Twayne Publishers
A Division of G. K. Hall & Co.
70 Lincoln St.
Boston, Massachusetts 02111

First Printing

Printed in Hong Kong

Library of Congress Cataloging in Publication Data
Dickens, Charles, 1812–1870.
    Selected letters of Charles Dickens.
Bibliography: p.
Includes index.
    1. Dickens, Charles, 1812–1870—Correspondence.
2. Novelists, English—19th century—Correspondence.
I. Paroissien, David.   II. Title.
PR4581.A4   1985   823′.8   84–19270
ISBN 0–8057–8536–1 (hardcover)
ISBN 0–8057–8537–X (paperback)

To Miriam

Contents

Acknowledgements

This volume owes an obvious debt to the outstanding scholarship of the editors of the Pilgrim Edition of *The Letters of Charles Dickens*, vols I–V, as well as to the important biographical and historical research of such eminent Dickensians as Michael Allen, Philip Collins, Angus Easson, K. J. Fielding and Edgar Johnson. I wish here to recognize also Michael Slater, whose *Dickens and Women* (1983) provides the most detailed and authoritative study of Dickens's relationship with his wife in print. Unfortunately Dr Slater's study appeared too late for me to use when I wrote the Introduction to Part I.

The interlibrary loan staff of the University of Massachusetts, Amherst, especially Edla Holm, helped me obtain important materials, as did John Kendall, the University librarian. To both I wish to record my particular appreciation of their unfailing co-operation and support. I am also indebted to other scholars and to a number of reference librarians, all of whom answered questions and generously contributed their help. Thus I owe particular thanks to Duane DeVries, Joseph Donohue, K. A. Doughty, Mary Drake McFeely, William McFeely, Claudia Fontaine, R. Howes, Paul Mariani, Elaine Miller, Alfred L. Nelson, Diana Orton, Bruce Sajdak, Peter Walne, Michael Wolff and Howard Ziff. I am grateful, as well, to the staff of the Beinecke Rare Book and Manuscript Library and to the Beinecke Library, Yale University, for permission to reproduce the sketch of Dickens by Harry Furniss on the cover. My thanks also go to Caroline Gouin and Mary Coty for their excellent typing. I wish also to record my thanks to the University of Massachusetts, Amherst, for a research grant to cover the cost of copying the three volumes of the Nonesuch *Letters*. To Everett Emerson, Thomas T. Beeler, Donna S. Sanzone, and Julia Steward I am most especially grateful for their support and encouragement throughout the various stages of the work.

Preface

Thomas Carlyle remarked that to the biographer the autograph letter represented what was 'once all luminous as a burning beacon, every word of it a live coal, in its time'. While selecting and arranging an author's letters cannot be equated with writing a biography, any compilation of Dickens's 'live coals' involves a degree of choice that implies a biographical perspective of the subject. In this selection of Dickens's letters I have, therefore, deliberately sought to structure the life I present here by substituting for the conventional chronological arrangement of letters one that seems to reflect most dramatically the main aspects of Dickens's life and work. In my judgement, three major 'beacons' coexist: the man as he was known to his family and friends, the author who saw himself as the public voice of conscience in Victorian England, and the writer who dedicated himself to his art.

By grouping the letters around these three focal points, I believe a clear picture of the private and public Dickens will emerge as Dickens describes, in his own words, some of the main highlights of his life. A brief introduction to each of the three sections serves to orient the reader and place the contents in an appropriate biographical, social and artistic setting. Following the three Introductions the text of the letters appears, to which I have added explanatory notes, either at the end of individual letters, or, where appropriate, at the end of a group of letters. An ellipses in square brackets [. . .] signifies passages I have dropped in the interest of brevity; otherwise I give Dickens's letters as they first appeared in my copy-text.

This selection is based on the three volumes of letters that were published in 1938 under the direction of Walter Dexter. The Nonesuch Letters, as these volumes are generally known, were part of an expensive collected edition of all Dickens's writings, an enterprise planned by its designers to 'end all editions of Dickens'. To make the project attractive to wealthy collectors a limited edition of 877 sets was prepared for sale to subscribers. As part of this edition, Walter Dexter assembled in three volumes the most extensive collection of Dickens letters hitherto published.

One consequence of the decision to include three volumes of letters as part of this limited edition is their relative unavailability, a source of constant frustration to the Dickens reader and to all except privileged owners of the Nonesuch Dickens or those with access to the letters through the rare book division of a major university library. In recent years, this situation has been much improved by the appearance of five volumes of the Pilgrim Edition of Dickens's letters, but the unavoidable slowness of this enterprise and the high price of each volume continue to leave the general reader at a disadvantage.

Redressing this situation appealed to me for two reasons. First, no broadly representative selection of letters was currently available, and, second, the letters that Dexter and his editors published in 1938 still constitute the most comprehensive compilation of Dickens's published correspondence extant today. Such riches, I concluded, deserved a wider audience, for among the Nonesuch volumes one finds not only letters which reveal Dickens as he actually was but portraits all the more memorable for their brilliant language. Through a special arrangement, the Nonesuch texts were placed at my disposal, allowing me to put together a selection from a range of correspondence unavailable to any previous editor. This selection is not likely to be superseded until such time as the Pilgrim editors make one from their own greater holdings of Dickens correspondence. At the publication of their most recent volume in 1981, the editors stated that the total number of letters known to them currently stands at 13 452, more than double the number known and published in 1938.

The magnitude of this addition to the canon of Dickens letters deserves further comment. During the years 1820 to 1849 – the period of correspondence so far covered in the five volumes published in the Pilgrim edition – the editors have added over fifteen hundred letters to those previously known and published for the same period. Without question, many of these letters advance our knowledge of Dickens's life and provide information formerly concealed or ignored. Dickens's letters to the de la Rues provide one instance, as do the recently discovered letters Dickens wrote to Richard Bentley and Thomas Mitton. Through these letters we learn at first hand of Dickens's passionate interest in mesmerism, follow in closer detail than we have done before his business dealings with Bentley, and discover more about the extent to which Dickens's relatives, especially his father, pestered him for money. For copyright reasons, I am unable to include samples of these letters in my selection.

Despite the obvious disadvantage in working from the less comprehensive Nonesuch Letters, I do not believe that, viewed as a whole, the Nonesuch volumes do Dickens a disservice. Until the last volume of the Pilgrim Letters is published, sometime in the twenty-first century, the letters assembled in 1938 will continue to represent more fully than any other collection the various sides of Dickens's personality his correspondence furnishes. Readers will see among these letters a multiplicity of self-portraits, whose lines emerge from each of the sections I have constructed. Unquestionably, the completed Pilgrim edition will extend that array and add fresh dimensions. But it will not, in any fundamental way, alter the authentic aspects of Dickens present in the Nonesuch Letters or indeed in the selection I have assembled.

A word of qualification about the number of new letters in the Pilgrim edition illustrates the point. The exciting prospect of recently-discovered correspondence loses some of its impact, for example, when one pauses to reflect that the phrase 'unpublished letter' often refers to a fragment of no more than a single sentence. Thanks for 'the most excellent paté,' Dickens wrote on 10 March 1848. 'I shall be much obliged to you,' he notified the same correspondent in May of the previous year, 'if you will have the goodness to send me round . . . half a dozen of good dry sherry, and half a dozen of dry old port.' And so on. One finds notes from Dickens to his banker about deposits and debits to his account, instructions to his printer to begin a chapter on a new page, notes accepting and notes rejecting social engagements, and many others making some appointments and cancelling or postponing others. 'I write 100 letters a day, about these plays,' Dickens complained to T. J. Thompson on 9 July 1847, referring to the benefit performances of *Every Man in His Humour* and *Comfortable Lodgings* that he organized on behalf of Leigh Hunt and John Poole.

While Dickens's statement is obviously an exaggeration, it accurately conveys the extent to which he, like any energetic Victorian, had to rely on putting pen to paper for the simplest order, question, or request for information. While we reach instinctively for the telephone, Victorians relied on the postal system. And if, like Dickens, they lived in central London, they had for their convenience twelve daily mail deliveries, as well as servants, whom they frequently pressed into service. Under those circumstances, Victorians could post a letter in the morning, receive an answer in the afternoon, and then send a response in the same evening.

I cite these instances of Victorian epistolary practice not to disparage the policy of the Pilgrim editors to include everything Dickens wrote but to make a central point. For the scholar and specialist, the Pilgrim volumes remain an indispensible tool, but, for the more general reader, a selection of letters based on the Nonesuch edition provides an introduction to the essential aspects of Dickens's life and career. That introduction, I contend, will remain true to Dickens even after all his known letters become available. One may forecast this with a reasonable degree of accuracy since all the letters relating to the one major area of Dickens's life biographers know least about – his relationship with Ellen Ternan – appear to have vanished long ago.

It is true that, unlike the team of scholars working for the Pilgrim edition Dexter and his associates reprinted letters from earlier editions of Dickens's letters without checking the text of each letter against either the original or a photograph copy of the same. Thus they inevitably perpetuated misreadings of Dickens's handwriting and other errors in their sources. For the letters in my selection written between 1833 and 1849, I have been able to check the Nonesuch texts against those in the Pilgrim volumes and have recorded significant substantive errors in the notes. But for those written from 1850 onwards, I have had to rely on the Nonesuch transcripts entirely. Fortunately, the proportion of substantive errors I detected does not appear to be high.

The editors of the Nonesuch Letters also laid down a policy quite different from that of the Pilgrim editors with respect to the treatment of Dickens's spelling, misspelling, capitalization, and punctuation. The general rule in transcribing letters for the Pilgrim edition is to follow the original exactly. The Nonesuch editors by contrast, systematically regularized Dickens's eighteenth-century use of capitals, making the novelist's practice conform more nearly to that of the present than the past. They also standardized Dickens's punctuation. When introductory phrases or clauses lacked a comma, they supplied one; non-restrictive clauses without commas received similar treatment, as did appositive phrases and interjections. Similarly, Dickens's misspellings were quietly corrected, commas often substituted for dashes, and arabic numerals spelled out. Some sense, therefore, of the writer's idiosyncracies vanished, including the system of punctuation Dickens introduced in 1846, which he designed for the oral delivery of his works but carried over into his letters of the period as well. Readers for whom exact transcripts are essential will need to consult the Pilgrim volumes for the letters published up to 1849 or wait for future volumes in that monumental project, if they want the text of letters written after 1849.

Meanwhile, the essential Dickens remains. His was too strong a personality, too characteristic an idiom, too powerful a voice to disappear from the paper once he set his pen to it. The *Selected Letters of Charles Dickens*, I believe, reveals that presence.

Columbus Day 1983   D. P.

Abbreviations

AR   *Annual Register: A Review of Public Events at Home and Abroad*
AYR   *All the Year Round*
DN   *Daily News*
DNB   *Dictionary of National Biography*
DSN   *Dickens Studies Newsletter*
Forster   John Forster's *Life of Charles Dickens*, ed. A. J. Hoppé (1969)
Hansard   *Hansard's Parliamentary Debates*
HW   *Household Words*
Lohrli   *The Household Words Office Book*, ed. Anne Lohrli (1973)
Johnson   Edgar Johnson's *Charles Dickens: His Tragedy and Triumph*, 2 vols (1952)
MHC   *Master Humphrey's Clock*
MP   *Miscellaneous Papers*, ed. B. W. Matz
N   Nonesuch Edition of *The Letters of Charles Dickens*, 3 vols (1938)
P   Pilgrim Edition of *The Letters of Charles Dickens*, 5 vols (1965–81)
Radzinowicz   Leon Radzinowicz's *History of English Criminal Law and Administration from 1750*, 4 vols (1948–68)
Speeches   *Speeches of Charles Dickens*, ed. K. J. Fielding (1960)
Stone   *Uncollected Writings of Charles Dickens: Household Words 1850–1859*, ed. Harry Stone. 2 vols (Harmondsworth: Penguin, 1969)
Wheatley   Henry B. Wheatley's *London Past and Present: A Dictionary of its History, Associations, and Traditions*. 3 vols (London: John Murray, 1891)

DICKENS'S MAJOR WORKS IN CHRONOLOGICAL ORDER

SB	*Sketches by Boz* (1836)
PP	*The Pickwick Papers* (1836–7)
OT	*Oliver Twist* (1837–9)
NN	*Nicholas Nickleby* (1838–9)
OCS	*The Old Curiosity Shop* (1840–1)
BR	*Barnaby Rudge* (1841)
AN	*American Notes* (1842)
MC	*Martin Chuzzlewit* (1843–4)
CC	*A Christmas Carol* (1843)
CH	*The Cricket on the Hearth* (1845)
PI	*Pictures from Italy* (1846)
DS	*Dombey and Son* (1846–8)
DC	*David Copperfield* (1849–50)
BH	*Bleak House* (1852–3)
HT	*Hard Times* (1854)
LD	*Little Dorrit* (1855–7)
RP	*Reprinted Pieces* (1858)
TTC	*A Tale of Two Cities* (1859)
GE	*Great Expectations* (1860–1)
UT	*The Uncommercial Traveller* (1861)
OMF	*Our Mutual Friend* (1864–5)
ED	*The Mystery of Edwin Drood* (1870)

Biographical Table: The Early Years

1809   13 June   John D and Elizabeth Barrow married.

1810   28 Oct.   Frances Elizabeth D – 'Fanny' – born (d. 1848).

1812   7 Feb.   Charles John Huffam D born at Mile End Terrace, Portsmouth.

   June   Family moves first to 16 Hawk Street and then to 39 Wish Street, Southsea, Portsmouth (Dec. 1813).

1814   28 Mar.   Alfred Allen D born (d. 5 Sep.).

1815   1 Jan.   JD recalled to the Admiralty Offices in Somerset House and removes his family to London.

1816   23 Apr.   Letitia Mary D born (d. 1893).

1817   Jan.–Mar.   JD stationed temporarily at Sheerness, Kent, where the family move.

   Apr.   JD sent to the Navy Pay Office in Chatham.

   Dec.   The family settled at 2 Ordnance Terrace.

1819   3 Sep.   Harriet D born (d. 1822).

1820   ? Aug.   Frederick William D born (d. 1868).

   CD receives instruction in the rudiments of English and Latin from his mother.

1821   Apr.   The family leaves Ordnance Terrace and moves to 18
       St. Mary's Place. CD attends William Giles's school nearby.

1822   11 Mar.   Alfred Lamert D born (d. 1860).

       Summer   JD recalled to Somerset House and moves his family
       to London. CD stays with his schoolmaster for about three
       months before joining his parents at 16 Bayham Street,
       Camden Town. CD withdrawn from school.

1823   9 Apr.   Fanny D admitted as a pupil to the Royal Academy of
       Music.

       Dec.   The family move to Gower Street North, where Mrs D
       opens a school, hoping to help their finances. The school
       fails.

1824   James Lamert, a relative, offers to employ CD at the shoe-
       blacking business he manages at 30 Hungerford Stairs, the
       Strand. CD begins work at Warren's.

       20 Feb.   JD arrested for debt and sent to the Marshalsea
       Prison.

       Mar.   Mrs D and the three younger children move into JD's
       quarters at the Marshalsea; Fanny stays at the Royal
       Academy and CD goes into lodgings.

       28 May   JD released from prison.

       Dec.   29 Johnson Street, Somers Town, London, becomes the
       new family home.

1825   9 Mar.   JD retires from the Navy Pay Office with a pension
       after 20 years of government service. Jonathan Warren's
       blacking business relocated at Chandos Street, Covent
       Garden. CD continues to work here until Mar. or Apr.

       ? Mar. or Apr.   CD resumes his formal education at Welling-
       ton House Academy.

1827   Mar.   CD works as a clerk for a legal firm in Gray's Inn,
       Holborn.

       Nov.   Augustus Newnham D born (d. 1866).

1828　Nov.　CD works for a solicitor in New Square, Lincoln's Inn.

1829　? Resigns as a clerk and learns shorthand, finding work as a freelance reporter at Doctors' Commons.

1830　8 Feb.　Admitted to the British Museum as a reader.

Biographical Table: The Professional Years 1830–1870

PERSONAL	POLITICAL AND SOCIAL INTERESTS	PUBLICATIONS
1830–33 Courts Maria Beadnell.	1831–32 Works for the *Mirror of Parliament* and later joins the *True Sun* as a Parliamentary reporter.	1833 1 Dec. 'A Dinner at Poplar Walk', CD's first story in the *Monthly Magazine*.
1834 Meets Catherine Hogarth.	Aug. 1834–Nov. 1836 Reporter on the *Morning Chronicle*	26 Sep.–15 Dec. 1834 'Street Sketches' in the *Morning Chronicle*.
21 Nov. JD arrested for debt again. CD secures his release from Abraham Sloman's detention house for debtors.		
1835 ? May Engaged to Catherine Hogarth.		31 Jan.–20 Aug. 'Street Sketches of London' in the *Evening Chronicle*.
Dec. CD leaves his parents' home and rents chambers at 13 Furnival's Inn.		
1836 17 Feb. CD moves to 17 Furnival's Inn.		8 Feb. *SB*, First Series published.
2 Apr. Marries Catherine Hogarth.		12 Feb. Chapman and Hall agree to publish *PP*.

PERSONAL	POLITICAL AND SOCIAL INTERESTS	PUBLICATIONS
		31 Mar.–30 Oct. 1837 *PP* appears in 20 monthly instalments.
		4 Nov. Signs a contract to edit *Bentley's Miscellany*. (Resigns as editor 31 Jan. 1839.)
1837 6 Jan. Charles Culliford Boz D born (d. 1896).		31 Jan.–Apr. 1839 *OT* published in *Bentley's Miscellany* in 24 monthly parts.
Mar. Moves to 48 Doughty Street.		*PP* and *OT* suspended for one month.
7 May Death of Mary Hogarth.		
1838 6 Mar. Mary ('Mamie') D born (d. 1896).	30 Jan.–? 6 Feb. Expedition to the Yorkshire schools with H. K. Browne.	31 Mar.–1 Oct. 1839 *NN* appears in 20 monthly instalments.
1839 Mar. At Exeter to find a house for his parents		
29 Oct. Catherine ('Katey') Elizabeth Macready D born (d. 1929).		
1840		31 Mar. Signs a contract with Chapman and Hall to edit *MHC*.
		4 Apr. *MHC* begins.
		25 Apr.–6 Feb. 1841 *OCS* published in *MHC* in 40 weekly

1841	8 Feb. Walter Landor D born (d. 1863).	
	29 May Invited to stand as a Liberal MP for Reading, but declines.	13 Feb.–27 Nov. *BR* published in *MHC* in 42 weekly numbers.
	19 Sep. Tells Forster of his decision to go to America.	
1842	4 Jan. Sails to Boston with Catherine: the first American trip.	
	8 July Expresses an interest in writing for the *Courier* and in working for political reform.	19 Oct. *AN* published.
	7 June Sails home from New York.	31 Dec.–30 June 1844 *MC* appears in 20 monthly instalments.
	14 Sep. Visits Field Lane Ragged School and enters an informal philanthropic partnership with Miss Coutts. (Their work together continues until about 1858.)	
	? Nov. Georgina Hogarth stays with the family and becomes a permanent member of CD's household.	
	24 Sep. Expresses a willingness to serve as a Police Magistrate.	
1843	Nov. Tells Forster of his plan to go abroad again and spend a year on the Continent.	
	5 Oct. Speaks at the Manchester Athenaeum.	19 Dec. *CC* published.
1844	15 Jan. Francis Jeffrey D born (d. 1886).	
	26 Feb. Speaks at the Liverpool Mechanics' Institution.	16 Dec. *The Chimes* published.
	2 July CD and his family leave London for Genoa, Italy.	
	28 Feb. Speaks at Birmingham Polytechnic Institution.	
	6 Nov.–20 Dec. CD travels in Northern Italy, goes to London to read *The Chimes* (3 & 5 Dec.), and returns to Genoa.	

PERSONAL	POLITICAL AND SOCIAL INTERESTS	PUBLICATIONS
1845 19 Jan.–9 Apr. Travels in Italy with Catherine.	24 July Offers to write a paper on the punishment of death for the *Edinburgh Review*.	20 Dec. *CH* published.
9 June The family leaves Genoa and returns home.	Oct.–Nov. Formulates plans for *The Daily News* and undertakes the paper's editorship.	
25 Oct. Alfred D'Orsay Tennyson D born (d. 1912).		
1846 31 May Leaves for Switzerland with his family. In Lausanne from June to Nov.	21 Jan. First number of *The Daily News*. CD remains as editor until 9 Feb. After resigning, CD continues to publish his 'Travelling Letters' and contributes 'Crime and Education' and five letters on capital punishment (Feb.–Mar.)	18 May *PI* published.
		June At work on *The Life of Our Lord* (pub. 1934).
16 Nov. Leaves for Paris with the family. Remains in Paris until 28 Feb. 1847.		28 June Begins to write *DS*.
	26 May Responds to Miss Coutts's interest in an asylum for women, pledging help and advice.	19 Dec. *The Battle of Life* published.
	20 June Repeats his desire to serve as a Police Magistrate in London.	
1847 28 Feb. The family returns from Paris.	5 June Arranges the lease of a house in Shepherd's Bush for Urania Cottage.	? Oct. 'An Appeal to Fallen Women'.
18 Apr. Sydney Smith Haldimand D born (d. 1872).	26 & 28 July Amateur theatricals in Manchester and Liverpool (benefit performances for Leigh Hunt and John Poole).	
Mar.–Apr. Forster learns of CD's childhood and youth.		

1848	2 Sep. CD's sister Fanny dies.	May–June Amateur theatricals.	19 Dec. *The Haunted Man* published.
1849	15 Jan. Henry Fielding D born (d. 1933).	20 Jan.–21 Apr. Contributes 4 essays to the *Examiner* about abuses to children at a juvenile asylum in Tooting, London.	Jan. Genesis of *DC*.
	20 Jan. Forster sees CD's autobiographical fragment 'in its connected shape'. N.B. Forster also gives 7 May 1848 as another date for this occurrence.	May–June Various public speaking engagements.	30 Apr.–30 Oct. 1850 *DC* appears in 20 monthly instalments.
		14 & 18 Nov. Two letters opposing public hangings published in *The Times*.	Sep.–Oct. Discusses the idea of editing a cheap weekly periodical. Forster encourages the project.
1850	16 Aug. Dora Annie D born (d. 1851).	6 Feb. Addresses the Metropolitan Sanitary Association.	30 Mar. *HW* begins and runs continuously until 28 May 1859.
		Nov. Begins his partnership with Bulwer Lytton in aid of the Guild of Literature and Art.	21 Dec. *HW* Christmas number, 'A Christmas Tree'.
1851	3 Mar. JD dies.	10 May Addresses the Metropolitan Association.	25 Jan. Begins *A Child's History of England* in *HW*. (Continues irregularly until 10 Dec. 1853.)
	14 Apr. Dora Annie D dies.	16 May Royal performance of Bulwer's 'Not So Bad as We Seem', followed by a provincial tour to raise funds for the Guild.	Nov. Genesis of *BH*.
	July Purchases Tavistock House; the family moves in late in Nov.		20 Dec. *HW* Extra Christmas number, 'What Christmas is as We Grow Older' in *Showing What Christmas Is to Everybody*.

PERSONAL	POLITICAL AND SOCIAL INTERESTS	PUBLICATIONS
1852 13 Mar. Edward Bulwer Lytton ('Plorn') D born (d. 1902).		Mar.–Sep. 1853 *BH* appears in 20 monthly instalments.
Oct. Visits Boulogne.		18 Dec. *HW* Extra Christmas number, 'The Poor Relation's Story' and 'The Child's Story' in *A Round of Stories by the Christmas Tree*.
1853 June–Sep. The family at Boulogne.	27–30 Dec. First public readings of *CC* in aid of charity.	19 Dec. *HW* Extra Christmas Number, 'The Schoolboy's Story' and 'Nobody's Story' in *Another Round of Stories by the Christmas Tree*.
Mid-Oct.–mid-Dec. CD tours Switzerland and Italy with W. Collins and A. Egg.		
1854 June–Oct. CD and his family reside in Boulogne.	23 Jan. Visits Preston to gather information about the industrial trouble.	11 Feb. 'On Strike', *HW*.
		1 Apr.–12 Aug. *HT* appears in *HW* in weekly instalments.
		14 Dec. *HW* Extra Christmas Number, 'The First' and 'The Road' in *The Seven Poor Travellers*.
1855 9 Feb. Receives a letter from Mrs Maria Beadnell Winter.	May Joins the Administrative Reform Association.	July Genesis of *LD*.
25 Feb. CD and Maria meet in private.	27 June Addresses the Association.	15 Dec. *HW* Extra Christmas Number, 'The Guest' and 'The Boots' in *The Holly Tree Inn*.

15 June Produces W. Collins's play, 'The Lighthouse'.

Oct.–May 1856 The family resides in Paris.

1856 14 Mar. Buys Gad's Hill Place, Rochester.

Apr. Confides in Forster about his marital troubles.

June–Sep. Boulogne.

6 Dec. *HW* Extra Christmas Number, 'The Captain's Account' in *The Wreck of the Golden Mary*.

1857 6 Jan. Produces W. Collins's play 'The Frozen Deep' at Tavistock House.

June CD revives the play to raise money for Douglas Jerrold's widow and family. After public performances in London CD hires professionals to act when he takes the production to Manchester (21 & 22 Aug.). Mrs Ternan and her daughters Maria and Ellen join the cast.

7–22 Sep. Tours Northern England with W. Collins. CD returns to Gad's Hill, avoiding Catherine at Tavistock House. From Rochester, he instructs Mrs Cornelius to oversee the alterations to his bedroom at Tavistock House.

3–31 Oct. 'A Lazy Tour of Two Idle Apprentices', *HW* (a joint production with Collins).

15 Oct. CD leaves Tavistock House and walks to Gad's Hill after a serious domestic quarrel.

CD gives serious thought to reading from his novels for his own profit.

7 Dec. *HW* Extra Christmas Number, *The Perils of Certain English Prisoners* (with Collins).

PERSONAL	POLITICAL AND SOCIAL INTERESTS	PUBLICATIONS
1858 29 Apr. The public readings for CD's own profit begin. First London season (to 22 July).		12 June 'Personal' statement in *HW*.
May Catherine leaves Tavistock House, living henceforth at Gloucester Crescent, Regent's Park. (d. 22 Nov. 1879).		7 Dec. *HW* Extra Christmas Number, 'Going into Society' and 'Let at Last' in *A House to Let*.
14 May Mark Lemon, acting on Catherine's behalf, accepts CD's proposed settlement. Rumours circulated by Mrs Hogarth and her daughter Helen upset the negotiations.		
22 May Catherine agrees to CD's terms.		
29 May Mrs Hogarth and Helen sign a statement retracting their belief in the rumours.		
2 Aug. First provincial reading tour (to 13 Nov.).		
Oct. Ellen Ternan and her sister Maria in family lodgings at 31 Berners Street, Oxford Street.		

1859 Breaks with Bradbury and Evans because they opposed CD's use of *HW* to air private matters.

July Ellen Ternan now at 2 Houghton Place, Ampthill Square. (Last payment of the rates, Apr. 1865.)

10–27 Oct. Second provincial tour.

24 Dec.–2 Jan. 1860 London Christmas readings.

1860 17 July Katey D marries Charles Collins.

21 Aug. CD sells Tavistock House and Gad's Hill becomes the new family home.

Sep. Sydney D goes to sea as a Naval midshipman.

1861 14 Mar.–18 Apr. Readings in London.

28 Oct.–30 Jan. 1862 Readings in the provinces, second series.

Nov. Charles D, Jr., marries Bessie Evans.

30 Apr. *TTC* begins in *AYR*, appearing weekly until 26 Nov.

28 May Last number of *HW*: CD announces its incorporation into *AYR*.

Dec. *AYR* Extra Christmas Number, 'The Mortals in the House', 'The Ghost in Master B's Room', and 'The Ghost in the Corner Room' in *The Haunted House*.

28 Jan. *UT* series begins in *AYR*; irregular contributions continue until 5 June 1869.

Genesis of *GE*

1 Dec.–3 Aug. 1861 *GE* appears in weekly parts in *AYR*.

Dec. *AYR* Extra Christmas Number, Chapters I, and III, and parts of II and V of *A Message from the Sea*.

Dec. *AYR* Extra Christmas Number, 'Picking up Soot and Cinders', 'Picking up Miss Kimmeens', and 'Picking up the Tinker' in *Tom Tiddler's Ground*.

PERSONAL	POLITICAL AND SOCIAL INTERESTS	PUBLICATIONS
1862 13 Mar.–27 June Readings in London.		Dec. *AYR* Extra Christmas Number, 'His Leaving it till Called for', 'His Boots', 'His Brown-Paper Parcel' and 'His Wonderful End' in *Somebody's Luggage*.
Mid-Oct.–mid-Dec. Resides in Paris, taking Georgina and Mamie.		
		Aug. Genesis of *OMF*.
1863 15 Jan. CD returns to Paris, remaining there until early Feb.	17, 29, 30 Jan. Readings for Charity at the British Embassy, Paris.	Dec. *AYR* Extra Christmas Number, 'How Mrs. Lirriper carried on the business' and 'How the Parlours added a few words' in *Mrs. Lirriper's Lodgings*.
2 Mar.–13 June Readings in London.		
12 Sep. Elizabeth D dies.		
Dec. Francis D leaves England to join the Bengal Mounted Police.		
31 Dec. Walter D dies in Calcutta.		
1864 Dec. CD's health increasingly troublesome.		May–Nov. 1865 *OMF* appears in 20 monthly instalments.
		Dec. *AYR* Extra Christmas Number, 'Mrs. Lirriper relates how she went in and over' and 'Mrs. Lirriper relates how Jemmy topped up' in *Mrs. Lirriper's Legacy*.
1865 29 May Alfred D emigrates to Australia.	29 July Speaks at Knebworth on behalf of the Guild of Literature and Art.	Dec. *AYR* Extra Christmas Number, 'To be taken immediately', 'To be taken with a Grain of Salt', and 'To be taken for Life' in *Doctor
? May–June In France with Ellen Ternan.		

9 June Staplehurst railway accident.

1866 ? Jan.–July 1867 CD takes a house in Slough for Ellen Ternan under the assumed name of Tringham.

10 Apr.–12 June First Chappell season.

May Considers proposals to read in America.

1867 15 Jan.–13 May Second Chappell season.

June–July 1870 CD takes Windsor Lodge, Peckham, for Ellen Ternan and pays the rates under the assumed names of Turnham and Tringham.

3 Aug. George Dolby sails to America to assess the possibility of a reading tour before CD commits himself.

9 Nov. CD sails for Boston: the American reading tour (2 Dec.–20 Apr. 1868).

Dec. *AYR* Extra Christmas Number, 'Barbox Brothers', 'Barbox Brothers and Co.', 'Main Line' and 'No. 1 Branch Line, The Signalman' in *Mugby Junction*.

June Writing *George Silverman's Explanation and A Holiday Romance* (first published in 1868 in USA).

Aug. Collaborates with W. Collins on *No Thoroughfare*, their joint contribution to the Christmas number of *AYR*.

PERSONAL	POLITICAL AND SOCIAL INTERESTS	PUBLICATIONS
1868 22 Apr. CD leaves New York and returns home.		Oct. Prepares the *Sikes and Nancy* version of *OT* for a private, trial performance (14 Nov.).
Sep. Charles D, Jr., assumes some of Wills's routine duties at the *AYR* office. After CD's death, Charley becomes the editor and owner of *AYR*.		
26 Sep. Plorn emigrates to Australia.		
Oct. Henry Fielding D wins a scholarship and goes to Trinity Hall, Cambridge.		
6 Oct.–20 Apr. 1869 The Farewell reading tour.		
1869 22 Apr. CD's health breaks down at Preston. The remaining readings cancelled.	27 Sep. Inaugural address at the Birmingham and Midland Institute.	Sep. Genesis of *ED*.
1870 11 Jan.–15 Mar. London Farewell Readings.	6 Jan. Distributes prizes at Birmingham Town Hall as President of the Birmingham and Midland Institute.	Apr.–Sep. *ED* (only 6 of the planned 12 instalments written before CD died).
9 June CD dies at Gad's Hill.		
14 June Buried at Westminster Abbey.		

Part I
Personal Letters

Introduction

Answering a letter from a distant friend in June 1848, Dickens exchanged family news and summarized his affairs as they appeared at the time. His two daughters and five sons, he informed his correspondent, were 'all well, all good, and all happy'. While he was not rich, Dickens continued, he had got ahead of the world 'by some few thousand pounds' owing to the success of *Dombey and Son* (1846–8), a work which had also reaffirmed his popularity, despite his sense that in England literature 'as a profession' had no distinct status. At the same time, he added, he felt bound to say that in his own person he experienced ample recognition throughout society. 'Go where I will,' he wrote to D. M. Moir, 'in out of the way places and odd corners of the country, I always find something of personal affection in people whom I have never seen, mixed up with my public reputation. This is the best part of it, and makes me very happy.'[1]

Financial success and public recognition represent two goals Dickens never relinquished. Less noteworthy were his domestic fortunes, either in marriage until he separated from his wife in 1858, or outside of it, in his apparently unhappy liason with Ellen Ternan in the last decade of his life. Lacking what John Forster termed a ' "city of the mind" against outward ills, for inner consolation and shelter,'[2] Dickens sought innumerable distractions from the increasing stress he and Catherine Hogarth Dickens endured from the 1850s onwards. Foreign travel, private and public theatricals, public speaking and various philanthropic interests, as the following selection of letters reveals, constitute variations of the work formula Dickens applied to ease the strain of his personal life before finally confessing to Forster in April 1856 that the skeleton in his domestic closet had become 'a pretty big one' (N, II, 765).

One discerns no hint of marital tension – actual or impending – in the letter Dickens wrote Moir in 1848. On the contrary, that letter and much of his correspondence up through the early 1850s suggest a characteristically affirmative outlook.[3] In part, we glimpse a man whose interests, curiosity and sympathies provide a vibrant sense of someone whose life knows no harness, the man whom Lord Shaftesbury called a great 'phenomenon' of his time.[4] Recorded in these letters the reader will find Dickens the Great Victorian: the philanthropist, the family man, the social critic, the traveller, the novelist concerned with his public standing, the artist committed to his craft, the figure whom his contemporaries also knew as a journalist, editor, actor, director, public speaker and dramatic reader of his own fiction.

At the same time, Dickens's letters occasionally portray a shadowy figure, an intimate Dickens whom the writer took pains to disguise, protecting this private self from public scrutiny. When asked directly on two occasions to supply biographical information for public use, Dickens responded with a mixture of reticence and candour.[5] His father, he informed a German scholar in 1838, 'was not a rich man', one consequence of which, the novelist continued, was that he (Dickens) had to begin life the hard way. 'I have been abroad in the world from a mere child,' he added, a half revelation that tells almost as much as it conceals about the novelist who thought of himself as an orphan and whose imaginative legacy includes some of the most moving portraits of forsaken children in the world's literature.

This same letter also alludes to his 'irregular rambling education', another fact about Dickens's early life he did his best to hide. One of his first acts on becoming eighteen was to apply to the British Museum for a reader's ticket[6] so that he could gain for himself such knowledge that a conventionally-schooled middle-class youth might be anticipated to have. Satisfying thus both social expectations and his own 'higher personal cravings', as Forster characterized Dickens's motive, he became a devoted occupant of the reading room at this period of his life. In his chair every morning as the clock struck ten,[7] Dickens spent there days 'decidedly the usefullest' to himself that he had ever passed, a judgement Forster also corroborated. 'No man who knew him in later years,' wrote his biographer, 'and talked to him familiarly of books and things' would have suspected that his education was almost entirely self-acquired (Forster, I, iii, 45).

On other occasions, insights into the self Dickens kept from sight burst out unexpectedly and even indirectly, so much so that the unwary reader of his letters might pass them by. For example, shortly before Dickens committed himself to a series of public readings in the United States in the winter of 1867, we find him characteristically involved in several projects. In August 1867 he had sent forth George Dolby, his tour manager, on a field report to assess American interest in the readings and to inspect possible locations where Dickens might perform. While these inquiries went forward, Dickens worked with Wilkie Collins to complete *No Thoroughfare*, a story they wrote conjointly for the forthcoming Christmas number of *All the Year Round*. At the same time, Dickens offered to keep an eye on the preparations for a revival of Bulwer Lytton's *Maid of Lyons*, scheduled to open at the Lyceum Theatre in London in September. Because Dickens knew and liked the play and because his friend Charles Fechter was both acting in it and directing it, Dickens agreed to attend an advanced rehearsal to assess the effects of the 'slight alterations' Fechter proposed. Dickens watched the performance and reported back to Bulwer, full of praise for the pains Fechter had taken with this romantic comedy set in nineteenth-century France, in which the protagonist, the son of a humble gardener, eventually distinguishes himself in Napoleon's army, becomes rich, and wins the hand of the daughter of his father's wealthy employer. But on the day of the opening, going over the prompt-book, Dickens noticed a slight cut in the protagonist's speech in Act III. 'I positively object,' Dickens wrote to Fechter, explaining that the change was 'highly injudicious', one that struck out 'the best known line[s] in the play' (N, III, 549).

Superlatives and charged language often characterize Dickens's letters, particularly when he combines personal feeling with some sense of affront or injustice. In this case, Fechter had unwittingly given offence by removing lines Dickens prized. Dickens noted, of course, that 'Lytton would not' let the cancelled passage go; most significantly, neither would he. 'I must stipulate for your restoring it thus,' Dickens commanded:

> Then did I seek to rise
> Out of the prison of my mean estate;
> And, with such jewels as the exploring mind
> Brings from the caves of knowledge, buy me ransom
> From those twin jailers of the daring heart –
> Low birth and iron fortune.
>
> (*The Lady of Lyons*, III, ii)

As if to clinch his argument, Dickens added that there would not be a man in the Lyceum from any newspaper 'who would not detect mutilations in that speech, moreover'.

The fact that Dickens himself nearly thirty years ago had been one such newspaper man, first at Covent Garden, when the play opened in 1838, and later at a subsequent revival of the play at the Haymarket in

1840, which he attended as part of a journalistic assignment for the *Examiner*,[8] adds interest to the story. But its real importance, I suggest, lies in the lines themselves. To them Dickens displays an apparently passionate dedication, presumably because they capture something with which he identified. Like Bulwer's protagonist, Claude Melnotte, Dickens had been imprisoned by a mean estate, until his daring heart challenged his 'low birth' and 'iron fortune' and his exploring mind wrested jewels from the caves of knowledge.[9] By objective standards the lines constitute no truly memorable verse, but they can certainly stand as an epigraph, one that Dickens himself might have selected, if pressed, or that we, looking back at his career, might adopt. Turning briefly to the events of his childhood and youthful privations – aspects of his life rarely seen in the correspondence – helps us understand further their private resonance.

Dickens was born on 7 February 1812, the second of eight children raised by John Dickens and Elizabeth Barrow Dickens. On his mother's side, family members took pride in the Barrows' relative affluence and middle-class status, a feeling of security denied to Dickens's father, a self-styled gentleman of more humble origin. Probably through the intervention of Lord Crewe of Crewe Hall, Cheshire, for whom John Dickens's parents worked as servants, their son had received some education and later obtained a post in the Navy pay office in Somerset House, London.[10] Working as a government clerk represented a modest accomplishment, but the job carried pay rises and increasing prospects for the steady employee willing to work his way towards greater responsibility and authority.

Unfortunately for his family, John Dickens was no such man. Ebullient, expansive, fond of convivial occasions, financially irresponsible and apparently incapable of saving hardly a penny, John Dickens proved a poor provider for the six surviving children born to him and Elizabeth after their marriage in 1809. As parents and children shuttled about south-east England from one naval base to another, John Dickens led them into a series of financial muddles. Professional reasons dictated the moves, first from Portsmouth, where Dickens was born, to London, and thence via Sheerness to Chatham in 1817, where they remained for the next five years, but each relocation seemed to fit a developing pattern: between 1812 and 1824 the family houses became successively meaner, more cramped, and less attractive, until finally reaching their nadir. On 24 February 1824 a London bailiff arrested John Dickens for debt. Taken first to a sponging house, where offenders had their last opportunity to raise money, John Dickens was later escorted to the Marshalsea, a prison for debtors in the High Street, Southwark, London. Mrs Dickens and the younger children soon followed, crowding into the cramped prison quarters and taking up residence as well, as families of debtors often did at the time. Only Charles and Fanny, his elder sister, escaped this fate. Fanny, a pupil at the Royal Academy of Music remained there, while Charles went into lodgings in Camden Town with 'a reduced old lady', who made a living by boarding children.

Dickens felt this separation from his family keenly, but perhaps no more sharply than the blow he had received shortly before his father's arrest. Early in 1824 Dickens began his business life at Warren's blacking factory in Hungerford Street, just off the Strand. He had been put to work with his parents' consent at the hint of a relative, who offered to find a situation for Charles as a means of easing the family's 'domestic circumstances'. Since there was no money to school the boy at present – Dickens's education had begun in Chatham but ceased when he arrived in London – the proposal made sense, at least to the parents. But to Dickens the suggestion was a nasty shock. 'No words can express the secret agony of my soul,' he recorded in his abandoned autobiography written at a later date,[11] as he sunk into the companionship of the common boys with whom he had to work, covering pots of paste-blacking and affixing the company's printed label. Warren's produced a preparation for giving shoes and boots a shining black surface in premises Dickens described as 'a crazy, tumble-down old house . . . literally overrun with rats'.

Existing records suggest that Dickens spent at least four months in this job,[12] a relatively short period if one measures by duration but an age if one judges by the intensity of the experience. The long work days sank iron teeth into him, as did his off-work hours, during which the young boy lounged about the streets of London 'insufficiently and unsatisfactorily fed'. Some days he wandered over to Covent Garden, London's fruit and vegetable market, where he stared at pineapples. On others, he haunted cheap coffee shops in search of food and warmth. 'From that hour, until this, my father and my mother have been stricken dumb upon it,' Dickens later wrote of the period he spent working at Warren's. 'I have never heard the least allusion to it, however far off and remote, from either of them. I have never, until I now impart it to this paper, in any burst of confidence with anyone, my own wife not excepted, raised the curtain I then dropped, thank God.' (Forster, I, ii, 32–33)[13]

Release for the father followed in the ensuing months. Under the provisions of the Insolvent Debtors' Act of 1821, John Dickens set up a schedule to pay his creditor and so was freed from the Marshalsea on 28 May 1824.[14] Charles, meanwhile, continued at the blacking factory until he resumed his schooling. Money was somehow found to send him as a day scholar to Wellington House Academy, which he attended for two or three years until the family's finances again rendered education an unaffordable luxury. In March 1827, Charles left school for good.

Dickens's second foray into the working world proved less traumatic. He began somewhat inauspiciously as an office boy working for an attorney, first at Gray's Inn, Holborn, and then at New Square, Lincoln's Inn, before he quit after less than two years, resolving to teach himself shorthand and look for another situation. This decision paid off handsomely. After a trying interval of freelance reporting for the proctors of Doctors' Commons, a college or 'common house' of doctors of law near St. Paul's Cathedral, Dickens obtained work in the reporters' gallery of the House of Commons. In a brief period he distinguished himself among the eighty or ninety parliamentary reporters, rising to the highest rank and graduating from transcribing speeches verbatim to covering various events for different London newspapers.[15] About this time, his 'first effusion[s]', as he referred to his earliest compositions, began to appear anonymously and then later under the pen name of 'Boz', as Dickens gained a reputation in the newspaper world. These pieces, in turn, attracted John Macrone, a London publisher who saw a profitable opportunity in collecting Dickens's essays and publishing them in book form. One day after Dickens's twenty-fourth birthday – 8 February 1836 – *Sketches by Boz*, first series, appeared. The book met with success, established Dickens's name among London publishers, and signalled the beginning of his career as a writer of fiction. Between 1836 and 1870 he published fourteen novels, dying about half way through his fifteenth, the incomplete *Mystery of Edwin Drood*.

*   *   *

The same years that saw Dickens laying the foundation of his literary career also widened his experiences in other ways. Perhaps the most intensive, if we turn to evidence from the correspondence, was his emotional response to Maria Beadnell, 'the object of my first and my last love' (N, I, 17). Dickens and Maria Beadnell evidently met in May 1830 (P, I, 16n). He fell in love almost immediately and for the next three years lived in emotional turmoil.

Of the two, Dickens unquestionably loved the more ardently, pursuing Maria in spite of her displays of 'heartless indifference' and in opposition to her parents, who cooled to Dickens once the courtship became serious. Possibly rumours of John Dickens's former imprisonment for debt reached them, possibly the Beadnells viewed the seemingly irregular life of a parliamentary reporter with suspicion. In any event, Dickens appears not to have been the son-in-law the Beadnells had in mind, so that an 'unhappy misunderstanding' between the lovers developed. When Maria was sent away to a finishing school in Paris, they communicated for a while by passing letters through friends until time and distance accomplished the parents' goal – the termination of the relationship.[16]

Their unsuccessful courtship, however, had a curious sequel some twenty-five years later. Sorting through his mail as he sat alone by the fire one evening in February 1855, Dickens experienced an extraordinary sensation when the sight of Maria's handwriting before him made the past vanish in an instant. Before him stood a young woman of twenty, a vision of loveliness, he later wrote, in 'a sort of raspberry coloured dress with a little black trimming at the top'. Maria – now Mrs Henry Winters and mother of two daughers – had unexpectedly written to Dickens to remind him of their youthful days together. 'I opened it [the letter],' Dickens wrote to her, 'with the touch of my young friend David Copperfield when he was in love.' (N, II, 625–26)

For a brief interval, the former lovers fanned each others' memories, conducting an epistolary flirtation almost as intense as their first exchanges a quarter of a century ago. They even went so far as agreeing to meet privately, 'in perfect innocence and good faith', emphasized Dickens, he cherishing the memory of the raspberry coloured dress and she, more realistically, disparaging herself as 'toothless, fat, old and ugly'. When they came face to face Dickens confronted a woman closer to Maria's self-description, dashing his expectations of her beauty and leaving him awkwardly extracting himself from her eager declarations of friendship, happy to deflect Maria's attentions to his wife.

Catherine Hogarth displaced Dickens's infatuation with Maria Beadnell about two years after he and Maria had parted in 1833. This second courtship proved more satisfactory, at least in the immediate outcome of their marriage in March 1836 and ensuing years together. Before the partnership faltered, Catherine bore ten children – the last was born in 1852 – and lived harmoniously with an exacting and difficult man.

Perspective on this marriage is not easy to obtain. Because Catherine Dickens left no record of her view of the relationship we have only her husband's occasional references to their difficulties in his letters to Forster. Other accounts include allusions Dickens made when he forced his domestic troubles before the public, providing testimony that was far from objective in the 'PERSONAL' statement on the front page of *Household Words* in 1858 and in the 'violated letter'.[17] We are also without detailed information from those whose closeness to Dickens and his wife would have enabled them to add their observations, had they been willing to share them. Lacking the present-day willingness to discuss the intimate aspects of the lives of others, these friends maintained a discreet silence, declining to speak or write about the difficulties Dickens and his wife experienced in any detail.[18] Forster, for example, refers to the separation but only in passing, committed to the Victorian biographers' belief that intimate matters should remain private even when the subject belonged, as Dickens did, to the public domain.

Reading the correspondence, however, provides some important clues, pieces of information which document Dickens's growing sense of dissatisfaction with his wife and his frequent attempts to blow off superfluous steam and cool the 'inimitable's brain'. From the early 1850s, he began to report signs of 'Hypochondriacal whisperings', complaining that his head would 'split like a fired shell' if he remained at home and failed to get away (N, II, 463).

In part, Dickens speaks here of being overworked, but as he continued to record these moods in the letters he wrote Forster, a greater frankness began to appear, leading him to lament the 'one happiness' he missed in life and the 'one friend and companion' he had never made. Lacking that companion at home, Dickens turned away, busying himself in work-related activities. He also began to play harder. To this period belongs his friendship with Wilkie Collins, with whom he spent many 'theatrical and other lounging evenings' dining out and relaxing over cigars and glasses of gin and hot water.

Catherine cannot have remained blind to her husband's behaviour, which she appears to have endured silently and miserably. Without the physical appeal that had formerly captivated Dickens, she was now middle-aged and ample. She was also, in the malign words of her husband, incompetent as both a housewife and mother. In addition, she had two parents whose 'imbecility' Dickens eventually found himself unable to contemplate, a reaction he developed over a long period of helping the Hogarths financially and often accommodating them in his own house.[19]

Dickens had few options with which to meet these accumulating tensions. On one occasion in April 1856 he stayed for several days at a hotel in Dover rather than return to London, where the Hogarths were living in his house. The sight of his in-laws at breakfast, he explained to a friend, undermined his constitution (N, II, 764). But escaping from Catherine proved more difficult. Under the Matrimonial Causes Act of 1857, divorce became possible, but only in very restricted circumstances, so that he and his wife had to make the best of their situation.[20] By exchanging confidences with Forster – 'Poor Catherine and I are not made for each other,' he wrote in September 1857 – and by explaining his feverish need 'to escape from myself' to Collins, Dickens managed to control his emotions. Forster offered his heartfelt sympathies, while Collins agreed to accompany Dickens to the north of England for 'a foray upon the fells of Cumberland'.

This fragile balance between confession and activity failed to last. When Dickens returned to London in September 1857, he avoided his wife at their family home and went directly to his recently purchased 'summer retreat' at Gad's Hill, Rochester.[21] From there in October he wrote the letter that signalled the end of his marriage: henceforth, he instructed a trusted family servant, the door between his bedroom and Catherine's in Tavistock House, London, should be sealed and given the aspect of permanence by substituting a new plain door and disguising the recess with a set of shelves. Later that month, Dickens returned, when, one evening at Tavistock House, an altercation of uncertain origin occurred. Afterwards he retired to bed but failed to sleep, so at two in the morning arose 'very much put out' and set off to walk thirty miles back to Gad's hill.[22] That was the last time Dickens visited the family home until the Hogarths were gone for good (Johnson, II, 912).

No further crises occurred as Dickens prepared for the first of his paid public readings, his latest attempt to wear and toss his domestic unhappiness away, as he commented in August 1858 (N, III, 38). Forster opposed the readings because he disapproved of putting oneself before the public as a paid performer, but Dickens's overrode these objections and went ahead, taking his place on the stage for the first occasion on 29 April 1858. About this time, his marital troubles appear to have come to an unexpected climax when a London jeweller mistakenly delivered a bracelet Dickens had purchased for Ellen Ternan to his wife. Catherine refused to believe that it was an innocent keepsake, a gift to a young actress for her services in a play Dickens had recently acted in and directed.

When charged with misconduct, Dickens responded indignantly, furious with his wife's obduracy in making her accusations and hysterically angry that Ellen Ternan could be defiled by any suggestion of improper behaviour. Catherine, he insisted, must prove her belief in his and Ellen's innocence by calling on the actress and her mother.[23] She complied but Mrs Hogarth showed more mettle by insisting that her daughter demand a separate allowance and leave Tavistock House immediately.

A temporary lull descended as the details of a formal separation were worked out. Initially Dickens and Forster attempted to 'recon-struct and rearrange' the unhappy marriage in order to preserve a façade of domestic unity (N, III, 22). Catherine, it was suggested, might continue to appear as Dickens's hostess on public occasions; in private, husband and wife would alternate separate periods at Tavistock House and Gad's Hill. Mrs Hogarth, however, held out for a complete separation and urged her daughter to reject face-saving compromises (Johnson, II, 920). Soon afterwards, Dickens proposed that Catherine should take a house of her own, receive £600 a year expenses, and live with her eldest son, Charley. The other children would remain with Dickens, but Catherine would have free access to them and they to their mother.

Catherine had scarcely accepted the terms of the proposed settle-ment when members of her family caused further trouble. Mrs Hogarth and her youngest daughter, Helen, Dickens learned, were responsible for the gossip in London that Ellen Ternan was his mistress. 'My father,' recalled his daughter Katey in later years, 'was like a madman,'[24] as he tried to make Mrs Hogarth and Helen accountable for their talk. Unless they retracted their wicked accusa-tions, he threatened, and pledged themselves in writing to contradict their statements affecting his moral character, Dickens refused to give Catherine a penny or sign any deed. For a brief period the Hogarths held out before giving in to Dickens's ultimatum and signing on 29 May 1858 the special statement he had prepared. Shortly afterwards, Dickens and his wife were formally separated.

*   *   *

By breaking up their marriage, Dickens changed his circumstances considerably, so much so that the events of the last decade stand apart, a strange life, as he himself noted, of travelling, dinners, the readings, and 'everything else' (N, III, 59). In 1859 he put Tavistock House, the family's former home, up for sale and retired to Gad's Hill, keeping out of London except when business matters required his presence in the city. He established there what he called a 'temporary Town Tent' in his office headquarters of *All the Year Round*, to which he commuted from Kent to edit the new weekly journal. *All the Year Round* incorporated *Household Words*, its predecessor, whose ownership Dickens acquired from his former partners and publishers, Bradbury and Evans, as retribution for their failure to side with him against his wife and their opposition to his using the journal as a forum for airing his conjugal differences.[25] This next decade also saw the deepening and eventual consummation of Dickens's relationship with Ellen Ternan. Of their life together and movements the letters reveal almost nothing.[26]

The correspondence, however, does document other aspects of Dickens's life, particularly the different professional focus we associate with the latter part of his career: his debut on stage as a reader of specially prepared scenes and episodes from his fiction. Certainly the readings appealed to Dickens as an antidote to the stress he felt when his marriage deteriorated, but once separated he did not lose interest in them. On the contrary, his commitment to the readings increased, extending to over four hundred performances during the next ten years of his life.[27]

The reading tours proved extremely lucrative, a fact which accounts for much of their appeal to Dickens, who lacked Forster's gentlemanly inhibitions about making money from the hard work the performances demanded. To Forster, the paid public readings constituted something of a threat to Dickens's literary reputation. By substituting 'lower for higher aims', he argued, Dickens ran the danger of undermining the esteem with which he was held by appearing too frequently in public. Forster's fears were unfounded, as the popularity of the tours demonstrated. His scruples also sounded a little self-indulgent and perhaps stuffy to a self-made man like Dickens, who liked to work hard and who also needed the money.[28] In addition to his own sons and daughters, he had to provide for a large extended family of widows, nephews, nieces and other relations who clung to his skirts, he remarked, for financial help. 'I never had anything left to me but relations,' he noted in 1860, after learning of the death of his brother

Alfred Lamert Dickens, who left a widow and five children 'you may suppose to whom' (N, III, 172). Improving Gad's Hill, his 'plain, old-fashioned, two-story, brick-built house,' also required capital as Dickens added bedrooms, rebuilt the drawing-room, and improved the property outside. Thus once Dickens established himself on the reading circuit, the 'golden prospect[s]' held before him constituted a powerful incentive to continue, enabling him to become rich and also meet what he called his 'enormous expenses'.[29]

Other factors about the readings deserve consideration as well. Making a success of the performances for their own sake became a challenge Dickens could not resist. As was his lifelong habit in everything, Dickens took immense pains with the texts he selected for reading. He chose each piece with care, reworking the narrative to heighten its dramatic appeal, tightening the dialogue, and adding special stage directions to remind himself of points to emphasize during each performance. 'Do every thing at your best,' Dickens urged his son Henry when he wrote to him from the United States in 1868. 'It was but this last year,' he continued, 'that I set to and learned every word of my readings; and from ten years ago to last night, I have never read to an audience but I have watched for an opportunity of striking out something better somewhere. Look at such of my manuscripts as are in the library at Gad's, and think of the patient hours devoted year after year to single lines' (N, III, 620). One attended to self-improvement in Dickens's world not because it led to fortune, but because it was right.[30]

Recent commentators tend to view Dickens's commitment to success more ambiguously, seeing in the exhaustive demands he imposed upon himself evidence of self-destructiveness, an unconscious but powerful impulse to shorten his life by undertaking arduous performances and exacting travel schedules. Edgar Johnson, for example, goes so far as to argue that in adding the strenuous 'Sikes and Nancy' episode from *Oliver Twist* to his repertoire in 1868, Dickens was 'sentencing himself to death'. He took this course, Johnson contends, because by this late stage of his life Dickens had 'ceased to care what happened'. His marriage had proved unsuccessful, Ellen Ternan, in some way, had 'failed his need', his children worried and disappointed him, and his earlier 'gleaming hopes' for a better world had given way to pessimism about Britain's apparent decline. (Johnson, II, 1104–05)

By aligning Dickens with self-destructiveness and disorder, we glimpse him through modern eyes but run the danger of losing Dickens the Victorian to the contemporary myth of the alienated artist. Johnson's Dickens also contradicts what the letters of this decade substantiate, that despite the hectic pace, Dickens's fears of railway travel after the Staplehurst accident in 1865, and his declining health, Dickens did his best to take care of himself. Instead of squandering his resources, as some imply,[31] he evolved a set of 'Spartan principles' designed to reduce 'to the smallest possible amount' the wear and tear of the episodical hotel-life he endured while on tour. It was his inflexible practice, he frequently explained to friends offering him private accommodations, always to live in his hotel and to keep close to the secretary and assistants who accompanied him. 'Knowing that I am never away, they are always at their posts,' he told those who urged him to make personal visits. (N, III, 514–15)

This thorough professionalism – together with the implied insistence on exactness and punctuality – characterize Dickens, the Victorian author and performer of his works who never neglected his responsibility to either his readers or listeners. As one who believed that art should 'sweeten the lives and fancies of others' and increase the world's stock of 'harmless cheerfulness',[32] reading from his fiction, he contended, helped rather than thwarted these goals. 'When I first entered on this interpretation of myself . . . [as a public reader] I was sustained by the hope that I could drop into some hearts,' Dickens explained to a friend in 1867, 'some new expression of the meaning of my books, that would touch . . . [audiences] in a new way. To this hour that purpose is so strong in me, and so real are my fictions to myself, that, after hundreds of nights, I come with a feeling of perfect freshness to that little red table, and laugh and cry with my hearers, as if I had never stood there before.' (N, III, 523)

Failing health checked these ambitions in 1869 when bouts of lameness, giddiness, and an inability to raise his hand to his head prompted Dickens's doctor to cancel the final reading tour before its projected completion. Cutting out twenty-seven performances disappointed Dickens greatly, causing him to agitate for permission from his medical advisers to give a short Farewell series of twelve readings in London in the spring of 1870. When Dickens's health recovered, his doctors consented, allowing him to bring this phase of his career to a close on 15 March. That evening a tearful Dickens told the spectators that he retired from 'the full-flood tide' of their favour with 'feelings of very considerable pain'.[33] At the same time, he added, he looked forward to renewing 'those old associations' with them as he rejoined his readers when *The Mystery of Edwin Drood* began the first of its twelve monthly instalments on 1 April of that same year.

The decision to write a shorter novel and the resolution to add to the contract a clause for repaying the publishers a portion of the money they advanced if he died or became incapable of completing the book indicate how Dickens himself assessed his health. At the time, Forster opposed the clause as 'altogether needless'; as he noted afterwards, it was 'sadly pertinent' because the novel ends abruptly, two pages short of the completion of the sixth monthly number.

Dickens worked on *Edwin Drood* to within hours of his death. He spent the morning of 8 June writing and then returned to his desk after lunch, 'much against his usual custom', noted Forster, to write his final words. At dinner that evening, Georgina Hogarth observed 'a singular expression of trouble and pain in his face'. Dickens attempted to leave the table, supported by the sister-in-law who had remained dedicated to him for most of her life. ' "On the ground" ' were the last words he spoke as he slid to the floor shortly after six that evening, suffering from an aneurysm in the brain. (Forster, xii, i, 415) Twenty-four hours later he died and the world mourned as the news spread. So great was the outpouring of public feeling in England and the sense that he deserved the highest honours the nation could bestow that he was buried in Westminster Abbey, despite his own instructions for a private funeral without monument or memorial. But the stone that was placed over his grave accorded perfectly with the injunction in his will that his 'name be inscribed in plain English letters' on his tomb 'without the addition of "Mr." or "Esquire" ':

CHARLES DICKENS
BORN FEBRUARY THE SEVENTH, 1812
DIED JUNE THE NINTH, 1870.

NOTES

1. Dickens to D. M. Moir, *The Letters of Charles Dickens*, ed. Walter Dexter, The Nonesuch Dickens (Bloomsbury: The Nonesuch Press, 1938), ii, 102–3. Future references to this edition will be supplied parenthetically throughout this *Selection*, using the abbreviation N and volume and page number.

2. John Forster, *The Life of Charles Dickens*, ed. A. J. Hoppé (London: Dent, 1969), ii, 200. Cf. Byron's 'Oh Rome! my country! city of the soul!' (*Childe Harold*, iv, 78), which Forster appears to misquote. Future references to this edition will appear throughout as Forster, followed by his book and chapter numbers and the pagination of the 1969 Everyman edition.

3. One possible exception is Dickens's correspondence with the de la Rues, letters which, as Kathleen Tillotson notes, might be 'open to misrepresentation by sensation-seekers'. Dickens, she adds, was 'sincerely concerned with her "recovery and happiness" '. *The Letters of Charles Dickens*, ed. Kathleen Tillotson, The Pilgrim Edition, iv (Oxford: Clarendon Press, 1977), xi.

4. Edwin Hodder, *The Life and Work of the Seventh Earl of Shaftesbury, K.G.* (London: Cassell, 1887), iii, 298.

5. For the full text of these letters, see pp 43–6.

6. Edgar Johnson, *Charles Dickens: His Tragedy and Triumph* (New York: Simon and Schuster, 1952), i, 56. References to Johnson, by volume and page, will appear parenthetically in the text.

7. 'Shabby-Genteel People', *Sketches by Boz*.

8. *The Letters of Charles Dickens*, ed. Madeline House and Graham Storey, The Pilgrim Edition, ii (Oxford: Clarendon Press, 1969), 103n. Future references to this edition will appear parenthetically, using the abbreviation P with the volume and page number.

9. Cf. the language of Redlaw's reverie in 'The Gift Bestowed', *The Haunted Man* (1848). The Spectre's references to his neglected past, poverty, suffering, and attempts to hew knowledge 'from the mine where it was buried' echo this passage and strike a similar autobiographical resonance. Speaking at the Birmingham and Midland Institute on 27 Sep. 1869, Dickens returned to this notion of self-help and improvement, citing Lytton's lines about 'those twin gaolers' as a fine expression of truths familiar both to himself and his audience. See *The Speeches of Charles Dickens*, ed. K. J. Fielding (Oxford: Clarendon Press, 1960), p. 400.

10. William Dickens (1719–85) and Elizabeth Ball Dickens (1745?–1824) were steward and housekeeper to John Crewe, MP, later Lord Crewe. See P, i, 43n.

11. The varying dates given by Forster for the composition of the autobiographical fragment suggest that Dickens spread the writing of it over several years (P, iv, 653n), perhaps beginning in 1845 and continuing to 1847 or later. See also Forster i, ii, 19; i, i, 14n; and vi, vi, 74.

12. See the Biographical Table in P, i, xliii. Recent biographical research by Michael Allen, however, allows him to make a convincing case for assuming that the period at the blacking factory lasted until Mar. or Apr. 1825. See 'The Dickens Family in London, 1824–1827', *The Dickensian*, 76 (Spring 1983), 8–14. Allen's revision of the estimate of the length of time Dickens spent at Warren's also means that Dickens received less schooling than biographers have previously assumed (i.e., two rather than three years at Wellington House Academy) and demands, as he notes, 'serious re-assessment of this period of his life, and the consequential reactions to it'.

13. In his introduction to a Macmillan reprint of *DC* published in 1892, Charles Dickens, Jr., acting on his mother's wishes, noted that his father *had* shared the autobiographical fragment 'in strict confidence' with his wife. Her eldest son wrote: 'I have my mother's authority for saying . . . that the story was eventually read to her . . . by my father, who at the time intimated his intention of publishing it by and by as a portion of his autobiography.' Because Dickens spoke so harshly of his parents, Charley continues, Catherine persuaded her husband against publishing the story as a portion of his autobiography. Instead, as we know, he worked a part of the fragment into *DC*. Preparing his *Life* of Dickens, Forster did not consult with Catherine and so recounted Dickens's words without realising that he could have read the fragment to his wife *after* showing it to Forster.

14. See Angus Easson, ' "I, Elizabeth Dickens": Light on John Dickens's Legacy', *The Dickensian*, 67 (Jan. 1971), 35–40, and David Paroissien, 'Release from the Marshalsea and Warren's: A Rejoinder', *DSN*, 13 (Sep. 1982), 71–73. Economic misfortune continued to follow John Dickens on his release. In 1825 he retired from the civil service, supplementing his annual pension of £145 with journalistic work. Later he fell into debt again but was bailed out by Dickens in 1834 (see pp 24–5), who tried to remove his parents to the country to keep them out of harm (see pp 46–8).

15. For a note on Dickens's early career as a journalist, see pp 22–3. Dickens spoke of the benefits of his apprenticeship on 20 May 1865 in his address to the Newspaper Press Fund and again on 18 Apr. 1868 at the banquet in his honour given by the New York Press. See *The Speeches of Charles Dickens*, ed. K. J. Fielding, pp 346–7 and 379–80.

16. See Johnson, I, 72–3 and P, I, 16n. Evidence to support this plausible though unproved account of the role played by Maria's parents in the termination of Dickens's courtship of their daughter is scant. Lacking Maria's letters to Dickens in 1855, we can only infer from his letter to her on 22 Feb. that what she said in the letter to which he replied referred to obstacles not of Maria's making. '[I]f you had ever told me then what you tell me now,' Dickens wrote, 'I know . . . that the simple truth and energy which were in my love would have overcome everything.' This interpretation, of course, assumes that Maria correctly ascribes their difficulties to unspecified external causes and that, doing so, she overlooks the part her own cruel flirtatiousness also played in ending their relationship.

17. For the text of Dickens's letter, see pp 129–31. Cf. also 'PERSONAL' (Dickens's statement about the 'domestic trouble'), HW, 12 June 1858.

18. Referring to the difficulty of assessing accurately the reasons leading to the separation between Catherine and Dickens, K. J. Fielding comments that 'no understanding can be reached without appreciating what those who took part in the affair were like, and with the exception of the overshadowing figure of Dickens they all remain obscure'. See his 'Dickens and the Hogarth Scandal', *Nineteenth-Century Fiction*, 10 (June 1955), 74. Further useful comments by Fielding appear in his 'Charles Dickens and his Wife: Fact or Forgery?' *Etudes Anglaises*, 8 (1955), 212–22.

19. George Hogarth appears to have been at the height of his career when he first met Dickens in 1834; as his success as a music critic and journalist gradually dissipated, he became something of a dependant, relying on his famous son-in-law for work and financial assistance. See P, IV, 437, and Anne Lohrli, comp., *Household Words ... Contents ... Contributors* (Toronto: Univ. of Toronto Press, 1973), pp. 304–5.

20. The revolutionary impact of the Matrimonial Causes Act of 1857 (20 – 21 Vict. c. 85) lay in the constitution of a civil court in London to replace the ecclesiastical courts, which had had a monopoly over the granting of decrees dissolving marriages since Henry VIII. By the new Act, civil procedures became possible which formerly had been limited only to those who could afford the elaborate and costly practice of appealing to Parliament to dissolve a marriage. The main grounds for divorce stipulated in 1857 enabled a husband to dissolve his marriage if his wife were guilty of adultery but did not allow wives the reciprocal privilege of bringing suit against guilty husbands.

21. Dickens bought Gad's Hill on 14 Mar. 1856. For a note on the property, see pp 102–3. For a note on the date of Dickens's return from his tour with Collins, see p. 120.

22. 'Shy Neighborhoods,' *All the Year Round*, 26 May 1860 (also repr. in *UT*) opens with some general remarks about walking and an allusion to 'My last special feat' which make possible the dating of this incident. Dickens writes that he turned out of bed at two, 'after a hard day, pedestrian, and otherwise,' and walked 'thirty miles into the country to breakfast' (i.e., from Tavistock House, London, to Gad's Hill). The essay continues with a description of Dickens's mental state as he walked, dozed and dreamed. Forster, commenting on the piece, adds that Dickens was particularly impressed with a striking equinoctial dawn, and gives 15 Oct. 1857 as the date of the walk (Forster, VIII, v, 232). Edgar Johnson, citing an unpublished letter of Dickens to Mrs Watson of 7 Dec. 1857, notes that Dickens's row and walk took place 'some six or eight weeks previous to the date of the letter,' a date which agrees with Forster's (Johnson, II, lxxv).

23. I should stress the conjectural nature of the chronology implicit in my summary. Recounting the well-known anecdote of Katey's discovery of her mother weeping because Dickens had asked her to visit Ellen Ternan, Gladys Storey dates the occasion imprecisely as occurring one afternoon 'at the commencement of the affair' (*Dickens and Daughter*, p. 96). That phrase, in its context, refers not to Dickens's affair with Ellen Ternan but to the 'domestic disagreements' that made life so unhappy for everyone at Tavistock House since Ellen entered his life in July 1857, when he hired her to act in *The Frozen Deep*. A probable interpretation is that some months elapsed since the performance of the play in Manchester in Aug. 1857, during which period tension mounted, first as Dickens ordered his bedroom to be sealed off from his wife's, followed by his apparent refusal to live at Tavistock House shortly afterwards. Then, as word of Dickens's domestic troubles spread, perhaps linking him and Ellen, he may have felt compelled to show the world that his wife and Ellen were on friendly terms. Possibly confusion over the present followed, causing the final

rupture, a view taken by Johnson (II, 916–7) and others. In *Dickens and Daughter*, Storey specifies that Dickens asked Catherine to call on Ellen; in her working notes, she states that it was Mrs Ternan. See David Parker and Michael Slater, 'The Gladys Storey Papers', *The Dickensian*, 76 (Spring 1980), p. 4 and note 2.

24. Quoted by Gladys Storey, *Dickens and Daughter* (London: Muller, 1939), p. 96.

25. Bradbury and Evans refer to the dispute in a statement published in June 1859 in the front part of Thackeray's *Virginians*, which they published in monthly numbers from 31 Oct. 1857 to 1 Oct. 1859. Hoppé's edition of Forster's *Life* provides a slightly abridged version of their summary (vol. II, 465–6).

   Dickens also tried, with less success, to wage his war with Evans on a personal level by inserting an injunction into the Deed of Separation forbidding his children to see the publisher, to speak to him, or go to his house. See Charles Dickens, Jr, to Mrs Dickens, 13 July 1858 (*Mr. and Mrs. Charles Dickens*, ed. Dexter, pp. 280–1). Charley, however, courted and married Evan's daughter, Bessie. Dickens did not attend their wedding in Nov. 1861 and even expressed his 'earnest hope' that Charley's godfather, Thomas Beard, would not enter 'Mr. Evan's house on that occasion' (N, III, 250). A year later, Dickens relented by welcoming Charley, his wife, and their baby daughter at Gad's Hill for Christmas. K. J. Fielding discusses the quarrel with Evans in his 'Bradbury v. Dickens,' *The Dickensian*, 50 (1954), 73–82.

26. Ada B. Nisbet provides a brief but comprehensive account of Dickens's relationship with Ellen Ternan in her study *Dickens and Ellen Ternan* (Berkley and Los Angeles: Univ. of California Press, 1952). See also Hoppé's extended note in his edition of Forster's *Life* (II, 454–65), where he provides a short account of Dickens's friendship with the actress and refers to the evidence discovered by scholars of their liaison since the appearance in print of the first revelations about Ellen Ternan by Thomas Wright between 1934 and 1936.

27. Because no accurate record of the readings exists different accounts do not tally. George Dolby, *Charles Dickens as I Knew Him* (London: T. Fisher Unwin, 1885), pp. 450–1, gives 423 as the total; Philip Collins, ed., *Charles Dickens: The Public Readings* (Oxford: Clarendon Press, 1975), pp. xxv–vi, estimates that Dickens gave 'about 472 public readings'.

28. I should add in fairness to Forster that he later saw the readings from Dickens's perspective and defended him from possible charges of greed. 'No man could care essentially less for mere money than he did,' he observed, referring to the last contract that tempted Dickens to make his farewell readings and then read 'No More'. Yielding to the proposal, he thought, was a fatal mistake but 'not an ignoble one' (Forster, XI, i, 355).

29. Dickens died a wealthy man. Philip Collins, who bases his judgement on evidence supplied by Dolby, writes in his Preface to *The Public Readings* that 'Altogether the Readings earned Dickens about £45 000 – nearly half of the estate which he left in 1870 (£93 000)', p. xxix.

30. Dickens, speaking at the Birmingham Midland Institute, 27 Sep. 1869. See *Speeches*, ed. Fielding, p. 405. This observation, comments Forster,

expresses 'a principle that at all times guided' Dickens (Forster, XII, iii, 398). Elsewhere, Forster notes that Dickens's secret of success lay in his lifting himself to the level of his hero, David Copperfield, whose 'golden rules' included always trying in his heart to do well whatever he set himself to accomplish. See Forster, I, iii, 45.

31. See, for example, James Olney, reviewing Edgar Johnson's revised and abridged biography of Dickens in *DSN*, 10 (Mar. 1979), 23, and John Romano reviewing the MacKenzies' *Dickens: A Life*, in *Saturday Review*, 21 July 1979, p. 49.

32. Dickens to Miss Coutts, 8 Apr. 1860, *The Heart of Charles Dickens*, ed. Edgar Johnson (New York: Duell, Sloan and Pearce, 1952), p. 370; *Speeches*, ed. Fielding, p. 9.

33. *Speeches*, ed. Fielding, p. 413.

The Letters 1832–1869

MY DEAR KOLLIE, [sic]¹—I owe you ten thousand apologies for not having seen you last night, but the fact is that I found out late in the evening that I could not leave the House until a quarter past ten, and I thought it would be useless to endeavour to make my way into the city at that hour. As I was not aware of the melancholy fact in sufficient time to send for you (I mean *to* you, but I do not like scratching out) I hope I need not ask you to excuse the apparent inattention on my part. It is equally unnecessary to add that I was very much disappointed, as I looked forward to having a very comfortable couple of hours.

I fear, until the House is up, I can name no certain night on which I can go to play, except Saturday. However, I leave the selection of another day to your taste, always promising that if I accept your next invitation, no consideration shall induce me to depart from it.

With my best remembrances to [?], believe me, my dear Kollie, —Very truly yours.

I see there are two superfluous I's in this note, but I suppose you are not particular to a shade. The Sun² is so obscured that I intend living under the planet no longer than Saturday week next.

1. Henry William Kolle (?1808–81), a bank clerk engaged to Anne Beadnell. Kolle later delivered messages between Charles Dickens and Maria Beadnell. See p. 29. Dickens worked for the *True Sun*, an evening paper which began publication on 5 Mar. 1832, as a Parliamentary reporter.
2. Accounts about the beginning of Dickens's career as a journalist differ. In his letter to Kuenzel (see p. 43), he states that he began his reporting on the *Mirror of Parliament*; later, in a letter to Wilkie Collins (see p. 45), he added that he made his début in the gallery working for the *Mirror* 'at about eighteen, I suppose'. See also *Speeches*, ed. K. J. Fielding, p. 347, where Dickens makes the same statement when he addressed members of the Newspaper Press Fund on 20 May 1856. Forster, however, states that Dickens's 'first parliamentary service' was given to the *True Sun* in 1831 and that afterwards he was engaged for the *Mirror of Parliament* (Forster, I, iv, 49). Charles Kent, in 'Charles Dickens as a Journalist', *Time*, 5 (July 1881), points out that Forster's date is wrong because the *True Sun* did not

begin publication until the following year (p. 362). Kent also states that Dickens did not fill a regular and recognized position in the gallery until the parliamentary session of 1832, during which he worked for both the *Sun* and the *Mirror* (pp. 363–6). The Pilgrim editors suggest that possibly Dickens worked for the *Mirror* in 1831 (P, I, 2 and n.).

18 BENTINCK STREET, CAVENDISH SQUARE
Thursday, June 6th [1833]

SIR,[1]—I trust you will pardon the very great liberty I take in troubling you with any application on my own behalf, but as you have been kind enough to express an opinion in favour of my abilities as a reporter, and as you have had opportunities of perusing my Reports, and being enabled to judge of their accuracy, &c.,[2] I am induced to make a request of a strictly private nature—and I can only plead my reliance on your kindness, and a natural wish on my part to enlarge the field of my exertions as an excuse of making it.

I am always entirely unemployed during the recess. I need hardly say that I have many strong inducements for wishing to be so as little as possible, and thinking that perhaps in the course of the business with which you are connected, you are frequently to a certain extent engaged in the formation of commissions or other Public Boards on which the services of a Short Hand Writer are required, I have made up my mind to take the liberty of asking you, should you ever have an opportunity of recommendation if you would object to mentioning my name—Of course the value of a recommendation from such a quarter would be incalculable, and I trust the recommendation itself would not be misplaced.

I will not detain you further than by again apologising for writing to you, and venturing to express a hope that you will not consider my application impertinent, and consequently unworthy of notice.—I am Sir—Your most obliged servant.

1. Richard Earle (1796–1848), private secretary to Edward Stanley (later 14th Earl of Derby), Secretary of State for Ireland. The letter is crossed with the note: 'Not likely to have opportunity, but shd one occur, shd not hesitate to recommend.'
2. Stanley spoke in favour of the Suppression of Disturbances (Ireland) Bill during the debate in the Commons on 28 Feb. 1833 when the bill was first moved. Eight reporters, each working in spells of forty-five minutes, took down Stanley's long and famous speech. By chance it fell to Charles Dickens to cover the opening and closing portions; and when Stanley saw his speech in the newspaper, he was dissatisfied with what he found, except for the beginning and ending. Enquiries at the *Morning Chronicle* produced Dickens's name, and Stanley sent for him, asking Dickens to go

over the whole speech with him and write it out. 'Without further pause,' Dickens later recalled, 'he began and went rapidly on, hour after hour, to the end, often becoming very much excited and frequently bringing down his hand with great violence upon the desk near which he stood.' See James T. Fields, *In and Out of Doors with Charles Dickens* (1876; repr. New York: AMS Press Inc., 1976), pp. 143–5. See also P, I, 126 and n.

[October 1834]

MY DEAR EDITOR,[1]—I celebrated a christening a few months ago in the Monthly, and I find that Mr. Buckstone has officiated as self-elected godfather, and carried off my child to the Adelphi, for the purpose, probably, of fulfilling one of its sponsorial duties, viz. of teaching it the vulgar tongue.[2]

Now, as I claim an entire right to do "what I like with my own" and as I contemplated a dramatic destination for my offspring, I must enter my protest against the kidnapping process.

It is very little consolation to me to know, when my handkerchief is gone, that I may see it flaunting with renovated beauty in Field Lane;[3] and if Mr. Buckstone has too many irons in the fire to permit him to get up his own "things," I don't think he ought to be permitted to apply to my chest of drawers.

Just give him a good "blow up" in your "magazine"—will you?—I remain—Yours,—BOZ.

1. Capt. J. B. Holland, owner and editor of the *Monthly Magazine*, in which Dickens's first sketches appeared. 'The Bloomsbury Christening' was published in Apr. 1834.
2. John Baldwin Buckstone (1802–79; *DNB*), adapted Dickens's sketch to the stage as *The Christening*, which ran at the Adelphi from 13 Oct. 1834 to 6 Apr. 1835. Bills for the play credited neither Buckstone nor Dickens. This letter marks the beginning of Dickens's problems with plagiarists.
3. Field Lane, Holborn, a narrow street running from Holborn Hill to Saffron Hill. Its filthy shops, Dickens wrote in *OT*, ch. 26, exposed for sale 'huge bunches of second-hand silk handkerchiefs'.

BENTINCK STREET
Friday Morning [1834]

DEAR TOM,[1]—On waking this morning I was informed that my father (whom I have not seen, for he had gone out) had just been arrested by Shaw and Maxwell, the quondam wine people.[2] Will you have the goodness the moment you receive this to go over to Sloman's in Cursitor Street, and see him for me, and ascertain whether anything can be done?

I must work this morning, but tell him, please, I shall be with him about six—I dine at 5, if you can come up.

I fear it is an awkward business and really I have no idea of the extent of his other embarrassments.—Believe me, sincerely yours.

I have not yet been taken, but no doubt that will be the next act in this "domestic tragedy."

1. Thomas Mitton (1812–78), solicitor, and close early friend of Dickens.
2. This occasion represents John Dickens's second arrest for debt (cf. Introduction, p. 7). Sloman's in Cursitor Street, Chancery Lane was a house kept by a bailiff or sheriff's officer for the temporary confinement of debtors. Dickens draws on Sloman's for his fictional sponging house in 'A Passage in the Life of Mr. Watkins Tottle,' ch. 2 (*SB*) and for Coavinses' in *BH*, for whom Neckett worked as 'a follower', (chs 6, 10, and 15).

BENTINCK STREET
Saturday Evening [29th November 1834]
DEAR TOM,[1]—I arrived from Birmingham at 7 this morning and remained at the office until 10, correcting the proofs of the *whack*[2] for a second edition. I am rather fagged as you may suppose, having perpetrated four columns in as many hours before I left the town of dirt, iron-works, radicals, and hardware.

If I had not a little business to transact on my own account to night, I should, tired as I am, run the chance of finding you at home, for the purpose of saying a few words to you on a very distressing subject. My mother appears most anxious that your sister and yourself should be made acquainted with the situation in which she is placed. Knowing the anxiety of her feelings on this head, and concurring most sincerely with her, in valuing the friendship of yourself and family, most highly, I think it better to spare her the pain of making any communication by writing to you myself at once. I do this with the less reluctance as I have already, more than once, hinted to you my fears that the state of my father's affairs, and his want of attention to them, would render a change in our situation imperative.

The fact is simply this—for a time, at all events, we must disperse ourselves as best we can, consistently with a reasonable hope of consulting the interests of all.

My father, I apprehend, will not rejoin his family for some time; my mother and two sisters will reside in the immediate neighbourhood of our present lodgings—I hope in comfortable quarters, where they are not strangers—and I, taking Frederick with me, to instruct and provide for as best I can, shall repair to chambers in Furnival's Inn.[3]

This is no great mystery after all, and perhaps will prove a source of but little surprise to you; but as I wish to know the real state of the case without delay, and as I know my mother does the same, I have no hesitation in confiding it to you, to disclose just as much, or as little, or, as you think proper. There may be something of selfishness in this; for one never values friends so highly as in seasons of adversity, when their loss would be most felt. You may attribute this communication to what cause you please—as far as I am concerned I can have no wish for concealment, and to my mother and sisters I know it will be a relief to find, that you, and yours, know the worst.

I will conclude this long and gloomy epistle by saying that after such[4] trouble and anxiety, I think I have, in conjunction with a friend of ours, succeeded in making the best general arrangement that could possibly be effected. We have much more cause for cheerfulness than despondency after all; and as I for one am determined to see everything in as bright a light as possible, having thank God little at present to fear on my own score, and not much on theirs, I will not add another word on the subject.

I suppose I shall have the pleasure of seeing you before long. I shall be at home all to-morrow.

All here desire loves and so forth. Will you add my remembrances, and accept my assurances that I am,—Most sincerely yours.

1. Thomas Beard (1807–91), journalist. Beard and Dickens met in 1832 and became close friends. Beard was best man at his wedding and godfather to his eldest son.
2. *Whack*: a share of the report covering a meeting of Liberals in Birmingham (*OED*).
3. On 4 Dec. 1834 John Dickens told Beard that his wife and daughters were leaving Bentinck Street for more economical quarters, that Charles would look after his brother Frederick, and that he would go 'to the winds'. See Walter Dexter, ed., *Dickens to His Oldest Friend* (London: Putnam, 1932), p. 265. Frederick Dickens (1820–68) stayed temporarily with Charles at 13 Furnival's Inn, Holborn; Dickens found work for Frederick and supervised his early progress.
4. Much (P, i, 48).

BLACK BOY HOTEL, CHELMSFORD
Sunday Morning [11th January 1835]
DEAR TOM,—I am more anxious than I can well express to know the result of your Interview with Hodgkin [sic],[1] having set my heart on its being favourable. If you are not engaged to morrow, will you write me a line by return of Post, and resolve my doubts. I go into Suffolk on

Tuesday Morning early but my Head Quarters will be here, and I have no doubt I shall receive at once any letter that arrives, directed as above.

I wish of all things that you were with me. Barring the grime of solitude I have been very comfortable since I left town and trust I shall remain so until I return, which I shall do about the latter end of the week, unless I receive orders from the office to the contrary.

Owing to the slippery state of the roads on the morning I started, I magnanimously declined the honor of driving myself, and hid my dignity in the Inside of a Stage Coach. As the Election here had not commenced, I went on to Colchester (which is a very nice town) and returned here on the following morning. Yesterday I had to start at 8 o'clock for Braintree—a place 12 miles off: and being unable to get a saddle horse, I actually ventured on a gig,—and what is more, I actually did the four and twenty miles without upsetting it. I wish to God you could have seen me tooling in and out of the banners, drums, conservative emblems, horsemen, and go-carts with which every little green was filled as the processions were waiting for Sir John Tyrell and Baring.[2] Every time the horse heard a drum he bounced into the hedge, or the left side of the road; and every time I got him out of that, he bounded into the hedge on the right side. When he *did* go however, he went along admirably. The road was clear when I returned, and with the trifling exception of breaking my whip, I flatter myself I did the whole thing in something like style.

If any one were to ask me what in my opinion was the dullest and most stupid spot on the face of the Earth, I should decidedly say Chelmsford. Though only 29 miles from town, there is a not a single shop where they sell Sunday Papers. I can't get an Athenæum, a Literary Gazette—no not even a penny Magazine, and here I am on a wet Sunday looking out of a damned large bow window at the rain as it falls into the puddles opposite; wondering when it will be dinner time, and cursing my folly in having put no books into my Portmanteau. The only book I have seen here is one which lies upon the sofa. It is entitled "Field Exercises and Evolutions of the Army, by Sir Henry Torrens" [1824]. I have read it through so often, that I am sure I could drill a hundred recruits from memory. There is not even anything to look at in the place, except two immense prisons, large enought to hold all the Inhabitants of the county—whom they can have been built for I can't imagine.

I fear among the gloomy reflections which will present themselves to my mind this day that of having entailed upon you the misery of decyphering such an unconnected mass as this, will not be the least. As I thought it very likely however, that you would never get beyond the first three sentences I have comprised in them, the whole object of my letter, knowing that whether you come to the end of it or not, you would believe without a written assurance that I am—Most sincerely yours.

My best remembrances to all.

1. Thomas Hodgskin (1786–1869), journalist, and editor of *Hansard*, 1834-7, to whom Beard had presumably applied for a job.
2. Sir John Tyssen Tyrell (1795–1877) and Alexander Baring (1774–1848), the Tory candidates for North Essex.

13 FURNIVALS INN

Tuesday evening Twentieth January 1835

MY DEAR SIR,[1]—As you have begged me to write an original sketch for the first number of the new evening paper, and as I trust to your kindness to refer my application to the proper quarter, should I be unreasonably or improperly trespassing upon you, I beg to ask whether it is probable that if I commenced a series of articles, written under some attractive title, for the Evening Chronicle, its conductors would think I had any claim to *some* additional remuneration (of course, of no great amount) for doing so?[2]

Let me beg of you not to misunderstand my meaning. Whatever the reply may be, I promised you an article, and shall supply it with the utmost readiness, and with an anxious desire to do my best, which I honestly assure you would be the feeling with which I shall always receive any request coming personally from yourself. I merely wish to put it to the proprietors, first, whether a continuation of light papers in the style of my Street Sketches[3] would be considered of use to the new paper; and, secondly, if so, whether they do not think it fair and reasonable that, taking my share of the ordinary reporting business of the Chronicle besides, I should receive something for the papers beyond my ordinary salary as a reporter.

Begging you to excuse my troubling you, and taking this opportunity of acknowledging the numerous kindnesses I have already received at your hands since I have had the pleasure of acting under you, I am, my dear Sir,—Very sincerely yours.

1. George Hogarth (1783–1870), Dickens's future father-in-law. Music critic of the *Morning Chronicle*; appointed co-editor of the *Evening Chronicle* in 1835.

2. Dickens's 20 'Sketches of London' began on 31 Jan. 1835 and continued until 20 Aug. in the *Evening Chronicle*. During this period his salary increased from five to seven guineas.
3. A series of five published in the *Morning Chronicle* from 26 Sep. to 15 Dec. 1834.

FITZROY STREET
Thursday morning [1832]

MY DEAR KOLLE,—I would really feel some delicacy in asking you again to deliver the enclosed as addressed, were it not for two reasons. In the first place, you know so well my existing situation that you must be almost perfectly aware of the general nature of the note, and in the second, I should not have written it, for I should have communicated its contents verbally, were it not that I lost the opportunity of keeping the old gentleman out of the way as long as possible last night. To these reasons you may add that I have not the slightest objection to your knowing its contents from the first syllable to the last.

I trust under these circumstances that you will not object to doing me the very essential service of delivering the enclosed as soon this afternoon as you can, and perhaps you will accompany the delivery by asking Miss Beadnell only to read it when she is quite alone. Of course in this sense I consider you as nobody.

By complying with this request you will confer a very great favour on, dear Kolle,—Yours most truly.
Excuse haste.

18 BENTINCK STREET
March 18th [1833]

DEAR MISS BEADNELL,[1]—Your own feelings will enable you to imagine far better than any attempt of mine to describe the painful struggle it has cost me to make up my mind to adopt the course which I now take—a course than which nothing can be so directly opposed to my wishes and feelings, but the necessity of which becomes daily more apparent to me. Our meetings of late have been little more than so many displays of heartless indifference on the one hand, while on the other they have never failed to prove a fertile source of wretchedness and misery; and seeing, as I cannot fail to do, that I have engaged in a pursuit which has long since been worse than hopeless and a further perseverance in which can only expose me to deserved ridicule, I have made up my mind to return the little present I received from you some time since (which I have always prized, as I still do, far beyond anything I ever possessed) and the other enclosed mementos of our past correspondence which I am sure it must be gratifying to you to receive, as after our recent situations they are certainly better adapted for your custody than mine.

Need I say that I have not the most remote idea of hurting your feelings by the few lines which I think it necessary to write with the accompanying little parcel? I must be the last person in the world who could entertain such an intention, but I feel that this is neither a matter nor a time for cold, deliberate, calculating trifling. *My* feelings upon any subject more especially upon this, must be to you a matter of very little moment; still *I have* feelings in common with other people—perhaps so far as they relate to you they have been as strong and as good as ever warmed the human heart—and I do feel that it is mean and contemptible of me to keep by me one gift of yours or to preserve one single line or word of remembrance, or affection from you. I therefore return them, and I can only wish that I could as easily forget that I ever received them.

I have but one more word to say and I say it in my own vindication. The result of our past acquaintance is indeed a melancholy one to me. I have felt too long ever to lose the feeling of utter desolation and wretchedness which has succeeded our former acquaintance. Thank God I can claim for myself and *feel* that I deserve the merit of having ever throughout our intercourse acted fairly, intelligibly and honourably, under[2] kindness and encouragement one day and a total change of conduct the next I have ever been the same. I have ever acted without reserve. I have never held out encouragement which I knew I never meant; I have never indirectly sanctioned hopes which I well knew I did not intend to fulfil. I have never made a mock confidante to whom to entrust a garbled story for my own purposes, and I think I never should (though God knows I am not likely to have the opportunity) encourage one danger as a useful shield for—an excellent set off against—others more fortunate and doubtless more deserving. I have done nothing that I could say would be very likely to hurt you. If (I can hardly believe it possible), I have said anything which can have that effect I can only ask you to place yourself for a moment in my situation, and you will find a much better excuse than I can possibly devise. A wish for your happiness altho' it comes from me may not be the worse for being sincere and heartfelt. Accept it as it is meant, and believe that nothing will ever afford me more real delight than to hear that you, the object of my first and my last love are happy. If you are as happy as I hope you may be, you will indeed possess every blessing that this world can afford.

1. Maria Sarah Beadnell (1810–86), Dickens's first love, and the third and youngest daughter of George and Maria Beadnell. When he wrote *DC* (1849–50), he recalled in Copperfield's courtship of Dora some of his own youthful ardour. Maria, much changed, re-entered Dickens's life in Feb. 1855 as Mrs Henry L. Wibter. See pp 106–17. Dickens records a changed perspective in *LD* (1855–7), where Flora Finching derives from the same original, now middle-aged, talkative, and 'extremely fat', as Dickens wrote to the Duke of Devonshire on 5 July 1856 (N, II, 785).
2. Under . . . New sentence (P, I, 17).

18 BENTINCK STREET
Sunday morning [19th May 1833]

DEAR MISS BEADNELL,—I am anxious to take the earliest opportunity of writing you again, knowing that the opportunity of addressing you through Kolle—now my only means of communicating with you—will shortly be lost, and having your own permission to write to you—I am most desirous of forwarding a note which had I received such permission earlier, I can assure you you would have received ere now. Before proceeding to say a word upon the subject of my present note let me beg you to believe that your request to see Marianne Leigh's answer is rendered quite unnecessary by my previous determination to shew it you, which I shall do immediately on receiving it—that is to say, if I receive any at all. If I know anything of her art or disposition however you are mistaken in supposing that her remarks will be directed against yourself. *I* shall be the mark at which all the anger and spleen will be directed—and I shall take it very quietly for whatever she may say I shall positively decline to enter into any further controversy with *her*. I shall have no objection to break a lance, paper or otherwise, with any champion to whom she may please to entrust her cause but I will have no further correspondence or communication with her personally or in writing. I have copied the note and done up the parcel which will go off by the first Clapton Coach tomorrow morning.

And now to the object of my present note. I have considered and reconsidered the matter, and I have come to the unqualified determination that I will allow no feeling of pride, no haughty dislike to making a conciliation to prevent my expressing it without reserve. I will advert to nothing that has passed, I will not again seek to excuse any part I have acted or to justify it by any course you have ever pursued; I will revert to nothing that has ever passed between us—I will only openly and at once say that there is nothing I have more at heart, nothing I more sincerely and earnestly desire, than to be reconciled to you. It would be useless for me to repeat here what I have so often said before; it would be equally useless to look forward and state my hopes for the future—all that anyone can do to raise himself by his own exertions and unceasing assiduity I have done, and will do. I have no guide by which to ascertain your present feelings and I have, God knows, no means of influencing them in my favour. I never have loved and I can never love any human creature breathing but yourself. We have had many differences, and we have lately been entirely separated. Absence, however, has not altered my feelings in the slightest degree, and the Love I now tender you is as pure and as lasting as at any period of our former correspondence. I have now done all I can to remove our most unfortunate and to me most unhappy misunderstanding. The matter now of course rests solely with you, and you will decide as your own feelings and wishes direct you. I could say much for myself and I could entreat a favourable consideration on my own behalf but I purposely abstain from doing so because it would be only a repetition of an oft told tale and because I am sure that nothing I could say would have the effect of influencing your decision in any degree whatever. Need I say that to me it is a matter of vital import and the most intense anxiety?—I fear that the numerous claims which must necessarily be made on your time and attention next week will prevent you answering this note within anything like the time which my impatience would name.

Let me entreat you to consider your determination well whatever it be and let me implore you to communicate it to me as early as possible. As I am anxious to convey this note into the City in time to get it delivered today, I will at once conclude by begging you to believe me,—Yours sincerely.

FURNIVALS INN
Wednesday Evening [10th February 1836]
MY DEAREST KATE,[1]—The house is up; but I am very sorry to say that I *must* stay at home. I have had a visit from the Publishers this morning, and the story[2] cannot be any longer delayed—it must be done tomorrow. As there are more important considerations than the mere payment for the story, involved too, I must exercise a little self denial, and set to work.

They (Chapman & Hall) have made me an offer of *£14 a month* to write and edit a new publication they contemplate, entirely by myself; to be published monthly and each number to contain four wood cuts. I am to make my estimate and calculation, and to give them a decisive answer on Friday morning. The work will be no joke, but the emolument is too tempting to resist. . . .

1. Catherine Hogarth (1815–79), eldest daughter of George and Georgina Hogarth, later Dickens's wife.
2. Edward Chapman (1840–80) and William Hall (?1801–47), booksellers and publishers. Dickens had agreed to contribute 'The Tuggs's at Ramsgate' for their *Library of Fiction*, to be published at the end of Mar. 1836. Their proposal led to the publication of *PP* as a monthly serial.

15 FURNIVALS INN
Thursday, March 31st, 1836

MY DEAR UNCLE,[1]—The great success of my book,[2] and the name it has established for me among the publishers, enables [*sic*] me to settle at an earlier period than I at first supposed possible; I have, therefore, fixed Saturday next for my marriage with Miss Hogarth, the daughter of a gentleman who has recently distinguished himself by a celebrated work on music,[3] who was the most intimate friend and companion of Sir Walter Scott, and one of the most eminent among the literati of Edinburgh.[4]

There is no member of my family to whom I should be prouder to introduce my wife than yourself, but I am compelled to say—and I am sure you cannot blame me for doing so—that the same cause which has led me for a long time past to deny myself the pleasure and advantage of your society prevents my doing so. If I could not as a single man, I cannot as a married one, visit at a relation's house from which my father is excluded,[5] nor can I see any relatives here who would not treat him as they would myself.

This is a very painful subject, and I have many associations connected with you which render it much more painful in this case than in any other. I cannot forget that I was once your little companion and nurse, through a weary illness, nor shall I ever cease to remember the many proofs you have given me in later days of your interest and affection.

When I say, uncle, that I should be more happy than I can possibly express if you would place it in my power to know you once again on those terms of intimacy and friendship I so sincerely desire, I hope you will not misunderstand my meaning. I do not ask you—I should conceive that I lowered and disgraced myself if I did—to alter your determination. I may think that time might have softened the determined animosity . . .[6] I may . . . an injustice (. . . I have no doubt) to my father's real character. I cannot, however, be an impartial judge because I cannot be an unprejudiced one; and I do not presume, therefore, to arraign your decision.

Nothing that has occurred to me in my life has given me greater pain than thus denying myself the society of yourself and aunt. I have only to add that the contents of this letter are unknown to everybody but Aunt Charlton, to whom I have written on the same subject, and that come what may, I shall ever be at heart,—dear Uncle,—Your most affectionate nephew.

1. Thomas Culliford Barrow (?1793–1857), Mrs John Dickens's eldest brother. Charles and Catherine became engaged in May 1835; they were married on 2 Apr. 1836 at St. Luke's Church, Chelsea.
2. *SB*, First Series (1836).
3. George Hogarth, Dickens's father-in-law; lawyer, musician, music critic, journalist, and author of *Musical History, Biography, and Criticism* (1835). Hogarth married Georgina Thomson (1793–1863) in 1814 and had ten children.
4. Through his sister Christian's marriage to James Ballantyne, Hogarth became Scott's trusted friend and adviser.
5. Trouble had arisen between Barrow and John Dickens because the latter failed to pay an annuity, guaranteed by Barrow in 1819, to a third party in return for £200. In 1821 Barrow was called upon to repay both the principal and six months' arrears of the annuity (P, I, 144n). W. J. Carlton writes about this episode in ' "The Deed" in *David Copperfield*', *The Dickensian*, 48 (June 1952), 101–6. Dickens visited his uncle several times in 1823 after Barrow broke his thigh. See Carlton, 'The Barber of Dean Street', *The Dickensian*, 48 (Dec. 1951), 8–12.
6. Letter torn here.

FURNIVALS INN
Wednesday Morning [July 1836]

MY DEAR MACRONE,[1]—If you still think that Fred would be of any use to you, I have made up my mind that I should very much like him to be initiated into business habits, in your Accounting[2] House. I know you will find him very quick and steady; and if you really want any sharp young fellow, you can not have one better suited to your purpose. I have deliberated a long time about the propriety of keeping him at his present study, but I am convinced that at his present period of life, it is really only so much waste time. If you write me word that you will give him a stool, he shall sit himself upon it forthwith. [. . .]

1. John Macrone (1809–37), publisher of Dickens's *SB*. For Frederick Dickens, see p. 26, n. 3.
2. Counting House (P, I, 157).

COLLIN'S FARM. NORTH END. HAMPSTEAD
Wednesday Evening [17th May 1837]

MY DEAR AINSWORTH,[1]—I have been so much unnerved and hurt by the loss of the dear girl whom I loved,[2] after my wife, more deeply and fervently than anyone on earth, that I have been compelled for once to give up all idea of my monthly work and to try a fortnight's rest and quiet. I have hired a very small cottage here, and have repaired hither for a little change of air and scene.

I believe there is some cross road which leads out very near your house. I wish you would show me the way by coming here. You cannot think how glad I should be to see you just now. I have given you the address above, and must leave the rest to you.—With compliments to the Ladies,—Believe me—Most Faithfully Yours.

1. William Harrison Ainsworth (1805–82), historical novelist.
2. Mary Scott Hogarth (1819–37), Catherine's next younger sister, spent long periods with Catherine and Charles after their marriage. On 6 May 1837, Charles, Catherine and Mary went to St. James's theatre, where they saw Dickens's curtain raiser, 'Is She His Wife? Or, Something Singular', a 'new and grand operatic burletta', *The Eagle's H*[a]*unt*, by Edward Fitzball, and an afterpiece called *The Illustrious Stranger*, presumably a revival of the play by that name by Kenney and Millingen that appeared at Drury Lane in 1827. Mary was suddenly taken ill later that night, and she died in Dickens's arms at 3 p.m. on 7 May. His intense grief at her death forced him to postpone the June instalment of *PP* and *OT*.

   Mary was buried in Kensal Green Cemetery on 13 May; Dickens composed the inscription for her tomb. 'Mary Scott Hogarth / Died 7th May 1837 / Young Beautiful and Good / God in His Mercy / Numbered Her with His Angels / At the Early Age of / Seventeen.' Dickens expressed a wish to be buried in the same grave, but he gave up the idea when her brother George died in 1841. The impact of Mary and her death can be seen in his fictional portraits of Rose Maylie (*OT*) and Little Nell (*OCS*).

COLLINS'S FARM, NORTH END, HAMPSTEAD
Wednesday evening [17th May 1837]

MY DEAR BEARD,—I received your kind letter in due course. I should have written to you myself to communicate the dreadful occurrence but I had so many distressing appeals to my attention and exertions, that I was compelled to postpone doing so for a time.

I presume you heard from my father, that on the Saturday Night we had been to the Theatre—that we returned home as usual—that poor Mary was in the same health and spirits in which you have so often seen her—that almost immediately after she went upstairs to bed she was taken ill—and that next day she died. Thank God she died in my arms, and the very last words she whispered were of me.

Of our sufferings at the time, and all through the dreary week that ensued, I will say nothing—no one can imagine what they were. You have seen a good deal of her, and can feel for us, and imagine what a blank she has left behind. The first burst of my grief has passed, and I can think and speak of her calmly and dispassionately. I solemnly believe that so perfect a creature never breathed. I knew her inmost heart, and her real worth and values. She had not a fault.

Mrs. Hogarth has suffered and still continues to suffer most deep and bitter anguish. Kate, I am glad to say, made such strong efforts to console her, that she unconsciously summoned up all her fortitude at the same time, and brought it to her own assistance. She knows that if ever a mortal went to heaven, her sister is there, she has nothing to remember but a long course of affection and attachment, perhaps never exceeded. Not one cross word or angry look on either side even as children rests in judgment against her, and she is now so calm and cheerful that I wonder to see her.

I have been so shaken and unnerved by the loss of one whom I so dearly loved that I have been compelled to lay aside all thoughts of my usual monthly work, for once, and we have come here for quiet and change. We have a cottage of our own, with large gardens, and everything else on a small scale. Kate is very anxious indeed to see you, and I can assure you that you will derive anything but pain from seeing her. I hope you will join us in the old way. Name your own time, and believe me that there is no one whom it would give us so much pleasure to welcome as yourself.—Believe me, my dear Beard,—Ever faithfully yours.

48 DOUGHTY STREET
Wednesday Morning [12th July 1837][1]

MY DEAR JOHNS,[2]—I should have written either to you or Mrs. Johns long ere this, had I not had so many painful and distressing demands on my time and exertions, as to render me for a time apparently unmindful of many kind and esteemed friends.

The loss we deplore and to which the Pickwick notice bears reference,[3] is the sudden death in this house, of our dear sister Mary Hogarth. On the day previous to that on which you dined with us she had gone home—to see her Mama. On the day after, she returned. On the Saturday Evening we went to the Saint James's Theatre; she went upstairs to bed at about one o'clock in perfect health and her usual delightful spirits; was taken ill before she had undressed and died in my arms next afternoon at 3 o'clock. Everything that could possibly be done *was* done but nothing could save her. The medical men imagine it was a disease of the heart.

From the day of our marriage the dear girl had been the grace and life of our home, our constant companion, and the sharer of all our little pleasures. The love and affection which subsisted between her and her sister, no one can imagine the extent of. We might have known that we were too happy together to be long without a change.

The change has come, and it has fallen heavily upon us. I have lost the dearest friend I ever had. Words cannot describe the pride I felt in her, and the devoted attachment I bore her. She well deserved it, for with abilities far beyond her years, with every attraction of youth and beauty, and conscious as she must have been of everybody's admiration, she had not a single fault, and was in life almost as far above the foibles and vanity of her sex and age as she is now in Heaven.

Mrs. Dickens has had a trying task, for in the midst of her own affliction she has had to soothe the sufferings of her bereaved mother who was called here in time to see her child expire, and remained here in a state of total insensibility for a week afterwards. She has borne up through here severe trial like what she is—a fine-hearted noble-minded girl. I have removed her to a quiet cottage at Hampstead where we think of staying for some weeks to come; and the first anguish of her grief being passed she is quite resigned and cheerful. From their earliest infancy to this moment she can call up no single recollection of an unkind word or look having ever passed between them, and she looks forward to being mercifully permitted one day to rejoin her sister in that happy world for which God adapted her better than for this.

I should have said that the affliction we have suffered brought on a miscarriage but that she has perfectly recovered from it.

Pray present my best remembrances to Mrs. Johns, and believe me that it will afford me the very greatest gratification if you will make this house your own when you next come to London.—My dear Johns,—Very faithfully yours.

1. Misdated in N; the date should be 31 May 1837.
2. Richard Johns (1805–51), Lieut., Royal Marines.
3. The Pilgrim editors suggest that the Pickwick notice refers to an announcement (untraced) sent by Dickens's publishers to booksellers about the temporary suspension of *PP* (P, I, 263n).

DOUGHTY STREET
Thursday Night, October 26th, 1837

MY DEAR MRS. HOGARTH,—I need not thank you for your present of yesterday, for you know the sorrowful[1] pleasure I shall take in wearing it, and the care with which I shall prize it, until—so far as relates to this life—I am like her.[2]

I have never had her ring off my finger by day or night, except for an instant at a time, to wash my hands, since she died. I have never had her sweetness and excellence absent from my mind so long. I can solemnly say that, waking or sleeping, I have never lost the recollection of our hard trial and sorrow, and I feel that I never shall.

It will be a great relief to my heart when I find you sufficiently calm upon this sad subject to claim the promise I made you when she lay dead in this house, never to shrink from speaking of her, as if her memory must be avoided, but rather to take a melancholy pleasure in recalling the times when we were all so happy—so happy that increase of fame and prosperity has only widened the gap in my affections, by causing me to think how she would have shared and enhanced all our joys, and how proud I should have been (as God knows I always was) to possess the affections of the gentlest and purest creature that ever shed a light on earth. I wish you could know how I weary now for the three rooms in Furnival's Inn, and how I miss that pleasant smile and those sweet words which, bestowed upon our evening's work, in our merry banterings round the fire, were more precious to me than the applause of a whole world would be. I can recall everything she said and did in those happy days, and could show you every passage and line we read together.

I see *now* how you are capable of making great efforts, even against the afflictions you have to deplore, and I hope that, soon, our words may be where our thoughts are, and that we may call up those old memories, not as shadows of the bitter past, but as lights upon a happier future.[3]—Believe me, my dear Mrs. Hogarth.—Ever truly and affectionately yours.

1. Mournful (P, I, 323).
2. Dickens had received from Mrs Hogarth 'a chain of Mary Hogarth's hair' on 25 Oct. in remembrance of Mary's birthday (P, I, 323).
3. Dexter makes no reference in N to a preceding sentence in the last paragraph referring to Catherine's 'coming confinement.' See P, I, 323 and n.

Sunday, Twenty-fourth October, 1841
MY DEAR MRS. HOGARTH,—For God's sake be comforted, and bear this well, for the love of your remaining children.

I had always intended to keep poor Mary's grave for us and our dear children, and for you. But if it will be any comfort to you to have poor George[1] buried there, I will cheerfully arrange to place the ground at your entire disposal. Do not consider me in any way. Consult only your own heart. Mine seems to tell me that as they both died so young and so suddenly, they ought both to be buried together.

Try—do try—to think that they have but preceded you to happiness, and will meet you with joy in heaven. There *is* consolation in the knowledge that you have treasure there, and that while you live on earth, there are creatures among the angels, who owed their being to you.—Always yours with true affection.

1. George Thompson Hogarth (1821–41), Mrs Hogarth's son, had died suddenly on 24 Oct. George Hogarth was buried in Mary's grave. See the next letter.

25th October 1841
[John Forster][1]. . . As no steps had been taken towards the funeral I thought it best at once to bestir myself; and not even you could have saved my going to the cemetery. It is a great trial to me to give up Mary's grave;[2] greater than I can possibly express. I thought of moving her to the catacombs and saying nothing about it; but then I remembered that the poor old lady is buried next her at her own desire,[3] and could not find it in my heart, directly she is laid in the earth, to take her grandchild away. The desire to be buried next her is as strong upon me now, as it was five years ago; and I *know* (for I don't think there ever was love like that I bear her) that it will never diminish. I fear I can do nothing. Do you think I can? They would move her on Wednesday, if I resolved to have it done. I cannot bear the thought of being excluded from her dust; and yet I feel that her brothers and sisters, and her mother, have a better right than I to be placed beside her.[4] It is but an idea. I neither think nor hope (God forbid) that our spirits would ever mingle *there*. I ought to get the better of it, but it is very hard. I never contemplated this—and coming so suddenly, and after being ill, it disturbs me more than it ought. It seems like losing her a second time. . . .

1. John Forster (1812–76), historian, biographer and Dickens's closest

friend. Soon after the two met in 1836–7, Forster aided Dickens in his disputes with publishers and took on the role of negotiator and literary adviser. In the mid fifties Dickens began to turn more to Wilkie Collins for recreation, but Forster remained his 'right hand and cool shrewd head too' (N, I, 817).
2. To make room for George T. Hogarth. See last letter.
3. Mrs George Thompson, Mrs Hogarth's mother, who died 13 Oct. 1841 and who was buried in the grave adjoining Mary's. Dickens wrote a special epitaph for Mrs Thompson's tombstone, but the inscription was never used. See P, II, 432n.
4. Mary's mother and father were also buried in her grave.

GRETA BRIDGE

Thursday, February 1st, 1838

MY DEAREST KATE,—I am afraid you will receive this later than I could wish, as the mail does not come through this place until two o'clock to-morrow morning. However, I have availed myself of the very first opportunity of writing, so the fault is that mail's, and not this.

We reached Grantham between nine and ten on Tuesday night, and found everything prepared for our reception in the very best inn I have ever put up at.[1] It is odd enough that an old lady, who had been outside all day and came in towards dinner time, turned out to be the mistress of a Yorkshire school returning from the holiday stay in London. She was a very queer old lady, and showed us a long letter she was carrying to one of the boys from his father, containing a severe lecture (enforced and aided by many texts of Scripture) on his refusing to eat boiled meat. She was very communicative, drank a great deal of brandy and water, and towards evening became insensible, in which state we left her.

Yesterday we were up again shortly after seven A.M., came on upon our journey by the Glasgow mail, which charged us the remarkably low sum of six pounds fare for two places inside. We had a very droll male companion until seven o'clock in the evening, and a most delicious lady's-maid for twenty miles, who implored us to keep a sharp look-out at the coach-windows, as she expected the carriage was coming to meet her and she was afraid of missing it. We had many delightful vauntings of the same kind; but in the end it is scarcely necessary to say that the coach did not come, but a very dirty girl did.

As we came further north the mire[2] grew deeper. About eight o'clock it began to fall heavily, and, as we crossed the wild heaths hereabout, there was no vestige of a track. The mail kept on well, however, and at eleven we reached a bare place with a house standing alone in the midst of a dreary moor, which the guard informed us was Greta Bridge. I was in a perfect agony of apprehension, for it was fearfully cold, and there were no outward signs of anybody being up in the house. But to our great joy we discovered a comfortable room, with drawn curtains and a most blazing fire. In half an hour they gave us a smoking supper and a bottle of mulled port (in which we drank your health), and then we retired to a couple of capital bedrooms, in each of which there was a rousing fire halfway up the chimney.

We have had for breakfast, toast, cakes, a Yorkshire pie, a piece of beef about the size and much the shape of my portmanteau, tea, coffee, ham, and eggs; and are now going to look about us. Having finished our discoveries, we start in a postchaise for Barnard Castle, which is only four miles off, and there I deliver the letter given me by Mitton's friend. All the schools are round about that place, and a dozen old abbeys besides, which we shall visit by some means or other to-morrow. We shall reach York on Saturday I hope, and (God willing) I trust I shall be at home on Wednesday morning. [. . .]

A thousand loves and kisses to the darling boy, whom I see in my mind's eye crawling about the floor of this Yorkshire inn. Bless his heart, I would give two sovereigns for a kiss. Remember me too to Frederick, who I hope is attentive to you.[3]

Is it not extraordinary that the same dreams which have constantly visited me since poor Mary died follow me everywhere? After all the change of scene and fatigue, I have dreamt of her ever since I left home, and no doubt shall till I return. I should be sorry to lose such visions, for they are very happy ones, if it be only the seeing her in one's sleep. I would fain believe, too, sometimes, that her spirit may have some influence over them, but their perpetual repetition is extraordinary.[4]—Love to all friends.—Ever, my dear Kate,—Your affectionate Husband.

1. Dickens and Hablot Knight Browne, the illustrator of all his novels (except *OT*) up to and including *TTC*, left London on 30 Jan. 1838 for their expedition to gather materials about the Yorkshire Schools for use in *NN*.
2. Snow. P, I, 365.
3. Dexter's transcription of this paragraph in N omits Dickens's injunction to Kate not to leave their son alone 'too much' and his reminder to his 'dearest' to take care of herself. See P, I, 366.
4. Telling Catherine about the dreams stopped them. Dickens's next recorded dream of Mary was in Sep. 1844.

48 DOUGHTY STREET
12 February 1838

SIR,[1]—Mrs. Macrone the widow of the late publisher of St. James's Square, is left, after several meetings of her deceased husband's creditors in a state of utter destitution; not one farthing remaining for her support and that of two infant children.[2]

This distressing circumstance having become known to Mr. Ainsworth and myself, it has occurred to us that if some small collection of papers in one volume could be made for this young widow's benefit, the produce of the sale of an edition to some respectable bookseller would afford her the means of setting on foot some little scheme for her future support.[3] If this be done at all, it must be done immediately.

Mr. George Cruikshank has kindly offered his gratuitious assistance in illustrating this book.[4] For its literary contents we can appeal only to those who were on any occasion connected, however slightly, with poor Mr. Macrone in business.

May we venture to ask whether your engagements will admit of your assistance with any trifle from your pen? I need scarcely say how much it would aid the project, nor can I describe to you how much of real charity you would be instrumental in promoting.

I may add that besides lending our humble assistance in the same way, we are willing to take upon ourselves the entire arrangements of the volume and to negotiate for its sale and publication, which we trust is a sufficient security to you that no improper use would be made of your contribution. I trust the urgency of this distressing case is a sufficient excuse, both for my troubling you with this letter, and begging the favor of a reply, *at your earliest convenience.*—I am Sir—Your obedient Servant.

1. Allan Cunningham (1784–1842), journalist and author.
2. Eliza Adeline Bordwine married Macrone in Jan. 1835. Macrone died on 9 Sep. 1837, leaving his wife and children without support. John Macrone (1809–37), published Dickens's *SB*.
3. The *Pic Nic Papers*, 1841, edited by Dickens, raised £450 for her.
4. George Cruikshank (1792–1878), artist, caricaturist and by 1835 the leading book illustrator of the day, contributed two illustrations, one of which, 'The Philosopher's Stone', was for Dickens's 'The Lamplighter's Story'.

Monday Evening [July 1838]

MY DEAR SIR,[1]—Pray keep the English Authors as long as you please. I only wish the collection were a more comprehensive and interesting one.

I am ashamed to confess that, in the hurry of many engagements, I have quite forgotten your request.[2] That I may forget it no longer, I will tell you "all I know" at once.

I was born at Portsmouth, an English seaport town, principally remarkable for mud, Jews, and sailors,[3] on the 7th of February, 1812. My father holding in those days a situation under Government in the Navy Pay Office, which called him in the discharge of his duty to different places, I came to London a child of two years old, left it again at six, and then left it again for another seaport town—Chatham,[4] where I remained some six or seven years, and then came back to London with my parents and half-a-dozen brothers and sisters, whereof I was second in seniority.

I had begun an irregular rambling education under a clergyman at Chatham, and I finished it at a good school in London—tolerably early, for my father was not a rich man, and I had to begin the world. So I began it in a lawyer's office—which is a very little world, and a very dull one—and leaving it at the expiration of two years, devoted myself for some time to the acquirement of such general literature as I could pick up in the Library of the British Museum—and to the study of shorthand, with a view of trying what I could do as a reporter—not for the newspapers, but legal authorities in our Ecclesiastical Courts. I was very successful in this pursuit—was induced to join the Mirror of Parliament, a publication which was at that time devoted solely to the debates[5]—and afterwards to attach myself to the Morning Chronicle,[6] where I remained until the four or five first numbers of The Pickwick Papers had appeared, and in the columns of which journal most of my shorter sketches were originally published.[7] Some few appeared in the old Monthly Magazine. I may tell you that I was considered very remarkable at the Chronicle, for an extraordinary facility in writing and so forth—that I was very liberally paid during my whole connection with the paper, and that when I quitted it, Pickwick was rapidly approaching the zenith of its fame and popularity.

The rest of my career up to this time, you know. I may add for your guidance in any little notes you may throw together of my "Life and Adventures," that I was a great reader as a child, being well versed in most of our English novelists before I was ten years old; that I wrote tragedies and got other children to act them; that I won prizes at school; and great fame; that I am positively assured I was a very clever boy; that I am now married to the eldest daughter of Mr. Hogarth, of Edinburgh, a gentleman who has published two well-known works on music,[8] and was a great friend and companion of Sir Walter Scott's; and that, being now in my twenty-seventh year, I hope, with God's blessing, to retain my health, spirits, fancy and perseverance (such as they are) for many years to come.

As to my means of observation, they have been pretty extensive. I have been abroad in the world from a mere child, and have lived in London, and travelled by fits and starts through a great part of England, a little of Scotland, and less of France, with my eyes open. Heaven send that some kind wind may ere long blow me to Germany!

There—I have said more about myself in this one note than I should venture to say elsewhere in twenty years. If you can make anything of such a jumble of matter, and—more than all—interest anybody in it, your ability, my dear Sir, will have exalted your subject.—Believe me,—Very truly yours.

If it be any consolation to the German ladies to know that I have two children, pray tell them so.

The Sketches, I should have told you, had been previously collected and published with amazing success, and have since gone through many editions.

1. Johann Heinrich Kuenzel (1810–73), German scholar and author.
2. Kuenzel requested Dickens for particulars about himself for his article about the author and *PP* in *Konversationslexikon*, one of the earliest appraisals of the novelist to appear in Germany. See P, I, 423n. German translations of *PP* and *SB* were published in 1837 and 1838. See E. N. Gummer, *Dickens' Works in Germany* (1940), p. 7.
3. Cf. Mr Pickwick's description of 'The principal productions' of Stroud, Rochester, Chatham, and Brompton in *PP*, ch. 2.
4. For documentary evidence about the family's movements after John Dickens's transfer from Portsmouth to the Admiralty headquarters in Somerset House, see M. Allen, 'The Dickens Family at London and Sheerness, 1815–1817', *The Dickensian*, 78 (Spring 1982), 3–7.
5. John Henry Barrow, Dickens's maternal uncle, founded *The Mirror of Parliament* in Jan. 1828. The journal provided a full weekly record of the debates in both Houses of Parliament.
6. Dickens served on the *Morning Chronicle* from Aug. 1834 to Nov. 1836. By then, eight numbers of *PP* had appeared.
7. See Appendix F, P, I, 692–4, for a complete list of Dickens's sketches and their places of publication.

8. *Musical History, Biography and Criticism*, 1835, and *Memoirs of the Musical Drama*, 1838.

TAVISTOCK HOUSE
Sixth June, 1856

MY DEAR COLLINS,[1]—I have never seen anything about myself in print which has much correctness in it—any biographical account of myself I mean. I do not supply such particulars when I am asked for them by editors and compilers, simply because I am asked for them every day. If you want to prime Forgues,[2] you may tell him without fear of anything wrong, that I was born at Portsmouth on the Seventh of February, 1812; that my father was in the Navy Pay Office; that I was taken by him to Chatham when I was very young, and lived and was educated there till I was twelve or thirteen, I suppose; that I was then put to a school near London, where (as at other places) I distinguished myself like a brick; that I was put in the office of a solicitor, a friend of my father's, and didn't much like it: and after a couple of years (as well as I can remember) applied myself with a celestial or diabolical energy to the study of such things as would qualify me to be a first-rate parliamentary reporter—at that time a calling pursued by many clever men who were young at the Bar; that I made my début in the gallery (at about eighteen, I suppose), engaged on a voluminous publication no longer in existence, called The Mirror of Parliament; that when The Morning Chronicle was purchased by Sir John Easthope,[3] and acquired a large circulation, I was engaged there, and that I remained there until I had begun to publish Pickwick, when I found myself in a condition to relinquish that part of my labours; that I left the reputation behind me of being the best and most rapid reporter ever known, and that I could do anything in that way under any sort of circumstances, and often did. (I daresay I am at this present writing the best shorthand writer in the world.)

That I began, without any interest or introduction of any kind, to write fugitive pieces for the old Monthly Magazine, when I was in the gallery for The Mirror of Parliament; that my faculty for descriptive writing was seized upon the moment I joined The Morning Chronicle, and that I was liberally paid there and handsomely acknowledged, and wrote the greater part of the short descriptive Sketches by Boz in that paper; that I had been a writer when I was a mere baby, and always an actor from the same age; that I married the daughter of a writer to the signet in Edinburgh, who was the great friend and assistant of Scott, and who first made Lockhart[4] known to him.

And that here I am.

Finally, if you want any dates of publication of books, tell Wills[5] and he'll get them for you.

This is the first time I ever set down even these particulars, and, glancing them over, I feel like a wild beast in a caravan describing himself in the keeper's absence.—Ever faithfully.

P.S.—I made a speech[6] last night at the London Tavern, at the end of which all the company sat holding their napkins to their eyes with one hand, and putting the other into their pockets. A hundred people or so contributed nine hundred pounds then and there.

1. William Wilkie Collins (1824–89), novelist and close friend of Dickens.
2. Paul Emile Daurand Forgues (1813–83), author, critic and translator of Collins, Mrs Gaskell, Goldsmith, Hawthorne, and Macaulay. Forgues also edited the *Revue des Deux Mondes*, which earlier that year published Hippolyte Taine's 'Charles Dickens: son talent et ses oeuvres', 1 Feb. 1856, pp 618–47.

    Some measure of Dickens's popularity abroad may be gauged by the contract he signed on 14 Jan. 1856 with Louis Hachette, founder of the famous French publishing house, who arranged to pay Dickens £440 for the right to translate all his novels to that date (N, II, 729–30). 'Considering that I get so much for what is otherwise worth nothing,' Dickens commented to Forster after he and Hachette had made the financial arrangements, 'and get my books before so clever and important a people, I think this is not a bad move?' (N, II, 737).
3. John Easthope (1784–1865), liberal politician and chief proprietor of the *Morning Chronicle*. Created a baronet in 1841.
4. John Gibson Lockhart (1794–1854), editor of the *Quarterly Review* 1825–53. Hogarth introduced Lockhart to Scott's eldest daughter, Sophia, whom he married in 1820.
5. William Henry Wills (1810–80), journalist.
6. Dickens spoke on 5 June 1856 at the London Tavern, where he presided as chairman over the first anniversary dinner for the Royal Hospital for Incurables. See K. J. Fielding, *Speeches*, pp 222–5.

NEW LONDON INN, EXETER

Wednesday Morning, Sixth March, 1839

DEAR TOM,[1]—Perhaps you have heard from Kate that I succeeded yesterday in the very first walk, and took a cottage at a place called Alphington,[2] one mile from Exeter, which contains, on the ground-floor, a good parlour and kitchen, and above, a full-sized country drawing-room and three bedrooms; in the yard behind, coal-holes, fowl-houses, and meat-safes out of number; in the kitchen, a neat little range; in the other rooms, good stoves and cupboards; and all for twenty pounds a year, taxes included. There is a good garden at the side well stocked with cabbages, beans, onions, celery, and some flowers. The stock belonging to the landlady (who lives in the adjoining cottage), there was some question whether she was not entitled to half the produce, but I settled the point by paying five shillings, and becoming absolute master of the whole!

I do assure you that I am charmed with the place and the beauty of the country round about, though I have not seen it under very favourable circumstances, for it snowed when I was there this morning, and blew bitterly from the east yesterday. It is really delightful, and when the house is to rights and the furniture all in, I shall be quite sorry to leave it. I have had some few things second-hand, but I take it seventy pounds will be the mark, even taking this into consideration. I include in that estimate glass and crockery, garden tools, and such like little things. There is a spare bedroom of course. That I have furnished too.

I am on terms of the closest intimacy with Mrs. Samuell,[3] the landlady, and her brother and sister-in-law, who have a little farm hard by. They are capital specimens of country folks, and I really think the old woman herself will be a great comfort to my mother. Coals are dear just now—twenty-six shillings a ton. They found me a boy to go two miles out and back again to order some this morning. I was debating in my mind whether I should give him eighteenpence or two shillings, when his fee was announced—twopence!

The house is on the high road to Plymouth, and, though in the very heart of Devonshire, there is as much long-stage and posting life as you would find in Piccadilly. The situation is charming. Meadows in front, an orchard running parallel to the garden hedge, richly-wooded hills closing in the prospect behind, and, away to the left, before a splendid view of the hill on which Exeter is situated, the cathedral towers rising up into the sky in the most picturesque manner possible. I don't think I ever saw so cheerful or pleasant a spot. The drawing-room is nearly, if not quite, as large as the outer room of my old chambers in Furnival's Inn. The paint and paper are new, and the place clean as the utmost excess of snowy cleanliness can be.

You would laugh if you could see me powdering away with the upholsterer, and endeavouring to bring about all sorts of impracticable reductions and wonderful arrangements. He has by him two second-hand carpets; the important ceremony of trying the same comes off at three this afternoon. I am perpetually going backwards and forwards. It is two miles from here, so I have plenty of exercise, which so occupies me and prevents my being lonely that I stopped at home to read last night, and shall to-night, although the theatre is open. Charles Kean[4] has been the star for the last two evenings. He was stopping in this house, and went away this morning. I have got his sitting-room now, which is smaller and more comfortable than the one I had before.

You will have heard perhaps that I wrote to my mother to come down to-morrow. There are so many things she can make comfortable at a much less expense than I could, that I thought it best. If I had not, I could not have returned on Monday, which I now hope to do, and to be in town at half-past eight.

Will you tell my father that if he could devise any means of bringing him down, I think it would be a great thing for him to have Dash, if it be only to keep down the trampers and beggars. The cheque I send you below. . . .[5]

1. Thomas Mitton.
2. As a home for his parents. Charles's plan to establish them in the country and so keep his father out of mischief succeeded only temporarily. By 1842 John Dickens returned to London, presenting to Charles a continuation of the problems of helping his father find work and stay out of debt (Johnson, I, 258). For a note about John Dickens's financial difficulties after his release from debtors' prison, see p. 18 n. 14.
3. Mrs. Pannell (P, I, 524).
4. Charles Kean (?1811–68), actor; second son of Edmund Kean.
5. The N text omits a closing reference to Dickens's paying his father's rent in London and provides a slightly altered version of the paragraph to accommodate the omission. See P, I, 525 and n.

1 DEVONSHIRE TERRACE
Thursday Evening Dec[r] 19th 1839

MY DEAR SIR,[1]—One of the gentlemen who have so feelingly acquitted themselves of their melancholy duty in the letters which I now return to you, says it would be hopeless to offer you any consolation in the bereavement you have sustained in the loss of your dear son.[2] I differ from him, and confidently trust that in the very letters which brought to you the sad intelligence of his death, you have long ere this found a source of deep and lasting reflection—reflection, which, whenever the loss presents itself to your mind, will soften its first bitterness more and more, and render it less hard to bear.

It is nothing that death is inevitable; but it is something that it has been without pain; how much more that it has been resigned and tranquil, that the object of our love and regret has passed away in peace, leaving nothing behind but pleasant thoughts of his worth and excellence, and his timely reliance on that merciful Being who did not desert him in his hour of need. In the plain and honest tribute to his memory which his old companions pay, there is, I am sure, more lasting comfort to you, than they (who are not fathers) can conceive; and sharp as the pain must be of losing a child, and that child one so well deserving of your love and affection, even his high deserts will, I feel assured, reconcile you only the sooner to his untimely fate.

Remember, my dear Sir, that the barrier which divides you now, is nothing to the gulf which has been between you ever since his boyhood. It is impossible to separate the idea of the dead from the companionship of the living. His thoughts were with you in life, but in that state which succeeds to death,—in that happy state in which he surely is at this moment—, to whom can his spirit cleave so strongly as to his mother and father? If in the living, the affection[3] survive beyond the grave, it is but reasonable to hold that they survive with the dead. The Great Father who requires that His children should love Him, requires also that they should love their earthly parents; and when no fragment of our bodies perishes without producing something beautiful in its stead, it would be impious indeed to believe that a child's love and duty were buried in the grave, and that from their ashes nothing sprung again.

As his form is changed for one of whose brightness we can have no conception, so I believe his regard and care for you are exalted in like degree. He spoke of returning to England where at best he could have been with you but for a time. He is now with you always. The air about us has been said to be thick with guardian angels, and I believe it, in my soul. The meeting with you to which he now looks forward is darkened by no thought of separation. The idea of death, which would seem to have been frequently present to him, is passed, and he is happy.

That you and Mrs. Beadnell may be happy in your remaining children and in the recollection of him who is spared all further trials, is the heartfelt and earnest wish of,—My Dear Sir,—Your faithful friend.

1. George Beadnell (1773–1862), bank clerk and father of Maria.
2. Alfred Beadnell (1807–39), Maria Beadnell's eldest brother.
3. The affections (P, I, 620).

December 1840

[John Forster]. . . In the midst of this child's death,[1] I, over whom something of the bitterness of death has passed, not lightly perhaps, was reminded of many old kindnesses, and was sorry in my heart that men who really liked each other should waste life at arm's length. . . .[2] I have laid it down as a rule in my judgment of men, to observe narrowly whether some (of whom one is disposed to think badly) don't carry all their faults upon the surface, and others (of whom one is disposed to think well) don't carry many more beneath it. I have long ago made sure that our friend is in the first class; and when I know all the foibles a man has, with little trouble in the discovery, I begin to think he is worth liking. . . .

1. Nell's, whose death Dickens described in *OCS*, ch. 70, originally published in *MHC* as part of No. 43 on 24 Jan. 1841.
2. Forster notes that Dickens described here 'the motive, as well as the principle that guided him' in his reconciliation of two friends, doubtlessly Forster and Ainsworth, who had been temporarily estranged since spring 1838. See P, II, 170–1n.

DEVONSHIRE TERRACE
Friday Evening, March the Twelfth, 1841
MY DEAR MACLISE,[1]—You will be greatly shocked and grieved to hear that the Raven is no more.[2]

He expired to-day at a few minutes after twelve o'clock at noon. He had been ailing (as I told you t'other night) for a few days, but we anticipated no serious result, conjecturing that a portion of the white paint he swallowed last summer might be lingering about his vitals without having any serious effect upon his constitution. Yesterday afternoon he was taken so much worse that I sent an express for the medical gentleman (Mr. Herring),[3] who promptly attended, and administered a powerful dose of castor oil. Under the influence of this medicine, he recovered so far as to be able at eight o'clock p.m. to bite Topping.[4] His night was peaceful. This morning at daybreak he appeared better; received (agreeably to the doctor's directions) another dose of castor oil; and partook plentifully of some warm gruel, the flavor of which he appeared to relish. Towards eleven o'clock he was so much worse that it was found necessary to muffle the stable-knocker. At half-past, or thereabouts, he was heard talking to himself about the horse and Topping's family, and to add some incoherent expressions which are supposed to have been either a foreboding of his approaching dissolution, or some wishes relative to the disposal of his little property: consisting chiefly of half-pence which he had buried in different parts of the garden. On the clock striking twelve he appeared slightly agitated, but he soon recovered, walked twice or thrice along the coach-house, stopped to bark, staggered, exclaimed *Halloa old girl!* (his favourite expression), and died.

He behaved throughout with a decent fortitude, equanimity, and self-possession, which cannot be too much admired. I deeply regret that being in ignorance of his danger I did not attend to receive his last instructions. Something remarkable about his eyes occasioned Topping to run for the doctor at twelve. When they returned together our friend was gone. It was the medical gentleman who informed me of his decease. He did it with great caution and delicacy, preparing me by the remark that "a jolly queer start had taken place"; but the shock was very great notwithstanding.

I am not wholly free from suspicions of poison. A malicious butcher has been heard to say that he would "do" for him: his plea was that he would not be molested in taking orders down the mews, by any bird that wore a tail. Other persons have also been heard to threaten: among others, Charles Knight,[5] who has just started a weekly publication price fourpence: Barnaby being, as you know, threepence. I have directed a post-mortem examination, and the body has been removed to Mr. Herring's school of anatomy for that purpose.

I could wish, if you can take the trouble, that you would inclose this to Forster when you have read it. I cannot discharge the painful task of communication more than once. Were they ravens who took manna to somebody in the wilderness? At times I hope they were, and at others I fear they were not, or they would certainly have stolen it by the way.—In profound sorrow,—I am ever your bereaved friend.

Kate is as well as can be expected, but terribly low as you may suppose. The children seem rather glad of it. He bit their ankles. But that was play.—Faithfully Yours.

1. Daniel Maclise (?1806–70), painter.
2. One of two ravens who served as the originals of Grip (see Preface to *BR*, cheap Edition, 1849).
3. William Herring, dealer in birds and live animals (P, II, 231n).
4. William Topping, Dickens's groom.
5. Charles Knight (1791–1873), journalist. Editor of *London*, a weekly periodical published between 6 Mar. 1841 and 2 Mar. 1844.

1 DEVONSHIRE TERRACE
April the Twenty-First 1841

MY DEAR SIR,[1]—There is no man in the world who could have given me the heartfelt pleasure you have, by your kind note of the thirteenth of last month. There is no living writer, and there are very few among the dead, whose approbation I should feel so proud to earn. And with everything you have written, upon my shelves, and in my thoughts, and in my heart of hearts, I may honestly and truly say so. If you could know how earnestly I write this, you would be glad to read it—as I hope you will be, faintly guessing at the warmth of the hand I autobiographically[2] hold out to you over the broad Atlantic.

I wish I could find in your welcome letter some hint of an intention to visit England. I can't. I have held it at arm's length, and taken a bird's-eye view of it, after reading it a great many times, but there is no greater encouragement in it this way than on a microscopic inspection. I should love to go with you—as I have gone, God knows how often—into Little Britain, and Eastcheap, and Green Arbour Court, and Westminster Abbey[3] I should like to travel with you, outside the last of the coaches down to Bracebridge Hall.[4] It would make my heart glad to compare notes with you about that shabby gentleman in the oilcloth hat and red nose, who sat in the nine-cornered back-parlour of the Masons' Arms; and about Robert Preston and the tallow-chandler's widow, whose sitting-room is second nature to me;[5] and about all those delightful places and people that I used to walk about and dream of in the daytime, when a very small and not over-particularly-taken-care-of-boy. I have a good deal to say, too, about that dashing Alonzo de Ojeda,[6] that you can't help being fonder of than you ought to be; and much to hear concerning Moorish legend, and poor unhappy Boabdil.[7] Diedrich Knickerbocker[8] I have worn to death in my pocket, and yet I should show you his mutilated carcass with a joy past all expression.

I have been so accustomed to associate you with my pleasantest and happiest thoughts, and with my leisure hours, that I rush at once into full confidence with you, and fall, as it were naturally and by the very laws of gravity, into your open arms. Questions come thronging to my pen as to the lips of people who meet after long hoping to do so. I don't know what to say first or what to leave unsaid, and am constantly disposed to break off and tell you again how glad I am this moment has arrived.

My dear Washington Irving, I cannot thank you enough for your cordial and generous praise, or tell you what deep and lasting gratification it has given me. I hope to have many letters from you, and to exchange a frequent correspondence. I send this to say so. After the first two or three I shall settle down into a connected style, and become gradually rational.

You know what the feeling is, after having written a letter, sealed it, and sent it off. I shall picture your reading this, and answering it before it has lain one night in the post-office. Ten to one that before the fastest packet could reach New York I shall be writing again.

Do you suppose the post-office clerks care to receive letters? I have my doubts. They get into a dreadful habit of indifference. A postman, I imagine, is quite callous. Conceive his delivering one to himself, without being startled by a preliminary double knock!—Always your faithful Friend.

1. Washington Irving (1783–1859), sent Dickens 'a very hearty letter . . . about little Nell and the *Curiosity Shop*' (see Forster, III, i, 171).
2. Autographically (P, II, 267).
3. See *The Sketch-Book*, in which Irving, under the pseudonym of Geoffrey Crayon, published his observations as an American visitor in England.
4. For the coach-journey and Christmas at Bracebridge Hall, see 'Westminster Abbey' and 'The Christmas Dinner'.
5. For the Mason's Arms and Robert Preston, see 'The Boar's Head Tavern'. The tallow chandler's widow appears in the last-mentioned sketch.
6. Alonzo De Ojeda, a Spanish adventurer in Irving's *Voyages and Discoveries of the Companions of Columbus*, 1831.
7. Boabdil el Chico, Moorish King of Granada, described in *A Chronicle of the Conquest of Granada*, 1829.
8. Diedrich Knickerbocker, the fictitious chronicler of Irving's humorous *History of New York*, 1809.

BROADSTAIRS
22nd September 1841

[John Forster]. . . I wrote to Chapman and Hall asking them what they thought of it,[1] and saying I meant to keep a note-book, and publish it for half a guinea or thereabouts, on my return. They instantly sent the warmest possible reply, and said they had taken it for granted I would go, and had been speaking of it only the day before. I have begged them to make every enquiry about the fares, cabins, berths, and times of sailing; and I shall make a great effort to take Kate *and* the children.[2] In that case I shall try to let the house furnished, for six months (for I shall remain that time in America); and if I succeed, the rent will nearly pay the expenses out, and home. I have heard of family cabins at £100; and I think one of these is large enough to hold us all. A single fare, I think, is forty guineas. I fear I could not be happy if we had the Atlantic between us; but leaving them in New York while I ran off a thousand miles or so, would be quite another thing. If I can arrange all my plans before publishing the Clock address,[3] I shall state therein that I am going: which will be no unimportant consideration, as affording the best possible reason for a long delay. How I am to get on without you for seven or eight months, I cannot, upon my soul, conceive. I dread to think of breaking up all our old happy habits, for so long a time. The advantages of going, however, appear by steady looking-at so great, that I have come to persuade myself it is a matter of imperative necessity. Kate weeps whenever it is spoken of. Washington Irving has got a nasty low fever. I heard from him a day or two ago. . . .

1. Dickens's proposal to visit America and return after four or five months with a 'One volume book'. See P, II, 383. This proposal led eventually to *AN*, which Chapman and Hall published in Oct. 1842. The American trip was made possible by the contract Dickens signed with Chapman and Hall on 7 Sep. 1841, whereby the publishers agreed to advance him £150 a month in return for a new novel in monthly parts, which Dickens would begin after a break from fiction.
2. Dickens and his wife went alone to America, leaving their children in London, much to Kate's reluctance. During the five months of their stay (Jan.–June 1842), they toured New England, journeyed south to Richmond, Virginia, west to St. Louis, and then returned to the northeast via Canada.
3. For the text of Dickens's Address 'To the Readers of *Master Humphrey's Clock*', as it appeared in *MHC*, no. 80, 9 Oct. 1841, see J. Butt and K. Tillotson, *Dickens at Work*, 1957, pp. 88–9. In the Address, Dickens explained his decision to close the periodical with the completion of *BR*, go to America in Jan. 1842, and begin a new book in monthly parts on 1 Nov. 1842. *MC* began in Jan. 1843.

BANKS OF NEWFOUNDLAND

Monday the seventeenth January 1842

[John Forster] . . . We have 86 passengers; and such a strange collection of beasts never was got together upon the sea, since the days of the Ark. I have never been in the saloon since the first day; the noise, the smell, and the closeness being quite intolerable. I have only been on deck *once!*—and then I was surprised and disappointed at the smallness of the panorama. The sea, running as it does and has done, is very stupendous, and viewed from the air or some great height would be grand no doubt. But seen from the wet and rolling decks, in this weather and these circumstances, it only impresses one giddily and painfully. I was very glad to turn away, and come below again.

I have established myself, from the first, in the ladies' cabin—you remember it? I'll describe its other occupants, and our way of passing the time, to you.

First, for the occupants. Kate, and I, and Anne[1]—when she is out of bed, which is not often. A queer little Scotch body, a Mrs. P——, whose husband is a silversmith in New York. He married her at Glasgow three years ago, and bolted the day after the wedding; being (which he had not told her) heavily in debt. Since then she has been living with her mother; and she is now going out under the protection of a male cousin, to give him a year's trial. If she is not comfortable at the expiration of that time, she means to go back to Scotland again. A Mrs. B——, about twenty years old, whose husband is on board with her. He is a young Englishman domiciled in New York, and by trade (as well as I can make out) a woollen-draper. They have been married a fortnight. A Mr. and Mrs. C——, marvellously fond of each other, complete the catalogue. Mrs. C——, I have settled, is a publican's daughter, and Mr. C—— is running away with her, the till, the time-piece off the bar mantel-shelf, the mother's gold watch from the pocket at the head of the bed; and other miscellaneous property. The women are all pretty; unusually pretty. I never saw such good faces together, anywhere. . . .

Apropos of rolling, I have forgotten to mention that in playing whist we are obliged to put the tricks in our pockets, to keep them from disappearing altogether; and that five or six times in the course of every rubber we are all flung from our seats, roll out at different doors, and keep on rolling until we are picked up by stewards. This has become such a matter of course, that we go through it with perfect gravity; and when we are bolstered up on our sofas again, resume our conversation or our game at the point where it was interrupted.

1. Charles, Catherine and his wife's maid, Anne Brown, left England on 4 Jan. 1842 on the SS Britannia and arrived in Boston on 22 Jan. The initials used here, Forster notes, 'are in no case those of the real names' (Forster III, ii, 177n).

TREMONT-HOUSE, BOSTON
Saturday the 28th[1] of January [1842]

[John Forster] . . . As the Cunard boats have a wharf of their own at the custom-house, and that a narrow one, we were a long time (an hour at least) working in. I was standing in full fig on the paddle-box beside the captain, staring about me, when suddenly, long before we were moored to the wharf, a dozen men came leaping on board at the peril of their lives, with great bundles of newspapers under their arms; worsted comforters (very much the worse for wear) round their necks; and so forth. "Aha!" says I, "this is like our London-bridge": believing of course that these visitors were news-boys. But what do you think of their being EDITORS? And what do you think of their tearing violently up to me and beginning to shake hands like madmen? Oh! If you could have seen how I wrung their wrists! And if you could but know how I hated one man in very dirty gaiters, and with very protruding upper teeth, who said to all comers after him, "So you've been introduced to our friend Dickens—eh?" There was one among them, though, who really was of use; a Doctor S, editor of the——. He ran off here (two miles at least), and ordered rooms and dinner. And in course of time Kate, and I, and Lord Mulgrave[2] (who was going back to his regiment at Montreal on Monday, and had agreed to live with us in the meanwhile) sat down in a spacious and handsome room to a very handsome dinner, 'bating peculiarities of putting on table, and had forgotten the ship entirely. A Mr. Alexander,[3] to whom I had written from England, promising to sit for a portrait, was on board directly we touched the land, and brought us here in his carriage. Then, after sending a present of most beautiful flowers, he left us to ourselves, and we thanked him for it.

How can I tell you what has happened since that first day?[4] How can I give you the faintest notion of my reception here; of the crowds that pour in and out the whole day; of the people that line the streets when I go out; of the cheering when I went to the theatre; of the copies of verses, letters of congratulation, welcomes of all kinds, balls, dinners, assemblies without end? There is to be a public dinner to me here in Boston, next Tuesday, and great dissatisfaction has been given to the many by the high price (three pounds sterling each) of the tickets. There is to be a ball next Monday week at New York, and 150 names appear on the list of the committee. There is to be a dinner in the same place, in the same week, to which I have had an invitation with every known name in America appended to it. But what can I tell you about any of these things which will give you the slightest notion of the enthusiastic greeting they give me, or the cry that runs through the whole country! I have had deputations from the Far West, who have come from more than two thousand miles distance: from the lakes, the rivers, the back-woods, the log-houses, the cities, factories, villages, and towns. Authorities from nearly all the States have written to me. I have heard from the universities, congress, senate, and bodies, public and private, of every sort and kind. "It is no nonsense, and no common feeling," wrote Dr. Channing[5] to me yesterday. "It is all heart. There never was, and never will be, such a triumph." And it is a good thing, is it not . . . to find those fancies it has given me and you the greatest satisfaction to think of, at the core of it all? It makes my heart quieter, and me a more retiring, sober, tranquil man to watch the effect of those thoughts in all this noise and hurry, even than if I sat, pen in hand, to put them down for the first time. I feel, in the best aspects of this welcome, something of the presence and influence of that spirit which directs my life, and through a heavy sorrow has pointed upward with unchanging finger for more than four years past. And if I know my heart, not twenty times this praise would move me to an act of folly. . . .

1. Correct date 29 Jan.
2. George Constantine Phipps (1819–90), Earl of Mulgrave.
3. Francis Alexander (1800–?81), portrait painter, to whom Dickens had promised to sit upon arriving in Boston. Alexander's portrait hangs in the Boston Museum of Fine Arts.
4. Dickens's first impressions of Boston caused him to think well of the city and to write enthusiastically of its intellectual attainments and enlightened institutional support for the poor and the destitute. See *AN*, chs 1 and 3.
5. William Ellery Channing, DD (1780–1842).

Twenty-fourth February
[John Forster . . .] I have still a horrible cold, and so has Kate, but in other respects we are all right. I proceed to my third head: the international copyright question.

I believe there is no country, on the face of the earth, where there is less freedom of opinion on any subject in reference to which there is a broad difference of opinion than in this. . . . There!—I write the words with reluctance, disappointment, and sorrow; but I believe it from the bottom of my soul.[1] I spoke, as you know, of international copyright, at Boston;[2] and I spoke of it again at Hartford.[3] My friends were paralysed with wonder at such audacious daring. The notion that I, a man alone by himself, in America, should venture to suggest to the Americans that there was one point on which they were neither just to their own countrymen nor to us, actually struck the boldest dumb! Washington Irving, Prescott,[4] Hoffmann,[5] Bryant,[6] Halleck,[7] Dana,[8] Washington Allston[9]—every man who writes in this country is devoted to the question, and not one of them *dares* to raise his voice and complain of the atrocious state of the law. It is nothing that of all men living I am the greatest loser by it. It is nothing that I have a claim to speak and be heard. The wonder is that a breathing man can be found with temerity enough to suggest to the Americans the possibility of their having done wrong. I wish you could have seen the faces that I saw, down both sides of the table at Hartford, when I began to talk about Scott.[10] I wish you could have heard how I gave it out. My blood so boiled as I thought of the monstrous injustice that I felt as if I were twelve feet high when I thrust it down their throats.

I had no sooner made that second speech than such an outcry began (for the purpose of deterring me from doing the like in this city) as an Englishman can form no notion of. Anonymous letters; verbal dissuasions; newspaper attacks making Colt[11] (a murderer who is attracting great attention here) an angel by comparison with me; assertions that I was no gentleman, but a mere mercenary scoundrel; coupled with the most monstrous mis-representations relative to my design and purpose in visiting the United States; came pouring in upon me every day. The dinner committee here (composed of the first gentlemen in America, remember that) were so dismayed, that they besought me not to pursue the subject *although they every one agreed with me*. I answered that I would. That nothing should deter me. . . . That the shame was theirs, not mine; and that as I would not spare them when I got home, I would not be silenced here. Accordingly, when the night came, I asserted my right, with all the means I could command to give it dignity, in face, manner, or words; and I believe that if you could have seen and heard me, you would have loved me better for it than ever you did in your life. [. . .]

I will tell you what *I* should like, my dear friend, always supposing that your judgment concurs with mine; and that you would take the trouble to get such a document. I should like to have a short letter addressed to me, by the principal English authors who signed the international copyright petition, expressive of their sense that I have done my duty to the cause.[12] I am sure I deserve it, but I don't wish it on that ground. It is because its publication in the best journals here would unquestionably do great good. As the gauntlet is down, let us go on. Clay[13] has already sent a gentleman to me express from Washington (where I shall be on the 6th or 7th of next month) to declare his strong interest in the matter, his cordial approval of the "manly" course I have held in reference to it, and his desire to stir in it if possible. I have lighted up such a blaze that a meeting of the foremost people on the other side (very respectfully and properly conducted in reference to me, personally, I am bound to say) was held in this town t'other night. And it would be a thousand pities if we did not strike as hard as we can, now that the iron is so hot.

I have come at last, and it is time I did, to my life here, and intentions for the future. I can do nothing that I want to do, go nowhere where I want to go, and see nothing that I want to see. If I turn into the street, I am followed by a multitude. If I stay at home, the house becomes, with callers, like a fair. If I visit a public institution, with only one friend, the directors come down incontinently, waylay me in the yard, and address me in a long speech. I go to a party in the evening, and am so inclosed and hemmed about by people, stand where I will, that I am exhausted for want of air. I dine out, and have to talk about everything, to everybody. I go to church for quiet, and there is a violent rush to the neighbourhood of the pew I sit in, and the clergyman preaches *at* me. I take my seat in a railroad car, and the very conductor won't leave me alone. I get out at a station, and can't drink a glass of water, without having a hundred people looking down my throat when I open my mouth to swallow. Conceive what all this is! Then by every post, letters on letters arrive, all about nothing, and all demanding an immediate answer. This man is offended because I won't live in his house; and that man is thoroughly disgusted because I won't go out more than four times in one evening. I have no rest or peace, and am in a perpetual worry. [. . .]

1. The 'huge dissonance' Dickens stirred up by speaking publicly about the refusal of American publishers to pay British authors royalties for the sales of their books in the US marks the beginning of the tension Dickens experienced throughout the remainder of his trip, particularly in his relations with American journalists, many of whom resented the criticism and hit back with unexpected ferocity.
2. Dickens spoke at Boston on 1 Feb. See *Speeches*, pp 17–22.
3. Dickens spoke at Hartford on 7 Feb. See *Speeches*, pp 22–6.
4. William Hickling Prescott (1796–1859), historian.
5. Charles Fenno Hoffman (1806–84), author and editor.
6. William Cullen Bryant (1794–1878), poet.
7. Fitz-Greene Halleck (1790–1867), poet.
8. Richard Henry Dana, Jr. (1815–82), author.
9. Washington Allston (1779–1843), painter and writer.
10. In his speech Dickens pictured Sir Walter Scott on his deathbed, 'crushed both in mind and body by his honourable struggle' to recover from his financial misfortunes while the characters from his books hovered around him, ashamed that none of his admirers would come forth and help him. Much of Scott's final suffering, Dickens believed, could have been eased had he received adequate payment for his books. See *Speeches*, p. 25.
11. John Caldwell Colt (1810–42), found guilty in Jan. 1842 of murdering Samuel Adams.
12. Helped by Bulwer Lytton, Forster procured the letter Dickens requested signed by twelve British writers. For the text, see Appendix A, P, III, 621–2.
13. Henry Clay (1777–1852), US Senator from Kentucky. Clay, a strong Congressional advocate of international copyright, had presented a petition to the senate in 1837 signed by 56 British authors. Efforts to introduce an effective international copyright law between Britain and

America did not succeed, however, until the Chase Act of 1891 and a revised US law in 1909. See International Copyright, Appendix II, *Oxford Companion to English Literature*, pp 929–30.

FULLER'S HOTEL, WASHINGTON
March the Tenth 1842

MY DEAR COLDEN,[1]—We reached this place safely last night: having sustained no more damage by the way, than the presence of a miraculously fractious child in the railroad car from Philadelphia to Baltimore; who, leaving us at the last-named place, was relieved by another child in the same frame of mind, in whose cheerful company we arrived here. He (it was a boy) set in so very heavily at Baltimore that I thought it impossible he could last; especially as his friends tempted him from time to time with a tin mug of milk and water, and other refreshment, from a basket. But contrary to my expectations, he cried the whole forty miles through; and when he was taken out at the station the crown of his head was covered with crimson pimples—the consequence of his supernatural exertion.

We were very comfortably lodged at Philadelphia—and indeed we deserved to be; for the landlord not only charged us half rent for the rooms during the time he had expected us (which was quite right) but charged us also—when I say us, I mean Kate, her maid, and I [*sic*]— for board during the whole of the same period. As I could not help regarding the statement that he had paid for our food while we were paying for it at New York, in the light of a pleasant fiction or ingenious jest, I *did* suggest through my factotum[2] the slightest possible insinuation to that effect. It appeared, however, that it was "the custom;" and as strangers in Rome do as they do in Rome, I bowed to the custom, and paid.

I passed a whole day in the Penitentiary[3]—where, as you know, the principle of solitary confinement is observed, in the strictest manner, in every case. It is inexpressibly painful to see so many of the prisoners as I did, and to converse with them; but I fear that to a certain extent the system is a good one. I use the expression "I fear," because it is dreadful to believe that it is ever necessary to impose such a torture of the mind upon our fellow creatures. But it seems, from all one can learn, to do good: and now and then to effect that reclamation which gives joy in Heaven. In the case of a very long term of imprisonment, however, I cannot but think it cruel, though I know it is mercifully and well intended. One man had been shut up by himself in the same cell, for nearly twelve years. His time is just expiring. I asked him how he felt at the prospect of release—and he answered—plucking in a strange way at his fingers, and looking restlessly about the walls and floor—that he didn't care: that it was all the same to him now: that he had looked forward to it once, but that was so long ago, that he had come to have no regard for anything. And so, with a heavy sigh, he went about his work, and would say no more. We are accustomed to hear it said sometimes that such a person must have felt in a minute, a year of suffering. But if ever twelve years of the most intense mental anguish were written in the small compass of one face, I saw it in this prisoner's. Indeed the men, however unlike naturally, become alike, and strikingly alike, in this place. There is the same bright eye, and haggard look, in them all; and an indescribable something—distantly resembling the attentive and sorrowful expression you see in the blind—which is never to be forgotten. The women bear it better, and acquire a patient and subdued look that makes you very sad, but not distressingly so. Each of them seems a better creature than one feels one's-self to be, and that's a comfort. The prison is beautifully—exquisitely—kept, and thoroughly well managed: but I never in my life was more affected by anything which was not strictly my own grief, than I was by this sight. It will live in my recollection always. When I come to tell you something of my brief experience there, you will often think of it too. [. . .]

1. David Cadwallader Colden (1797–1850), lawyer and philanthropist.
2. George W. Putnam. See p. 83 n. 1.
3. Philadelphia's Eastern Penitentiary, run on the separate system, by which prisoners were separated from their fellows on the assumption that isolation would encourage their repentance. Seven wings radiated from a central tower, a feature which the architect, John Haviland, adopted from Jeremy Bentham's Panopticon.

BALTIMORE
Twenty-Second March 1842

MY DEAR FRIEND,[1]—I beg your pardon, but you were speaking of rash leaps at hasty conclusions. Are you quite sure you designed that remark for me? Have you not, in the hurry of correspondence, slipped a paragraph into my letter which belongs of right to somebody else? When did you ever find me leap at wrong conclusions? I pause for a reply. [. . .]

My dear Macready, I desire to be so honest and just to those who have so enthusiastically and earnestly welcomed me, that I burned that last letter I wrote to you—even to you to whom I could speak as to myself—rather than let it come with anything that might seem like an ill-considered word of disappointment. I preferred that you should think me neglectful (if you could imagine anything so wild) rather than I should do wrong in this respect. Still it is of no use. I *am* disappointed. This is not the republic I came to see; this is not the republic of my imagination. I infinitely prefer a liberal monarchy—even with its sickening accompaniments of court circulars—to such a government as this.[2] The more I think of its use[3] and strength, the poorer and more trifling in a thousand aspects it appears in my eyes. In everything of which it has made a boast—excepting its education of the people and its care for poor children—it sinks immeasurably below the level I had placed it upon; and England, even England, bad and faulty as the old land is, and miserable as millions of her people are, rises in the comparison.

You live here, Macready, as I have sometimes heard you imagining! *You!* Loving you with all my heart and soul, and knowing what your disposition really is, I would not condemn you to a year's residence on this side of the Atlantic for any money. Freedom of opinion! Where is it? I see a press more mean, and paltry, and silly, and disgraceful than any country I ever knew. If that is its standard, here it is. [. . .]

Freedom of opinion! Macready, if I had been born here and had written my books in this country, producing them with no stamp of approval from any other land, it is my solemn belief that I should have lived and died poor, unnoticed, and a "black sheep" to boot. I never was more convinced of anything than I am of that.

The people are affectionate, generous, open-hearted, hospitable, enthusiastic, good-humoured, polite to women, frank and candid to all strangers, anxious to oblige, far less prejudiced than they have been described to be, frequently polished and refined, very seldom rude or disagreeable. I have made a great many friends here, even in public conveyances, whom I have been truly sorry to part from. In the towns I have formed perfect attachments. I have seen none of that greediness and indecorousness on which travellers have laid so much emphasis. I have returned frankness with frankness; met questions not intended to be rude, with answers meant to be satisfactory; and have not spoken to one man, woman, or child of any degree who has not grown positively affectionate before we parted. In the respects of not being left alone, and of being horribly disgusted by tobacco chewing and tobacco spittle, I have suffered considerably. The sight of slavery in Virginia, the hatred of British feeling upon the subject, and the miserable hints of the impotent indignation of the South, have pained me very much! on the last head, of course, I have felt nothing but a mingled pity and amusement; on the other, sheer distress. But however much I like the ingredients of this great dish, I cannot but come back to the point upon which I started, and say that the dish itself goes against the grain with me, and that I don't like it.

You know that I am truly a Liberal. I believe I have as little pride as most men, and I am conscious of not the smallest annoyance from being "hail fellow well met" with everybody. I have not had greater pleasure in the company of any set of men among the thousands I have received than in that of the carmen of Hertford, who presented themselves in a body in their blue frocks, among a crowd of well-dressed ladies and gentlemen, and bade me welcome through their spokesman. They had all read my books, and all perfectly understood them. It is not these things I have in my mind when I say that the man who comes to this country a Radical and goes home again with his opinions unchanged, must be a Radical on reason, sympathy, and reflection, and one who has so well considered the subject that he has no chance of wavering.

1. William Charles Macready (1793–1873), actor.
2. N text omits two sentences from this paragraph. In one, Dickens makes a laudatory reference to the national support for education he finds in the US; in the other, he expresses his willingness to reject his new love for America 'without a pang or moment's hesitation' if one could 'strike down the established church' in England. See P, III, 156.
3. Youth (P, III, 156).

Friday, Fifteen April, 1842

[John Forster] They won't let me alone about slavery. A certain Judge in St. Louis went so far yesterday, that I fell upon him (to the indescribable horror of the man who brought him) and told him a piece of my mind. I said that I was very averse to speaking on the subject here, and always forbore, if possible: but when he pitied our national ignorance of the truths of slavery, I must remind him that we went upon indisputable records, obtained after many years of careful investigation, and at all sorts of self-sacrifice; and that I believed we were much more competent to judge of its atrocity and horror, than he who had been brought up in the midst of it. I told him that I could sympathise with men who admitted it to be a dreadful evil, but frankly confessed their inability to devise a means of getting rid of it: but that men who spoke of it as a blessing, as a matter of course, as a state of things to be desired, were out of the pale of reason; and that for them to speak of ignorance or prejudice was an absurdity too ridiculous to be combated. . . .

It is not six years ago, since a slave in this very same St. Louis, being arrested (I forget for what), and knowing he had no chance of a fair trial be his offence what it might, drew his bowie knife and ripped the constable across the body. A scuffle ensuing, the desperate negro stabbed two others with the same weapon. The mob who gathered round (among whom were men of mark, wealth, and influence in the place) overpowered him by numbers; carried him away to a piece of open ground beyond the city; *and burned him alive*. This, I say, was done within six years in broad day; in a city with its courts, lawyers, tipstaffs, judges, jails, and hangman; and not a hair on the head of one of those men has been hurt to this day.[1] And it is, believe me, it is the miserable, wretched independence in small things; the paltry republicanism which recoils from honest service to an honest man, but does not shrink from every trick, artifice, and knavery in business; that makes these slaves necessary, and will render them so, until the indignation of other countries sets them free.

They say the slaves are fond of their masters. Look at this pretty vignette[2] (part of the stock-in-trade of a newspaper), and judge how you would feel, when men, looking in your face, told you such tales with the newspaper lying on the table. In all the slave districts, advertisements for runaways are as much matters of course as the announcement of the play for the evening with us. The poor creatures themselves fairly worship English people: they would do anything for them. They are perfectly acquainted with all that takes place in reference to emancipation; and *of course* their attachment to us grows out of their deep devotion to their owners. I cut this illustration out of a newspaper which had a leader in reference to *the abominable and hellish doctrine of Abolition—repugnant alike to every law of God and Nature*. "I know something," said a Dr. Bartlett[3] (a very accomplished man), late a fellow-passenger of ours: "I know something of their fondness for their masters. I live in Kentucky; and I can assert upon my honour, that, in my neighbourhood, it is as common for a runaway slave, retaken, to draw his bowie knife and rip his owner's bowels open, as it is for you to see a drunken fight in London."

1. Dickens's details of this incident prove sketchy. On 28 Apr. 1836, Mackintosh, a free negro who worked as a steward on a steamboat docked in St. Louis, rescued an escaped slave from his captors. As a result, Mackintosh was arrested; on his way to prison he killed one peace-officer and wounded another. The citizens of St. Louis responded by demanding

the free negro, whom they took to the woods, tried, and burnt to death. American papers chose to ignore the incident, as did the judge responsible for investigating the case because the deed was committed not by a few, who could be punished, but by the many, whose deeds on this occasion were above and beyond the law. See P, III, 197n.

2. Dickens enclosed an advertisement headed 'Runaway Negro in Jail'. See Forster, III, vi, 238n.

3. Elisha Bartlett, MD (1804–55), Quaker physician and writer.

BROADSTAIRS, KENT
Third August 1842

MY DEAR FRIEND,[1]—I date this letter from a little fishing town on the sea coast, whither we have retired (according to our annual custom) for a couple of months. It is a very delicious place, and I wish I could meet you on the beach in one of my long walks hereabouts.

The receipt of your letter gave me inexpressible pleasure. I have read the lines in which you recall our parting many times—always with new interest, and a still more eager looking forward to that bright day when we shall meet again on this side of the ocean. For I make a point of taking it for granted that that day is to come, and is to come moderately soon. There is nothing like assuming a fact stoutly in such a case as this. The comfort is unspeakable.

When we sat down in our own dear home again, we did just as you would have imagined. I never in my life felt so keenly as on the night of our reaching it. When we had expended ourselves upon the children, I hurried away to see Macready, who had had charge of them in our absence.[2] He was sitting in a dark room by an open window, and had no idea who it was then until I laid my hand upon his sleeve and spoke. Such a scene as we had then. I bustled off to see another most intimate friend.[3] He was dining out. Thereupon I drove to the place where he was dining, and, admonishing the servant not to say who it was, told him to carry in the message that a gentleman wished to speak to him. Guessing directly what it was, he came flying out of the house, got into the carriage, pulled up the window, and began to cry. We had gone a couple of miles before he remembered he had left his hat behind him.

It would have been worth going anywhere—far less going where I have gained such friends as you—to feel the affection and attachment I have been made sensible of in ten thousand quiet ways since I came home. As to the pleasures of home itself, they are unspeakable.

We found our darlings heartily well and delighted beyond all telling to see us. They were in bed, but we very quickly had them up, you may believe. Charley (our eldest boy) told his mother that he was "too glad," as indeed he was, for he soon afterwards fell into violent convulsions. Dr. Elliotson[4] told us afterwards that the sudden joy had perfectly turned his brain and overthrown his system, and that he had never seen the like in a child.[5] I can see him now from the window at which I am writing, digging up the sand on the shore with a small spade, and compressing it into a perfectly impossible wheelbarrow. The cliffs being high and the sea pretty cold, he looks a mere dot in creation. It is extraordinary how many hopes and affections we may pile up on such a speck, small as it is.

I have decided on writing an account of my journeyings in America, and am at this moment busily engaged upon the book. It will be published in a couple of volumes—whether in October (I hope) or November next, I shall be very curious and eager to get your first letter after reading it.[6]

As I fear I may miss the next packet, even at the best, I must make this a very short epistle. But as I never should feel, though I made it a mile long, that I had said anything I want to say, I have the least scruple in closing it. Mrs. Dickens desires her best regards to yourself and Mrs. Chapman. The children, hearing us speak of you, look very hard at this sheet of paper and repeat the message. So I will add Mary's love and Katy's and Walter's, and take upon myself the responsibility of sending Charley's also. God Bless you.—Ever believe me, affectionately your friend.

1. Jonathan Chapman (1807–48), Mayor of Boston 1840–2.
2. During Dickens's absence, his four children, Charles Culliford Boz (b. 6 Jan. 1837), Mary (b. 6 Mar. 1838), Kate Macready (b. 29 Oct. 1839), and Walter Landor (b. 8 Feb. 1841) stayed at the Macreadys'.
3. Forster.
4. For Dr. Elliotson, see p. 333 n. 1.
5. N omits the next sentence: 'Thank God he soon got well again.' See P, III, 302.
6. *AN* in two vols, was published on 19 Oct. 1842 by Chapman and Hall.

DEVONSHIRE TERRACE
Twenty-Sixth July, 1843

DEAR MISS COUTTS,[1]—I don't know whether you have seen an advertisement in the papers of this morning,[2] signed by me, and having reference to the family of Mr. Elton[3] the actor, who was drowned in the Pegasus. I consented last night to act as chairman of a committee for the assistance of his children: and I assure you that their condition is melancholy and desolate beyond all painting.

He was a struggling man through his whole existence—always very poor, and never extravagant. His wife died mad, three years ago, and he was left a widower with seven children—who were expecting his knock at the door, when a friend arrived with the terrible news of his Death.

If in the great extent of your charities, you have a niche left to fill up, I believe in my heart this is as sad a case as could possibly be put into it. If you have not, I know you will not mind saying so to me.

Do not trouble yourself to answer this, as I will call upon you to day between one and two. I called on Sunday last, to enquire after Miss Meredith;[4] but seeing your carriage at the door, I left my card. By the way—lingering at the street corner, was a very strange looking fellow, watching your house intently.[5]—Dear Miss Coutts,—always Yours faithfully and obliged.

1. Angela Georgina Burdett Coutts. See p. 185 n. 1.
2. For the text of the first advertisement to appear in the papers on 26 July, see P, III, 527n.
3. Edward William Elton (1794–1843), actor, who went down with 47 others on the Pegasus on 19 July 1843. Elton left seven children. By 25 Nov., Dickens's Benefit Committee had collected £2380 (P, III, 541n.).
4. Hannah Meredith, Miss Coutts's companion.
5. Possibly Richard Dunn. See P, III, 528 and n.

DEVONSHIRE TERRACE
Seventeenth September 1845

[Miss Coutts] . . . With a smaller sum, my dear Miss Coutts, I think I can do, on your behalf, an infinitely greater service. George Cruikshank came to me some weeks ago, and told me the facts of the melancholy little history I am going to state to you. He asked me if I thought I could influence any rich friend in the sufferer's behalf. You were not in the way. I do not know that I should have had the courage to come to you, if you had been, and I told him, No; I would not then; but if I ever could, I would. I should premise that Cruikshank is one of the best creatures in the world in his own odd way (he is a live caricature himself); and that to the extent of his means, he had rendered assistance here, already, from his own purse.

I don't know if you ever saw a book called Mornings at Bow Street. It is a collection of Bow Street reports that appeared, years and years ago, in the Morning Herald; and did the paper immense service at that time. The writer is a Mr White,[1] who from that time until very recently, has been connected with the Herald as one of its sub-editors. The paper changed hands within this year and a Half, or so—he was not wanted in the new arrangements—and at 60 years of age was suddenly discharged, with a month's salary, from the establishment that had not only been his income but his whole prospect; for he thought himself (quite naturally) a leaf of the tree, and believed he would never be shaken off until he died. He had lived upon his salary, but had done no more—I really don't see how he could have done more—and this was a blow, as if his Bank had failed, or he had become paralyzed.

His daughter had been engaged to be married, *Fourteen Years*. Her lover was not rich—was fighting his way, very slowly, to the Bar—and they had always said they would be married when he was "called." After all these many years, he was called, at last; and her wedding clothes were being made, when one night, (just at the time of this discharge) after they had been to the opera together, he went home to his chambers and was seized with congestion of the Brain. In a very few hours she was sent for. If she wished to see him before he died, the message said, she must come without delay. She was taken down to the Adelphi (where the chambers were) by her mother; and they arrived in the Bedroom, just in time to see him die. Quite frantic, she ran out of the chamber; opened a window, four tall stories high; and plunged herself, head-foremost from it! By a kind of miracle, she fell into a tank of water at the back of one of the neighbouring houses; and was taken out, insensible, but unhurt. Since that time, she has been watched, day and night. Her mother has never been told the Truth, but the father knows it. The poor girl sits all day in a sort of dream, repeating little scraps of comfort from the Bible. She has never shed a tear.

The wretched father is oppressed with some small debts. But they are very small; and if he could release his plate, which he has pawned for Thirty Pounds, I have no doubt Cruikshank could compound for every one of them with the produce of its sale; and then he could, with an easier mind, seek some employment: or at the worst, go away to live with his son who is a poor curate—I think in Wales. My dear Miss Coutts, these are all miserable facts within my knowledge. Thirty Pounds here, will be like Help from Heaven. There is no possibility of imposition; Cruikshank has known the parties twenty years at least; and the circumstances surely are peculiarly affecting and distressful.

My letter is so long already, that I will tell of the other Eltons in my next. We have never had the least trouble with them; and they are all as well, as happy, and as full of promise—thank God for it!—as we could possibly desire. . . .

1. John Wight, former sub-editor of the *Morning Herald* and author of *Mornings in Bow Street*, 1824, *More Mornings in Bow Street*, 1827, and *Sunday in London*, 1833, all of which were illustrated by Cruikshank.

2nd November 1843

[John Forster] . . . I expected you to be startled. If I was startled myself, when I first got this project of foreign travel into my head, MONTHS AGO, how much more must you be, on whom it comes fresh: numbering only hours! Still, I am very resolute upon it—very. I am convinced that my expenses abroad would not be more than half of my expenses here; the influence of change and nature upon me, enormous.[1] You know, as well as I, that I think Chuzzlewit in a hundred points immeasurably the best of my stories. That I feel my power now, more than I ever did. That I have a greater confidence in myself than I ever had. That I *know*, if I have health, I could sustain my place in the minds of thinking men, though fifty writers started up to-morrow. But how many readers do *not* think! How many take it upon trust from knaves and idiots, that one writes too fast, or runs a thing to death! How coldly did this very book go on for months, until it forced itself up in people's opinion, without forcing itself up in sale! If I wrote for forty thousand Forsters, or for forty thousand people who know I write because I can't help it, I should have no need to leave the scene. But this very book warns me that if I *can* leave it for a time, I had better do so, and must do so. Apart from that again, I feel that longer rest after this story would do me good. You say two or three months, because you have been used to see me for eight years never leaving off. But it is not rest enough. It is impossible to go on working the brain to that extent for ever. The very spirit of the thing, in doing it, leaves a horrible despondency behind, when it is done; which must be prejudicial to the mind, so soon renewed and so seldom let alone. What would poor Scott have given to have gone abroad, of his own free will, a young man, instead of creeping there, a driveller, in his miserable decay![2] I said myself in my note to you—anticipating what you put to me—that it was a question *what* I should come out with, first. The travel-book, if to be done at all, would cost me very little trouble; and surely would go very far to pay charges, whenever published. We have spoken of the baby, and of leaving it here with Catherine's mother.[3] Moving the children into France could not, in any ordinary course of things, do them anything but good. And the question is, what it would do to that by which they live: not what it would do to them. [. . .]

1. Falling sales with *MC* in June 1843 upset Dickens and prompted thoughts of going abroad again and travelling. Italy, he reasoned, would provide cheap quarters and a suitable base from which to explore the continent. In mid July of the next year Dickens and his family settled first in Albaro and then in Genoa, where they stayed in the Palazzo Peschiere until June 1846. During this period, he wrote *The Chimes*, travelled south to Naples in 1845 with his wife, and wrote many of the letters to friends at home that subsequently became part of the text of *PI*, his second travel book (1846).
2. Scott went abroad in his last illness in Oct. 1831, returning home the following July to die in Sep. 1832.
3. Catherine was pregnant with Francis Jeffrey, who was born 15 Jan. 1844. The baby accompanied the family to Italy in the following summer.

ALBARO
3rd August 1844

...[1] The story goes that it is in autumn and winter, when other countries are dark and foggy, that the beauty and clearness of this are most observable. I hope it may prove so; for I have postponed going round the hills which encircle the city, or seeing any of the sights, until the weather is more favourable. I have never yet seen it so clear, for any long time of the day together, as on a bright, lark-singing, coast-of-France-discerning day at Broadstairs; nor have I ever seen so fine a sunset, *throughout*, as is very common there. But the scenery is exquisite, and at certain periods of the evening and the morning the blue of the Mediterranean surpasses all conception or description. It is the most intense and wonderful colour, I do believe, in all nature. . . .

. . . This, my friend, is quite accurate.[2] Allow me to explain it. You are standing, sir, in our vineyard, among the grapes and figs. The Mediterranean is at your back as you look at the house: of which two sides, out of four, are here depicted. The lower story (nearly concealed by the vines) consists of the hall, a wine-cellar, and some store-rooms. The three windows on the left of the first floor belong to the sala, lofty and whitewashed, which has two more windows round the corner. The fourth window *did* belong to the dining-room, but I have changed one of the nurseries for better air; and it now appertains to that branch of the establishment. The fifth and sixth, or two right-hand windows, sir, admit the light to the inimitable's (and uxor's) chamber; to which the first window round the right-hand corner, which you perceive in shadow, also belongs. The next window in shadow, young sir, is the bower of Miss H[ogarth].[3] The next, a nursery window; the same having two more round the corner again. The bowery-looking place stretching out upon the left of the house is the terrace, which opens out from a French window in the drawing-room on the same floor of which you see nothing, and forms one side of the court-yard. The upper windows belong to some of those uncounted chambers upstairs; the fourth one, longer than the rest, being in Fletcher's[4] bedroom. There is a kitchen or two up there besides, and my dressing-room; which you can't see from this point of view. The kitchens and other offices in use are down below, under that part of the house where the roof is longest. On your left, beyond the bay of Genoa, about two miles off, the Alps stretch out into the far horizon; on your right, at three or four miles distance, are mountains crowned with forts. The intervening space on both sides is dotted with villas, some green, some red, some yellow, some blue, some (and ours among the number) pink. At your back, as I have said, sir, is the ocean; with the slim Italian tower of the ruined church of St. John the Baptist rising up before it, on the top of a pile of savage rocks. You go through the court-yard, and out at the gate, and down a narrow lane to the sea. Note. The sala goes sheer up to the top of the house; the ceiling being conical, and the little bedrooms built round the spring of its arch. You will observe that we make no pretension to architectural magnificence, but that we have abundance of room. And here I am, beholding only vines and the sea for days together. . . . Good Heavens! How I wish you'd come for a week or two, and taste the white wine at a penny farthing the pint. It is excellent. . . .

1. 'He opened [this] letter by telling me there was a thick November fog, that rain was pouring incessantly, and that he did not remember to have seen in his life, at that time of year, such cloudy weather as he had seen beneath Italian skies . . .' – Forster.
2. Referring 'to a sketch, from a pencil outline by Fletcher of [his residence] which bore the imposing name of the Villa di Bella Vista, but which he called by the homelier one of its proprietor, Bagnerello.' – Forster.
3. Georgina Hogarth. See p. 80 n. 1.
4. Angus Fletcher (1799–1862), sculptor.

["in the middle of October"]
[John Forster] . . . If I come, I shall put up at Cuttris's[1] that I may be close to you. Don't say to anybody, except our immediate friends, that I am coming. Then I shall not be bothered. If I should preserve my present fierce writing humour, in any pass I may run to Venice, Bologna, and Florence, before I turn my face towards Lincoln's-inn-fields; and come to England by Milan and Turin. But this of course depends in a great measure on your reply. . . .

. . . Notwithstanding what you say, I am still in the same mind about coming to London.[2] Not because the proofs concern me at all (I should be an ass as well as a thankless vagabond if they did), but because of that unspeakable restless something which would render it almost as impossible for me to remain here and not see the thing complete, as it would be for a full balloon, left to itself, not to go up. I do not intend coming from *here*, but by way of Milan and Turin (previously going to Venice), and so, across the wildest pass of the Alps that may be open, to Strasburg. . . . As you dislike the Young England gentleman I shall knock him out,[3] and replace him by a man (I can dash him in at your rooms in an hour) who recognizes no virtue in anything but the good old times, and talks of them, parrot-like, whatever the matter is. A real good old city tory, in a blue coat and bright buttons and a white cravat, and with a tendency of blood to the head. File away at Filer, as you please,[4] but bear in mind that the Westminster Review considered Scrooge's presentation of the turkey to Bob Cratchit as grossly incompatible with political economy.[5] I don't care at all for the skittle-playing. . . .

GENOA

Third of November, 1844. Half-past two, afternoon
. . . Thank God! I have finished the Chimes. This moment. I take up my pen again to-day, to say only that much; and to add that I have had what women call "a real good cry!" . . .

Fourth November

. . . Here is the brave courier[6] measuring bits of maps with a carving-fork, and going up mountains on a tea-spoon. He and I start on Wednesday for Parma, Modena, Bologna, Venice, Verona, Brescia, and Milan.[7] Milan being within a reasonable journey from here, Kate and Georgy will come to meet me when I arrive there on my way towards England; and will bring me all letters from you. I shall be there on the 18th. . . . Now, you know my punctiwality. Frost, ice, flooded rivers, steamers, horses, passports, and custom-houses may damage it. But my design is, to walk into Cuttris's coffee-room on Sunday the 1st of December, in good time for dinner. I shall look for you at the farther table by the fire—where we generally go. [. . .]

1. George Cuttriss's Piazza Coffee House and Hotel, Covent Garden, where Dickens intended to stay if he carried out his plan to visit London.
2. Forster had replied to Dickens's letter by 'dwelling on the fatigue and cost' of a visit to London (Forster, IV, v, 343).
3. Dickens intended the young England gentleman as a satirical comment on Disraeli's young England Tories. For the cancelled passages from the MS, see Michael Slater's App. A, *CB*, vol. 1, 247–52. Slater also discusses these

changes in 'Dickens (and Forster) at work on *The Chimes*', *Dickens Studies*, 2 (1966), 106–40.

4. Forster made only a slight change to Filer, the story's economist.

5. The reviewer of R. H. Horne's *New Spirit of the Age* commented in the *Westminster Review*, 44 (June 1844), on the naïve generosity of Scrooge in *CC* and the author's unwillingness to spoil the denouement by allowing real problems like the process 'whereby poor men are to be enabled to earn good wages' to enter into account (p. 376).

6. Louis Roche (d. 1849), the courier who accompanied Dickens to Italy in 1844 and to Switzerland in 1846.

7. Dickens's Italian trip went as planned, except he went from Verona to Mantua. He arrived in London on 1 Dec. and read *The Chimes* twice at Forster's rooms in Lincoln's Inn Fields (3 and 5 Dec.).

FRIBOURG

Saturday Night, Twenty-Third November, 1844

MY DEAREST KATE,—For the first time since I left you I am sitting in a room of my own hiring, with a fire and a bed in it. And I am happy to say that I have the best and fullest intentions of sleeping in the bed, having arrived here at half-past four this afternoon, without any cessation of travelling, night or day, since I parted from Mr. Bairr's cheap firewood.

The Alps appeared in sight very soon after we left Milan—by eight or nine o'clock in the morning; and the brave C. was so far wrong in his calculations that we began the ascent of the Simplon that same night, while you were travelling (as I would I were) towards the Peschiere. Most favourable state of circumstances for journeying up that tremendous pass! The brightest moon I ever saw, all night, and daybreak on the summit. The glory of which, making great wastes of snow a rosy red, exceeds all telling. We *sledged* through the snow on the summit for two hours or so. The weather was perfectly fair and bright, and there was neither difficulty nor danger—except the danger that there always must be, in such a place, of a horse stumbling on the brink of an immeasurable precipice. In which case no piece of the unfortunate traveller would be left large enough to tell his story in dumb show. You may imagine something of the rugged grandeur of such a scene as this great passage of these great mountains, and indeed Glencoe, well sprinkled with snow, would be very like the ascent. But the top itself, so wild, and bleak, and lonely, is a thing by itself, and not to be likened to any other sight. The cold was piercing; the north wind high and boisterous; and when it came driving in our faces, bringing a sharp shower of little points of snow and piercing it into our very blood, it really was, what it is often said to be, "cutting"—with a very sharp edge too. There are houses of refuge here—bleak, solitary places—for travellers overtaken by the snow to hurry to, as an escape from death; and one great house, called the Hospital, kept by monks, where wayfarers get supper and bed for nothing. We saw some coming out and pursuing their journey. If all monks devoted themselves to such uses, I should have little fault to find with them.[1]

The cold in Switzerland, since, has been something quite indescribable. My eyes are tingling to-night as one may supposed cymbals to tingle when they have been lustily played. It is positive pain[2] to me to write. The great organ[3] which I was to have had "pleasure in hearing" don't play on a Sunday, at which the brave is inconsolable. But the town is picturesque and quaint, and worth seeing. And this inn (with a German bedstead in it about the size and shape of a baby's linen-basket) is perfectly clean and comfortable. Butter is so cheap hereabouts that they bring you a great mass like the squab of a sofa for tea. And of honey, which is most delicious, they set before you a proportionate allowance.[4]

Swiss towns, and mountains, and the Lake of Geneva, and the famous suspension bridge at this place, and a great many other objects (with a very low thermometer conspicuous among them), are dancing up and down me, strangely. But I am quite collected enough, notwithstanding, to have still a very distinct idea that this hornpipe travelling is uncomfortable, and that I would gladly start for my palazzo out of hand without any previous rest, stupid as I am and much as I want it.—Ever, my dear love,—Affectionately yours.

P.S.—I hope the dancing lessons will be a success. Don't fail to let me know.

1. Dickens also describes his journey over the Simplon Pass in *PI* (1846).
2. Purgatory (P, iv, 229).
3. In Fribourg Cathedral.
4. The N text omits a sentence and a paragraph in which Dickens refers to his family in Genoa. See P, iv, 229.

NAPLES
11th February 1845

[John Forster] . . . The condition of the common people here is abject and shocking. I am afraid the conventional idea of the picturesque is associated with such misery and degradation that a new picturesque will have to be established as the world goes onward. Except Fondi there is nothing on earth that I have seen so dirty as Naples. I don't know what to liken the streets to where the mass of the lazzaroni live. You recollect that favourite pig-stye of mine near Broadstairs? They are more like streets of such apartments heaped up story on story, and tumbled house on house, than anything else I can think of, at this moment. . . . What would I give that you should see the lazzaroni as they really are—mere squalid, abject, miserable animals for vermin to batten on; slouching, slinking, ugly, shabby, scavenging scarecrows! And oh the raffish counts and more than doubtful countesses, the noodles and the blacklegs, the good society! And oh the miles of miserable streets and wretched occupants, to which Saffron-hill or the Borough-mint[1] is a kind of small gentility, which are found to be so picturesque by English lords and ladies; to whom the wretchedness left behind at home is lowest of the low, and vilest of the vile, and commonest of all common things. Well! well! I have often thought that one of the best chances of immortality for a writer is in the Death of his language, when he immediately becomes good company: and I often think here,—What *would* you say to these people, milady and milord, if they spoke out of the homely dictionary of your own "lower orders." [. . .]

In Naples, the burying place of the poor people is a great paved yard with three hundred and sixty-five pits in it: every one covered by a square stone which is fastened down. One of these pits is opened every night in the year; the bodies of the pauper dead are collected in the city; brought out in a cart (like that I told you of at Rome); and flung in, uncoffined. Some lime is then cast down into the pit; and it is sealed up until a year is past, and its turn again comes round. Every night there is a pit opened; and every night that same pit is sealed up again, for a twelvemonth. The cart has a red lamp attached, and at about ten o'clock at night you see it glaring through the Streets of Naples: stopping at the doors of hospitals and prisons, and such places, to increase its freight: and then rattling off again. Attached to the new cemetery (a very pretty one, and well-kept: immeasurably better in all respects than Père-la-Chaise) there is another similar yard, but not so large. . . . About Naples, the dead are borne along the street, uncovered, on an open bier; which is sometimes hoisted on a sort of palanquin, covered with a cloth of scarlet and gold. This exposure of the deceased is not peculiar to that part of Italy; for about midway between Rome and Genoa we encountered a funeral procession attendant on the body of a woman, which was presented in its usual dress, to my eyes (looking from my elevated seat on the box of a travelling carriage) as if she were alive, and resting on her bed. An attendant priest was chanting lustily—and as badly as the priests invariably do. Their noise is horrible. . . .

1. Saffron Hill, Holborn and the Borough Mint, Southwark, two filthy and notorious criminal haunts in London.

GENEVA

October Twenty-First 1846

MY DEAR BEARD,—Having run over here[1] for a day or two, to escape from a headache consequent upon the completion of the Christmas Book,[2] I take up my pen (I employ that phrase as a new one) to report myself alive and hearty. Also to report everybody else alive and hearty. Also to report that I mean to strike my encampment at Lausanne about the tenth or fifteenth of next month, and go to Paris,[3] where I shall take a house, and where, if you will make holiday, and come and unbend that bow which is kept strung in Shoe Lane,[4] you shall have your old welcome and everything else you like. *This is a thing that must be done*, so turn it over in your mind before I run over to England in December.

Dombey is a prodigious success.[5] Enthusiastic bulletins reach me daily. I hope you get yours as of old and like it.

There are two men standing under the balcony of the hotel in which I am writing, who are really good specimens, and have amused me mightily. An immense Frenchman, with a face like a bright velvet pincushion, and a very little Englishman, whose head comes up to about the middle of the Frenchman's waistcoat. They are travelling together. I saw them at Mont Blanc, months ago. The Englishman can't speak a word of French, but the Frenchman can speak a very little English, with which he helps the Englishman out of abysses and ravines of difficulty. The Englishman, instead of being obliged by this, condescends goodhumouredly to correct the Frenchman's pronunciation, patronises him, would pat him on the head if he could reach so high, and screeches at his mistakes. There he is now, staggering over the stones in his little boots, and falling up against a watchmaker's window, in perfect convulsions of joy, because the beaming giant, without whom he couldn't get a single necessary of life, has made some mistake in the English language! I never saw such a fellow. The last time I met them was at the other end of the Lake by Chillon, disembarking from the steamer. It is done in little boats, the water being shallow close in shore, and in the confusion, the Giant had got into one boat and the Dwarf in another. A hairy sailor on board the steamer found the Dwarf's greatcoat on deck and gave a great roar to him; upon which the Dwarf, standing up in the boat, cried out (in English): "Put it down. Keep it. I shall be back in an hour." The hairy sailor, of course not understanding one word of this, roared again and shook the coat in the air. "Oh you damned fool!" said the Dwarf (still in English). "Oh you precious jackass! Put it down, will you?" The Giant, perceiving from the other boat what was the matter, cried out to the hairy sailor what it was necessary for him to know, and then called out to the Dwarf: "I have tell him to cap it!" I thought the Dwarf would have died with delight. "Oh my God!" he said to himself. "You're a nice man! Tell him to cap it, have you? Yes yes. Ha ha ha! Cap it, indeed! Oh Lord!" And never left off chuckling till he landed. [. . .]

1. Dickens visited Geneva while staying in Lausanne, where he had settled his family in June 1846 for a second continental sojourn.
2. *The Battle of Life* (1846), the final part of which Dickens sent Forster on 18 Oct.
3. The family left Lausanne on 16 Nov. and took up residence in Paris, where they remained until 28 Feb. 1847.
4. Shoe Lane, Fleet Street, where Beard worked as a journalist.
5. Dickens began *DS* on 27 June; sales of the first no. (Oct. 46), as reported by Forster, account for his elation. See Forster, v, vi, 428 and P, iv, 631n.

Fifth July 1848

[John Forster] . . . A change took place in poor Fanny,[1] about the middle of the day yesterday, which took me out there last night. Her cough suddenly ceased almost, and, strange to say, she immediately became aware of her hopeless state; to which she resigned herself, after an hour's unrest and struggle, with extraordinary sweetness and constancy. The irritability passed, and all hope faded away; though only two nights before, she had been planning for "after Christmas." She is greatly changed. I had a long interview with her to-day, alone; and when she had expressed some wishes about the funeral, and her being buried in unconsecrated ground,[2] I asked her whether she had any care or anxiety in the world. She said No, none. It was hard to die at such a time of life, but she had no alarm whatever in the prospect of the change; felt sure we should meet again in a better world; and although they had said she might rally for a time, did not really wish it. She said she was quite calm and happy, relied upon the mediation of Christ, and had no terror at all. She had worked very hard, even when ill; but believed that was in her nature, and neither regretted nor complained of it. Burnett had been always very good to her; they had never quarrelled; she was sorry to think of his going back to such a lonely home; and was distressed about her children, but not painfully so. She showed me how thin and worn she was; spoke about an invention she had heard of that she would like to have tried, for the deformed child's back; called to my remembrance all our sister Letitia's[3] patience and steadiness; and, though she shed tears sometimes, clearly impressed upon me that her mind was made up, and at rest. I asked her very often, if she could ever recall anything that she could leave to my doing, to put it down, or mention it to somebody if I was not there; and she said she would, but she firmly believed that there was nothing—nothing. Her husband being young, she said, and her children infants,[4] she could not help thinking sometimes, that it would be very long in the course of nature before they were reunited; but she knew that was a mere human fancy, and could have no reality after she was dead. Such an affecting exhibition of strength and tenderness, in all that early decay, is quite indescribable. I need not tell you how it moved me. I cannot look round upon the dear children here, without some misgiving that this sad disease will not perish out of our blood with her; but I am sure I have no selfishness in the thought, and God knows how small the world looks to one who comes out of such a sick-room on a bright summer day. I don't know why I write this before going to bed. I only know that in the very pity and grief of my heart, I feel as if it were doing something. . . .

1. Frances Elizabeth Dickens (1810–48), Charles's eldest sister. Fanny studied music at the Royal Academy of Music; she married Henry Burnett, a singer and music teacher, in 1837, and she died of consumption on 2 Sep.
2. As a Dissenter, Fanny was buried in the unconsecrated part of Highgate Cemetery (P, v, 366n).
3. Letitia Mary Dickens (1816–93), Dickens's younger sister.
4. Fanny had two children: Henry Augustus, a cripple (1839–49) and Charles Dickens Kneller Burnett (b. 1841).

BONCHURCH
[September 1849]

[John Forster] . . . Before I think of beginning my next number,[1] I perhaps cannot do better than give you an imperfect description of the results of the climate of Bonchurch after a few weeks' residence.[2] The first salubrious effect of which the Patient becomes conscious is an almost continual feeling of sickness, accompanied with great prostration of strength, so that his legs tremble under him, and his arms quiver when he wants to take hold of any object. An extraordinary disposition to sleep (except at night, when his rest, in the event of his having any, is broken by incessant dreams) is always present at the same time; and, if he have anything to do requiring thought and attention, this over-powers him to such a degree that he can only do it in snatches: lying down on beds in the fitful intervals. Extreme depression of mind, and a disposition to shed tears from morning to night, developes itself at the same period. If the Patient happen to have been a good walker, he finds ten miles an insupportable distance; in the achievement of which his legs are so unsteady, that he goes from side to side of the road, like a drunken man. If he happen to have ever possessed an energy of any kind, he finds it quenched in a dull, stupid languor. He has no purpose, power, or object in existence whatever. When he brushes his hair in the morning, he is so weak that he is obliged to sit upon a chair to do it. He is incapable of reading, at all times. And his bilious system is so utterly overthrown, that a ball of boiling fat appears to be always behind the top of the bridge of his nose, simmering between his haggard eyes. If he should have caught a cold, he will find it impossible to get rid of it, as his system is wholly incapable of making any effort. His cough will be deep, monotonous, and constant. "The faithful watch-dog's honest bark"[3] will be nothing to it. He will abandon all present idea of overcoming it, and will content himself with keeping an eye upon his blood-vessels to preserve them whole and sound. *Patient's name, Inimitable B* . . . . It's a mortal mistake!—That's the plain fact. Of all the places I ever have been in, I have never been in one so difficult to exist in, pleasantly. Naples is hot and dirty, New York feverish, Washington bilious, Genoa exciting, Paris rainy—but Bonchurch, smashing. I am quite convinced that I should die here, in a year. It's not hot, it's not close, I don't know what it is, but the prostration of it is *awful*. Nobody here has the least idea what I think of it; but I find from all sorts of hints from Kate, Georgina, and the Leeches,[4] that they are all affected more or less in the same way, and find it very difficult to make head against. I make no sign, and pretend not to know what is going on. But they are right. I believe the Leeches will go soon, and small blame to 'em!—For me, when I leave here at the end of this September, I must go down to some cold place; as Ramsgate for example, for a week or two; or I seriously believe I shall feel the effects of it for a long time. [. . .]

1. *DC*, no. VI.
2. Dickens rented a house in Bonchurch, Isle of Wight, for the summer of 1849.
3. Byron, *Don Juan*, I, stanza 123.
4. John Leech (1817–64), artist and illustrator of Dickens's Christmas books. Leech and his wife shared the house with Dickens and his family.

Tuesday, Third September, 1850

MY DEAREST KATE,—I enclose a few lines from Georgy,[1] and write these to say that I purpose going home at some time on Thursday, but I cannot say precisely when, as it depends on what work I do to-morrow. Yesterday Charles Knight,[2] White,[3] Forster, Charley, and I walked to Richborough Castle[4] and back. Knight dined with us afterwards; and the Whites, the Bicknells,[5] and Mrs. Gibson[6] came in in the evening and played vingt-et-un.

Having no news I must tell you a story of Sydney.[7] The children, Georgy, and I were out in the garden on Sunday evening (by-the-bye, I made a beautiful passage down, and got to Margate a few minutes after one), when I asked Sydney if he would go to the railroad and see if Forster was coming. As he answered very boldly "Yes," I opened the garden gate, upon which he set off alone as fast as his legs would carry him; and being pursued, was not overtaken until he was through the Lawn House Archway, when he was still going on at full speed—I can't conceive where. Being brought back in triumph, he made a number of fictitious starts, for the sake of being overtaken again, and we made a regular game of it. At last, when he and Alley[8] had run away, instead of running after them, we came into the garden, shut the gate, and crouched down on the ground. Presently we heard them come back and say to each other with some alarm, "Why, the gate's shut, and they're all gone," Alley began in a dismayed way to cry out, but the Phenomenon shouting, "Open the gate!" sent an enormous stone flying into the garden (among our heads) by way of alarming the establishment. I thought it a wonderful piece of character, showing great readiness of resource. He would have fired a perfect battery of stones, or very likely have broken the pantry window, I think, if we hadn't let him in.

They are all in great force, and send their loves. They are all much excited with the expectation of receiving you on Friday, and would start me off to fetch you now if I would go.—Ever my Dearest Kate—Most affectionately yours.

1. Georgina Hogarth (1827–1917), Dickens's sister-in-law who, since his return from America in 1842, became a part of his household. In the 'Violated letter' of 25 May 1858 (p. 129), he describes her as having 'from the age of fifteen . . . devoted herself to our house and our children'.
2. Charles Knight, see p. 51 n. 5.
3. Revd James White (1800–62), author.
4. A former Roman fort about 9 miles west of Broadstairs.

5. Elhanan Bicknell (1788–1861), and his wife.
6. Susanna Arethusa Gibson (1814–85).
7. Sydney Smith Haldimand Dickens (b. 18 Apr. 1847).
8. Alley, a nickname for Alfred D'Orsay Tennyson Dickens (b. 28 Oct. 1845).

DEVONSHIRE TERRACE
Tuesday Morning Fifteenth April 1851

MY DEAREST KATE,—Now observe. You must read this letter, very slowly and carefully. If you have hurried on thus far without quite understanding (apprehending some bad news), I rely on your turning back, and reading again.

Little Dora,[1] without being in the least pain, is suddenly stricken ill. She awoke out of a sleep, and was seen, in one moment, to be very ill. Mind! I will not deceive you. I think her *very* ill.

There is nothing in her appearance but perfect rest. You would suppose her quietly asleep. But I am sure she is very ill, and I cannot encourage myself with much hope of her recovery. I do not—why should I say I do, to you my dear!—I do not think her recovery at all likely.

I do not like to leave home. I can do nothing here, but I think it right to stay here. You will not like to be away, I know, and I cannot reconcile it to myself to keep you away. Forster with his usual affection for us comes down to bring you this letter and to bring you home. But I cannot close it without putting the strongest entreaty and injunction upon you to come home with perfect composure—to remember what I have often told you, that we never can expect to be exempt, as to our many children, from the afflictions of other parents—and that if— *if*—when you come, I should even have to say to you "our little baby is dead," you are to do your duty to the rest, and to shew yourself worthy of the great trust you hold in them.

If you will only read this, steadily, I have a perfect confidence in your doing what is right.—Ever affectionately.

1. Dora Annie Dickens (b. 16 Aug. 1850), had been unwell for some time and died suddenly on 14 Apr. 1851 shortly after Dickens left her bedside to give a speech at the General Theatrical Fund. Forster broke the news to Dickens after the speech and then travelled to Malvern, where Catherine was staying, to escort her home. Dickens wrote this letter to prepare his wife for Dora's death.

BROADSTAIRS, KENT
Thursday Twenty-Fourth July, 1851

MY DEAR MR. PUTNAM,[1]—I have received your letter with very great pleasure, as it is quite delightful to me to have a new assurance of your attachment, and a reminder (though I need none) of your old fidelity and zeal. I have often travelled, in fancy, over the old ground and water in America, and have over and over again beheld you coming at dusk into the stern-galley of a Western steamer, with a little jug of some warm mixture intended for my very little cabin. Sometimes (this present year for instance) I have had an impression that you would come to England, and should not have been in the least surprised to behold you bodily entering my study.

Whether we look as we used to look, I can't quite determine. I am much redder and browner, I believe, than I was in those times—more robust—less interesting—shorter haired—a more solid-looking personage—and not younger. But I take great exercise, and am very strong. Mrs. Dickens is stouter, though not quite so well in health as she used to be then. Anne,[2] who has been with us in Italy and in Switzerland, is with us still, and looks (in my eyes) much the same. They both desire to be kindly remembered to you—and an immense sensation has been created in their minds by your allusion to your daughter—which has given unbounded satisfaction.

I write from the seaside—from a fishing village and small watering-place to which we generally come at this time of the year. We still reside, however, in London—our headquarters being always there. We have eight children, and have had nine—a little girl died suddenly, not long ago.[3] The picture of the four we had when we were in America, hangs in our dining room at home.[4] It is in a gay round frame now, and has these many years forgotten the sliding lid of the box you used to take off before you set it up on a side table at each of the four and twenty thousand Inns we stayed at. I wonder whether you recollect the Inn at Hartford where the "Levee" wouldn't go away—or at Newhaven where they kicked the staircase, to express impatience—or at Columbus where they came in, arm in arm, at about midnight—or at St. Louis where we had (I think) a ball—or at Pittsburgh, where I recollect one man with very large buttons on his waistcoat, who got behind the door and couldn't be got out—or at Philadelphia, where a little hatter with black whiskers did the honors? I feel as if I should like to see all those places again, so much—and to have another ride on a corduroy coach, and to sit at another very long table with nothing particular to eat upon it, aboard the Messenger.

I see many Americans in London, and find them the old good-humoured kind-hearted people. We never quarrel, but "get along" (as you would say) quite merrily and pleasantly. If I ever find one, in travelling about, I try to make him more at home, in remembrance of my old welcome. Sometimes he seems disposed to consider me a sort of Monster, at first, but he soon gets over it. I want to save the next leaf for the autographs you ask for. Therefore I will only ask you to give my cordial regards to your wife (quite a Matron, I suppose, since I saw her at the Tremont House[5]) and a kiss to the little girl, and to believe me always Faithfully Your friend.—Faithfully Yours.

1. George Washington Putnam (1812–96), Dickens's American secretary in 1842. See Putnam's account, 'Four Months with CD. During his First Visit to America (in 1842). By his secretary', *Atlantic Monthly*, 26 (Oct. and Nov. 1870), 476–82; 591–99.
2. Anne Brown, Catherine's maid, who accompanied Dickens and his wife to America in 1842.
3. P. Collins lists Dickens's nine children and provides brief particulars of their careers in *Dickens and Education*, pp 27–8. For Dora's death, see p. 81.
4. A crayon drawing by D. Maclise of the four Dickens children, done at Catherine's request in the autumn of 1841. See P, II, 393n. Johnson reproduces the drawing in his biography (vol. I, pl. 30).
5. Boston, where Dickens and his wife stayed in 1842.

BROADSTAIRS
Sunday, Seventh September, 1851

MY DEAR HENRY,[1]—I am in that state of mind which you may (once) have seen described in the newspapers as "bordering on distraction;" the house given up to me,[2] the fine weather going on (soon to break, I daresay), the painting season oozing away, my new book waiting to be born,[3] and

NO WORKMEN ON THE PREMISES,

along of my not hearing from you!! I have torn all my hair off, and constantly beat my unoffending family. Wild notions have occurred to me of sending in my own plumber to do the drains. Then I remember that you have probably written to prepare *your* man, and restrain my audacious hand. Then Stone[4] presents himself, with a most exasperatingly mysterious visage, and says that a rat has appeared in the kitchen, and it's his opinion (Stone's, not the rat's) that the drains wasn't "compo-ing;"[5] for the use of which explicit language I could fell him without remorse. In my horrible desire to "compo" everything, the very postman becomes my enemy because he brings no letter from you; and, in short, I don't see what's to become of me unless I hear from you to-morrow which I have not the least expectation of doing.

Going over the house again, I have materially altered the plans—abandoned conservatory and front balcony—decided to make Stone's painting-room the drawing-room (it is nearly six inches higher than the room below), to carry the entrance passage right through the house to a back door leading to the garden, and to reduce the once intended drawing-room—now school-room—to a manageable size, making a door of communication between the new drawing-room and the study. Curtains and carpets, on a scale of awful splendour and magnitude, are already in preparation, and still—still—.

NO WORKMEN ON THE PREMISES.

To pursue this theme is madness. Where are you? When are you coming home? Where is THE man who is to do the work? Does he know that an army of artificers must be turned in at once, and the whole thing finished out of hand? O rescue me from my present condition. Come up to the scratch, I entreat and implore you!

I send this to Lætitia to forward,

Being, as you well know why,
Completely floored by N. W., I
Sleep.

I hope you may be able to read this. My state of mind does not admit of coherence.—Ever affectionately.

P.S.—NO WORKMEN ON THE PREMISES!
Ha! ha! ha! (I am laughing demoniacally.)

1. Henry Austin (?1812–61), architect and civil engineer; married Letitia Dickens in 1837.
2. Dickens had recently purchased Tavistock House in London, putting his brother-in-law in charge of the extensive alterations while he and his family remained at Broadstairs until the house was ready for occupation.
3. *BH*, which Dickens began writing in Nov.
4. Frank Stone (1800–59), painter, from whom Dickens bought Tavistock House.
5. The *OED* lists *compo* as a verb – to cover with compo, a mixture of whiting, resin, and glue – in 1809.

BROADSTAIRS, KENT
Friday Twenty-Sixth September 1851

SIR,[1]—I have decided as follows:

To abandon the chairs altogether. To have the centre recess in the drawing-room fitted with one plate of the best glass (according to your estimate) "with a space of nine inches left on each side to correspond

with the two side recesses, and a little additional ornament at the top."
Also to have the plate under Console table, and the two glasses from
Devonshire Terrace[2] fixed in the side recesses regilt where necessary,
and additional ornaments at the top. All this agreeably to your
estimate. I do not require any such pendant from these, as you
mention.

The large chimney-glass in Devonshire Terrace will require a little
regilding here and there. Please take it down, and have it done.

At the same time, you may fetch away if you please the large dining
table (substituting some other, on loan, in its place) and the rosewood
Card tables from the best bedroom. These to have such repair, as they
need.

I also wish the Console glass from Devonshire Terrace, to be taken
away, for the following purpose:

The maker of the Bookcase will have learnt from Mr Austin that that
side of it *which will be opposite to the windows of the study*, is to have
two recesses in it, instead of one, on account of our having altered the
position of the proposed doorway. Now, midway between these two
recesses, I wish this looking-glass to be let into the bookcase—of
course without its gilt frame. The bookshelves all round it being
finished off in mahogany, it will be in a mahogany frame, and built in
on all four sides with the books; the bookshelves below it (two rows,
probably for rather large books) being finished off at the top with a
mahogany slab, so that there will be a shelf before the looking-glass, as
in the case of a chimney piece; and the centre and higher part of the
Bookcase being over it, on account of the glass being itself in the
middle of that side of the room.

I shall be glad to know that you quite understand this.

As dispatch is very important to me with a view to my avocations, I
have to request that no time may be lost in executing this work and I
rest on your assurance that it shall be promptly done. The ornamental
papering of the drawing room, of course cannot be executed until the
glasses are fixed: nor can I get at my books (at present packed in a
number of boxes) until they can be arranged on their shelves.—Yours.

1. Unidentified.
2. Dickens's former London home, where he lived, 1839–51.

HOUSEHOLD WORDS OFFICE
Wednesday Evening, Twenty-Second October, 1851

MY DEAR MR. EELES,[1]—I send you the list I have made for the book-backs. I should like the History of a Short Chancery Suit[2] to come at the bottom of one recess, and the Catalogue of Statues of the Duke of Wellington[3] at the bottom of the other. If you should want more titles, and will let me know how many, I will send them to you.—Faithfully yours.

LIST OF IMITATION BOOK-BACKS.[4]

Five Minutes in China. 3 vols.
Forty Winks at the Pyramids. 2 vols.
Abernethy on the Constitution. 2 vols.
Mr. Green's Overland Mail. 2 vols.
Captain Cook's Life of Savage. 2 vols.
A Carpenter's Bench of Bishops. 2 vols.
Toots' Universal Letter-Writer. 2 vols.
Orson's Art of Etiquette.
Downeaster's Complete Calculator.
History of the Middling Ages. 6 vols.
Jonah's Account of the Whale.
Captain Parry's Virtues of Cold Tar.
Kant's Ancient Humbugs. 10 vols.
Bowwowdom. A Poem.
The Quarrelly Review. 4 vols.
The Gunpowder Magazine. 4 vols.
Steele. By the Author of "Ion."
The Art of Cutting the Teeth.
Matthew's Nursery Songs. 2 vols.
Paxton's Bloomers. 5 vols.
On the Use of Mercury by the Ancient Poets.
Drowsy's Recollections of Nothing. 3 vols.
Heavyside's Conversations with Nobody. 3 vols.
Commonplace Book of the Oldest Inhabitant. 2 vols.
Growler's Gruffiology, with Appendix. 4 vols.
The Books of Moses and Sons. 2 vols.
Burke (of Edinburgh) on the Sublime and Beautiful. 2 vols.
Teazer's Commentaries.
King Henry the Eighth's Evidences of Christianity. 5 vols.
Miss Biffin on Deportment.
Morrison's [sic] Pills Progress. 2 vols.

Lady Godiva on the Horse.

Munchausen's Modern Miracles. 4 vols.

Richardson's Show of Dramatic Literature. 12 vols.

Hansard's Guide to Refreshing Sleep. As many volumes as possible.

1. Thomas Robert Eeles, bookbinder (P, IV, 517n).
2. Chancery suits, as Dickens makes clear in *BH*, were notoriously long, tenacious, and certain to cost suitors dearly, a fact which is reflected in contemporary pugilistic slang and in the figurative use of 'in chancery' to signify an awkward fix or predicament.
3. On 18 June 1822 Sir Richard Westmacott's 'Statute of Achilles' was erected in Hyde Park, 'inscribed by the women of England to Arthur, Duke of Wellington, and his brave companions in arms'. Achilles's nudity, and the fact that British ladies defrayed the cost of the statue, caused a public stir, which Cruikshank humorously exploited in 'Making Decent!!—A Hint to the Society for the Suppression of Vice' two months later. This drawing satirizes the extremists worried about the possible harmful consequences of nude statues by showing William Wilberforce, the great Evangelical moralist, covering Achilles's genitals (already decorously hidden behind a fig leaf) with his hat. As an intimate of Cruikshank's and admirer of his work, Dickens perhaps alluded to this episode in his mock title.
4. Not all of the imaginary titles were devised by Dickens, notes E. Johnson, who refers to an overlapping collection of mock titles in the Forster collection, noted there as inventions of Dickens, Forster, and B. W. Proctor (*Johnson*, vol. II, lxiv). For a detailed list of all the titles, see F. G. Kitton, *Charles Dickens by Pen and Pencil* (London: F. T. Sabin, 1890–2), 34–6.

   Several of these titles, as Johnson suggests, are purely facetious (vol. II, 749). Among these are: *Five Minutes in China*, 3 vols; *Forty Winks at the Pyramids*, 2 vols; *History of the Middling Ages*, 6 vols; *Bowwowdom. A Poem*; *The Art of Cutting the Teeth*; *Drowsy's Recollections of Nothing*, 3 vols; *Heavyside's Conversations with Nobody*, 3 vols; *Commonplace Book of the Oldest Inhabitant*, 2 vols; *Growler's Gruffiology, with Appendix*, 4 vols; other puns on titles are easily accessible to modern readers: *Captain Cook's Life of Savage*; *Jonah's Account of the Whale*; *The Quarrelly [Quarterly] Review*; *The Gunpowder Magazine*; *The Book of Moses and Sons*; and *Teazer's Commentaries*.

   Several need some explanation: John Abernethy (1764–1831), surgeon and well-known lecturer on anatomy and physiology; Charles Green (1785–1870), aeronaut and balloonist; John Carpenter (d. 1476), bishop of Worcester; *Toots'/Tout Universal Letter-Writer*; Orson, brought up by a bear and reared as a wildman in *Valentine and Orson*; Sir William Edward Parry (1790–1855), Arctic explorer and author of Captain Parry's *Arctic Voyages*, 1821–6; tarwater, an infusion of tar in cold water, was formerly in repute as a medicine and was praised by George Berkeley in his *Philosophical Reflexions and Inquiries concerning the Virtues of Tar-water* (1744); a Down-Easter lives in New England, especially Maine, where people have a reputation for frugality and thrift; Immanuel (cant) Kant

(1724–1804), philosopher; 'Ion', a pseudo-Greek tragedy published by Sir Thomas Noon Talford in 1835; (Steel) Sir Richard Steele (1672–1729), dramatist and journalist; Sir Joseph Paxton (1803–65), architect famous for his use of glass and iron, whose two greenhouses at Chatsworth, Derbyshire, served as models for the 1851 Crystal Palace; Mercury, the Roman messenger of the gods (mercury also served as a cure for syphilis); William Burke (1792–1829), murderer, who, with William Hare in Edinburgh, sold dead bodies to surgeons; Edmund Burke (1729–97) published his *Philosophical Inquiry into the Sublime and Beautiful* in 1756; Henry VIII (1509–47) signed the Act of Supremacy (1534), by which England repudiated the supremacy of the Pope and declared the King to be the supreme Head on earth of the Church of England; Miss Biffin (1784–1850), a painter born without arms or legs, who held her brush between her teeth and specialised in miniatures; Morison's Pills, the 'vegetable universal medicines', invented in 1825 by James Morison (1770–1840), which consisted principally of gamboge. The pills became popular and Morison set up an establishment for their sale called 'The British College of Health'. Carlyle scornfully referred to Morison's Pills in *Past and Present*; Lady Godiva (fl. 1040–80), wife of Leofric, earl of Mercia, famous for her legendary ride through the city of Coventry, which she and her husband founded. The chronicle in which the reference to her ride appears states that her husband agreed to remit the heavy tax on the people if she would ride naked through Coventry on a white horse; Rudolphe E. Raspe published in English a version of Baron Munchausen's exaggerated experiences called *Baron Munchausen, Narrative of his Marvelous Travels* (1785). Among them are stories of a horse being cut in two, drinking from a fountain, and then being sewn together; of a stag shot with a cherry stone who afterwards grew a cherry-tree in his forehead, and so on; John Richardson (1767?–1837), itinerant showman with whom many actors rose to distinction; Luke Hansard (1752–1828), founder of the House of Commons' Journals in 1774. *Hansard* became the familiar title for the summaries of Parliamentary debates and was used until 1892, when the name was dropped. In 1943, the name *Hansard* was reinstated.

BROADSTAIRS
Eighth September, 1851

[Frank Stone][1] . . . You never saw such a sight as the sands between this and Margate presented yesterday.[2] This day fortnight a steamer laden with cattle going from Rotterdam to the London market, was wrecked on the Goodwin[3]—on which occasion, by-the-bye, the coming in at night of our Salvage Luggers laden with dead cattle, which were hoisted up upon the pier, where they lay in heaps, was a most picturesque and striking sight. The sea since Wednesday has been very rough, blowing in straight upon the land. Yesterday, the shore was strewn with hundreds of oxen, sheep, and pigs (and with bushels upon bushels of apples,) in every state and stage of decay—burst open, rent asunder, lying with their stiff hoofs in the air, or with their great ribs yawning like the wrecks of ships—tumbled and beaten out of shape, and yet with a horrible sort of humanity about them. Hovering among these carcases was every kind of water-side plunderer, pulling the horns out, getting the hides off, chopping the hoofs with poleaxes, etc. etc., attended by no end of donkey carts, and spectral horses with scraggy necks, galloping wildly up and down as if there were something maddening in the stench. I never beheld such a demoniacal business!—Very faithfully yours.

1. Frank Stone (1800–59), painter. See also p. 84 n. 4.
2. On 7 Sep. 1851 gales caused several disastrous shipwrecks around the coast, including the 'Apollo', another cattleboat from Rotterdam, which foundered about 40 miles from the entrance to the Thames that day ('Chronicle', *AR*, 1851, p. 145). The same source carries no reference to the earlier wreck Dickens refers to.
3. The Goodwin Sands, a stretch of shoals and sand bars about ten miles off the east coast of Kent, claimed many vessels.

SUNDERLAND
29th August 1852

[John Forster] . . . The play[1] is so far improved by the reductions which your absence and other causes have imposed on us, that it acts now only two hours and twenty-five minutes, all waits included, and goes "like wildfire," as Mr. Tonson says.[2] [. . .] When we got here at noon, it appeared that the hall was a perfectly new one, and had only had the slates put upon the roof by torchlight over night. Farther, that the proprietors of some opposition rooms had declared the building to be unsafe, and that there was a panic in the town about it; people having had their money back, and being undecided whether to come or not, and all kinds of such horrors. I didn't know what to do. The horrible responsibility of risking an accident of that awful nature seemed to rest only upon me; for I had only to say we wouldn't act, and there would be no chance of danger. I was afraid to take Sloman[3] into council lest the panic should infect our men. I asked W.[4] what *he* thought, and he consolingly observed that his digestion was so bad that death had no terrors for him! I went and looked at the place; at the rafters, walls, pillars, and so forth; and fretted myself into a belief that they really were slight! To crown all, there was an arched iron roof without any brackets or pillars, on a new principle! The only comfort I had was in stumbling at length on the builder, and finding him a plain practical north-countryman with a foot rule in his pocket. I took him aside, and asked him should we, or could we, prop up any weak part of the place: especially the dressing-rooms, which were under our stage, the weight of which must be heavy on a new floor, and dripping wet walls. He told me there wasn't a stronger building in the world; and that, to allay the apprehension, they had opened it, on Thursday night, to thousands of the working people, and induced them to sing, and beat with their feet, and make every possible trial of the vibration. Accordingly there was nothing for it but to go on. I was in such dread, however, lest a false alarm should spring up among the audience and occasion a rush, that I kept Catherine and Georgina out of the front. When the curtain went up and I saw the great sea of faces rolling up to the roof, I looked here and looked there, and thought I saw the gallery out of the perpendicular, and fancied the lights in the ceiling were not straight. Rounds of applause were perfect agony to me, I was so afraid of their effect upon the building. I was ready all night to rush on in case of an alarm—a false alarm was my main dread—and implore the people for God's sake to sit still. I had our great farce-bell[5] rung to startle Sir Geoffrey[6] instead of throwing down a piece of wood, which might have raised a sudden apprehension. I had a palpitation of the heart, if any of our people stumbled up or down a stair. I am sure I never acted better, but the anxiety of my mind was so intense, and the relief at last so great, that I am half dead to-day, and have not yet been able to eat or drink anything or to stir out of my room. I shall never forget it. As to the short time we had for getting the theatre up; as to the upsetting, by a runaway pair of horses, of one of the vans at the Newcastle railway station *with all the scenery in it, every atom of which was turned over*; as to the fatigue of our carpenters, who have now been up four nights, and who were lying dead asleep in the entrances last night; I say nothing, after the other gigantic nightmare, except that Sloman's splendid knowledge of his business, and the good temper and cheerfulness of all the workmen, are capital. I mean to give them a supper at Liverpool, and address them in a neat and appropriate speech. We dine at two to-day (it is now one) and go to Sheffield at four, arriving there at about ten. I had been as fresh as a daisy; walked from Nottingham to Derby, and from Newcastle here; but seem to have had my nerves crumpled up last night, and have an excruciating headache. That's all at present. I shall never be able to bear the smell of new deal and fresh mortar again as long as I live. . . .

1. Bulwer Lytton's five-act comedy, 'Many Sides to a Character, or Not so Bad as We Seem', written for performance by an amateur cast organized by Dickens. After the play opened at Devonshire House (16 May 1851), Dickens, as the actor-manager, took the company on tour to raise money for the Guild of Literature and Art, whose aims he describes in 'The Guild

of Literature and Art', *HW*, 10 May 1851. See also *Speeches*, pp 116–7 and
N, II, 275–7, where Dickens outlines the scheme in a letter to the Duke of
Devonshire. Forster played Hardman, *MP*, in the original cast but retired
from the company when illness and his work disabled him (Forster, VI, vi,
71).
2. Jacob Tonson, a bookseller in the play.
3. Unidentified.
4. Wilkie Collins, who played Smart, Lord Wilmot's valet.
5. Used in 'Mr. Nightingale's Diary', a one-act farce by Dickens and Mark
   Lemon.
6. Sir Geoffrey Thornside, a character in 'Many Sides', played by Mark
   Lemon.

DOVER

Thursday, Twenty-Third September, 1852

[Miss Coutts] . . . The whole Public seems to me to have gone mad
about the funeral of the Duke of Wellington. I think it a grievous
thing[1]—a relapse into semi-barbarous practices—an almost ludicrous
contrast to the calm good sense and example of responsibility set by the
Queen Dowager—a pernicious corruption of the popular mind, just
beginning to awaken from the long dream of inconsistencies, mons-
trosities, horrors and ruinous expenses, that has beset all classes of
society in connexion with Death—and a folly sure to miss its object and
to be soon attended by a strong re-action on the memory of the
illustrious man so *mis*respected.

But to say anything about it now, or to hope to leaven with any grain
of sense such a mass of wrong-doing, would be utterly useless.
Afterwards, I shall try to present the sense of the case in Household
Words.[2] At present, I think I might as well whistle to the sea. . . .

1. Arthur Wellesley, 1st Duke of Wellington (b. 1769), Fieldmarshal and
   Statesman, died 14 Sep. 1852.
2. Dickens expressed his disapproval of the competition among the middle
   classes for 'superior gentility in Funerals' and 'the demoralizing practice of
   trading in Death' evident in the way people profited by state funerals in
   'Trading in Death', *HW*, 27 Nov. 1852.

H.M.S. TAVISTOCK

Second January, 1853

[Clarkson Stanfield][1] . . . Yoho, old salt! Neptun' ahoy! You don't
forget, messmet, as you was to meet Dick Sparkler[2] and Mark Porpuss[3]
on the fok'sle of the good ship Owssel Words,[4] Wednesday next,
half-past four? Not you; for when did Stanfell ever pass his word to go
anywheers and not come? Well. Belay, my heart of oak, belay! Come

alongside the Tavistock same day and hour, 'stead of Owssel Words. Hail your shipmets, and they'll drop over the side and join you, like two new shillings a-droppin' into the purser's pocket. Damn all lubberly boys and swabs, and give *me* the lad with the tarry trousers, which shines to me like di'mings bright! . . .

1. Clarkson Stanfield (1793–1867), marine and landscape painter. From 1844 onwards, Dickens's letters to Stanfield frequently included passages of nautical humour like this one. See P, IV, 18n. Stanfield joined the Merchant Marine in 1808; in 1812 he was pressed into the navy.
2. Dick Sparkler, a comic name for Dickens.
3. Mark Lemon. See p. 336 n. 1.
4. The journal *HW*.

CHATEAU DES MOULINEAUX, RUE BEAUREPAIRE, BOULOGNE[1]

Thursday, Twenty-Third June, 1853

MY DEAR PUMPION,[2]—I take the earliest opportunity, after finishing my number[3]—ahem!—to write you a line, and to report myself (thank God!) brown, well, robust, vigorous, open to fight any man in England of my weight, and growing a moustache. Any person of undoubted pluck, in want of a customer, may hear of me at the bar of Bleak House, where my money is down.

I think there is an abundance of places here that would suit you well enough; and Georgina is ready to launch on voyages of discovery and observation with you. But it is necessary that you should consider for how long a time you want it, as the folks here let much more advantageously for the tenant when they know the term—don't like to let without. It seems to me that the best thing you can do is to get a paper of the South Eastern tidal trains, fix your day for coming over here in five hours, let me know the day, and come and see how you like the place. *I* like it better than ever. We can give you a bed (two to spare, at a pinch three), and show you a garden and a view or so. The town is not so cheap as places farther off, but you get a great deal for your money, and by far the best wine at tenpence a bottle that I have ever drunk anywhere. I really desire no better.

I may mention for your guidance (for I count upon your coming to overhaul the general aspect of things), that you have nothing on earth to do with your luggage when it is once in the boat, *until after you have walked ashore*. That you will be filtered with the rest of the passengers through a hideous, whitewashed, quarantine-looking custom-house, where a stern man of military aspect will demand your passport. That you will have nothing of the sort, but will produce your card with this addition: "Restant à Boulogne, chez M. Charles Dickens, Château des Moulineaux." That you will then be passed out at a little door, like one of the ill-starred prisoners on the bloody September night, into a yelling and shrieking crowd, cleaving the air with the names of the different hotels, exactly seven thousand six hundred and fifty-four in number. And that your heart will be on the point of sinking with dread, then you will find yourself in the arms of the Sparkler of Albion.—Ever affectionately.

1. Dickens and his family first visited Boulogne in 1852, when they stayed for the first two weeks in Oct. at the Hotel Des Bains. 'It is as quaint, picturesque, good a place as I know,' Dickens wrote Forster, with delightful country walks, and 'the best mixture of town and country (with sea air into the bargain) I ever saw' (N, II, 417–18). Dickens and the family returned in the summers of 1853, 1854 and 1856, renting houses each time from Ferdinand Beaucourt-Mutuel (1805–81). Dickens describes his impressions of the town, its environs, and his landlord, whom he calls M. Loyal Devasseur, in 'Our French Watering-Place', *HW*, 4 Nov. 1854 (see also *RP*). W. J. Carlton in 'Dickens's Forgotten Retreat in France', *The Dickensian*, 62 (May, 1966), 69–86, describes the different houses Dickens stayed in and gives full details of his French landlord.
2. Frank Stone.
3. Dickens had just finished *BH*, no. 18 (N, II, 465).

HOTEL DE LA VILLE, MILAN
Tuesday Twenty-Fifth October, 1853

MY DEAR GEORGY,[1]—First of all the main thing I have to tell you is, that the word describing a sparkling wine—the word synonymous with mousseux—which I vaguely remembered at Boulogne but could not recall, turned up at Domo d'Ossola, the very first Italian place we stayed at. As follows:

Inimitable (to waiter) C'e un vino che vido scritto sulla carta "Vino d'Asti." C'e il vecchio vino che ho spesse volte bevuto, un vino come champagne, non e vero?

Waiter (to Inimitable)—Si Signore. Un vino bianco, Italiano, un vino spumante.

Inimitable (apart)—Ecco la parola! L'ho trovato!

The next thing you will be interested in hearing of is the progress of the cumulative moustaches of the two other members of the Triumvirate.[2] They are more distressing, more comic, more sparse and meagre, more straggling, wandering, wiry, stubbly, formless, more given to wandering into strange places and sprouting up noses and dribbling under chins, than anything in that nature ever produced, as I believe, since the Flood. Collins has taken to wiping his (which are like the Plornishghenter's[3] eye-brows) at dinner; and Egg's are not near his nose, but begin at the corners of his mouth, like those of the Witches in Macbeth. I have suffered so much from the contemplation of these terrific objects from grey dawn to night in little carriages, that this morning, finding myself with a good looking-glass, and a good light, I seized my best razor, and as a great example, shaved off the whole of the Newgate fringe from under my chin! The moustache remains, and now looks enormous; but the beard I have sacrificed as a dread warning to competitors—which I am bound to add does not produce the least effect; they merely observing with complacency that "it looks much better so."

I have walked to that extent in Switzerland (walked over the Simplon on Sunday, as an addition to the other feats) that one pair of the new strong shoes has gone to be mended this morning, and the other is in but a poor way; the snow having played the mischief with them.

1. Miss Georgina Hogarth.
2. Wilkie Collins and Augustus Leopold Egg (1816–63), painter, accompanied Dickens on a tour of Switzerland and Italy which lasted from mid Oct. to early Dec. 1853.
3. 'Plornishghenter', or more simply, 'Plorn', a nickname for Edward Bulwer Lytton Dickens, Charles's seventh son and last child (the tenth) born on 13 Mar. 1852.

FLORENCE
Monday, Twenty-First November, 1853
H.W.

MY DEAR WILLS,[1]—I sent you by post from Rome, on Wednesday last, a little story for the Christmas number, called The Schoolboy's Story. I have an idea of another short one to be called Nobody's Story, which I hope to be able to do at Venice, and to send you straight home before this month is out.[2] I trust you have received the first safely. [. . .]

Will you write to Ryland[3] if you have not heard from him, and ask him what the Birmingham reading-nights are really to be? For it is ridiculous enough that I positively don't know. Can't a Saturday Night in a Truck District, or a Sunday Morning among the Ironworkers (a fine subject) be knocked out in the course of the same visit?[4]

If you should see any managing man you know in the Oriental and Peninsular Company, I wish you would very gravely mention to him from me that if they are not careful what they are about with their steamship Valetta, between Marseilles and Naples, they will suddenly find that they will receive a blow one fine day in The Times, which it will be a very hard matter for them ever to recover. When I sailed in her from Genoa, there had been taken on board, *with no caution in most cases from the agent, or hint of discomfort*, at least forty people of both sexes for whom there was no room whatever. I am a pretty old traveller as you know, but I never saw anything like the manner in which pretty women were compelled to lie among the men in the great cabin and on the bare decks. The good humour was beyond all praise, but the natural indignation very great; and I was repeatedly urged to stand up for the public in Household Words, and to write a plain description of the facts to The Times. If I had done either, and merely mentioned that all these people paid heavy first-class fares, I will answer for it that they would have been beaten off the station in a couple of months. I did neither, because I was the best of friends with the captain and all the officers, and never saw such a fine set of men; so admirable in the discharge of their duty, and so zealous to do their best by everybody. It is impossible to praise them too highly. But there is a strong desire at all the ports along the coast to throw impediments in the way of the English service, and to favour the French and Italian boats. In these boats (which I know very well) great care is taken of the passengers, and the accommodation is very good. If the Peninsular and Oriental add to all this the risk of such an exposure as they are *certain* to get (if they go on so) in The Times, they are dead sure to get a blow from the public which will make them stagger again. I say nothing of the number of the passengers and the room in the ship's boats, though the frightful consideration the contrast presented must have been in more minds than mine. I speak only of the taking people for whom there is no sort of accommodation as the most decided swindle, and the coolest, I ever did with my eyes behold.—Ever, my dear Wills, faithfully yours.

1. William Henry Wills (1810–80), journalist. In the latter part of 1845, Wills served as Dickens's secretary during his establishment of *The Daily News*. Wills also worked on the staff under Dickens and remained with the paper when Dickens left. Forster later suggested Wills as the assistant editor of *HW*, where Wills served as sub-editor until 1859, and then as sub-editor of *AYR* until 1868, when poor health forced him to retire from active work.
2. Dickens's 'Schoolboy's Story' and 'Nobody's Story' appeared in the Extra Christmas Number of *HW* for 1853, 'Another Round of Christmas Stories by the Fire'.
3. Arthur Ryland (1807–77), solicitor; founder of the Birmingham and Midland Institute, 1858. When the project began in June 1852, Dickens

agreed to help raise money for it by reading his *CC* in Birmingham, where he read three times on 27–30 Dec. 1853.
4. Dickens appears to refer to the titles of two pieces he contemplated for *HW*; no contributions under those headings appeared in the journal.

TAVISTOCK HOUSE

Monday, Sixteenth January, 1854

MY DEAR MARY,[1]—It is all very well to pretend to love me as you do. Ah! If you loved as *I* love, Mary! But, when my breast is tortured by the perusal of such a letter as yours, Falkland, Falkland, madam, becomes my part in The Rivals,[2] and I play it with desperate earnestness.
As thus:

FALKLAND (*to Acres*). Then you see her, sir, sometimes?

ACRES. See her! Odds beams and sparkles, yes. See her acting! Night after night.

FALKLAND (*aside and furious*). Death and the devil! Acting, and I not there! Pray, sir (*with constrained calmness*), what does she act?

ACRES. Odds, monthly nurses and babbies! Sairey Gamp and Betsey Prig,[3] "which, wotever it is, my dear (*mimicking*), I likes it brought reg'lar and draw'd mild!" *That's* very like her.

FALKLAND. Confusion! Laceration! Perhaps, sir, perhaps she sometimes acts—ha! ha! perhaps she sometimes acts, I say—ch! sir?—a—ha, ha, ha! a fairy? (*With great bitterness.*)

ACRES. Odds, gauzy pinions and spangles, yes! You should hear her sing as a fairy. You should see her dance as a fairy. Tol de rol lol—la—lol—liddle diddle. (*Sings and dances.*) *That's* very like her.

FALKLAND. Misery! while I, devoted to her image, can scarcely write a line now and then, or pensively read aloud to the people of Birmingham. (*To him.*) And they applaud her, no doubt they applaud her, sir. And she—I see her! Curtsies and smiles! And they—curses on them! they laugh and—ha, ha, ha! and clap their hands—and say it's very good. Do they not say it's very good, sir? Tell me. Do they not?

ACRES. Odds, thunderings and pealings, of course they do! and the third fiddler, little Tweaks, of the country town, goes into fits. Ho, ho, ho, I can't bear it (*mimicking*); take me out! Ha, ha, ha! O what a one she is! She'll be the death of me. Ha, ha, ha, ha! *That's* very like her!

FALKLAND. Damnation! Heartless Mary! (*Rushes out.*)

Scene opens, and discloses coals of fire, heaped up into form of letters, representing the following inscription:

When the praise thou meetest
To thine ear is sweetest,
O then

REMEMBER JOE!

(Curtain falls.)

1. Mary Louisa Boyle (1810–90), writer. Dickens met Miss Boyle in 1849; he admired her as an amateur actress and was delighted by her performances in his theatricals. This letter typifies the mock flirtation he carried on with her after he lost his heart to her (P, v, 663n and App. H).
2. Dickens draws on R. B. Sheridan's *Rivals* (1775) for the names Faulkland and Acres, but improvises his own comic dialogue.
3. Sarah Gamp and her imaginary friend Mrs Betsey Prig appear in *MC*. A 'monthly nurse' was a midwife.

TAVISTOCK HOUSE
Thirtieth May, 1854

MY DEAR STONE,—I can*not* stand a total absence of ventilation, and I should have liked (in an amiable and persuasive manner; to have punched T——'s head, and opened the register stoves. I saw the supper tables, sir, in an empty state, and was charmed with them. Likewise I recovered myself from a swoon, occasioned by long contact with an unventilated man of a strong flavour from Copenhagen, by drinking an unknown species of celestial lemonade in that enchanted apartment.

I am grieved to say that on Saturday I stand engaged to dine, at three weeks' notice, with one B——, a man who has read every book that ever was written, and is a perfect gulf of information. Before exploding a mine of knowledge he has a habit of closing one eye and wrinkling up his nose, so that he seems perpetually to be taking aim at you and knocking you over with a terrific charge. Then he looks again, and takes another aim.[1] So you are always on your back, with your legs in the air. [. . .]

1. T—.and B—.unidentified. Dickens later incorporated B's peculiar mannerism of appearing to aim an invisible weapon in his portrait of the 'secret-looking man' in *GE*, who stirs his rum-and-water with the file Pip stole for Magwitch and who delivers the two one-pound notes from Pip's benefactor (ch. 10).

BOULOGNE
6th July 1856

[John Forster] The only thing new in this garden is that war is raging against two particularly tigerish and fearful cats (from the mill, I suppose), which are always glaring in dark corners, after our wonderful little Dick.[1] Keeping the house open at all points, it is impossible to shut them out, and they hide themselves in the most terrific manner: hanging themselves up behind draperies, like bats, and tumbling out in the dead of night with frightful caterwaulings. Hereupon French[2] borrows Beaucourt's[3] gun, loads the same to the muzzle, discharges it twice in vain and throws himself over with the recoil, exactly like a clown. But at last (while I was in town) he aims at the more amiable cat of the two, and shoots the animal dead. Insufferably elated by this victory, he is now engaged from morning to night in hiding behind bushes to get aim at the other. He does nothing else whatever. All the boys encourage him and watch for the enemy—on whose appearance they give an alarm which immediately serves as a warning to the creature, who runs away. They are at this moment (ready dressed for church) all lying on their stomachs in various parts of the garden. Horrible whistles give notice to the gun what point it is to approach. I am afraid to go out, lest I should be shot. Mr. Plornish says his prayers at night in a whisper, lest the cat should overhear him and take offence. The tradesmen cry out as they come up the avenue, "Me voici! C'est moi—boulanger—ne tirez pas, Monsieur Franche!" It is like living in a state of siege; and the wonderful manner in which the cat preserves the character of being the only person not much put out by the intensity of this monomania, is most ridiculous. . . .

1. Dick, a canary given to Katey and Mamie one summer in Broadstairs by their bathing woman, who reared birds. He lived for sixteen years and became an important member of the household, writes Mamie (*My Father as I Recall Him*), pp 91–2.
2. Dickens's man-servant.
3. The French landlord. See p. 93 n. 1.

VILLA DES MOULINEAUX
Wednesday Thirteenth August, 1856

[Miss Coutts] . . . Pray tell Mrs Brown[1] with my love, that the flowers are beautiful, and that Mary[2] is improving in her powers of floral arrangement every day. In two parts of the garden, we have sweet peas nearly seven feet high, and their blossoms rustle in the sun, like Peacocks' tails. We have honey-suckle that would be the finest in the world—if that were not at Gad's Hill.[3] The house is invisible at a few yards' distance, hidden in roses and geraniums. The little bird is gradually getting less afraid of his thimble, and draws a world of water this hot weather. He hangs in the drawing-room now, with the other birds; and a tremendous sensation was created yesterday just before dinner by his being found hanging by the leg, upside down, in the cord from which one of their cages depended—twirling round and round as if he were roasting for a course of poultry. It took about half an hour to untwist him. He was prodigiously ruffled, and staggered about as if he had been to the public house; but soon recovered. . . .

1. Mrs William Brown (Hannah Meredith), Miss Coutts's former governess and life-long companion and friend.
2. Mamie Dickens.
3. For Gad's Hill, see pp 102–3 and nn.

[August 1857][1]

[John Forster] I have been (by mere accident) seeing the serpents fed to-day, with the live birds, rabbits, and guinea pigs—a sight so very horrible that I cannot get rid of the impression, and am, at this present, imagining serpents coming up the legs of the table, with their infernal flat heads, and their tongues like the Devil's tail (evidently taken from that model, in the magic lanterns and other such popular representations), elongated for dinner. I saw one small serpent, whose father was asleep, go up to a guinea pig (white and yellow, and with a gentle eye—every hair upon him erect with horror); corkscrew himself on the tip of his tail; open a mouth which couldn't have swallowed the guinea pig's nose; dilate a throat which wouldn't have made him a stocking; and show him what his father meant to do with him when he came out of that ill-looking Hookah into which he had resolved himself. The guinea pig backed against the side of the cage—said "I know it, I know it!"—and his eye glared and his coat turned wiry, as he made the remark. Five small sparrows crouching together in a little trench at the back of the cage, peeped over the brim of it, all the time; and when they saw the guinea pig give it up, and the young serpent go away looking at him over about two yards and a quarter of shoulder, struggled which should get into the innermost angle and be seized last. Everyone of them hid his eyes in another's breast, and then they all shook together like dry leaves—as I daresay they may be doing now, for old Hookah was as dull as laudanum. . . . Please to imagine two small serpents, one beginning on the tail of a white mouse, and one on the head, and each pulling his own way, and the mouse very much alive all the time, with the middle of him madly writhing. . . .

1. Forster assigns 'August 1857' to the extract after noting that Dickens's visit to London Zoo was 'one of . . . [the] incidents' of that summer that made

'such an impression on [CD] that it will be worth while to preserve his description of it' (Forster, VIII, i, 189 and n.).

James T. Field notes that Dickens frequently visited London Zoological Gardens, and that he 'knew the zoological address of every animal, bird, and fish of distinction'. See his *In and Out of Doors with Charles Dickens* (p. 153). Cf. Dickens's letter to Miss Coutts on 14 Feb. 1857, in which he made similar reference to the spectacle of the serpents feeding at the Zoological Gardens (N, II, 835).

VILLA DES MOULINEAUX, BOULOGNE
Wednesday, Ninth July, 1856

MY DEAR STONE,—I have got a capital part for you in the farce,[1] not a difficult one to learn, as you never say anything but "Yes" and "No." You are called in the *dramatis personæ* an able-bodied British seaman, and you are never seen by mortal eye to do anything (except inopportunely producing a mop) but stand about the deck of the boat in everybody's way, with your hair immensely touzled, one brace on, your hands in your pockets, and the bottoms of your trousers tucked up. Yet you are inextricably connected with the plot, and are the man whom everybody is enquiring after. I think it is a very whimsical idea and extremely droll. It made me laugh heartily when I jotted it all down yesterday.—Ever affectionately.

1. The farce was never written.

PARIS
[1856]

[John Forster] B.[1] was with me the other day, and, among other things that he told me, described an extraordinary adventure in his life, at a place not a thousand miles from my "property" at Gadshill, three years ago. He lived at the tavern and was sketching one day when an open carriage came by with a gentleman and lady in it. He was sitting in the same place working at the same sketch, next day, when it came by again. So, another day, when the gentleman got out and introduced himself. Fond of art; lived at the great house yonder, which perhaps he knew; was an Oxford man and a Devonshire squire, but not resident on his estate, for domestic reasons; would be glad to see him to dinner tomorrow. He went, and found among other things a very fine library. "At your disposition," said the Squire, to whom he had now described himself and his pursuits. "Use it for your writing and drawing. Nobody else uses it." He stayed in the house *six months*. The lady was a mistress, aged five-and-twenty, and very beautiful, drinking her life away. The Squire was drunken, and utterly depraved and wicked; but an excellent scholar, an admirable linguist, and a great theologian. Two other mad visitors stayed the six months. One, a man well known in Paris here, who goes about the world with a crimson silk stocking in his breast pocket, containing a tooth-brush and an immense quantity of ready money. The other, a college chum of the Squire's now ruined; with an insatiate thirst for drink; who constantly got up in the middle of the night, crept down to the dining-room, and emptied all the decanters. . . . B. stayed on in the place, under a sort of devilish fascination to discover what might come of it. . . . Tea or coffee never seen in the house, and very seldom water. Beer, champagne, and brandy, were the three drinkables. Breakfast: leg of mutton, champagne, beer, and brandy. Lunch: shoulder of mutton, champagne, beer, and brandy. Dinner: every conceivable dish (Squire's income, £7,000 a-year), champagne, beer, and brandy. The Squire had married a woman of the town from whom he was now separated, but by whom he had a daughter. The mother, to spite the father, had bred the daughter in every conceivable vice. Daughter, then 13, came from school once a month. Intensely coarse in talk, and and always drunk. As they drove about the country in two open carriages, the drunken mistress would be perpetually tumbling out of one, and the drunken daughter perpetually tumbling out of the other. At last the drunken mistress drank her stomach away, and began to die on the sofa. Got worse and worse, and was always raving about Somebody's where she had once been a lodger, and perpetually shrieking that she would cut somebody else's heart out. At last she died on the sofa, and, after the funeral, the party broke up. A few months ago, B. met the man with the crimson silk stocking at Brighton, who told him that the Squire was dead "of a broken heart;" that the chum was dead of delirium tremens; and that the daughter was heiress to the fortune. He told me all this, which I fully believe to be true, without any embellishment—just in the offhand way in which I have told it to you.[2] . . .

1. B. not identified.
2. Forster cites this occurrence as one 'belonging to that wildly improbable class of realities which Dickens always held, with Fielding, to be (properly) closed to fiction. Only, he would add,' continues Forster, 'critics should not be so eager to assume that what had never happened to themselves could not, by any human possibility, ever be supposed to have happened to anybody else' (Forster, VII, v, 175).

TAVISTOCK HOUSE
Monday Night, Nineteenth January, 1857

MY DEAR CERJAT,[1]—So wonderfully do good (epistolary) intentions become confounded with bad execution, that I assure you I laboured under a perfect and most comfortable conviction that I had answered your Christmas Eve letter of 1855. More than that, in spite of your assertions to the contrary, I still strenuously believe that I did so! [. . .]

Down at Gad's Hill, near Rochester, in Kent—Shakespeare's Gad's Hill, where Falstaff engaged in the robbery—is a quaint little country-house of Queen Anne's time. I happened to be walking past, a year and a half or so ago, with my sub-editor of Household Words,[2] when I said to him: "You see that house? It has always a curious interest for me, because when I was a small boy down in these parts I thought it the most beautiful house (I suppose because of its famous old cedar-trees) ever seen. And my poor father used to bring me to look at it, and used to say that if I ever grew up to be a clever man perhaps I might own that house, or such another house. In remembrance of which, I have always in passing looked to see if it was to be sold or let, and it has never been to me like any other house, and it has never changed at all." We came back to town, and my friend went out to dinner. Next morning he came to me in great excitement, and said: "It is written that you were to have that house at Gad's Hill. The lady I had allotted to me to take down to dinner yesterday began to speak of that neighbourhood. 'You know it?' I said; 'I have been there to-day.' 'O yes,' said she, 'I know it very well. I was a child there, in the house they call Gad's Hill Place. My father was the rector, and lived there many years. He has just died, has left it to me, and I want to sell it.' So," says the sub-editor, "you must buy it. Now or never!" I did,[3] and hope to pass next summer there, though I may, perhaps, let it afterwards, furnished, from time to time. [. . .]

1. William Woodley Frederick de Cerjat (d. 1869), one of several English residents in Lausanne whom Dickens met in 1846.
2. Dickens's letter to Wills on 9 Feb. 1855 contradicts his statement to Cerjat that Wills accompanied him on his walk. The occasion was Dickens's forty-third birthday, which he celebrated with a small group of friends, who joined him at Waites's Hotel, Gravesend, for a 'festive Banquet' at 5 p.m. Earlier in the day, he travelled to Gravesend by train and then walked to Rochester, returning through Cobham woods to the hotel. On the way he noticed 'a little freehold to be sold', which two days later he asked Wills to inquire about. 'The spot and the very house,' he explained to his sub-editor, 'are literally "a dream of childhood" ' (N, II, 625). The house – Gad's Hill Place – had always held a prominent place in his imagination, Dickens

wrote in 'The German Chariot', *AYR*, 7 Apr. 1860 (see also 'Travelling Abroad', *UT*), since his father promised him that he might live in it or some such house when he grew up, if he would only work hard enough.

3. In Oct. 1855 Dickens began negotiating for its purchase (N, II, 699–700) after learning from Wills that not only was the house for sale, but that the owner, Mrs Lynn Linton, 'had been long known and much esteemed by himself' as a contributor to *HW*. 'Such curious chances,' comments Forster, 'led Dickens to the saying he so frequently repeated about the smallness of the world' (Forster, VIII, iii, 207). On 14 Mar. 1856 Dickens bought Gad's Hill for £1790 (N, II, 751), intending to improve the place as an investment, rent it, and use it only in the summers. 'A railroad opened from Rochester to Maidstone, which connects Gadshill at once with the whole sea coast, is certainly an addition to the place, and an enhancement of its value,' Dickens wrote to Forster in July 1856. 'By and by we shall have the London, Chatham and Dover, too; and that will bring it within an hour of Canterbury and an hour and a half of Dover' (Forster, VIII, iii, 207).

A little more than a year later, Gad's Hill provided an unexpected refuge when Dickens turned out of bed at two in the morning and walked from London to Rochester after quarrelling with Catherine and the Hogarths. After separating from his wife in 1858, he sold Tavistock House (1860) and transferred its contents to Gad's Hill, which became his home. Dickens's eldest son bought the house after his father's death. Although Gad's Hill now serves as a girls' school, the house is intact and the library, Leslie Staples noted in 1965, 'with Dickens's book-shelves, dummy book-backs, etc., is exactly as he left it'. (*Life*, ed. A. J. Hoppé, II, 465n).

Dickens's first act of ownership, writes Forster, was to place the following notice on the first-floor landing: 'THIS HOUSE, GADSHILL PLACE, stands on the summit of Shakespeare's Gadshill, ever memorable for its association with Sir John Falstaff in his noble fancy. *But, my lads, my lads, to-morrow morning, by four o'clock, early at Gadshill! there are pilgrims going to Canterbury with rich offerings, and traders riding to London with fat purses: I have vizards for you all; you have horses for yourselves.*' [*I Henry IV*, I, ii, 116ff] (Forster, VIII, iii, 209–10)

TAVISTOCK HOUSE

Tuesday, Sixteenth September, 1856

MY DEAR WILLS,—I have been thinking a good deal about Collins,[1] and it strikes me that the best thing we can just now do for H.W. is to add him on to Morley,[2] and offer him Five Guineas a week. He is very suggestive, and exceedingly quick to take my notions. Being industrious and reliable besides, I don't think we should be at an additional expense of £20 in the year by the transaction.

I observe that to a man in his position who is fighting to get on, the getting his name before the public is important. Some little compensation for its not being constantly announced is needed, and that I fancy might be afforded by *a certain engagement*. If you are of my mind, I wish you would go up to him this morning, and tell him this is what we have to propose to him today, and that I wish him, if he can, to consider beforehand. You could explain the nature of such an engagement to him, in half a dozen words, far more easily than we could all open it together. And he would then come prepared.

Of course he should have permission to collect his writings, and would be handsomely and generously considered in all respects. I think it would do him, in the long run, a world of good; and I am certain that by meeting together—dining three instead of two—and sometimes calling in Morley to boot—we should knock out much new fire.

What it is desirable to put before him, is the regular association with the work, and the means he already has of considering whether it would be pleasant and useful to him to work with me, and whether any mere trading engagement would be likely to render him as good service.—Ever faithfully.

TAVISTOCK HOUSE
Thursday, Eighteenth September, 1856
MY DEAR WILLS,—Don't conclude anything, *un*favourable with Collins, without previous reference of the subject, and the matter of your consultation, to me. And again put before him clearly, when he comes to you, that I do not interpose myself in this stage of the business, solely because I think it right that he should consider and decide without any personal influence on my part.

I think him wrong in his objection, and have not the slightest doubt that such a confusion of authorship (which I don't believe to obtain in half a dozen minds out of half a dozen hundred) would be a far greater service than dis-service to him. This I clearly see. But, as far as a long story is concerned, I see not the least objection to our advertising, at once, before it begins, that it is by him.[3] I *do* see an objection to departing from our custom of not putting names to the papers in H.W. itself; but to our advertising the authorship of a long story, as a Rider to all our advertisements, I see none whatever.

Now, as to a long story itself, I doubt its value to us. And I feel perfectly convinced that it is not one quarter so useful to us as detached papers, or short stories in four parts. But I am quite content to try the experiment. The story should not, however, go beyond six months, and the engagement should be for twelve.—Faithfully ever.

1. The friendship between Dickens and Collins grew quickly since they met in

1851, and Collins became, in Forster's words, 'for all the rest of Dickens's life, one of his dearest and most valued friends' (Forster, VI, v, 73). After contributing to *HW* for four and-a-half years, Dickens offered Collins a weekly salary and invited him to join the editorial staff.

2. Henry Morley, a member of the *HW* staff who received the same salary. For Morley's association with Dickens, see Lohrli, pp 370–80. See also pp 338–9 and n. 1.

3. Collins accepted the position at five guineas a week, but not before negotiating with Dickens to serialize a long story (*The Dead Secret*, which ran in *HW* from 3 Jan. 1857 to 13 June) and announce the novel as Collins's. See the next letter. In 1857 Dickens increased Collins's salary by £50 (see To Wills, 2 Oct. 1857, N, II, 888–9); he remained with *HW* for another two years, served on the editorial staff of *A YR*, helped Wills during Dickens's absence in America in 1867–8, and contributed *The Woman in White, No Name* and *The Moonstone* to the journal. A useful summary of Collins's contributions to *HW* appears in Lohrli, pp 232–7; for Collins's literary association with Dickens, see p. 311 n. 3.

TAVISTOCK HOUSE

Sunday Morning, Twenty-Eighth September, 1856

MY DEAR WILLS,—I suddenly remember this morning that in Mr. Carter's article, Health and Education,[1] I left a line which must come out. It is in effect that the want of healthy training leaves girls in a fit state to be the subjects of mesmerism. I would not on any condition hurt Elliotson's feelings (as I should deeply) by leaving that depreciatory kind of reference in any page of H.W.[2] He has suffered quite enough without a stab from a friend. So pray, whatever the inconvenience may be in what Bradbury calls "the Friars,"[3] take that passage out. By some extraordinary accident, after observing it, I forgot to do it.—Ever faithfully.

1. Robert Brudenell Carter (1828–1918), surgeon and frequent author of articles on medical subjects. His 'Health and Education' appeared in *HW* 18 Oct. 1856.
2. Dickens's concern for Dr John Elliotson (see p. 333 n. 1) typifies his readiness to stand by old friends.
3. *HW* was printed by Bradbury and Evans of Whitefriars, London.

TAVISTOCK HOUSE

Tuesday Night, Twenty-Fourth February 1857

MY DEAR BEARD,—I had heard of the first calamity, but not of the second.[1] Your letter is a painful surprise to me in so far as it concerns your own treatment—if I can say, without making an ass of myself, that anything would surprise me in that association.

If Saturday evening will suit you equally well, let me propose that we dine at the Garrick at 6. We will be alone of course. A glass of good wine may take the taste of that Scum out of our mouths—and it must be pretty strong in yours by this time. If this should not suit you, of course I am at your disposal in the morning of the same day; but the evening is better, as being more like one of our old Saturdays. Write me just a word in reply.

I went down yesterday to look at your country quarters. I said when I came home at night that they would set you up: and now I feel that they are fresh enough—ah! even to get you in training for another Baldwin—if there should be another in reserve for the sons of men and Holy Church.

Don't be cast down. Cheer up, and you will soon be the better for this. *If I were you, I would above all things leave a card for Delane without a day's delay*. You need do no more,—but do that.—Ever heartily.

1. Beard lost his job as a reporter when Edward Baldwin, the proprietor of the *Morning Herald* since 1844, sold the paper in 1857. Until Beard obtained his appointment as the official spokesman of Court News to the press, in Jan. 1864 (*Dickens to his Oldest Friend*, p. 228n), Dickens exerted himself on Beard's behalf in many ways. He gave Beard summer quarters at Gad's Hill in 1857, arranged a meeting with Beard and John Thadeus Delane, editor of *The Times* (1841–77), and wrote to Bulwer Lytton, who in 1859 was Colonial Secretary, in order to help Beard find permanent work. See *Dickens to his Oldest Friend*, pp 184, 186, and 203–4). Dickens also gave Beard opportunities to contribute to *AYR* (N, III, 213 and 215), offered to take him to Australia as his secretary if he accepted a proposal to read there (N, III, 314–5; 319–20), and provided other helpful services (N, III, 366–9).

TAVISTOCK HOUSE
Saturday, Tenth February 1855

MY DEAR MRS. WINTER,[1]—I constantly receive hundreds of letters in great varieties of writing, all perfectly strange to me, and (as you may suppose) have no particular interest in the faces of such general epistles. As I was reading by my fire last night, a handful of notes was laid down on my table. I looked them over, and, recognising the writing of no private friend, let them lie there and went back to my book. But I found my mind curiously disturbed, and wandering away through so many years to such early times of my life, that I was quite perplexed to account for it. There was nothing in what I had been reading, or immediately thinking about, to awaken such a train of thought, and at last it came into my head that it must have been suggested by something in the look of one of those letters. So I turned them over again—and suddenly the remembrance of your hand came upon me with an influence that I cannot express to you. Three or four and twenty years vanished like a dream, and I opened it with the touch of my young friend David Copperfield when he was in love.

There was something so busy and so pleasant in your letter—so true and cheerful and frank and affectionate—that I read on with perfect delight until I came to your mention of your two little girls. In the unsettled state of my thoughts, the existence of these dear children appeared such a prodigious phenomenon, that I was inclined to suspect myself of being out of my mind, until it occurred to me, that perhaps I had nine children of my own! Then the three or four and twenty years began to rearrange themselves in a long procession between me and the changeless Past, and I could not help considering what strange stuff all our little stories are made of.

Believe me, you cannot more tenderly remember our old days and our old friends than I do. I hardly ever go into the City but I walk up an odd little court at the back of the Mansion House and come out by the corner of Lombard Street.[2] Hundreds of times as I have passed the church there[3]—on my way to and from the Sea, the Continent, and where not—I invariably associate it with somebody (God knows who) having told me that poor Anne[4] was buried there. If you would like to examine me in the name of a good-looking Cornish servant you used to have (I suppose she has twenty-nine great grandchildren now, and walks with a stick), you will find my knowledge on the point, correct, though it was a monstrous name too. I forget nothing of those times. They are just as still and plain and clear as if I had never been in a crowd since, and had never seen or heard my own name out of my own house. What should I be worth, or what would labour and success be worth, if it were otherwise!

Your letter is more touching to me from its good and gentle associations with the state of Spring in which I was either much more wise or much more foolish than I am now—I never know which to think it—than I could tell you if I tried for a week. I will not try at all. I heartily respond to it, and shall be charmed to have a long talk with you, and most cordially glad to see you after all this length of time.

I am going to Paris to-morrow morning, but I propose being back within a fortnight.[5] When I return, Mrs. Dickens will come to you, to arrange a day for our seeing you and Mr. Winter (to whom I beg to be remembered) quietly to dinner. We will have no intruder or foreign creature on any pretence whatever, in order that we may set in without any restraint for a tremendous gossip.

Mary Anne Leigh[6] we saw at Broadstairs about fifty years ago. Mrs. Dickens and her sister, who read all the marriages in the papers, shrieked to me when the announcement of hers appeared, what did I think of *that*? I calmly replied that I thought it was time. I should have been more excited if I had known of the old gentleman with seven thousand a year, uncountable grown-up children, and no English grammar.

My mother has a strong objection to being considered in the least old, and usually appears here on Christmas Day in a juvenile cap which takes an immense time in the putting on. The Fates seem to have made up their minds that I shall never see your Father when he comes this way. David Lloyd[7] is altogether an imposter—not having in the least changed (that I could make out when I saw him at the London Tavern) since what I suppose to have been the year 1770, when I found you three on Cornhill, with your poor mother, going to St. Mary Axe[8] to order mysterious dresses—which afterwards turned out to be wedding garments. That was in the remote period when you all wore green cloaks, cut (in my remembrance) very round, and which I am resolved to believe were made of Merino. I escorted you with native gallantry to the Dress Maker's door, and your mother, seized with an apprehension—groundless upon my honor—that I might come in, said emphatically: "And now, Mr. Dickin"—which she always used to call me—:"We'll wish *you* good morning."

When I was writing the word Paris just now, I remembered that my existence was once entirely uprooted and my whole Being blighted by the Angel of my soul being sent there to finish her education! If I can discharge any little commission for you, or bring home anything for the darlings,[9] whom I cannot yet believe to be anything but a delusion of yours, pray employ me. I shall be at the Hotel Meurice—locked up when within, as my only defence against my country and the United States—but a most punctual and reliable functionary, if you will give me any employment.

My Dear Mrs. Winter, I have been much moved by your letter; and the pleasure it has given me has some little sorrowful ingredient in it. In the strife and struggle of this great world where most of us lose each other so strangely, it is impossible to be spoken to out of the old times without a softened emotion. You so belong to the days when the qualities that have done me most good since, were growing in my boyish heart that I cannot end my answer to you lightly. The associations my memory has with you made your letter more—I want a word—invest it with a more immediate address to me than such a letter could have from anybody else. Mr. Winter will not mind that. We are all sailing away to the sea, and have a pleasure in thinking of the river we are upon, when it was very narrow and little.—Faithfully your friend.

1. Mrs Henry Louis Winter (Maria Beadnell), Dickens's first love. See pp 29–32.
2. Maria's father worked at a bank in George Street, Mansion House. The family home was nearby in Lombard Street.
3. St. Swithin's, Cannon Street.
4. Anne Beadnell, Maria's sister, who married Henry Kolle in 1833 and died in 1836.
5. Dickens stayed in Paris for just over a week, visiting the theatre and relaxing with Wilkie Collins before returning on 20 Feb.
6. Mary Anne Leigh, a friend of Maria.
7. David Lloyd married Maria's eldest sister, Margaret, in 1831.
8. A street running from Leadenhall Street to Houndsditch.
9. Maria's two young daughters.

HOTEL MEURICE, PARIS
Thursday, Fifteenth February 1855

MY DEAR MRS. WINTER,—(I had half a mind when I dipped my pen in the ink, to address you by your old natural Christian name.)

The snow lies so deep on the Northern Railway, and the Posts have been so interrupted in consequence, that your charming note arrived here only this morning. I reply by return of post—with a general idea that Sarah[1] will come to Finsbury Place with a basket and a face of good-humoured compassion, and carry the letter away, and leave me as desolate as she used to do.

I got a heartache when I read your commission written in the hand which I find now to be not in the least changed and yet it is a great pleasure to be entrusted with it, and to have that share of your gentler remembrances which I cannot find it still my privilege to have without a stirring of the old fancies. I need not tell you that it shall be executed to the letter—with as much interest as I once matched a little pair of gloves for you which I recollect were blue ones. (I wonder whether people generally wore blue gloves when I was nineteen or whether it was only you!) I am very, very sorry you mistrusted me in not writing before your little girl was born; but I hope now you know me better you will teach her, one day, to tell her children, in times to come when they may have some interest in wondering about it, that I loved her mother with the most extraordinary earnestness when I was a boy.

I have always believed since, and always shall to the last, that there never was such a faithful and devoted poor fellow as I was. Whatever of fancy, romance, energy, passion, aspiration and determination belong to me, I never have separated and never shall separate from the hard-hearted little woman—you—whom it is nothing to say I would have died for, with the greatest alacrity! I never can think, and I never seem to observe, that other young people are in such desperate earnest or set so much, so long, upon one absorbing hope. It is a matter of perfect certainty to me that I began to fight my way out of poverty and obscurity, with one perpetual idea of you. This is so fixed in my knowledge that to the hour when I opened your letter last Friday night I have never heard anybody addressed by your name, or spoken of by your name, without a start. The sound of it has always filled me with a kind of pity and respect for the deep truth that I had, in my silly hobbledehoyhood, to bestow upon one creature who represented the whole world to me. I have never been so good a man since, as I was when you made me wretchedly happy. I shall never be half so good a fellow any more.

This is all so strange now both to think of, and to say, after every change that has come about; but I think, when you ask me to write to you, you are not unprepared for what it is so natural to me to recall, and will not be displeased to read it. I fancy—though you may not have thought in the old time how manfully I loved you—that you may have seen in one of my books a faithful recollection of the passion I had for you, and may have thought that it was something to have been loved so well, and may have seen in little bits of "Dora" touches of your old self sometimes and a grace here and there that may be revived in your little girls, years hence, for the bewilderment of some other young lover—though he will never be as terribly in earnest as I and David Copperfield were. People used to say to me how pretty all that was, and how fanciful it was, and how elevated it was above the little foolish loves of very young men and women. But they little thought what reason I had to know it was true and nothing more nor less.

There are things that I have locked up in my own breast and that I never thought to bring out any more. But when I find myself writing to you again "all to yourself," how can I forbear to let as much light in upon them as will shew you that they are there still! If the most innocent, the most ardent, and the most disinterested days of my life had you for their Sun—as indeed they had—and if I know that the Dream I lived in did me good, refined my heart, and made me patient and persevering, and if the Dream were all of you—as God knows it was—how can I receive a confidence from you, and return it, and make a feint of blotting all this out!

As I have said, I fancy that you know all about it quite as well as I do however. I have a strong belief—and there is no harm in adding hope to that—that perhaps you have once or twice laid down that book, and thought, "How dearly that boy must have loved me, and how vividly this man remembers it!"

I shall be here until Tuesday or Wednesday. If the snow allows this letter to come to you in the meantime, perhaps it would allow one to come to me, "all to myself," if you were to try it. A number of recollections came into my head when I began, and I meant to have gone through a string of them and to have asked you if they lived in your mind too. But they all belong to the one I have indulged in—half pleasantly, half painfully—and are all swallowed up in that, so let them go.—My Dear Mrs. Winter,—Ever Affectionately yours.

P.S.—I wonder what has become of a bundle of letters I sent you back once (according to order) tied with a blue ribbon, of the colour of the gloves.

1. Sarah, presumably one of the Beadnell servants who carried letters between the former lovers.

TAVISTOCK HOUSE
Thursday, Twenty-Second February 1855
MY DEAR MARIA,—The old writing is so plain to *me*, that I have read your letter with great ease (though it is just a little crossed) and have not lost a word of it. I was obliged to leave Paris on Tuesday morning before the Post came in; but I took such precautions to prevent the possibility of any mischance, that the letter came close behind me. I arrived at home last night, and it followed me this morning. No one but myself has the slightest knowledge of my correspondence, I may add in this place. I could be nowhere addressed with stricter privacy or in more absolute confidence than at my own house.

Ah! Though it is so late to read in the old hand what I never read before, I have read it with great emotion, and with the old tenderness softened to a more sorrowful remembrance than I could easily tell you. How it all happened as it did, we shall never know on this side of Time; but if you had ever told me then what you tell me now, I know myself well enough to be thoroughly assured that the simple truth and energy which were in my love would have overcome everything. I remember well that long after I came of age—I say long; well! it seemed long then—I wrote to you for the last time of all, with a dawn upon me of some sensible idea that we were changing into man and woman, saying would you forget our little differences and separations and let us begin again? You answered me very coldly and reproachfully—and so I went my way.

But nobody can ever know with what a sad heart I resigned you, or after what struggles and what conflict. My entire devotion to you, and the wasted tenderness of those hard years which I have ever since half loved, half dreaded to recall, made so deep an impression on me that I refer to it a habit of suppression which now belongs to me, which I know is no part of my original nature, but which makes me chary of showing my affections, even to my children, except when they are very young. A few years ago (just before Copperfield) I began to write my life, intending the manuscript to be found among my papers when its subject should be concluded. But as I began to approach within sight of that part of it, I lost courage and burned the rest.[1] I have never blamed you at all but I have believed until now that you never had the stake in that serious game which I had.

All this mist passes away before your earnest words; and when I find myself to have been in your mind at that thoughtful crisis in your life which you so unaffectedly and feelingly describe, I am quite subdued and strangely enlightened. When poor Fanny died[2] (I think she always knew that I never could bear to hear of you as of any common person) we were out of town, and I never heard of your having been in Devonshire Terrace—least of all in my room! I never heard of you in association with that time until I read your letter to-day. I could not however—really *could not*—at any time within these nineteen years, have been so unmindful of my old truth, and have so set my old passion aside, as to talk to you like a person in any ordinary relation towards me. And this I think is the main reason on my side why the few opportunities that there have been of ever seeing one another again have died out.

All this again you have changed and set right—at once so courage-ously, so delicately and gently, that you open the way to a confidence between us which still once more, in perfect innocence and good faith, may be between ourselves alone. All that you propose, I accept with my whole heart. Whom can you ever trust if it be not your old lover? Lady Olliffe[3] asked me in Paris the other day (we are, in our way, confidential you must know) whether it was really true that I used to love Maria Beadnell so very, very, very much? I told her that there was no woman in the world, and there were very few men, who could ever imagine how much.

You are always the same in my remembrance. When you say you are "toothless, fat, old and ugly" (which I don't believe), I fly away to the house in Lombard Street, which is pulled down, as if it were necessary that the very bricks and mortar should go the way of my airy castles, and see you in a sort of raspberry colored dress with a little black trimming at the top—black velvet it seems to be made of—cut in vandykes—an immense number of vandykes—with my boyish heart pinned like a captured butterfly on every one of them. I have never seen a girl play the harp, from that day to this, but my attention has been instantly arrested, and that drawing room has stood before me so plainly that I could write a most accurate description of it. I remember that there used to be a tendency in your eyebrows to join together; and sometimes in the most unlikely places—in Scotland, America, Italy—on the stateliest occasions and the most unceremonious—when I have been talking to a strange face and have observed ever such a slight association as this in it, I have been suddenly carried away at the rate of a thousand miles a second, and have thought "Maria Beadnell"! When we were falling off from each other, I came from the House of Commons[4] many a night at two or three o'clock in the morning, only to wander past the place you were asleep in. And I have gone over that ground within these twelve months hoping it was not ungrateful to consider whether any reputation the world can bestow is repayment to a man for the loss of such a vision of his youth as mine. You ask me to treasure what you tell me, in my heart of hearts. O see what I have cherished there, through all this time and all these changes!

In the course of Saturday I will write to you at Artillery Place,[5] sending the little brooches and telling you when Catherine will come—not forgetting the little niece, though I don't expect her to remind me of Somebody or Anybody. And now to what I have reserved for the last.

I am a dangerous man to be seen with, for so many people know me. At St. Paul's the Dean and the whole chapter know me. In Paternoster Row of all places, the very tiles and chimney pots know me. At first, I a little hesitated whether or no to advise you to forego that interview or suggest another—principally because what would be very natural and probable a fortnight hence seems scarcely so probable now. Still I should very much like to see you before we meet when others are by—I feel it, as it were, so necessary to our being at ease—and unless I hear from you to the contrary, you may expect to encounter a stranger whom you may suspect to be the right person if he wears a moustache. You would not like better to call here on Sunday asking first for

Catherine and then for me? It is almost a positive certainty that there will be none here but I, between 3 and 4. I make this suggestion, knowing what odd coincidences take place in streets when they are not wanted to happen; though I know them to be so unlikely that I should not think of such a thing if any one but you were concerned. If you think you would not like to come here, make no change. I will come there.

I cannot trust myself to begin afresh, or I should have my remembrances of our separation, and think yours hard on me. I remember poor Anne writing to me once (in answer to some burst of low-spirited madness of mine), and saying "My Dear Charles, I really cannot understand Maria, or venture to take the responsibility of saying what the state of her affection is"—and she added, I recollect, God bless her, a long quotation about Patience and Time. Well, Well! It was not to be until Patience and Time should bring us round together thus.

Remember, I accept all with my whole soul, and reciprocate all.—Ever your affectionate friend.

1. Dickens, however, did not destroy the fragment detailing his hard experiences as a young boy in the blacking factory. See Forster, I, ii, 20–33.
2. Frances Dickens. See p. 78 n. 1.
3. Lady Laura Olliffe, second daughter of Sir William Cubitt; wife of Sir Joseph Olliffe, physician to the British Embassy in Paris.
4. Where Dickens worked as a parliamentary reporter in 1832. Living in Finsbury Place, he could easily arrange his route home so as to pass Maria's house.
5. Artillery Place, Finsbury Square, the Winters' house.

TAVISTOCK HOUSE

Tuesday Evening Thirteenth March 1855

MY DEAR LITTLE FRIEND,[1]—Only think of my having had your nice little letter one whole week tomorrow, and not having answered it until now! What a careless rascal I should have been, if I had not been busy all the time. Having been busy all the time, what an agreeable man I am!

I am very glad indeed that you like the small present so much; because it is such a very small present in itself that when you tell me so, I begin to think you like me, and think the present a much better one than it is, for my sake. Once upon a time when the Fairies used to give presents to Queens' daughters (if your Mama had lived in those days *she* might have been a Queen perhaps, though I don't think she would ever have been a tall one), they used to say at the christenings, "I give this little girl goodness"—"I give this little girl sweet temper"—"I give this little girl a tender heart"—and so on. Now I am not a Fairy myself, and indeed I never heard of a Fairy with a moustache and Wellington Boots, and I never gave anything at a christening except a Mug, and I didn't even give that to a cousin of yours when He was christened;[2] but when I gave you that little brooch, I gave you my best wishes for all sorts of virtues. So, I expect you to grow up the best—and therefore of course the happiest—of tiny women; and when everybody loves you and you come to see a very old gentleman in a black velvet cap, reading a big book in a (there I am, blotting again!) in a big arm-chair, you will think of these words, and you will find that identical old gentleman to be myself.

I was dreadfully cross on Sunday, when I came home and found you had been here and were gone. My Owl said, "what do you think? She knocked me down, but she didn't hurt me—and she peeped all over the table." When you come again, I will shew you a Raven, alive and pecking. He will peck little holes in your legs if you like, and make a complete cribbage-board of each of your stockings. He breaks all the kitchen-windows every day, and flies at everybody except the cook. What a dear bird he is to be sure.

My little children send you their loves. It's the Baby's birthday,[3] and he says he don't want many happy returns of the Measles—which he has got at present. He keeps upon his bed, and goes to sleep among a large cart of real timber drawn by two grey horses; a Noah's Ark with all the animals out walking, in company with Noah, Ham, Shem and Japhet, Mrs. N., Mrs. H., Mrs. S. and Mrs. J.; the Camp at Chobham and four brass cannon; a farm-yard; a box of bricks; a clown in a washing-tub, driving two geese; four crusts of buttered toast; all the cannon-balls (which roll into bed and tickle him); and I don't know what besides.—Ever affectionately yours.

(what do you think of *that* for a flourish!)

1. Maria's daughter, Ella.
2. Henry Kolle, the first child of Anne and H. W. Kolle, to whom Dickens became godfather.
3. Edward Bulwer Lytton Dickens (b. 13 Mar. 1852).

Tuesday, Third April, 1855

MY DEAR MARIA,—Going down to Ashford this day week,[1] already with a bad cold, I increased it so much by getting into the intense heat consequent upon a reading of three hours and then coming up in the night (which I was obliged to do, having business in Town next morning), that I was very unwell all the week, and on Friday night was so completely knocked up that I came home at 9 o'clock to bed. A necessity is upon me now—as at most times—of wandering about in my own wild way, to think. I could no more resist this on Sunday or yesterday, than a man can dispense with food, or a horse can help himself from being driven. I hold my inventive capacity on the stern condition that it must master my whole life, often have complete possession of me, make its own demands upon me, and sometimes for months together put everything else away from me. If I had not known long ago that my place could never be held unless I were at any moment ready to devote myself to it entirely, I should have dropped out of it very soon. All this I can hardly expect you to understand—or the restlessness or waywardness of an author's mind. You have never seen it before you, or lived with it or had occasion to think or care about it, and you cannot have the necessary consideration for it. "It is only half an hour"—"it is only an afternoon"—"it is only for an evening"—people say to me over and over again—but they don't know that it is impossible to command one's self sometimes to any stipulated and set disposal of five minutes—or that the mere consciousness of an engagement will sometimes worry a whole day. These are the penalties paid for writing books. Whoever is devoted to an Art must be content to deliver himself wholly up to it, and to find his recompense in it. I am grieved if you suspect me of not wanting to see you, but I can't help it; I must go my way, whether or no. [. . .]

I am going off, I don't know where or how far, to ponder about I don't know what. Sometimes I am half in the mood to set off for France, sometimes I think I will go and walk about on the sea shore for three or four months, sometimes I look towards the Pyrenees, sometimes Switzerland. I made a compact with a great Spanish authority last week, and vowed I would go to Spain. Two days afterwards Layard[2] and I agreed to go to Constantinople when Parliament rises. To-morrow I shall probably discuss with somebody else, the idea of going to Greenland or the North Pole. The end of all this, most likely will be that I shall shut myself up in some out of the way place I have never yet thought of, and go desperately to work there.

Once upon a time I didn't do such things, you say. No, but I have done them through a good many years now, and they have become myself and my life.—Ever affectionately.

1. Dickens read the *CC* on 27 March 1855 for the employees of the locomotive and carriage works of the South-Eastern & Chatham Railway at Ashford, Kent (N, II, 645).
2. Austen Henry Layard (1817–94), excavator of Nineveh; MP for Aylesbury, 1852–7.

TAVISTOCK HOUSE

Wednesday, Thirteenth June 1855

MY DEAR MRS. WINTER,—I am truly grieved to hear of your affliction in the loss of your darling baby. But if you be not, even already, so reconciled to the parting from that innocent child for a little while, as to bear it gently and with a softened sorrow, I know that that not unhappy state of mind must soon arise. The death of infants is a release from so much chance and change—from so many casualties and distress—and is a thing so beautiful in its serenity and peace—that it should not be a bitterness even in a mother's heart. The simplest and most affecting passage in all the noble history of our Great Master, is his consideration for little children. And in reference to yours, as many millions of bereaved mothers poor and rich will do in reference to theirs until the end of time, you may take the comfort of the words "And he took a child, and set it in the midst of them."[1]

In a book by one of the greatest English writers, called A Journey from this World to the Next,[2] a parent comes to the distant country beyond the grave, and finds the little girl he had lost so long ago, engaged in building a bower to receive him in, when his aged steps should bring him there at last. He is filled with joy to see her—so young—so bright—so full of promise—and is enraptured to think that she never was old, wan, tearful, withered. This is always one of the sources of consolation in the deaths of children. With no effort of the fancy, with nothing to undo, you will always be able to think of the pretty creature you have lost, *as a child* in Heaven.

A poor little baby of mine[3] lies in Highgate Cemetery—and I laid her, just as you think of laying yours, in the catacombs there until I made a resting-place for all of us in the free air.

It is better that I should not come to see you. I feel quite sure of that, and will think of you instead.

God bless and comfort you! Mrs. Dickens and her sister send their kindest condolences to yourself and Mr. Winter. I add mine with all my heart—Affectionately your friend.

1. Mark 9. 36.
2. Henry Fielding's *Journey from this World to the Next*, 1743.
3. Dora. See p. 81, n. 1.

PARIS
[*Circa* December 1855]

[John Forster] . . . I don't quite apprehend what you mean by my over-rating the strength of the feeling of five-and-twenty years ago.[1] If you mean of my own feeling, and will only think what the desperate intensity of my nature is, and that this began when I was Charley's age;[2] that it excluded every other idea from my mind for four years, at a time of life when four years are equal to four times four; and that I went at it with a determination to overcome all the difficulties, which fairly lifted me up into that newspaper life, and floated me away over a hundred men's heads: then you are wrong, because nothing can exaggerate that. I have positively stood amazed at myself ever since!—And so I suffered, and so worked, and so beat and hammered away at the maddest romances that ever got into any boy's head and stayed there, that to see the mere cause of it all, now, loosens my hold upon myself. Without for a moment sincerely believing that it would have been better if we had never got separated, I cannot see the occasion of so much emotion as I should see any one else. No one can imagine in the most distant degree what pain the recollection gave me in Copperfield. And, just as I can never open that book as I open any other book, I cannot see the face (even at four-and-forty), or hear the voice, without going wandering away over the ashes of all that youth and hope in the wildest manner. . . .

1. Writing about the parallels between Copperfield's and Dickens's early career, Forster notes how 'I used to laugh and tell him [CD] I had no belief in any [idol] but the book Dora, until the incidence of a sudden reappearance of the real one in his life, nearly six years after *Copperfield* was written'. Forster then found himself convinced that the Dora chapters were founded upon Dickens's life, but still expressed scepticism that he could be so profoundly affected many years later, to which Dickens replied in the extract from Paris. See Forster, I, iii, 47.
2. Dickens's eldest son was now 18.

TAVISTOCK HOUSE
Saturday Evening, Thirteenth December, 1856

MY DEAREST MACREADY,—[. . .] You may faintly imagine, my venerable friend, the occupation of these also gray hairs,[1] between Golden Marys, Little Dorrits, Household Wordses, four stage-carpenters entirely boarding on the premises, a carpenter's shop erected in the back garden, size always boiling over on all the lower fires, Stanfield perpetually elevated on planks and splashing himself from head to foot, Telbin[2] requiring impossibilities of smart gasmen, and a legion of prowling nondescripts for ever shrinking in and out. Calm amidst the wreck, your aged friend glides away on the Dorrit stream, forgetting the uproar for a stretch of hours, refreshing himself with a ten or twelve miles' walk, pitches headforemost into foaming rehearsals, placidly emerges for editorial purposes, smokes over buckets of distemper with Mr. Stanfield aforesaid, again calmly floats upon the Dorrit waters. —Ever, my dear Macready, most affectionately yours.

1. Dickens refers to the preparations for his production of Wilkie Collins's melodrama *The Frozen Deep* for Charley's twentieth birthday on Twelfth Night. Besides producing the play and learning his own role as Richard Wardour, Dickens continued to write *LD*, edit *HW*, and collaborate with Collins on *The Wreck of the Golden Mary*, a special contribution to the Extra Christmas Number of *HW* for 1856.
2. William Telbin (1815–73), painter, who helped Stanfield with the scenery.

5th July 1857

[John Forster] . . . My gracious sovereign was so pleased that she sent round begging me to go and see her and accept her thanks.[1] I replied that I was in my Farce dress, and must beg to be excused. Whereupon she sent again, saying that the dress "could not be so ridiculous as that," and repeating the request. I sent my duty in reply, but again hoped her Majesty would have the kindness to excuse my presenting myself in a costume and appearance that were not my own. I was mighty glad to think, when I woke this morning, that I had carried the point. . . .

1. When Douglas Jerrold (see p. 261 n. 1) died on 8 June 1857, Dickens and other friends set up a Committee to raise money for Jerrold's widow and family. Among the suggestions for help, Dickens proposed public subscription performances of *The Frozen Deep* both in London and the provinces. The Queen as asked to give her name to the cause, but she declined because assent would have involved 'either perpetual compliance or the giving of perpetual offence' (quoted by Forster, XI, iii, 390). She did, however, ask Dickens to produce the play at Buckingham Palace; he excused himself because he did not feel easy, he explained, 'as to the social position' of his daughters. Instead, he proposed that the Queen should come to a private performance at the Gallery of Illustration, Waterloo Place, London.

Dickens's offer was accepted and the Queen saw both the melodrama and J. B. Buckstone's farce *Uncle John* on 9 July 1857 (*Dickens to His Oldest Friend*, p. 188). During the interval the Queen sent for Dickens to express her thanks, but he declined the opportunity for the reasons he states in the letter. See Forster, XI, iii, 390–1. Dickens also parried the Queen's invitation to hear him read the *CC* in private; but he did meet with her in Mar. 1870 and attend her levee on 2 Apr. 1870. See Johnson, II, 1146–8.

TAVISTOCK HOUSE

Saturday, Twenty-Ninth August, 1857

MY DEAR COLLINS,—Partly in the grim despair and restlessness of this subsidence from excitement, and partly for the sake of Household Words, I want to cast about whether you and I can go anywhere—take any tour—see anything—whereon we could write something together. Have you any idea tending to any place in the world? Will you rattle your head and see if there is any pebble in it which we could wander away and play at marbles with? We want something for Household Words, and I want to escape from myself. For when I *do* start up and stare myself seedily in the face, as happens to be my case at present, my blankness is inconceivable—indescribable—my misery amazing.

I shall be in town on Monday. Shall we talk then? Shall we talk at Gad's Hill? *What* shall we do?[1] As I close this I am on my way back by train.—Ever faithfully.

1. Dickens and Collins left for the Lake District on 7 Sep. and returned on 22 Sep. *The Lazy Tour of Two Idle Apprentices* grew out of their excursion, and appeared in *HW* from 3 Oct. 1857 to 31 Oct.

LANCASTER

Saturday Night, Twelfth September, 1857

MY DEAR GEORGY,—I received your letter at Allonby yesterday, and was delighted to get it. We came back to Carlisle last night (to a capital inn, kept by Breach's[1] brother), and came on here to-day. We are on our way to Doncaster; but, although it is not a hundred miles from here, we shall have, as well as I can make out the complicated list of trains, to sleep at Leeds to-morrow night.

Accustomed as you are to the homage which men delight to render to the Inimitable, you would be scarcely prepared for the proportions it assumes in this northern country. Station-masters assist him to alight from carriages, deputations await him in hotel entries, inn-keepers bow down before him and put him into regal rooms, the town goes down to the platform to see him off, and Collins's ankle goes into the newspapers!!![2]

It is a great deal better than it was, and he can get into new hotels and up the stairs with two thick sticks, like an admiral in a farce. His spirits have improved in a corresponding degree, and he contemplates cheerfully the keeping house at Doncaster. I thought (as I told you) he would never have gone there, but he seems quite up to the mark now. Of course he can never walk out, or see anything of any place.

The landlady of the little inn at Allonby lived at Greta Bridge, in Yorkshire, when I went down there before Nickleby,[3] and was smuggled into the room to see me, when I was secretly found out. She is an immensely fat woman now. "But I could tuck my arm round her waist then, Mr. Dickens," the landlord said when she told me the story as I was going to bed the night before last. "And can't you do it now," I said, "you insensible dog? Look at me! Here's a picture!" Accordingly, I got round as much of her as I could; and this gallant action was the most successful I have ever performed, on the whole. I think it was the dullest little place I ever entered; and what with the monotony of an idle sea, and what with the monotony of another sea in the room (occasioned by Collins's perpetually holding his ankle over a pail of salt water, and laving it with a milk jug), I struck yesterday, and came away.

We are in a very remarkable old house here with genuine old rooms and an uncommonly quaint staircase. I have a state bedroom, with two enormous red four-posters in it, each as big as Charley's room at Gad's Hill. Bellew[4] is to preach here to-morrow. "And we know he is a friend of yours, sir," said the landlord, when he presided over the serving of the dinner (two little salmon trout; a sirloin steak; a brace of partridges; seven dishes of sweets; five dishes of dessert, led off by a bowl of peaches; and in the centre an enormous bride-cake—"We always have it here, sir," said the landlord, "custom of the house"). Collins turned pale, and estimated the dinner at half a guinea each.

This is the stupidest of letters, but all description is gone or going, into The Lazy Tour of Two Idle Apprentices.—Ever affectionately, my dearest Georgy.

1. Breach, unidentified.
2. Collins sprained his ankle on Carrick Fell on their first walking expedition.
3. See pp 40–1.
4. Revd John Chippendale Montesquieu Bellew (1823–74), author and popular preacher. Bellew was born in Lancaster; in 1855 he became the incumbent of Bedford Chapel, Bloomsbury, London. The Revd J. M. Bellew, according to the author of 'Literary Gossip' (*London Review*, 15 June 1876, p. 687), was 'one of our best public readers', who gave benefit readings from Shakespeare, Scott, Dickens, Macaulay and Tennyson.

5th September 1857

[John Forster] . . . To the most part of what you say—Amen! You are
not so tolerant as perhaps you might be of the wayward and unsettled
feeling which is part (I suppose) of the tenure on which one holds an
imaginative life, and which I have, as you ought to know well, often
only kept down by riding over it like a dragoon—but let that go by. I
make no maudlin complaint. I agree with you as to the very possible
incidents, even not less bearable than mine, that might and must often
occur to the married condition when it is entered into very young. I am
always deeply sensible of the wonderful exercise I have of life and its
highest sensations, and have said to myself for years, and have honestly
and truly felt, this is the drawback to such a career, and is not to be
complained of. I say it and feel it now as strongly as ever I did; and, as I
told you in my last, I do not with that view put all this forward. But the
years have not made it easier to bear for either of us; and, for her sake
as well as mine, the wish will force itself upon me that something might
be done. I know too well it is impossible. There is the fact, and that is all
one can say.[1] Nor are you to suppose that I disguise from myself what
might be urged on the other side. I claim no immunity from blame.
There is plenty of fault on my side, I dare say, in the way of a thousand
uncertainties, caprices, and difficulties of disposition; but only one
thing will alter all that, and that is, the end which alters everything. . . .

What do you think of my paying for this place,[2] by reviving that old
idea of some Readings from my books.[3] I am very strongly tempted.
Think of it.

. . . Hop-picking is going on, and people sleep in the garden, and
breathe in at the keyhole of the house door. I have been amazed,
before this year, by the number of miserable lean wretches, hardly able
to crawl, who go hop-picking. I find it is a superstition that the dust of
the newly picked hop, falling freshly into the throat, is a cure for
consumption. So the poor creatures drag themselves along the roads,
and sleep under wet hedges, and get cured soon and finally. . . .

1. While Dickens turned to his younger friend Collins as a companion with
   whom to seek relief from his marriage through restless activity, he appears
   to have relied on Forster as the one person with whom he could freely
   discuss his discontent with Catherine. Responding to Dickens's letters at
   this time, Forster consistently advocated 'the moderate middle course', his
   phrase for urging him to accept his situation (as Dickens appears to here)
   and commit himself to thinking how the marriage could be saved not
   abandoned.

2. Gad's Hill. On Dickens's purchase, see p. 103 n. 3.
3. P. Collins (*The Public Readings*, 1975) traces the origins of the idea of the readings back to the late 1840s, when Dickens first confided to Forster his long preoccupation with the stage. Collins also provides (pp xvii–xxii) a full discussion of the events leading to Dickens's turning professional reader, a move Forster consistently opposed because he saw in the readings dangerous symptoms of Dickens's abandoning 'every hope of resettling his disordered home' (Forster, viii, ii, 200–1).

[September 1857]

[John Forster] . . . Your letter of yesterday was so kind and hearty, and sounded so gently the many chords we have touched together, that I cannot leave it unanswered, though I have not much (to any purpose) to say. My reference to "confidences" was merely to the relief of saying a word of what has long been pent up in my mind. Poor Catherine and I are not made for each other, and there is no help for it. It is not only that she makes me uneasy and unhappy, but that I make her so too—and much more so. She is exactly what you know, in the way of being amiable and complying; but we are strangely ill-assorted for the bond there is between us. God knows she would have been a thousand times happier if she had married another kind of man, and that her avoidance of this destiny would have been at least equally good for us both. I am often cut to the heart by thinking what a pity it is, for her own sake, that I ever fell in her way; and if I were sick or disabled to-morrow, I know how sorry she would be, and how deeply grieved myself, to think how we had lost each other. But exactly the same incompatibility would arise, the moment I was well again; and nothing on earth could make her understand me, or suit us to each other. Her temperament will not go with mine. It mattered not so much when we had only ourselves to consider, but reasons have been growing since which make it all but hopeless that we should even try to struggle on. What is now befalling me I have seen steadily coming, ever since the days you remember when Mary was born;[1] and I know too well that you cannot, and no one can, help me. Why I have even written I hardly know; but it is a miserable sort of comfort that you should be clearly aware how matters stand. The mere mention of the fact, without any complaint or blame of any sort, is a relief to my present state of spirits—and I can get this only from you, because I speak of it to no one else. . . .

[October 1857]

. . . Too late to say, put the curb on, and don't rush at hills—the wrong man to say it to.[2] I have now no relief but in action. I am become incapable of rest. I am quite confident I should rust, break, and die, if I spared myself. Much better to die, doing. What I am in that way, nature made me first, and my way of life has of late, alas! confirmed. I must accept the drawback—since it is one—with the powers I have; and I must hold upon the tenure prescribed to me. . . .

1. Their second child, born in 1838. This statement sounds more like exaggerated hindsight than an accurate comment on twenty years of marriage. Forster's observation that Dickens's marital discontent – 'An unsettled feeling greatly in excess of what was usual with Dickens' – dated from the time of his first summer residence in Boulogne (1853) perhaps comes closer to approximating the beginning of Dickens's real unhappiness with his wife (Forster, VIII, ii, 193).
2. A possible reference to Forster's negative counsel about the public readings and to Forster's advising Dickens to avoid impetuous actions at home. See the next letter, some hint of which Dickens may have communicated to Forster.

GAD'S HILL PLACE
Sunday Eleventh October 1857

MY DEAR ANNE,[1]—I want some little changes made in the arrangement of my dressing-room and the Bathroom.[2] And as I would rather not have them talked about by comparative strangers, I shall be much obliged to you, my old friend, if you will see them completed before you leave Tavistock House.

I wish to make the Bathroom my washing-room also. It will be therefore necessary to carry into the Bathroom, to remain there, the two washing-stands from my Dressing-Room. Then, to get rid altogether, of the chest of drawers in the Dressing-Room I want the recess of the doorway between the Dressing-Room and Mrs. Dickens's room, fitted with plain white deal shelves, and closed in with a plain light deal door, painted white. Rudkin can do this—or Lillie,[3] being in the house, can do it if he likes. The sooner it is done, the better.

My wardrobe will then stand where the chest of Drawers stands now, and a small iron bedstead will go behind the door, with its side against the wall, as you enter the Dressing-Room; its head towards the stairs, and its foot towards the window. I have ordered the bedstead and bedding, and they will be sent to Tavistock House to you. The chest of Drawers shall come down here, when the van comes down to bring our luggage home at the end of the month.

They all send you their love.—Ever Faithfully yours.

1. Anne Brown Cornelius, Catherine's maid since 1841, who remained with

the family until her marriage in 1855. Two years later, she returned, staying on at Tavistock House after Dickens and Catherine separated. See P, II, 392n.

2. Dickens appears to have contemplated making some symbolic but significant change in his married life sometime between leaving for Cumberland with Collins on 7 Sep. and the interval following his return to Gad's Hill on ?22 Sep. (see To Wills, 20 Sep. 1857, N, II, 886). Ostensibly Dickens went directly to Gad's Hill upon returning to prepare the account of their tour for publication in *HW*, a task which kept him away from Tavistock House, where Catherine stayed with the family, until he resolved on the step he describes in the letter.

3. Rudkin and Lillie unidentified.

TAVISTOCK HOUSE, TAVISTOCK SQUARE, LONDON W.C.

Tuesday, March 16th 1858

DEAR EVANS,[1]—I want you to consider this letter as being strictly private and confidential between you and me. I am anxious to have your soundest opinion on the point it refers to you, and I shall give it great weight—though I do not, of course, pledge myself to be bound by it.

The Reading idea that I had, sometime ago, sticks to me. Let me read where I will, an effect is produced which seems to belong to nothing else; and the number of people who want to come, cannot by any means be got in. I have in mind this project:—after reading in London on the 15th of next month for the Benefit of the Children's Hospital,[2] to announce by advertisement (what is quite true) that I cannot answer the applications that are made to me, so numerous are they, and that compliance with ever so few of them is in any reason impossible. That therefore I have resolved upon a course of readings both in town and country, and that those in London will take place at St Martins Hall on certain evenings—four or six Thursdays—through May and just into June. Then, in August, September and October, in the Eastern Counties, the West of England, Lancashire, Yorkshire and Scotland, I should read from 35 to 40 times.[3] At each place where there was a great success, I should myself announce that I should come back, on the turn of Christmas, to read a new Christmas Story written for the purpose (and which I should first read in London).[4] Unless I am gigantically mistaken by March or April *a very large sum of money* would be cleared and Ireland would be still untouched; not to speak of America where I believe I could make (if I could resolve to go there) ten thousand pounds.[5]

Now, the question I want your opinion on is this:—Assuming these hopes to be well grounded, would such an use of the personal (I may almost say affectionate) relations which subsist between me and the public and make my standing with them very peculiar, at all affect my position with them as a writer? Would it be likely to have any influence on my next book? If it had any influence at all, would it be likely to be of a weakening or a strengthening kind?

(It is not the purpose of this point, to remark that I should confide the whole of the Business arrangements to Arthur Smith.[6] I merely mention it that you may have the whole case.)—Faithfully.

1. Frederick Mullet Evans, partner of William Bradbury, whose firm Chapman and Hall used as printers for all the works of Dickens's they published up to 1844. Thereafter, Bradbury and Evans took over, both publishing and printing all Dickens's works until 1858, when he quarrelled with Bradbury and Evans because they refused to side in public with him over his separation from Catherine. See Introduction, p. 2 and n. 25. Dickens retaliated by switching back to Chapman and Hall.
2. Held as scheduled in St. Martin's Hall. Dickens's last charity reading before turning professional.
3. Dickens gave his first paid reading on 29 Apr. 1858 in St. Martin's Hall. See *Speeches*, p. 264, for the text of his short prefatory address. In June and July 16 more readings in London followed before he set off on his first provincial tour. (2 Aug.–13 Nov.) comprising 83 readings. See Collins, *The Public Readings*, p. xxvi.
4. Dickens contributed to *A House to Let*, the Christmas number of *HW*, but he did not read from it during the eight London readings at the end of the year.
5. Later events proved Dickens correct, both as to the popularity of the readings and their remuneration. See subsequent letters and p. 161.
6. Arthur W. W. Smith (1835–61), Dickens's first business manger.

[March] 1858

[John Forster] . . . It becomes necessary with a view to the arrangements that would have to be begun next month if I decided on the Readings, to consider and settle the question of the Plunge. Quite dismiss from your mind any reference whatever to present circumstances at home. Nothing can put *them* right, until we are all dead and buried and risen. It is not, with me, a matter of will, or trial, or sufferance, or good humour, or making the best of it, or making the worst of it, any longer. It is all despairingly over. Have no lingering hope of, or for, me in this association. A dismal failure has to be borne, and there an end. Will you then try to think of this reading project (as I do) apart from all personal likings and dislikings, and solely with a view to its effect on that particular relation (personally affectionate and like no other man's) which subsists between me and the public? I want your most careful consideration. If you would like, when you have gone over it in your mind, to discuss the matter with me and Arthur Smith (who would manage the whole of the Business, which I should never touch); we will make an appointment. But I ought to add that Arthur Smith plainly says, "Of the immense return in money, I have no doubt. Of the Dash into the new position, however, I am not so good a judge." I enclose you a rough note of my project, as it stands in my mind. [. . .]

[March] 1858

[John Forster] . . . Your view of the reading matter I still think is unconsciously taken from your own particular point. You don't seem to me to get out of yourself in considering it. A word more upon it. You are not to think I have made up my mind. If I had, why should I not say so? I find very great difficulty in doing so because of what you urge, because I know the question to be a balance of doubts, and because I most honestly feel in my innermost heart, in this matter (as in all others for years and years), the honour of the calling by which I have always stood most conscientiously. But do you quite consider that the public exhibition of oneself takes place equally, whosoever may get the money? And have you any idea that at this moment—this very time—half the public at least supposes me to be paid? My dear F, out of the twenty or five-and-twenty letters a week that I get about Readings, twenty will ask at what price, or on what terms, it can be done. The only exceptions, in truth, are when the correspondent is a clergyman, or a banker, or the member for the place in question. Why, at this very time half Scotland believe that I am paid for going to Edinburgh![1] [. . .]

1. A reference to Dickens's reading of *CC* to raise money for the Edinburgh Philosophical Institution on 26 Mar. 1858.

TAVISTOCK HOUSE, TAVISTOCK SQUARE, LONDON
Sunday, Tenth October, 1858

MY DEAR FORSTER,—As to the truth of the readings, I cannot tell you what the demonstrations of personal regard and respect are. How the densest and most uncomfortably-packed crowd will be hushed in an instant when I show my face. How the youth of colleges, and the old men of business in the town, seem equally unable to get near enough to me when they cheer me away at night. How common people and gentlefolks will stop me in the streets and say: "Mr. Dickens, will you let me touch the hand that has filled my home with so many friends?"[1] And if you saw the mothers, and fathers, and sisters, and brothers in mourning, who invariably come to Little Dombey, and if you studied the wonderful expression of comfort and reliance with which they hang about me, as if I had been with them, all kindness and delicacy, at their own little death-bed, you would think it one of the strangest things in the world.

As to the mere effect, of course I don't go on doing the thing so often without carefully observing myself and the people too in every little thing, and without (in consequence) greatly improving in it.

At Aberdeen, we were crammed to the street twice in one day. At Perth (where I thought when I arrived there literally could be nobody to come), the nobility came posting in from thirty miles round, and the whole town came and filled an immense hall. They were as full of perception, fire, and enthusiasm as any people I have seen. At Glasgow, where I read three evenings and one morning, we took the prodigiously large sum of six hundred pounds! And this at the Manchester prices, which are lower than St. Martin's Hall. As to the effect, if you had seen them after Lilian died, in The Chimes, or when Scrooge woke and talked to the boy outside the window, I doubt if you would ever have forgotten it. And at the end of Dombey yesterday afternoon, in the cold light of day, they all got up, after a short pause, gentle and simple, and thundered and waved their hats with that astonishing heartiness and fondness for me, that for the first time in all my public career they took me completely off my legs, and I saw the whole eighteen hundred of them reel on one side as if a shock from without had shaken the hall. Notwithstanding which, I must confess to you, I am very anxious to get to the end of my Readings, and to be at home again, and able to sit down and think in my own study. There has been only one thing quite without alloy.

The dear girls[2] have enjoyed themselves immensely, and their trip has been a great success. I hope I told you (but I forget whether I did or no) how splendidly Newcastle came out. I am reminded of Newcastle at the moment because they joined me there.

I am anxious to get to the end of my readings, and to be at home again, and able to sit down and think in my own study. But the fatigue, though sometimes very great indeed, hardly tells upon me at all. And although all our people, from Smith downwards, have given in, more or less, at times, I have never been in the least unequal to the work, though sometimes sufficiently disinclined for it. My kindest and best love to Mrs. Forster.[3]—Ever affectionately.

1. Cf. Sir Henry F. Dickens, who noted that walking in London with his father

'was in itself a revelation: a royal progress; people of all degrees and classes taking off their hats and greeting him as he passed' in the streets. See *Memoirs of My Father* (1929), pp 17–8.
2. Mamie and Katey Dickens.
3. In 1856 Forster married Eliza Ann Colburn the widow of Henry Colburn, the publisher, who died in 1855.

TAVISTOCK HOUSE, TAVISTOCK SQUARE, LONDON, W.C.
[Enclosure][1]   Tuesday, May 25, 1858

Mrs. Dickens and I have lived unhappily together for many years. Hardly any one who has known us intimately can fail to have known that we are, in all respects of character and temperament, wonderfully unsuited to each other. I suppose that no two people, not vicious in themselves, ever were joined together, who had a greater difficulty in understanding one another, or who had less in common. An attached woman servant[2] (more friend to both of us than a servant), who lived with us sixteen years, and is now married, and who was, and still is in Mrs. Dickens's confidence and in mine, who had the closest familiar experience of this unhappiness, in London, in the country, in France, in Italy, wherever we have been, year after year, month after month, week after week, day after day, will bear testimony to this.

Nothing has, on many occasions, stood between us and a separation but Mrs. Dickens's sister, Georgina Hogarth. From the age of fifteen, she has devoted herself to our house and our children.[3] She has been their playmate, nurse, instructress, friend, protectress, adviser and companion. In the manly consideration toward Mrs. Dickens which I owe to my wife, I will merely remark of her that the peculiarity of her character has thrown all the children on some one else. I do not know—I cannot by any stretch of fancy imagine—what would have become of them but for this aunt, who has grown up with them, to whom they are devoted, and who has sacrificed the best part of her youth and life to them.

She has remonstrated, reasoned, suffered and toiled, again and again to prevent a separation between Mrs. Dickens and me. Mrs. Dickens has often expressed to her her sense of her affectionate care and devotion in the house—never more strongly than within the last twelve months.

For some years past Mrs. Dickens has been in the habit of representing to me that it would be better for her to go away and live apart; that her always increasing estrangement made a mental disorder[4] under which she sometimes labors—more, that she felt herself unfit for the life she had to lead as my wife, and that she would be better far away. I have uniformly replied that we must bear our misfortune, and fight the fight out to the end; that the children were the first consideration, and that I feared they must bind us together "in appearance."

At length, within these three weeks, it was suggested to me by Forster that even for their sakes, it would surely be better to reconstruct and rearrange their unhappy home. I empowered him to treat with Mrs. Dickens, as the friend of both of us for one and twenty years. Mrs. Dickens wished to add on her part, Mark Lemon, and did so. On Saturday last Lemon wrote to Forster that Mrs. Dickens "gratefully and thankfully accepted" the terms I proposed to her.[5]

Of the pecuniary part of them, I will only say that I believe they are as generous as if Mrs. Dickens were a lady of distinction and I a man of fortune. The remaining parts of them are easily described—my eldest boy to live with Mrs. Dickens and take care of her; my eldest girl to keep my house; both my girls, and all my children but the eldest son, to live with me, in the continued companionship of their aunt Georgina, for whom they have all the tenderest affection that I have ever seen among young people, and who has a higher claim (as I have often declared for many years) upon my affection, respect and gratitude than anybody in this world.

I hope that no one who may become acquainted with what I write here, can possibly be so cruel and unjust, as to put any misconstruction on our separation, so far. My elder children all understand it perfectly, and all accept it as inevitable. There is not a shadow of doubt or concealment among us—my eldest son and I are one, as to it all.

Two wicked persons[6] who should have spoken very differently of me, in consideration of earned respect and gratitude, have (as I am told, and indeed to my personal knowledge) coupled with this separation the name of a young lady[7] for whom I have a great attachment and regard. I will not repeat her name—I honor it too much. Upon my soul and honor, there is not on this earth a more virtuous and spotless creature than that young lady. I know her to be innocent and pure, and as good as my own dear daughters. Further, I am quite sure that Mrs. Dickens, having received this assurance from me, must now believe it, in the respect I know her to have for me, and in the perfect confidence I know her in her better moments to repose in my truthfulness.

On this head, again, there is not a shadow of doubt or concealment between my children and me. All is open and plain among us, as though we were brothers and sisters. They are perfectly certain that I would not deceive them, and the confidence among us is without a fear.

                                                    29th May, 1858

It having been stated to us that in reference to the differences which have resulted in the separation of Mr. and Mrs. Charles Dickens, certain statements have been circulated that such differences are occasioned by circumstances deeply affecting the moral character of Mr. Dickens and compromising the reputation and good name of others, we solemnly declare that we now disbelieve such statements. We know that they are not believed by Mrs. Dickens, and we pledge ourselves on all occasions to contradict them, as entirely destitute of foundation.

[Here follow the signatures of Mrs. Hogarth and her youngest daughter.]

1. In addition to issuing a public statement about the reason for his separation from his wife on the front page of *HW* on 12 June 1858, Dickens prepared this more explicit letter of 25 May to give to Arthur Smith. Use it as a weapon against my detractors, Dickens explained. 'You have not only my full permission to show this,' he wrote about the enclosure, 'but I beg you to show to any one who wishes to do me right, or to any one who may have been misled into doing me wrong.' (N, III, 21–2) Smith took Dickens at his word, the result of which was that newspapers on both sides of the Atlantic disregarded Dickens's ambiguous instructions and printed copies of the letter after a journalist saw the original and sent a copy to the *New York Tribune*, where it was published on 16 Aug. 1858. Dickens referred to the document as the 'violated letter' because he never intended it for publication, hoping instead that the manager of his readings could use it to check any scandal that might harm the new series of public performances he projected.
2. Mrs Anne Cornelius.
3. According to Forster, Georgina became part of Dickens's household after his trip to America in 1842 and remained a member of it until he died. See Forster, IV, i, 276.
   Dickens's remarks here about his wife's putative lack of maternal feelings and Georgina's willingness to supply what her older sister lacked contrast with the assessment of Katey Dickens, who commented to Gladys Storey: 'she [Georgina] was useful to my mother, of course, but that was all'. Quoted by Storey in *Dickens and Daughter* (1939), p. 24.
4. When Dickens spoke of Catherine's illness in March 1851, he described it to Dr James Wilson as 'a nervous one . . . of a peculiar kind' (N, II, 278). 'Mental disorder' is surely much stronger and perhaps part of the letter's obvious yet sincerely felt rhetorical strategy on Dickens's part to justify his compliance with his wife's wish 'to go away and live apart'.

5. Working together, Forster and Lemon negotiated a settlement by which Catherine was to live apart in her own house and receive £600 a year. These arrangements were accepted by both parties and were about to be signed when Dickens learned of the rumours circulated by Mrs Hogarth and Helen falsely citing his relationship with Ellen Ternan as the reason for the separation. Before Dickens agreed to pay Catherine a penny, he insisted that Mrs Hogarth and Helen sign the retraction he prepared. For Lemon, see p. 336 n. 1.
6. Mrs Hogarth and Helen Hogarth.
7. An ambiguous reference in the context of the rumours current in London at the time, which not only linked Dickens with Ellen Ternan but also maliciously named Georgina Hogarth as his mistress, holding her, not Ellen, responsible for the break up. Thus when 'smashing slanders' about Georgina's supposed pregnancy came to him, Dickens evidently resolved to prepare this version of the story in an attempt to clear her of charges his solicitor described as so 'disgusting and horrible' that he thought it undesirable to write them down 'even for the purpose of denial'. K. J. Fielding, who has examined the papers left by Dickens's solicitor, notes that the documents reveal that Dickens firmly believed that the Hogarths were responsible for both sets of rumours. See 'Dickens and the Hogarth Scandal', *Nineteenth-Century Fiction*, 10 (June 1955), 68–9.

TAVISTOCK HOUSE, TAVISTOCK SQUARE, LONDON, W.C.

Monday, Fourteenth June 1858

MY DEAR MR. TAGART,[1]—I have had the greatest pleasure in the receipt of your kind and affectionate note. The only draw-back is, that I wasn't at home when you brought it, and should have been delighted to have seen you.

Though I have unquestionably suffered deeply from being lied about with a wonderful recklessness, I am not so weak or wrong-headed as to be in the least changed by it. I know the world to have just as much good in it as it had before; and no one has better reason to thank God for the friendship it contains, than I have.

So I hope to regain my composure in a steady manner, and to live to be good and true to my innocent people who have been traduced along with me. For the rest, I am already thoroughly sure that the change which has been made at home here, is a beneficial one for us all.

With kindest regards from all here to yourself, Mrs. Tagart, and all your house,—Believe me ever—affectionately yours.

1. Revd Edward Tagart (1804–58), Unitarian minister.

TAVISTOCK HOUSE, TAVISTOCK SQUARE, LONDON, W.C.

Wednesday, Twenty-Eight April, 1858

MY DEAR YATES,[1]—I send you an orthopædic shield, to defend your manly bosom from the pens of the enemy.

For a good many years I have suffered a great deal from charities, but never anything like what I suffer now. The amount of correspondence they inflict upon me is really incredible. But this is nothing. Benevolent men get behind the piers of the gates, lying in wait for my going out; and when I peep shrinkingly from my study-windows, I see their pot-bellied shadows projected on the gravel. Benevolent bullies drive up in hansom cabs (with engraved portraits of their benevolent institutions hanging over the aprons, like banners on their outward walls), and stay long at the door. Benevolent area-sneaks get lost in the kitchens and are found to impede the circulation of the knife-cleaning machine. My man has been heard to say (at The Burton Arms) "that if it wos a wicious place, well and good—*that* an't door work; but that wen all the Christian wirtues is always a-shoulderin' and a-helberin' on you in the 'all, a-tryin' to git past you and cut upstairs into Master's room, wy no wages as you couldn't name wouldn't make it up to you."—Persecuted Ever.

1. Edmund Yates (1831–94), journalist and miscellaneous writer.

3 HANOVER TERRACE
Monday, Eleventh March, 1861

MY DEAR WILLS,—I have had a begging letter from that Robert Barrow[1]—a very bad one by the way—with an awful affectation of Christian piety in it—a pretence of having known me and offended me, which is altogether a Lie—and the usual blaring assumption (of which I shall die at last) that I am immensely rich.

If you would not object to see him, I shall be very much obliged to you if you will do so once more, at that same wretched lodging hard by Holborn. He seems to have no idea of my having already relieved him. I wish you would tell him that you have already given him £2 and that you have £3 more in hand; but that you must impress upon him in the strongest manner that he has no hope in making any further appeal to me—that it is quite impossible and monstrous—that I am quite weighed down and loaded and chained in life, by the enormous drags upon me which are already added to the charges of my own large family—and that he must not deceive himself with the notion of my assisting him further. It is very important indeed that he should be got to understand this, quite apart from the question of his own necessities.

I declare to you that what with my mother—and Alfred's family[2] —and my wife—and a Saunders[3] or so—I seem to stop sometimes like a steamer in a storm, and deliberate whether I shall go on whirling, or go down.—Ever faithfully.

1. Unidentified.
2. Dickens's brother Alfred Lamart Dickens died unexpectedly in August 1860. He left five children and a widow.
3. Unidentified.

BRIGHTON

Saturday, Thirteenth November 1858

MY DEAR MRS. WINTER,—I have been so constantly and rapidly changing from place to place during the past week, that I am only just now in receipt of the intelligence of your misfortune. With the utmost sincerity and earnestness of which my heart is capable, I condole with you upon it and assure you of my true sympathy and friendship. It has distressed me greatly. Not because I am so worldly or so unjust as to couple the least reproach or blame with a reverse that I do not doubt to have been unavoidable, and that I know to be always easily possible of occurrence to the best and most fortunate of men, but because I know you feel it heavily.

I wish to Heaven it were in my power to help Mr. Winter to any new opening in life.[1] But you can hardly imagine how powerless I am in any such case. My own work in life being of that kind that I must always do it with my own unassisted hand and head, I have such rare opportunities of placing anyone, that for years and years I have been seeking in vain to help in this way a friend of the old days[2] when the old house stood unchanged in Lombard Street. To this hour, I have not succeeded, though I have strenuously tried my hardest, both abroad and at home. Commercial opportunities above all are so far removed from me, that I dare not encourage a hope of my power to serve Mr. Winter with my good word, ever coming within a year's journey of my will and wish to do it.

But I really think that your Father who could do so much in such a case, without drawing at all heavily upon his purse, might be induced to do what—I may say to you, Maria—it is no great stretch of sentiment to call his duty. Has not Margaret[3] great influence with him? Have you not *some*? And don't you think that if you were to set yourself steadily to exert whatever influence you can bring to bear upon him, you would do the best within your reach for your husband, your child, and yourself? Is it not all important that you should try your utmost with him, at this time?

Forgive my recommending this, if you have so anticipated the recommendation as to have done all that possibly can be done to move him. But what you tell me about George seems so strange, so hard, and so ill balanced, that I cannot avoid the subject.

I write in the greatest haste, being overwhelmed by business here. On Monday I hope to be at Gad's Hill, and to remain either there or at Tavistock House for months to come. I enclose a few lines to Mr. Winter, and am ever,—Your Faithful Friend.

BRIGHTON

Saturday, Thirteenth November 1858

MY DEAR MR. WINTER,—In the hope that friendly words of remembrance in season may not be unacceptable to you, I write to assure you of my sympathy with you in your trouble. Pray do not let it cast you down too much; what has happened to you has happened to many thousands of good and honourable men, and will happen again in a like manner to the end of all things. If you should feel the bitterness of losing belief in any nature you had previously trusted in, consider that the truth is always better than falsehood, even though the truth involves the detection of such skin-deep friendships as that which can cool towards a man in temporary misfortune. It is better lost than kept, as all things worthless are.

Be strong of heart for yourself, and look forward to a better time. You will not think I know, that I obtrude myself upon you in asking to be borne in mind among the friends who feel truly towards you. —Faithfully yours always.

1. When her husband failed in business, Mrs Maria Winter appealed for help without success to George Beadnell, her father, and then to Dickens. Winter, a saw-mill manager in Finsbury, was officially declared bankrupt in Mar. 1859.
2. Probably Beard. See pp 105–6.
3. Unidentified.

TAVISTOCK HOUSE

Monday Night, Fourteenth March, 1859

MY DEAR PANIZZI,[1]—If you should feel no delicacy in mentioning, or should see no objection to mentioning, to Signor Poerio,[2] or any of the wronged Neapolitan gentlemen to whom it is your happiness and honour to be a friend on their arrival in this country, an idea that has occurred to me, I should regard it as a great kindness in you if you would be my exponent. I think you will have no difficulty in believing that I would not, on any consideration, obtrude my name or projects upon any one of those noble souls, if there were any reason of the slightest kind against it. And if you see any such reason, I pray you instantly to banish my letter from your thoughts.

It seems to me probable that some narrative of their ten years' suffering will, somehow or other, sooner or later, be by some of them laid before the English people. The just interest and indignation alive here, will (I suppose) elicit it. False narratives and garbled stories will, in any case, of a certainty get about. If the true history of the matter is to be told, I have that sympathy with them and respect for them which would, all other considerations apart, render it unspeakably gratifying to me to be the means of its diffusion. What I desire to lay before them is simply this. If for my new successor to Household Words³ a narrative of their ten years' trial could be written, I would take any conceivable pains to have it rendered into English, and presented in the sincerest and best way to a very large and comprehensive audience. It should be published exactly as you might think best for them, and remunerated in any way that you might think generous and right. They want no mouthpiece and no introducer, but perhaps they might have no objection to be associated with an English writer, who is possibly not unknown to them by some general reputation, and who certainly would be animated by a strong public and private respect for their honour, spirit, and unmerited misfortunes. This is the whole matter; assuming that such a thing is to be done, I long for the privilege of helping to do it. These gentlemen might consider it an independent means of making money, and I should be delighted to pay the money.

In my absence from town, my friend and sub-editor, Mr. Wills (to whom I had expressed my feelings on the subject), has seen, I think, three of the gentlemen together. But as I hear, returning home to-night, that they are in your good hands, and as nobody can be a better judge than you of anything that concerns them, I at once decide to write to you and take no other step whatever. Forgive me for the trouble I have occasioned you in the reading of this letter, and never think of it again if you think that by pursuing it you would cause them an instant's uneasiness.—Believe me, very faithfully yours.

1. Antonio Panizzi (1797–1879), Principal Librarian at the British Museum and Italian patriot, who, during his official career from 1831–66, also occupied himself with the movement to liberate Italy. Panizzi sought refuge in England in 1822 after fleeing from Italy; later he returned at considerable personal risk to help the 20 000 Neapolitan State prisoners, who were gaoled in 1849 when Ferdinand II dissolved the constitution of the Kingdom of the Two Sicilies.

2. Carlo Poerio (1803–67), an Italian patriot and writer whom Gladstone saw chained to a murderer during a visit to one of Naples's prisons in the winter of 1850–1. Gladstone subsequently published three indignant letters exposing the atrocities and cruelty he witnessed; the letters aroused public opinion in Europe, and Lord Derby obtained Poerio's freedom in 1852.
3. *AYR*. Existing records identify no contribution by Poerio. Dickens, however, did publish his own piece, 'The Italian Prisoner', on 13 Oct. 1860.

GAD'S HILL PLACE
Saturday Sixth November 1858

MY DEAR SIR,—Will you and Mr. Bewsher[1] tell me whether you think the gigantic Sydney[2] really has any sort of call to the sea service? He has often talked of it at home here, and has lately written an odd characteristic letter to one of his sisters, entreating her to ask me to make the Navy his profession, as he is devoted to it "without any sham," and longs to follow it.

I cannot make out in my own mind how much of this ardour is in-bred in the boy, and how much of it is referable to the frequent appearance here, in the last holidays, of a young midshipman, the son of an Edinburgh friend of mine,[3] in glorious buttons and with a real steel weapon in his belt. As you have so many more opportunities of observing Sydney than I have, I should be very glad of your opinion: though of course I am not so unreasonable as to expect you to pronounce oracularly on so difficult a question.

But he is a boy of such remarkable energy and purpose, considering his years and inches, that if I supposed him to be quite in earnest and to have made up his small mind, I would give him his way, because I really believe he would then follow it out with spirit.[4]

My daughters and Miss Hogarth write in kind regard to yourself and Mr. Bewsher; and I am always—My Dear Sir—Very faithfully yours.

1. The Revds M. Gibson and J. Bewsher ran the English school in Boulogne to which Dickens also sent Frank, Alfred, and Henry Dickens. He thought highly of the school, observing to Mrs Watson on 14 Sep. 1860 that 'The teaching [was] unusually sound and good. The manner and conduct developed in the boys quite admirable. But I have never seen a gentleman so perfectly acquainted with boy-nature as the Eton master [Gibson]. There was a perfect understanding between him and his charges; nothing pedantic on his part, nothing slavish on their parts. The result was, that either with or away from him, the boys combined an ease and frankness with a modesty and sense of responsibility that was really above all praise.' (N, III, 177–8) For a general description of English schools on the northern coast of France, see Edmund S. Dixon, 'Our Boys and Girls', *HW*, 16 May 1857. Dixon points out various advantages such as nearness to London, good food, no corporal punishment, and good supervision; a French

education, Dickens also realised, was relatively cheap. 'I pay for each of my boys £40 a year,' he wrote in 1856, adding that the school in Boulogne was 'a *perfectly honorable* establishment as to extras, and not a sharking one' (N, II, 730–1).

2. Sydney Smith Haldimand Dickens (1847–72), Dickens's fifth son and seventh child, whose diminutive stature Dickens jokes about. Sydney, nicknamed 'Ocean Spectre', 'Hoshen Peck' or 'the Peck' because of a faraway look in his eyes, as if he saw some phantom at sea, wanted to join the Navy.

3. Unidentified.

4. Sydney went from Boulogne to North Grove House, Southsea, where he trained to become Naval Cadet. His promising career (naval midshipman, 1860, lieutenant 1867) ended in disgrace: debts almost ruined him, and the last letter Dickens wrote to him forbade Sydney to visit the family on his next leave (Johnson, II, p. 1112).

GAD'S HILL PLACE, HIGHAM BY ROCHESTER, KENT

Thursday night, Eighth September 1859

MY DEAR SIR,[1]—I am a little puzzled to know what to do with Frank.[2] I cannot quite understand him, and I take the cause to be that he does not quite understand himself. Before he went to Germany he was (as you may remember) all agog to be a Doctor. From Germany he wrote me that he wished to abandon the idea. Being at home he has the idea again. I do not think it prudent to conclude that he has any call that way, until he has thought of it more, and is a little older. I have asked him if he would like to come back to you for a time and he says yes.

If you would like to have him by "you," I mean you and Mr. Bewsher of course—I think he cannot do better than come. You understand him and he is used to you, and we may perhaps make out among us without hurrying him what he is best fitted for. I should particularly wish him not to lose his German and to acquire Italian. It would not be very difficult for me I think, to get him into the Foreign Office, when he is old enough; and whether we thought this advisable or no he must be all the better qualified for any station, by a good knowledge of European Languages. At present he is at home here and would probably lose ground soon. I did not think it wise to send him back to Germany for several reasons.

If it would be convenient to you and not inconsistent with your discipline, to give him a little extra liberty, so that he may look about him outside school a little more, it might do him good. He does not seem to me to have the self reliance and self helpfulness of the other boys.

I only await your consent to return him to your kind care.

You will be glad to know that Sydney is flourishing and that Mr.

Brackenbury[3] wrote to me strongly in praise of the manner in which Alfred[4] had been trained. He said he thought it decidedly advisable that he should not rest content with his direct appointment but should study for the competitive examination for Engineers with a view rather to the British or Indian Army. I gave my consent of course.

My daughters and their aunt unite with me in kind regard to Mr. Bewsher and yourself.—I am ever My Dear Sir,—Yours Faithfully and obliged.

1. Revd M. Gibson.
2. Francis Jeffrey 'Frank' Dickens (1844–86), Dickens's third son and fifth child, educated at Boulogne (1853–8) and Hamburg (1858–60), had difficulty settling down in a career of his choice. '[A]ll professions are barred against me,' he told his father in a letter sent to Dickens from Hamburg in May 1859, and stammering, Frank said, forced him to give up all thoughts of being a doctor. 'The only thing I should like to be is a gentleman-farmer, either at the Cape, in Canada, or Australia. With my passage paid, fifteen pounds, a horse, and a rifle, I could go two or three hundred miles up country, sow grain, buy cattle, and in time be very comfortable.' (N, III, 104)
   In 1861 Dickens thought that he had solved Frank's problem by taking him into the office of *AYR*. 'If I am not mistaken,' Dickens wrote to Cerjat, 'he has a natural literary taste and capacity, and may do very well with a chance so congenial to his mind, and being also entered at the Bar' (N, III, 209). Frank did not find the work to his liking; he joined the Bengal Mounted Police and went to India in 1863. He returned to England in 1871 and left again in 1874 to spend the remainder of his years in the Canadian Mounties, where he rose to the rank of Inspector and became well known as one of the 'coolest and most intrepid soldiers' in the North-west Mounted Police.' See *The Dickensian*, 15 (July 1919), 163.
3. Revd J. M. Brackenbury, co-owner (with Revd C. J. Wynne) of the school in Wimbledon Alfred attended.
4. Alfred D'Orsay Tennyson Dickens (1845–1912), Dickens's fourth son and sixth child. Educated at Boulogne (1853–9) and Wimbledon School (1859–62), Alfred prepared for an army career, but did not win a place at the Royal Military Academy at Woolwich. After two years in a mercantile house in London, Alfred sailed to Melbourne in May 1865. 'His object is,' Dickens explained, 'to become employed in some business-house in Australia, and gradually to make his way in the new world.' (N, III, 421) Two years later, Dickens learned, 'with great relief of mind', that Alfred 'had struck out the path in life for which he is best fitted' and that his interests seemed to be 'inseparable from a wholesome sense of responsibility' (N, III, 558). Alfred lived in Australia till 1911 and then went to the US on a lecture tour, where he died in 1912. Mary Lazarus provides full details of the later careers of Alfred and Edward Dickens after they emigrated to Australia in *A Tale of Two Brothers: Charles Dickens's Sons in Australia* (Sydney: Angus and Robertson, 1973).

TAVISTOCK HOUSE, LONDON
Wednesday Fourteenth March 1860

MY DEAR SIR,[1]—I am much obliged to you for your letter not desiring to unsettle Frank still more. I have not yet intimated to him that I contemplate new arrangements for him while they are as yet uncompleted. But I hope to remove him about Easter. When he was at last at home I thought him in a desultory unprofitable kind of state; and I have since had it in my mind to find an opportunity of setting him to work.

Next, as to Harry.[2] I am very reluctant to withdraw him from your care, but I fear I shall be obliged to do so at midsummer. His youngest brother,[3] as the only child at home, has become such an article of household furniture that my eldest daughter[4] is unwilling to send him as far as Boulogne. It is advisable that the two should be educated together; and I am inclined to think that the Rochester Grammar School, which is near my little country place, would reconcile the difficulties of the case. You will, I am sure, understand that if I remove Harry, it will be solely for this reason, and not because I have the slightest doubt of your establishment, or any but the very highest opinion of yourself and Mr Gibson. The friendly regard and interest with which you have inspired me, and the sense I entertain of your excellent training of the boys, could not be easily over-stated.

The gallant Sydney is in immense repute at Portsmouth, and is shewn (I hear) to visitors, as one of the curiosities of the place. When he is in the country with me, he usually lives up a tree or on the top of a pole.

With kind regards to Mr Gibson, and Believe me My Dear Sir,—Very faithfully Yours.

1. Revd J. Bewsher.
2. Henry Fielding 'Harry' Dickens (1849–1933), Dickens's eighth child and sixth son, educated at Boulogne (1858–60), Rochester Grammar School (?1860–1), and Wimbledon (1861–8). Harry resisted his father's wish to see him enter the Indian Civil Service and held out for going to Cambridge instead.
3. Plorn.
4. Mamie.

OFFICE OF ALL THE YEAR ROUND
Monday Night, Twenty-Fourth September, 1860

MY DEAREST GEORGY,—At the Waterloo station we were saluted with "Hallo! here's Dickens!" from divers naval cadets, and Sir Richard Bromley[1] introduced himself to me, who had his cadet son with him, a friend of Sydney's. We went down together, and the boys were in the closest alliance. Bromley being Accountant-General of the Navy, and having influence on board, got their hammocks changed so that they would swing side by side, at which they were greatly pleased. The moment we stepped on board, the "Hul-lo! here's Dickens!" was repeated on all sides, and the Admiral (evidently highly popular) shook hands with about fifty of his messmates. Taking Bromley for my model (with whom I fraternised in the most pathetic manner), I gave Sydney a sovereign before stepping over the side. He was as little overcome as it was possible for a boy to be, and stood waving the gold-banded cap as we came ashore in a boat.

There is no denying that he looks very small abroad a great ship, and that a boy must have a strong and decided speciality for the sea to take to such a life. Captain Harris[2] was not on board, but the other chief officers were, and were highly obliging. We went over the ship. I should say that there can be little or no individuality of address to any particular boy, but that they all tumble through their education in a crowded way. The Admiral's servant (I mean our Admiral's) had an idiotic appearance, but perhaps it did him injustice (a mahogany-faced marine by station). The Admiral's washing apparatus is about the size of a muffin-plate, and he could easily live in his chest. The meeting with Bromley was a piece of great good fortune, and the dear old chap could not have been left more happily.[3]—Ever, my dearest Georgy, your most affectionate.

1. Sir Richard Madox Bromley (1813–66), civil servant; from 1854, Accountant-General of the Navy.
2. Captain Robert Harris, RN (1809–65), commander of the *Illustrious* training ship, 1854–9, and the *Britannia*, on which Sydney shipped, until 1862.
3. After Sydney passed his exam as a naval cadet, he came home, Dickens reported on 14 Sep. to Mrs Watson, 'all eyes and gold buttons'. In the interval before joining his training ship, Dickens saw him outfitted and then sent him off for Portsmouth (N, III, 183), where he embarked on the *Britannia* on 24 Sept. Sydney passed out of the training ship a year later and sailed to America on the *Orlando* in Dec. 1861 (N, III, 268; 279).

QUEEN'S HEAD, NEWCASTLE-ON-TYNE
Saturday, Twenty-Third November, 1861
MY DEAREST MAMIE,—A most tremendous hall here[1] last night; something almost terrible in the cram. A fearful thing might have happened. Suddenly, when they were all very still over Smike,[2] my gas batten came down, and it looked as if the room was falling. There were

three great galleries crammed to the roof, and a high steep flight of stairs, and a panic must have destroyed numbers of people. A lady in the front row of stalls screamed, and ran out wildly towards me, and for one instant there was a terrible wave in the crowd. I addressed that lady laughing (for I knew she was in sight of everybody there), and called out as if it happened every night, "There's nothing the matter, I assure you; don't be alarmed; pray sit down;" and she sat down directly, and there was a thunder of applause. It took some few minutes to mend, and I looked on with my hands in my pockets; for I think if I had turned my back for a moment there might still have been a move. My people were dreadfully alarmed, Boycett[3] in particular, who I suppose had some notion that the whole place might have taken fire.

"But there stood the master," he did me the honour to say afterwards, in addressing the rest, "as cool as ever I see him a-lounging at a railway-station."—Ever affectionately.

P.S.—Duty to Mrs. Bouncer.[4]

1. The Newcastle reading occurred during Dickens's second series, a provincial tour lasting from 28 Oct. 1861 to 30 Jan. 1862.
2. For conflicting opinions on the rendering of Smike in *Nicholas Nickleby at Mr. Squire's School*, see Collins, *The Public Readings*, pp 251–2.
3. Unidentified.
4. A Pomeranian dog in the Dickens household.

CARRICK'S ROYAL HOTEL, GLASGOW
Tuesday, Third December, 1861

MY DEAR WILLS,—From a paragraph, a letter, and an advertisement in a Scotsman I send you with this,[1] you may form some dim guess at the scene we had in Edinburgh last night. I think I may say that I never saw a crowd before.

As I was quietly dressing, I heard the people (when the doors were opened) come in with a most unusual crash; and I was very much struck by the place's obviously filling to the throat within five minutes. But I thought no more of it, dressed placidly, and went in at the usual time. I then found that there was a tearing mad crowd in all the passages and in the street, and that they were forcing a great turbid stream of people into the already crammed hall. The moment I appeared, 50 frantic men addressed me at once, and 50 other frantic men got upon ledges and cornices, and tried to find private audiences of their own. Meantime the crowd outside still forced the turbid stream in, and I began to have some general idea that the platform would be driven through the wall behind it, and the wall into the street. You know that your Respected Chief has a spice of coolness in him, and is not altogether unaccustomed to public speaking. Without the exercise of the two qualities, I think we should all have been there now. But when the uproarious spirits (who, as we strongly suspect, didn't pay at all) saw that it was quite impossible to disturb me, they gave in, and there was a dead silence. Then I told them, of course in the best way I could think of, that I was heartily sorry, but that this was the fault of their own townsman (it was decidedly the fault of Wood's people, with maybe a trifle of preliminary assistance from Headland[2]); that I would do anything to set it right; that I would at once adjourn to the Music Hall, if they thought it best; or that I would alter my arrangements and come back and read to all Edinburgh if they would.[3] (Meantime Gordon,[4] if you please, is softening the crowd outside, and dim reverberations of his stentorian roars are audible.) At this there is great cheering, and they cry, "Go on, Mr. Dickens. Everybody will be quiet now." Uproarious spirit exclaims, "We *won't* be quiet. We won't let the reading be heard. We're ill-treated." Respected Chief says, "There's plenty of time, and you may rely upon it that the reading is in no danger of being heard until we are agreed." Thereupon good-humouredly shuts up book. Laugh turned against uproarious spirit, and uproarious spirit, shouldered out. Respected Chief prepares, amidst calm, to begin, when gentleman (with full dressed lady torn to ribbons on his arm) cries out: "Mr. Dickens!"—"Sir."—"Couldn't some people, at all events ladies, be accommodated on your platform?" "Most certainly." Loud cheering. "Which way can they come to the platform, Mr. Dickens?" "Round here to my left." In a minute the platform was crowded. Everybody who came up, laughed, and said it was nothing when I told them in a low voice how sorry I was; but the moment they were there, the sides began to roar, because they couldn't see! At least half the people were ladies, and I then proposed to them to sit down or lie down. Instantly they all dropped into recumbent groups, with Respected Chief standing up in the centre. I don't know what it looked like most—a battlefield—an impossible tableau—a gigantic picnic. There was one very pretty girl in full dress lying down on her side all night, and holding on to one leg of my table. So I read Nickleby and the Trial. From the beginning to the end they didn't lose one point, and they ended with a great burst of cheering.

Very glad to hear that Morley's American article is done.[5] Rather fagged today, but not very. So no more at present.—Ever faithfully.

Will you reply to enclosed letter. 200 Stalls let here for tonight.

1. The confusion attending Dickens's readings at the Queen Street Hall, Edinburgh, on 30 Nov. and 2 Dec. arose because he gave three different performances and because Headland issued tickets which could be used at any one. When an unexpected proportion of ticket holders chose the last night (*NN* and the trial scene from *PP*), chaos resulted. 'The misarrangement was no fault of his,' *The Scotsman* reported on 3 Dec. 1861, 'but was due to "a townsman of our own" ' (Wood), assisted, as Dickens says to Wills, by Headland. Evidently Dickens sent Wills a copy of this paragraph from the paper, together with a reader's letter to the Editor ('What the Dickens?') on the same day complaining about the faulty arrangements, and an advertisement from *The Scotsman* (30 Nov. 1861) about the readings.
2. Thomas Headland, Dickens's tour-manager after Arthur Smith died on 1 Oct. 1861 shortly before the second series began. Although Headland proved 'so anxious' to do well and 'so good-tempered" that Dickens could not be stormy with him (N, III, 258), Dickens chafed at his incompetence and replaced 'Blockheadland' (N, III, 340) after the completion of the London readings in the spring of 1863.
3. Dickens did indeed return, in fulfillment of his pledge, to read again at Queen's Street Hall on 7 Dec. (*The Scotsman*, 7 Dec. 1861).
4. John Thomson Gordon (1813–65), advocate; sheriff of Midlothian 1849–65.
5. Morley's 'American Disunion' appeared in *AYR*, 21 Dec. 1861. In it Morley commented favourably on James Spence's defence of the South, *The American Union: Its Effects on National Character and Policy, with an Inquiry into Secession as a Constitutional Right, and the Causes of Disruption*, London, 1861.

GAD'S HILL
Tuesday, Seventh October, 1862

[Mrs Henry Austin] . . . I do not preach consolation because I am unwilling to preach at any time, and know my own weakness too well. But in this world there is no stay but the hope of a better, and no reliance but on the mercy and goodness of God. Through those two harbours of a shipwrecked heart, I fully believe that you will, in time, find a peaceful resting-place even on this careworn earth.[1] Heaven speed the time, and do you try hard to help it on! It is impossible to say but that our prolonged grief for the beloved dead may grieve them in their unknown abiding-place, and give them trouble. The one influencing consideration in all you do as to your disposition of yourself (coupled, of course, with a real earnest strenuous endeavour to recover the lost tone of spirit) is, that you think and feel you *can* do. I do not in the least regard your change of course in going to Havre as any evidence of instability. But I rather hope it is likely that through such restlessness you will come to a far quieter frame of mind. The disturbed mind and affections, like the tossed sea, seldom calm without an intervening time of confusion and trouble.

But nothing is to be attained without striving. In a determined effort to settle the thoughts, to parcel out the day, to find occupation regularly or to make it, to be up and doing something, are chiefly to be found the mere mechanical means which must come to the aid of the best mental efforts.

It is a wilderness of a day, here, in the way of blowing and raining, and as darkly dismal, at four o'clock, as need be. My head is but just now, raised from a day's writing, but I will not lose the post without sending you a word. [. . .]

1. Henry Austin died in 1861. As the trustee of the estate, Dickens took the responsibility for helping Austin's widow, Letitia, and obtaining for her in June 1864 an annual pension from the London Sanitary Commission, where Austin worked as the Secretary. (N, III, 247, 254, and 391)

3 HANOVER TERRACE
Twenty-Fifth March 1861

MY DEAR BEARD,—Since you mentioned to me in the last note I had from you, that you were doing some little things for the Observer, I have been again and again turning over in my mind the old question whether there are not some kinds of articles that you surely could do for All the Year Round.

To make what I mean as practical and intelligible as possible in the shortest way, I send you a pamphlet I have lately received,[1] which in the main expresses the views I have often urged respecting Prison Discipline, which sensibly shews what evil is done by injudicious Jail-Chaplains, and points out in what glaring respects their pet ways of carrying on are wrong. Now, don't you think that you could write just such an abstract of this pamphlet, and accounts of this question according to its writer's views, as I want? And don't you think you could do it quite as well as another man? *I do*.

If you can find it in your heart to make the attempt, only fancy throughout that you are doing your utmost to tell some man something in the pleasantest and most intelligent way that is natural to you, and that he is on the whole a pleasant and intelligent fellow too, though rather afraid of being bored, and I really cannot doubt your coming out well. It is painful to me to consider that these subjects are constantly arising; that they must be done by someone; and that they are always going into other hands while yours are empty.

And talking of emptiness: why don't you come into my room at St. James's Hall where there is always a lump of Ice and a little old Brandy? Why do I see you sitting on the ends of rows whence you could glide out like the old Serpent, and sticking there like a fixture???—Ever affectionately.

1. Dickens asked Beard to summarize Charles Pennell Measor's *Convict Service: A Letter to Sir G[eorge] C[ornewall] Lewis*, London, 1861. At that time, Measor served as the Deputy-Governor of Chatham convict prison; Beard's article, 'A Dialogue Concerning Convicts,' *AYR*, 1 May 1861, summarized Measor's view that prisons should both reclaim and punish and that convicts should be put to useful work.

PARIS, RUE DU FAUBOURG ST. HONORE, 27
Fourth November 1862

MY DEAR BEARD,—Mary, Georgina, and I, are here until just before Christmas day.

I am going to ask you rather a startling, staggering question. Hold up, therefore!

If I were to decide to go and read in Australia, how stand your inclination and spirits for going with me?[1] Outside term of absence, a year. Period of departure May or June. Overland journey both ways. The journey and climate are said to be wonderful restorers. The work would be, seconding the Inimitable in the ring, delivering him at the scratch in fine condition, keeping off the crowd, polishing him up when at all punished, and checking the local accounts. The Arthur Smith class of arrangements would necessarily have to be made by the Colonial sharer, and my bottle holder would merely in all things represent me. A servant should go, to valet both of us, and make washing and dressing easy.

Observe. I don't in the least know that I shall go. But supposing I *did* re-open the question with the Australian people, and supposing the negotiations *did* proceed to the going point, and supposing you *did* like the notion of what such a trip would ensure you free of all expense, do you feel equal to it? There are not six men in the world, I would go with—and I don't know the other five!

I cannot too strongly put to you when I come bursting at you with this surprising question, the extreme uncertainty in which the matter stands. But I am wavering between reading in Australia and writing a book at home; that, in strict confidence, is the whole truth. If I were to go to Australia, I would not let myself out, but would go with my own capital and on my own account. The man who came over to bid for me, has gone back. "Shall I write out to him and ask him on what terms he will become my agent?" is the question that revolves in my mind. I may not write at all. I may write, and his reply may be such that it will all come to nothing three months hence. But constantly disturbed and dazzled by the great chances that seem to lie waiting over there, I am restless—and this mark of my confidence in my old comrade is the very first form my restlessness has shaped out for itself.

I parted with the bidder thus: "I cannot go now, I don't know that I ever *can* go, and therefore terms are not in question. But if I can ever make up my mind to go, I will certainly communicate with your Melbourne House." (He opened the business with me by producing a letter of credit for £10,000.)

Write me a word when you get your breath again.—Startlingly always,—THE INIMITABLE.

1. As soon as Dickens began his public readings in 1858, invitations to read abroad quickly followed. James T. Fields writes that he 'began to press [Dickens] very hard' that spring to come to America (*In and Out of Doors with Charles Dickens* (1876; repr. New York, Ams Press Inc. 1976), p. 42); in June 1862 an Australian in London offered Dickens £10 000 for an eight months' tour (N, III, 298). Dickens took this proposal seriously thinking at first he might take Charles Collins with him as his secretary (N, III, 312); later he asked Beard. The notion of the long separation from home led to Dickens's rejecting the possibility of going to Australia, and the outbreak of the Civil War in America (1861–5) forced him to postpone a serious consideration of reading there until the war finished.

According to Dolby, Dickens retained his interest in going to Australia even after the American visit of 1867–8. '[I]t was his earnest desire,' writes Dolby, who says that Dickens's 'strong paternal yearning' to see his sons in Australia added a further incentive. 'Without doubt . . . this voyage would have been made,' thought Dolby, had not Dickens's health given way in 1869 (*Charles Dickens As I Knew Him*, pp 416–7).

HOTEL DU HELDER, PARIS
Wednesday, Fourth February, 1863

MY DEAR WILLS,—[. . .]
MYSELF AND PARIS.

It is really the general Parisian impression that such a hit was never made here.[1] The curiosity and interest and general buzz about it are quite indescribable. They are so extraordinarily quick to understand a face and gesture, going together, that one of the remarkable points is, that people who don't understand English, positively understand the Readings! I suppose that such an audience for a piece of Art is not to be found in the world. I wish you could have seen them—firstly, for my effect upon them—secondly, for their effect upon me. You have no idea what they made of me. I got things out of the old Carol—effects I mean—so entirely new and so very strong, that I quite amazed myself and wondered where I was going next. I really listened to Mr. Peggotty's narrative in Copperfield, with admiration. When Little Emily's letter was read, a low murmur of irrepressible emotion went about like a sort of sea. When Steerforth made a pause in shaking hands with Ham, they all lighted up as if the notion fired an electric chain. When David proposed to Dora, gorgeous beauties all radiant with diamonds, clasped their fans between their two hands, and rolled about in ecstasy. They took the storm as if they were in it. As to the Trial,[2] their perception of the Witnesses, and particularly of Mr. Winkle, was quite extraordinary. And whenever they saw the old Judge coming in, they tapped one another and laughed with that amazing relish that I could hardly help laughing as much myself. All this culminated on the last night, when they positively applauded and called out expressions of delight, out of the room into the cloak room, out of the cloak room into their carriages, and in their carriages away down the Faubourg.

Of course, if I had gone on, I could have made a great deal of money. But I thought the dignified course was to stop. I could not reconcile myself to the notion of making the charitable help, the stepping-stone. So, for the present, I have done here. [. . .]

I leave here tomorrow morning long before post time.—Ever, My Dear Wills,—Faithfully yours.

1. Dickens gave readings for Charity at the British Embassy, Paris, on 17, 29 and 30 Jan.
2. *The Trial from Pickwick*, Dickens's most popular reading after the *Carol*.

16 HYDE PARK GATE, SOUTH KENSINGTON GORE, W.

Saturday, First March, 1862

MY DEAR CHORLEY,[1]—I was at your lecture this afternoon, and I hope I may venture to tell you that I was extremely pleased and interested. Both the matter of the materials and the manner of their arrangement were quite admirable, and a modesty and complete absence of any kind of affectation pervaded the whole discourse, which was quite an example to the many whom it concerns. If you could be a very little louder, and would never let a sentence go for the thousandth part of an instant until the last word is out, you would find the audience more responsive.

A spoken sentence will never run alone in all its life, and is never to be trusted to itself in its most insigificant member. See it *well out*—with the voice—and the part of the audience is made surprisingly easier. In that excellent description of the Spanish mendicant and his guitar, as well as the very happy touches about the dance and castanets, the people were really desirous to express very hearty appreciation; but by giving them rather too much to do in watching and listening for latter words, you stopped them. I take the liberty of making the remark, as one who has fought with wild beasts (oratorically) in divers arenas. For the rest nothing could be better. Knowledge, ingenuity, neatness, condensation, good sense, and good taste in delightful combination.—Affectionately always.

1. Henry Fothergill Chorley (1808–72), music critic for the *Athenaeum*, literary reviewer and writer. Chorley's lecture on 1 Mar. 1862 was the first of four he gave at the Royal Institution on 'The National Music of the World'. The lectures were subsequently edited by Henry G. Hewlett and published under same title in 1880.

GAD'S HILL PLACE, HIGHAM BY ROCHESTER, KENT
Monday Seventh November 1864

DEAR SIR,[1]—Mrs. Cary having mentioned to my sister-in-law that you would be glad to compare notes with me on likely means of ensuring relief in reading to a congregation, I very readily offer you a few slight words of suggestions out of my own practice and experience.

The main point is difficult to express, and will have, I am sensible, a very cold appearance on this paper. If you could form a habit of finding your voice *lower down*—in other words, of reading more from the chest and less from the throat—you would find yourself immensely relieved, and your voice greatly strengthened—when you experience any little distress or difficulty now, I think it is in the throat; and I think that is because the strain is in the wrong place. If you make the trial, reading aloud, of placing your hand on your chest, and trying as it were to sing with your voice behind the hand, you will probably soon find a capacity in it almost new to you—while the ease of speaking will be correspondingly increased.

I should have supposed your perfectly unaffected reading of the lessons to be generally audible throughout the church. If it is not so, it may pretty nearly be made so by addressing the last person in the Building and your being always watchful not to drop the voice towards the close of a sentence or a verse, but rather to sustain and prolong the distinctness of the concluding words, always supposing the words to be well separated and never run into one another. I believe that a very moderate voice, observing this method, may be heard with ease and pleasure in a large place, when a very powerful voice, neglecting it, might be quite ineffective. The habit of reading *downhill*, or dropping the voice as the sentence proceeds, is so extremely common, that perhaps even if Mrs. Cary were to happen to read a few pages to you by the fireside, you would detect yourself asking what this or that lost word towards the close of a sentence was. Imagine how fatal the fault must be to distinctness when there are listeners at various removed distances.

I should be more diffident than I am in offering these simple hints, if I had not habitually acted on them with the result that I am said to be always heard.

To be of the least service to you would be a great pleasure to me—with which sincere assurance—I am dear Sir—Faithfully yours.

1. Revd Christopher Cary, unidentified.

GAD'S HILL PLACE, HIGHAM BY ROCHESTER, KENT
Tuesday, Thirteenth June, 1865
MY DEAR MITTON,—I should have written to you yesterday or the day before, if I had been quite up to writing.

I was in the only carriage that did not go over into the stream.[1] It was caught upon the turn by some of the ruin of the bridge, and hung suspended and balanced in an apparently impossible manner. Two ladies[2] were my fellow-passengers, an old one and a young one. This is exactly what passed. You may judge from it the precise length of the suspense: Suddenly we were off the rail, and beating the ground as the car of a half-emptied balloon might. The old lady cried out, "My God!" and the young one screamed. I caught hold of them both (the old lady sat opposite and the young one on my left), and said: "We can't help ourselves, but we can be quiet and composed. Pray don't cry out." The old lady immediately answered: "Thank you. Rely upon me. Upon my soul I will be quiet." We were then all tilted down together in a corner of the carriage, and stopped. I said to them thereupon: "You may be sure nothing worse can happen. Our danger *must* be over. Will you remain here without stirring, while I get out of the window?" They both answered quite collectedly, "Yes," and I got out without the least notion what had happened. Fortunately I got out with great caution and stood upon the step. Looking down I saw the bridge gone, and nothing below me but the line of rail. Some people in the two other compartments were madly trying to plunge out of window, and had no idea that there was an open swampy field fifteen feet down below them, and nothing else! The two guards (one with his face cut) were running up and down on the down side of the bridge (which was not torn up) quite wildly. I called out to them: "Look at me. Do stop an instant and look at me, and tell me whether you don't know me." One of them answered: "We know you very well, Mr. Dickens." "Then," I said, "my good fellow, for God's sake give me your key, and send one of those labourers here, and I'll empty this carriage." We did it quite safely, by means of a plank or two, and when it was done I saw all the rest of the train, except the two baggage vans, down in the stream. I got into the carriage again for my brandy flask, took off my travelling hat for a basin, climbed down the brickwork, and filled my hat with water.

Suddenly I came upon a staggering man covered with blood (I think he must have been flung clean out of his carriage), with such a frightful cut across the skull that I couldn't bear to look at him. I poured some water over his face and gave him some drink, then gave him some brandy, and laid him down on the grass, and he said, "I am gone," and died afterwards. Then I stumbled over a lady lying on her back against a little pollard-tree, with the blood streaming over her face (which was lead colour) in a number of distinct little streams from the head. I asked her if she could swallow a little brandy and she just nodded, and I gave her some and left her for somebody else. The next time I passed her she was dead. Then a man, examined at the inquest yesterday (who evidently had not the least remembrance of what really passed) came running up to me and implored me to help him find his wife, who was afterwards found dead. No imagination can conceive the ruin of the carriages, or the extraordinary weights under which the people were lying, or the complications into which they were twisted up among iron and wood, and mud and water.

I don't want to be examined at the inquest and I don't want to write about it. I could do no good either way, and I could only seem to speak about myself, which, of course, I would rather not do. I am keeping very quiet here. I have a—I don't know what to call it—constitutional (I suppose) presence of mind, and was not in the least fluttered at the time. I instantly remembered that I had the MS. of a number with me, and clambered back into the carriage for it.[3] But in writing these scanty words of recollection I feel the shake and am obliged to stop.—Ever faithfully.

1. The railway accident Dickens refers to occurred around 3.15 p.m. on 9

June 1865 shortly after the fast tidal train from Folkestone to London had received the signal 'All right' at Headcorn, Kent, and passed on towards Staplehurst at 50 m.p.h. About 1½ miles along the track plate layers making routine repairs to the line had removed a section of rails on a low bridge crossing a small stream, unaware of the approaching train. The foreman had misread the train's departure time, which varied with the tides and awaited the arrival of boat passengers from Boulogne; when the driver saw the improperly posted warning signal, he could not stop. The engine leaped over the gap in the rails, travelling about 15 m.p.h., and the train broke in two. Five or six carriages plunged into the stream below and were severely crushed; Dickens's, the only first-class carriage to escape, rested precariously on the bridge. Ten people were killed and twenty wounded (see *The Times*, 10 June 1865, p. 9; 12 June, p. 5; and 13 June, p. 14, and T. W. Hill, 'The Staplehurst Railway Accident', *The Dickensian*, 38 (Summer 1942), 147–52.

Dickens and Ellen Ternan, with whom he was travelling after the two returned from a brief vacation in Paris at the end of May (Johnson, ii, 1018) received no injuries but both were shaken, especially Dickens. The effects of the accident, Forster thought, were 'for some time evident; and, up to the day of his death on its fatal fifth anniversary, were perhaps never wholly absent' (Forster, ix, v, 294). Dickens's energetic assistance to the wounded and dying was praised by a fellow passenger in 'A Passenger's Account of the Accident' published in the *Illustrated Police News* of 17 June 1865. Extracts of this letter appear in the *The Dickensian*, 67 (Sep. 1971), 159–60; the complete text can be found in the 'Chronicle', *AR*, 9 June 1865, p. 72. For his services to the injured, Dickens received a piece of plate from the South Eastern Railway.

2. Ellen Ternan and her mother.

3. In the 'Postscript in lieu of a preface' to *OMF*, Dickens describes how he climbed back into the carriage to rescue a part of the MS of *OMF* after assisting the injured.

OFFICE OF ALL THE YEAR ROUND
Friday, Ninth February, 1866

MY DEAREST GEORGY,— . . . Frank Beard[1] wrote me word that with such a pulse as I described, an examination of the heart was absolutely necessary, and that I had better make an appointment with him alone for the purpose. This I did. I was not at all disconcerted, for I knew well beforehand that the effect could not possibly be without that one cause at the bottom of it. There seems to be degeneration of some functions of the heart. It does not contract as it should. So I have got a prescription of iron, quinine, and digitalis, to set it a-going, and send the blood more quickly through the system. If it should not seem to succeed on a reasonable trial, I will then propose a consultation with someone else. Of course I am not so foolish as to suppose that all my work can have been achieved without *some* penalty, and I have noticed for some time a decided change in my buoyancy and hopefulness—in other words, in my usual "tone.". . .

1. Francis Carr Beard (1814–93), FRCS, the family doctor in 1859 and Dickens's medical adviser until the novelist's death. Beard, younger brother of Dickens's old friend Thomas, practised medicine in Welbeck Street, London.

GAD'S HILL PLACE
1st January 1867

[John Forster] . . . We had made a very pretty course, and taken great pains. Encouraged by the cricket matches experience,[1] I allowed the landlord of the Falstaff to have a drinking-booth on the ground. Not to seem to dictate or distrust, I gave all the prizes (about ten pounds in the aggregate) in money. The great mass of the crowd were labouring men of all kinds, soldiers, sailors, and navvies. They did not, between half-past ten, when we began, and sunset, displace a rope or a stake; and they left every barrier and flag as neat as they found it. There was not a dispute, and there was no drunkenness whatever. I made them a little speech from the lawn, at the end of the games, saying that please God we would do it again next year. They cheered most lustily and dispersed. The road between this and Chatham was like a Fair all day; and surely it is a fine thing to get such perfect behaviour out of a reckless seaport town. Among other oddities we had A Hurdle Race for Strangers. One man (he came in second) ran 120 yards and leaped over ten hurdles, in twenty seconds, *with a pipe in his mouth, and smoking it all the time*. "If it hadn't been for your pipe," I said to him at the winning-post, "you would have been first." "I beg your pardon, sir," he answered, "but if it hadn't been for my pipe, I should have been nowhere." . . . The sale of the Christmas number was, yesterday evening, 255,380.[2]. . .

1. In the summer of 1866 Dickens arranged two cricket matches involving local players, (N, III, 479); and encouraged by their success, he 'got up a quantity of footraces and rustic sports' on 26 Nov. 1866 (N, III, 494). Dickens also provided a drinking booth and cash prizes to add to the festivities, which went off so well that he resolved upon more field sports for New Year's day 1867. 'There were between two and three thousand people present,' wrote Mary Dickens of this second occasion, 'and by a kind of magical influence, my father seemed to rule every creature present to do his or her best to maintain order. The likelihood of things going wrong was anticipated, and despite the general prejudice of the neighbours against the undertaking, 'my father's belief and trust in his guests was not disappointed.' See *My Father as I Recall Him* (New York: E. P. Dutton, n.d.), p. 42.
2. *Mugby Junction*, Dec. 1866.

NEWCASTLE-ON-TYNE
Wednesday Sixth March 1867
[Georgina Hogarth] . . . The readings have made an immense effect in this place, and it is remarkable that although the people are individually rough, collectively they are an unusually tender and sympathetic audience; while their comic perception is quite up to the high London standard.[1] The atmosphere is so very heavy that yesterday we escaped to Tynemouth for a two hours' sea walk. There was a high north wind blowing, and a magnificent sea running. Large vessels were being towed in and out over the stormy bar, with prodigious waves breaking on it; and, spanning the restless uproar of the waters, was a quiet rainbow of transcendent beauty. The scene was quite wonderful. We were in the full enjoyment of it when a heavy sea caught us, knocked us over, and in a moment drenched us and filled even our pockets. We had nothing for it but to shake ourselves together (like Doctor Marigold),[2] and dry ourselves as well as we could by hard walking in the wind and sunshine. But we were wet through for all that, when we came back here to dinner after half-an-hour's railway drive. I am wonderfully well, and quite fresh and strong. . . .

1. The second Chappell season, arranged by Dickens's agents, Messrs S. Arthur Chappell and Thomas Chappell of Bond Street, London, lasted from 15 Jan. to 13 May 1867. See next letter.
2. Doctor Marigold, the travelling hawker who introduces the stories that make up the 1865 Christmas Number of *AYR, Doctor Marigold's Prescriptions*.

14th May 1867
[John Forster] . . . Last Monday evening I finished the 50 Readings with great success. You have no idea how I have worked at them. Finding it necessary, as their reputation widened, that they should be better than at first, I have *learnt them all*, so as to have no mechanical drawback in looking after the words. I have tested all the serious passion in them by everything I know; made the humorous points much more humorous; corrected my utterance of certain words; cultivated a self-possession not to be disturbed; and made myself master of the situation. Finishing with Dombey (which I had not read for a long time), I learnt that, like the rest; and did it to myself, often twice a day, with exactly the same pains as at night, over and over and over again. . . .

GAD'S HILL PLACE, HIGHAM BY ROCHESTER, KENT
Tuesday, Twenty-Fourth September, 1867

MY DEAR WILLS,—I send you, enclosed, a plain statement of the American question, deduced from a mass of notes and figures. Give me your opinion on it. To go, or not to go?

I have sent it to Forster in exactly the same way, with exactly the same request, and no hint of my own tending either way.

On Saturday I will call at the office sometime in the day, for a letter from you. I would rather make up on *Monday morning*, as on that day I must be in town to send off the decisive Telegram to Boston.[1]—Ever faithfully.

[The enclosure]
"THE CASE IN A NUTSHELL

"1. I think it may be taken as proved, that general enthusiasm and excitement are awakened in America on the subject of the Readings and that the people are prepared to give me a great reception. The *New York Herald*, indeed, is of opinion that 'Dickens must apologise first';[2] and where a *New York Herald* is possible, any thing is possible. But the prevailing tone, both of the press and of people of all conditions, is highly favourable. I have an opinion myself that the Irish element in New York is dangerous; for the reason that the Fenians[3] would be glad to damage a conspicuous Englishman. This is merely an opinion of my own.

"2. All our original calculations were based on 100 Readings. But an unexpected result of careful enquiry on the spot, is the discovery that the month of May is generally considered (in the large cities) bad for such a purpose. Admitting that what governs an ordinary case in this wise, governs mine, this reduces the Readings to 80,[4] and consequently at a blow makes a reduction of 20 per cent. in the means of making money within the half year—unless the objection should not apply in my exceptional instance.

"3. I dismiss the consideration that the great towns of America could not possibly be exhausted—or even visited—within 6 months, and that a large harvest would be left unreaped. Because I hold a second series of Readings in America is to be set down as out of the question: whether regarded as involving two more voyages across the Atlantic, or a vacation of five months in Canada.

"4. The narrowed calculation we have made, is this: What is the largest amount of clear profit derivable, under the most advantageous circumstances possible, as to their public reception, from 80 Readings and no more? In making this calculation, the expenses have been throughout taken on the New York scale—which is the dearest; as much as 20 per cent. has been deducted for management, including Mr. Dolby's[5] commission; and no credit has been taken for any extra payment on reserved seats, though a good deal of money is confidently expected from this source. But on the other hand it is to be observed that four Readings (and a fraction over) are supposed to take place every week, and that the estimate of receipts is based on the assumption that the audiences are, on all occasions, as large as the rooms will reasonably hold.

"5. So considering 80 Readings, we bring out the nett profit of that number, remaining to me after payment of all charges whatever, as £15,500.[6]

"6. But it yet remains to be noted that the calculation assumes New York City, and the State of New York, to be good for a very large proportion of the 80 Readings; and that the calculation also assumes the necessary travelling not to extend beyond Boston and adjacent places, New York City and adjacent places, Philadelphia, Washington, and Baltimore. But, if the calculation should prove too sanguine on this head, and if these places should *not* be good for so many Readings, then it may prove impracticable to get through 80 within the time: by reason of other places that would come into the list, lying wide asunder, and necessitating long and fatiguing journeys.

"7. The loss consequent on the conversion of paper money into gold (with gold at the present ruling premium) is allowed for in the calculation.[7] It counts seven dollars to the pound."

1. Dickens despatched the telegram to Boston on Monday 30 Sep. 'Yes. Go Ahead' (N, III, 555).
2. Made orally by James Gordon Bennett, the *Herald*'s founder and editor, who met with Dickens's manager to talk over the prospect of his visit. The following day, the *New York Herald* issued a special reprint of *AN*, free of cost, a generous and handsome act, Dolby thought. See Dolby (note below, pp 123–4). Other important newspaper editors Dolby met in New York both spoke and wrote favourably of the possibility of Dickens's returning to America to read from his works. See, for example, the *New York Tribune*, 29 Aug. 1867, p. 4 and the *New York Times*, 21 Aug. 1867, p. 4.
3. Members of an organization formed among the Irish in the US for promoting revolutionary movements opposed to English rule in Ireland. Reports of Fenian-inspired activities began to appear in the British press from the mid sixties onwards.
4. Collins, *The Public Readings*, p. xxvi, gives a total of 75 readings for the American tour between 2 Dec. and 20 Apr. 1868.

5. George Dolby, the tour-manager of the readings appointed by Messrs Chappell, who handled Dickens's readings from 1866 onwards. Dolby served from Apr. 1866 to Mar. 1870; he became Dickens's close and trusted associate and later wrote about the reading tours in *Charles Dickens as I knew Him: The Story of the Reading Tours in Great Britain and America (1866–1870)* (London: T. Fisher Unwin, 1885).
6. After paying all his expenses and Dolby's commission, Dickens banked nearly £19 000 on returning to England. See Dolby, pp 331–2, and Collins, p. xxix.
7. Collins notes that by insisting on converting dollars to gold Dickens unnecessarily incurred a loss of nearly 40 per cent of his original dollar profits of about £38 000 (p. xxix).

PARKER HOUSE, BOSTON
Thursday, Twenty-First November, 1867

MY DEAR WILLS,—A winter passage out here is, under the best circumstances (not to put too fine a point upon it) odious. But I had, in the Cuba, a fine run—was not sick for a moment—was highly popular on board—made no end of speeches after the last dinner of the voyage—sang no end of duets with the Captain (never known to come out before) and came over the side into the arms of Dolby (in a steam tug) illuminated with a blaze of triumph.

The Pilot brought the news on board that the people had stood with the greatest good temper in the freezing street, 12 hours, to buy tickets for the first four readings here (the only Readings announced), and that every ticket for every night was sold. I found it to be literally true. The gross receipts of those 4 nights are £250 beyond our calculation. New York tickets are not on sale until next week, but there are signs of the same excitement there. The Hall here is charming—I never saw a better. If I can only hit them hard with the Carol and Trial, I think our expectations may be far overpassed. Longfellow, Emerson, Holmes,[1] Agassiz,[2] and all Cambridge—Professors and Students—are booked in a phalanx for the body of the Hall on the 1st night, Monday, December the Second. Nothing can exceed the interest and heartiness of these men.

Boston, as a City, is enormously changed since I was here, and is far more mercantile. I do not yet notice any special difference in manners and customs between my old time and this time—except that there is more of New York in this fine City than there was of yore. The Hotel[3] I stayed at in my first visit has now become contemptible. This is an establishment like one of our Termini Hotels, with the addition of an immense quantity of white marble floors. I live on the third storey—our three rooms together—and have hot and cold water laid on in a bath in my bedroom, and other comforts not known in my former experience. The cuisine is very good. The cost of living is enormous. Ten Pounds sterling a day for Dolby and me is by no means a large estimate. (It was our original calculation.) Happily, Dolby has seen reason to make up his mind that the less I am shown—for nothing—the better for the Readings! So I am fended off and kept—so far—unexpectedly quiet. In addition to which I must say that I have experienced—so far—not the slightest intrusiveness, and everywhere the greatest respect and consideration. There is the utmost curiosity about the Readings, and I should not wonder if they proved to be a great surprise, seeing that the general notion stops at a mere "Reading," book in hand.

Even you, I think, will find it difficult to believe that at this moment ——[4] has not sent out the pamphlet with the Dinner Speeches!!!! Of course when it does come, it will be waste paper. The American journals all over the country have taken the account from the English Journals, and I am assured that my speech has given the highest satisfaction to the American people.

This is all my news at present—except that I am so well and so free of the ship, that I am worried by not having arranged to begin reading next Monday—for I yearn to begin to check the Readings off, and feel myself tending towards Home.

My love to Mrs. Wills, and my love to the personal and official Wilkie.[5] Fields[6] does not begin to publish the Holiday Romance until January. I will advise you in good time, when you can begin with it in A.Y.R. Take all my confidence and trust now and ever,—And Believe me,—Affectionately Yours always.

1. Henry Wadsworth Longfellow and Dickens became friends in 1842; Dickens had also met Ralph Waldo Emerson and Oliver Wendell Holmes on his first visit.
2. Jean Louis Rodolphe Agassiz (1807–73), Swiss-born scientist who was a professor of natural history at Harvard from 1848 until his death.
3. In 1842 Dickens and Catherine stayed at the Tremont House; he occupied rooms at the Parker House in 1867–8.
4. Frederick Chapman, identified by Fielding in a note (*Speeches*, p. 441). The pamphlet to which Dickens refers was prepared by Charles Kent and contained Dickens's conciliatory remarks about America and other speeches given at the Farewell Banquet of 2 Nov. 1867 prior to his departure. For the text of his address, see *Speeches*, pp 370–3 and Kent's pamphlet, *The Charles Dickens Dinner* (1867).
5. Collins helped Wills at the office of *AYR* during Dickens's absence.
6. James Thomas Fields (1817–81), writer and junior partner in Ticknor, Reed, and Fields, Dickens's main American publishers. Ticknor and Fields

published 'Holiday Romance' in *Our Young Folks; an Illustrated Magazine for Boys and Girls*, (Jan., Mar., Apr., and May, 1868); the story also appeared in *AYR*, 25 Jan.; 8 Feb.; 14 Mar.; and 4 Apr. 1868.

WESTMINSTER HOTEL, IRIVING PLACE, NEW YORK CITY
Monday, Sixteenth December, 1867

[Georgina Hogarth] ... We have been snowed up here, and the communication with Boston is still very much retarded. Thus we have received no letters by the Cunard steamer that came in last Wednesday, and are in a grim state of mind on that subject.

Last night I was getting into bed just at twelve o'clock, when Dolby came to my door to inform me that the house was on fire (I had previously smelt fire for two hours). I got Scott[1] up directly, told him to pack the books and clothes for the readings first, dressed, and pocketed my jewels and papers, while Dolby stuffed himself out with money. Meanwhile the police and firemen were in the house, endeavouring to find where the fire was. For some time it baffled their endeavours, but at last, bursting out through some stairs, they cut the stairs away, and traced it to its source in a certain fire-grate. By this time the hose was laid all through the house from a great tank on the roof, and everybody turned out to help. It was the oddest sight, and people had put the strangest things on! After a little chopping and cutting with axes and handing about of water, the fire was confined to a dining-room in which it had originated, and then everybody talked to everybody else, the ladies being particularly loquacious and cheerful. And so we got to bed again at about two.

The excitement of the readings continues unabated. They are a wonderfully fine audience, even better than Edinburgh, and almost, if not quite, as good as Paris.

Dolby continues to be the most unpopular man in America (mainly because he can't get four thousand people into a room that holds two thousand), and is reviled in print daily. Yesterday morning a newspaper proclaims of him: "Surely it is time that the pudding-headed Dolby retired into the native gloom from which he has emerged." [. . .]

1. Scott, Dickens's valet and one of the members of his reading tour party.

PHILADELPHIA
14th January 1868

[John Forster] ... I see *great changes* for the better, socially. Politically, no. England governed by the Marylebone vestry[1] and the penny papers, and England as she would be after years of such governing; is what I make of *that*. Socially, the change in manners is remarkable. There is much greater politeness and forbearance in all ways. . . . On the other hand there are still provincial oddities wonderfully quizzical; and the newspapers are constantly expressing the popular amazement at "Mr. Dickens's extraordinary composure." They seem to take it ill that I don't stagger on to the platform overpowered by the spectacle before me, and the national greatness. They are all so accustomed to do public things with a flourish of trumpets, that the notion of my coming in to read without somebody first flying up and delivering an "Oration" about me, and flying down again and leading me in, is so very unaccountable to them, that sometimes they have no idea until I open my lips that it can possibly be Charles Dickens. . . .

. . . The Irish element is acquiring such enormous influence in New York city, that when I think of it, and see the large Roman Catholic cathedral[2] rising there, it seems unfair to stigmatise as "American" other monstrous things that one also sees. But the general corruption in respect of the local funds appears to be stupendous, and there is an alarming thing as to some of the courts of law which I am afraid is native-born. A case came under my notice the other day in which it was perfectly plain, from what was said to me by a person interested in resisting an injunction, that his first proceeding had been to "look up the Judge." . . . Last night here in Philadelphia (my first night), a very impressible and responsive audience were so astounded by my simply walking in and opening my book that I wondered what was the matter. They evidently thought that there ought to have been a flourish, and Dolby sent in to prepare for me. With them it is the simplicity of the operation that raises wonder. With the newspapers "Mr. Dickens's extraordinary composure" is not reasoned out as being necessary to the art of the thing, but is sensitively watched with a lurking doubt whether it may not imply disparagement of the audience. Both these things strike me as drolly expressive. . . .

I think it reasonable to expect that as I go westward, I shall find the old manners going on before me, and may tread upon their skirts mayhap. But so far, I have had no more intrusion on boredom than I have when I lead the same life in England. I write this in an immense hotel, but I am as much at peace in my own rooms, and am left as wholly undisturbed, as if I were at the Station Hotel in York. I have now read in New York city to 40,000 people, and am quite as well known in the streets there as I am in London. People will turn back, turn again and face me, and have a look at me, or will say to one another, "Look here! Dickens coming!" But no one ever stops me or addresses me. Sitting reading in the carriage outside the New York post-office while one of the staff was stamping the letters inside, I became conscious that a few people who had been looking at the turn-out had discovered me within. On my peeping out good-humouredly, one of them (I should say a merchant's book-keeper) stepped up to the door, took off his hat, and said in a frank way: "Mr. Dickens, I should very much like to have the honour of shaking hands with you"—and, that done, presented two others. Nothing could be more quiet or less intrusive. In the railway cars, if I see anybody who clearly wants to speak to me, I usually anticipate the wish by speaking myself. If I am standing on the brake outside (to avoid the intolerable stove), people getting down will say with a smile: "As I am taking my departure, Mr. Dickens, and can't trouble you for more than a moment, I should like to take you by the hand, sir." And so we shake hands and go our ways. . . . Of course many of my impressions come through the readings. Thus I find the people lighter and more humorous than formerly; and there must be a great deal of innocent imagination among every class, or they never could pet with such extraordinary pleasure as they do, the Boots's[3] story of the elopement of the two little children. They seem to see the children; and the women set up a shrill undercurrent of half-pity and half-pleasure that is quite affecting. To-night's reading is my 26th; but as all the Philadel-phia tickets for four more are sold, as well as four at Brooklyn, you must assume that I am at—say—my 35th reading. I have remitted to Coutts's[4] in English gold £10,000 odd; and I roughly calculate that on this number Dolby will have another thousand pounds profit to pay me. These figures are of course between ourselves, at present; but are they not magnificent? The expenses, always recollect, are enormous. On the other hand we never have occasion to print a bill of any sort (bill-printing and posting are great charges at home); and have just now sold off £90 worth of bill-paper, provided beforehand, as a wholly useless incumbrance. . . .

The work is very severe. There is now no chance of my being rid of this American catarrh until I embark for England. It is very distressing. It likewise happens, not seldom, that I am so dead beat when I come off that they lay me down on a sofa after I have been washed and dressed, and I lie there, extremely faint, for a quarter of an hour. In that time I rally and come right. . . .

1. The Marylebone vestry: a body of parishioners elected by members of the congregation to conduct the business affairs of the parish.
2. The new St. Patrick's Cathedral, Fifth Avenue, New York. The corner-stone was laid in 1858 and the building dedicated in 1879.
3. 'The Boots', from *The Holly-Tree Inn*, the *HW* Christmas number for 1855.
4. Coutts's Bank, London, used by Dickens since Nov. 1837.

WASHINGTON
4th February 1868

[John Forster] . . . You may like to have a line to let you know that it is all right here, and that the croakers were simply ridiculous.[1] I began last night. A charming audience, no dissatisfaction whatever at the raised prices, nothing missed or lost, cheers at the end of the Carol, and rounds upon rounds of applause all through. All the foremost men and their families had taken tickets for the series of four. A small place to read in. £300 in it.

I am going to-morrow to see the President,[2] who has sent to me twice. I dined with Charles Sumner[3] last Sunday, against my rule; and as I had stipulated for no party, Mr. Secretary Stanton[4] was the only other guest, besides his own secretary. Stanton is a man with a very remarkable memory, and extraordinarily familiar with my books.[5] . . . He and Sumner having been the first two public men at the dying President's bedside, and having remained with him until he breathed his last, we fell into a very interesting conversation after dinner, when, each of them giving his own narrative separately, the usual discrepancies about details of time were observable. Then Mr. Stanton told me a curious little story[6] which will form the remainder of this short letter.

On the afternoon of the day on which the President was shot, there was a cabinet council at which he presided. Mr. Stanton, being at the time commander-in-chief of the Northern troops[7] that were concentrated about here, arrived rather late. Indeed they were waiting for him, and on his entering the room, the President broke off in something he was saying, and remarked: "Let us proceed to business, gentlemen." Mr. Stanton then noticed, with great surprise, that the President sat with an air of dignity in his chair instead of lolling about it in the most ungainly attitudes, as his invariable custom was; and that instead of telling irrelevant or questionable stories, he was grave and calm, and quite a different man. Mr. Stanton, on leaving the council with the Attorney-General, said to him, "That is the most satisfactory cabinet meeting I have attended for many a long day! What an extraordinary change in Mr. Lincoln!" The Attorney-General replied, "We all saw it, before you came in. While we were waiting for you, he said, with his chin down on his breast, 'Gentlemen, something very extraordinary is going to happen, and that very soon.' " To which the Attorney-General had observed, "Something good, sir, I hope?" when the President answered very gravely: "I don't know; I don't know. But it will happen, and shortly too!" As they were all impressed by his manner, the Attorney-General took him up again: "Have you received any information, sir, not yet disclosed to us?" "No," answered the President: "but I have had a dream. And I have now had the same dream three times. Once, on the night preceding the Battle of Bull Run.[8] Once, on the night preceding" such another (name a battle also not favourable to the North). His chin sank on his breast again, and he sat reflecting. "Might one ask the nature of this dream, sir?" said the Attorney-General. "Well," replied the President without lifting his head or changing his attitude, "I am on a great broad rolling river—and I am in a boat—and I drift—and I drift!—but this is not business—" suddenly raising his face and looking round the table as Mr. Stanton entered, "let us proceed to business, gentlemen." Mr. Stanton and the Attorney-General said, as they walked on together, it would be curious to notice whether anything ensued on this; and they agreed to notice. He was shot that night. . . .

1. All those forecasting that the impending impeachment of President Johnson would seriously disrupt Dickens's chances of success in Washington, D.C.
2. Andrew Johnson (1808–75), seventeenth President of the US (1865–9), who succeeded President Abraham Lincoln (1809–65) upon the latter's assassination by John Wilkes Booth on 14 Apr. 1865 at Ford's Theatre in Washington.
3. Charles Sumner (1811–74), statesman and leading Republican senator in the 1860s, first met Dickens in 1842.
4. Edwin McMasters Stanton (1814–69), US Secretary of War, 1862–8.
5. Sumner gave the dinner party at his house on 2 Feb.; Moorfield Storey, Sumner's secretary, who was also present, records how Stanton quoted accurately long passages from *PP* and how Dickens asked Stanton to offer his recollections of the night when Lincoln was shot. See Benjamin P. Thomas and Harold M. Hyman, *Stanton: The Life and Times of Lincoln's Secretary of War* (New York: Alfred A. Knopf, 1962), p. 577.
6. The anecdote, which Stanton, in turn, had from Lincoln's Attorney-General, James Speed (1812–87), appears to be based on Speed's interpretation of Mary Lincoln's cry, 'His dream was prophetic', when her husband died at 7.22 a.m. on 15 Apr. Speed and Stanton, both present during the all-night vigil by Lincoln's bedside in the room to which the President was removed after Booth shot him, did not know of the disturbing dream Mrs Lincoln referred to. Earlier in Apr., Lincoln had described to his wife and Ward Hill Lamon, a former law partner, a detailed

premonition of his death. Lincoln spoke of hearing people sobbing in his dream, and of finding the White House silent and deserted, except for a catafalque in the East Room. In answer to Lincoln's question, 'Who is dead in the White House?' one of the soldiers guarding the coffin replied that it was the President, 'killed by an assassin!' Lamon recorded the President's description of his dream immediately after the conversation, but he did not publish it until 1895 in his *Recollections of Lincoln*, pp 115–8. See Stephen B. Oates, *With Malice Toward None: The Life of Abraham Lincoln* (New York: Harper and Row, 1977), pp 425–6; and 433.

On the day of the cabinet meeting to which Dickens refers, the President woke, writes Oates, 'in a pleasant mood' because he had had *another* dream: the dream that had come to him several times 'on the eve of significant military events – especially Union victories like Antietam [a creek near Sharpsburg], Gettysburg, and Vicksburg. In the dream, he was on a phantom ship moving swiftly toward a dark and indefinite shore. It must portend favorable news today – no doubt that [Confederate General Joseph E.] Johnston had surrendered in North Carolina, thus ending organized rebel resistance.' (pp 426–7)

Speed, of course, heard Lincoln refer to this dream at the cabinet meeting on 14 Apr., but he appears to have drawn an entirely different inference from it after hearing Mrs Lincoln's comment about her husband's fate as it appeared to him in the dream Lamon recorded.

7. In 1864 Lincoln appointed Ulysses S. Grant commander in chief of the Union forces; Dickens appears to have misunderstood Stanton's position.
8. The Confederate army beat the Union Troops at the Battle of Bull Run twice: on 21 July 1861 and 30 Aug. 1862.

SPRINGFIELD, MASS.

Saturday, Twenty-First March 1868

MY DEAREST MACREADY,—What with perpetual reading and travelling, what with "a true American catarrh" (on which I am complimented almost boastfully), and what with one of the severest Winters ever known, your coals of fire received by the last mail did not burn my head so much as they might have done under less excusatory circumstances. But they scorched it too!

You would find the general aspect of America and Americans, decidedly much improved. You would find immeasurably greater consideration and respect for your privacy, than of old. . . . You would find a steady change for the better everywhere except, (oddly enough) in the Railways generally; which seem to have stood still, while everything else has moved. But there is an exception Westward. There, the Express trains have now a very delightful carriage called a "Drawing Room Car"—literally, a series of little private drawing rooms, with sofas and a table in each, opening out of a little corridor. In each, too, is a large plate glass window, with which you can do as you like. As you pay extra for this luxury, it may be regarded as the first move towards two classes of passengers. When the Railroad straight away to San Francisco (in 6 days) shall be opened through,[1] it will not only have these drawing rooms, but sleeping rooms too, a bell in every little apartment communicating with a steward's pantry, a Restaurant, a staff of servants, marble washing-stands and a barber's shop! I looked into one of these cars a day or two ago, and it was very ingeniously arranged and quite complete.

I left Niagara last Sunday and travelled on to Albany through 300 miles of flood—villages deserted, bridges broken, fences drifting away, nothing but tearing water, floating ice, and absolute wreck and ruin. The train gave in altogether at Utica and we passengers were let loose there for the night. As I was due at Albany, a very active superintendent of works did all he could to "get Mr. Dickens along," and in the morning we resumed our journey—through the water—with a hundred men in seven league boots pushing the ice from before us with long poles. How we got to Albany I can't say, but we got there somehow, just in time for a triumphant Carol, and Trial. All the tickets had been sold and we found the Albanians in a state of great excitement. You may imagine what the flood was when I tell you that we took the passengers out of two trains that had had their fires put out by the water, four and twenty hours before; and that we released a number of sheep and horned cattle from trucks that had been in the water—I don't know how long, but so long that the sheep had begun to eat each other. It was a horrible spectacle and the haggard human misery of their faces was quite a new study. There was a fine breath of Spring in the air concurrently with this great thaw; but lo and behold! last night it began to snow again with a strong wind; and today a snow drift covers this place with all the desolation of Winter once more. I never was so tired of the sight of snow. As to sleighing, I have been sleighing about to that extent, that I am sick of the sound of a sleighbell. . . .

God bless you and all dear to you, my dear old friend!—I am ever your affectionate and loving.

1. On 10 May 1869 the construction crews of America's first transcontinental railroad met and joined tracks at Promontory, Utah, in the mountains north of Great Salt Lake.

GAD'S HILL, HIGHAM BY ROCHESTER, KENT
Twenty-Fifth May, 1868

MY DEAR MRS. FIELDS,[1]—As you ask me about the dogs, I begin with
them. When I came down first, I came to Gravesend, five miles off. The
two Newfoundland dogs,[2] coming to meet me with the usual carriage
and the usual driver, and beholding me coming in my usual dress out at
the usual door, it struck me that their recollection of my having been
absent for any unusual time was at once cancelled. They behaved (they
are both young dogs) exactly in their usual manner; coming behind the
basket phaeton as we trotted along, and lifting their heads to have their
ears pulled—a special attention which they receive from no one else.
But when I drove into the stable-yard, Linda (the St. Bernard) was
greatly excited; weeping profusely, and throwing herself on her back
that she might caress my foot with her great fore-paws. Mamie's little
dog, too, Mrs. Bouncer, barked in the greatest agitation on being
called down and asked by Mamie, "Who is this?" and tore round and
round me, like the dog in the Faust outlines.[3] You must know that all
the farmers turned out on the road in their market-chaises to say,
"Welcome home, sir!" and that all the houses along the road were
dressed with flags; and that our servants, to cut out the rest, had
dressed this house so that every brick of it was hidden. They had asked
Mamie's permission to "ring the alarm-bell"(!) when master drove up,
but Mamie, having some slight idea that that compliment might
awaken master's sense of the ludicrous, had recommended bell
abstinence. But on Sunday the village choir (which includes the
bell-ringers) made amends. After some unusually brief pious reflections in the crowns of their hats at the end of the sermon, the ringers
bolted out, and rang like mad until I got home. There had been a
conspiracy among the villagers to take the horse out, if I had come to
our own station, and draw me here. Mamie and Georgy had got wind of
it and warned me.

Divers birds sing here all day, and the nightingales all night. The
place is lovely, and in perfect order. I have put five mirrors in the Swiss
chalet[4] (where I write) and they reflect and refract in all kinds of ways
the leaves that are quivering at the windows, and the great fields of
waving corn, and the sail-dotted river. My room is up among the
branches of the trees; and the birds and the butterflies fly in and out,
and the green branches shoot in, at the open windows, and the lights
and shadows of the clouds come and go with the rest of the company.
The scent of the flowers, and indeed of everything that is growing for
miles and miles, is most delicious. [. . .]

1. Annie Adams Fields (1834–1915), wife of James Thomas Fields, the Boston publisher and junior partner in Ticknor, Reed and Fields, Dickens's main American publishers.
2. Don and Bumble; Dickens also had Turk, a mastiff, and Linda, a gentle St. Bernard. Mrs Bouncer came next, writes Mamie Dickens in *My Father as I Recall Him*, a Pomeranian who was a special gift to her (pp 82–3). There was also Sultan, an Irish bloodhound, who had to be shot in 1866 after severely biting a little girl (N, III, 489).
3. Mephistopheles first appears to Faust in the guise of a poodle, when Faust, walking with Wagner, comments on how the dog circles around him casting, he thought, fine nooses of magic about his feet.
4. The Swiss chalet Charles Fechter sent Dickens in Dec. 1864 and later also furnished 'in a very handsome manner' was ready for use in Aug. 1865, according to *The Gad's Hill Gazette* of 19 Aug. 1865 (*The Dickensian*, 6 (July 1910), 177), although the 58 packing cases in which it arrived were opened and the building partially assembled soon after New Year 1864. See 'Mr. Marcus Stone, RA, and Charles Dickens', *The Dickensian*, 8 (Aug. 1912), 216–7. The chalet, which formerly stood in the wooded grounds Dickens owned on the other side of the Dover Road, can now be seen at Eastgate House Museum, Rochester. He used the upper room as a study in the summers and wrote parts of *OMF* and *ED* in it.

[26th September 1868]

MY DEAREST PLORN,—I write this note to-day because your going away[1] is much upon my mind, and because I want you to have a few parting words from me to think of now and then at quiet times. I need not tell you that I love you dearly, and am very, very sorry in my heart to part with you. But this life is half made up of partings, and these pains must be borne. It is my comfort and my sincere conviction that you are going to try the life for which you are best fitted.[2] I think its freedom and wildness more suited to you than any experiment in a study or office would ever have been; and without that training, you could have followed no other suitable occupation.

What you have always wanted until now has been a set, steady, constant purpose.[3] I therefore exhort you to persevere in a thorough determination to do whatever you have to do as well as you can do it. I was not so old as you are now when I first had to win my food, and to do it out of this determination, and I have never slackened in it since.

Never take a mean advantage of anyone in any transaction, and never be hard upon people who are in your power. Try to do to others, as you would have them do to you, and do not be discouraged if they fail sometimes. It is much better for you that they should fail in obeying the greatest rule laid down by our Saviour, than that you should.

I put a New Testament among your books, for the very same

reasons, and with the very same hopes that made me write an easy account of it for you,[4] when you were a little child; because it is the best book that ever was or will be known in the world, and because it teaches you the best lessons by which any human creature who tries to be truthful and faithful to duty can possibly be guided. As your brothers have gone away, one by one, I have written to each such words as I am now writing to you, and have entreated them all to guide themselves by this book, putting aside the interpretations and inventions of Man.

You will remember that you have never at home been harassed about religious observances or mere formalities. I have always been anxious not to weary my children with such things before they are old enough to form opinions respecting them. You will therefore understand the better that I now most solemnly impress upon you the truth and beauty of the Christian religion, as it came from Christ Himself, and the impossibility of your going far wrong if you humbly but heartily respect it.

Only one thing more on this head. The more we are in earnest as to feeling it, the less we are disposed to hold forth about it. Never abandon the wholesome practice of saying your own private prayers, night and morning. I have never abandoned it myself, and I know the comfort of it.

I hope you will always be able to say in after life, that you had a kind father. You cannot show your affection for him so well, or make him so happy, as by doing your duty.[5]—Your affectionate Father.

1. Plorn planned to leave Plymouth on 27 Sep., sailing for Australia aboard the *Sussex*. The ship was delayed until 2 Oct., when Plorn left England, taking with him this letter from Dickens, whom he was destined never to see again. The parting, as Dickens acknowledged to Charles Fechter, was hard. Plorn 'seemed to me to become once more my youngest and favourite little child as the day drew near, and I did not think I could have been so shaken' (N, III, 669).
2. Unlike four of his elder brothers, Plorn did not go to Boulogne, because, as Dickens explained, his youngest child was so much 'an article of household furniture' that his eldest daughter was unwilling to send him away (N, III, 153). Instead, Plorn attended various schools in England before he enrolled at sixteen at the Royal Agricultural College at Cirencester. Plorn stayed there for seven months, preparing for his life abroad as a settler.
3. Writing to one of Plorn's teachers in the previous year, Dickens commented on his youngest son: 'His want of application and continuity of purpose would be quite extraordinary to me if I had not observed the same defect in one of his brothers, and tried to trace it to its source. That a certain

amount of unsatisfactory and impracticable torpor is in his natural character, and consequently his misfortune, I am sure' (N, III, 526).

4. *The Life of Our Lord*, 1846–9. Dickens wrote this expressly for his own children, not intending it for publication, although an edition first appeared in 1934.

5. Plorn did not settle down quickly in Australia, poorly served, perhaps, by the wayward nature and 'unformed character' his father detected in him. Shortly before he died, Dickens noted that Plorn 'seems to have been born without a groove. It cannot be helped,' he added. 'If he cannot, or will not find one, I must try again, and die trying.' (N, III, 779).

Plorn went to Momba station on the Darling River, NSW early in 1869; later, he managed Mount Murchison station, Wilcannia. He married in 1880; in 1894 he was elected to the seat of Wilcannia in the Legislative Assembly, which he held until 1894. Afterwards he worked in the Lands Office at Moree, where he died in 1902. See *The Australian Encyclopaedia*, III, 246. In his chapter on Dickens's children, P. Collins notes that Plorn's achievements, like those of several of his brothers, seem 'unusually depressing': Walter died young in India, without ever having revisited England; after various failures at home, Francis Jeffery left England in 1874 and spent the remainder of his life in the Canadian Mounties; when Dickens died, Sydney was in disgrace and undistinguished in the Navy; while Charles and Alfred, after setbacks, settled down to modest successes. The oldest boy became the editor and owner of *AYR* after Dickens's death and Alfred earned his living as a businessman abroad. See *Dickens and Education*, p. 44.

ADELPHI HOTEL, LIVERPOOL
Thursday, Fifteenth October, 1868

MY DEAR HARRY,—I have your letter here this morning. I enclose you another cheque for twenty-five pounds, and I write to London by this post, ordering three dozen sherry, two dozen port, six bottles of brandy, and three dozen light claret, to be sent down to you. And I enclose a cheque in favour of the Rev. F. L. Hopkins[1] for £5:10:0.

Now, observe attentively. We must have no shadow of debt. Square up everything whatsoever that it has been necessary to buy. Let not a farthing be outstanding on any account, when we begin with your allowance. Be particular in the minutest detail.

I wish to have no secret from you in the relations we are to establish together, and I therefore send you Joe Chitty's[2] letter bodily. Reading it, you will know exactly what I know, and will understand that I treat you with perfect confidence. It appears to me that an allowance of two hundred and fifty pounds a year will be handsome for all your wants, if I send you your wines. I mean this to include your tailor's bills as well as every other expense; and I strongly recommend you to buy nothing in

Cambridge, and to take credit for nothing but the clothes with which your tailor provides you. As soon as you have got your furniture accounts in, let us wipe all those preliminary expenses clean out, and I will then send you your first quarter. We will count in it October, November, and December; and your second quarter will begin with the New Year. If you dislike, at first, taking charge of so large a sum as sixty-two pounds ten shillings, you can have your money from me half-quarterly.

You know how hard I work for what I get, and I think you know that I never had money help from any human creature after I was a child. You know that you are one of many heavy charges on me, and that I trust to your so exercising your abilities and improving the advantages of your past expensive education, as soon to diminish *this* charge. I say no more on that head.

Whatever you do, above all other things keep out of debt and confide in me. If ever you find yourself on the verge of any perplexity or difficulty, come to me. You will never find me hard with you while you are manly and truthful.

As your brothers have gone away one by one, I have written to each of them what I am now going to write to you. You know that you have never been hampered with religious forms of restraint, and that with mere unmeaning forms I have no sympathy. But I most strongly and affectionately impress upon you the priceless value of the New Testament, and the study of that book as the one unfailing guide in life. Deeply respecting it, and bowing down before the character of our Saviour, as separated from the vain constructions and inventions of men, you cannot go very wrong, and will always preserve at heart a true spirit of veneration and humility. Similarly I impress upon you the habit of saying a Christian prayer every night and morning. These things have stood by me all through my life, and remember that I tried to render the New Testament intelligible to you and lovable by you when you were a mere baby.

And so God bless you.[3]—Ever your affectionate Father.

1. Revd Frank Lawrence Hopkins, Fellow and Tutor of Trinity Hall.
2. Sir Joseph William Chitty (1828–99), judge.
3. 'I always feel so proud of Harry,' Georgina Hogarth wrote in 1877. 'He is such a *worthy* representative of his Father, thank God!' (Quoted by Collins, *Dickens and Education*, p. 44.) Henry Fielding Dickens attended Trinity Hall, Cambridge (1868–72), was called to the Bar (1873), became a KC and Common Serjeant, and was knighted in 1922.

October 1868

[John Forster] . . . I have made a short reading of the murder in Oliver Twist.[1] I cannot make up my mind, however, whether to do it or not. I have no doubt that I could perfectly petrify an audience by carrying out the notion I have of the way of rendering it. But whether the impression would not be so horrible as to keep them away another time, is what I cannot satisfy myself upon. What do you think? It is in three short parts: 1, Where Fagin sets Noah Claypole on to watch Nancy. 2, The scene on London Bridge. 3, Where Fagin rouses Claypole from his sleep, to tell his perverted story to Sikes: and the Murder, and the Murderer's sense of being haunted.[2] I have adapted and cut about the text with great care, and it is very powerful. I have to-day referred the book and the question to the Chappells as so largely interested. . . .

1. Some five years earlier, Dickens had experimented alone with the possibility of adapting the murder of Nancy for inclusion in his reading repertoire (N, III, 353); after returning from America he revived the idea, partly as an attraction to add to his final series of readings in Britain. To guage the effects of the scene, he arranged a special trial performance before an invited audience on 14 Nov. 1868. For Dickens's account of the results, see the next letter.
2. Acting on the advice of Charles Kent and Wilkie Collins, Dickens agreed to add, at their urging, a further scene in which the performance ended not with Sikes's exit after murdering Nancy but with his pursuit and death. Full details of the brilliant effects of the reading and Dickens's enthusiastic portrayal of the characters may be found in Collins, *The Public Readings*, pp 465–71.

GLASGOW

Wednesday, Sixteenth December, 1868

MY DEAR MRS. FIELDS,—. . . First, as you are curious about the Oliver murder, I will tell you about that trial of the same at which you *ought* to have assisted.[1] There were about a hundred people present in all. I have changed my stage. Besides that back screen which you know so well, there are two large screens of the same colour, set off, one on either side, like the "wings" at a theatre. And besides these again, we have a quantity of curtains of the same colour, with which to close in any width of room from wall to wall. Consequently, the figure is now completely isolated, and the slightest action becomes much more important. This was used for the first time on the occasion. But behind the stage—the orchestra being very large and built for the accommodation of a numerous chorus—there was ready, on the level of the platform, a very long table, beautifully lighted, with a large staff of men ready to open oysters and set champagne-corks flying. Directly I had done, the screens being whisked off by my people, there was disclosed one of the prettiest banquets you can imagine; and when all the people came up, and the gay dresses of the ladies were lighted by those powerful lights of mine, the scene was exquisitely pretty; the hall being newly decorated, and very elegantly; and the whole looking like a great bed of flowers and diamonds.

Now, you must know that all this company were, before the wine went round, unmistakably pale, and had horror-stricken faces. Next morning Harness[2] (Fields knows—Rev. William—did an edition of Shakespeare—old friend of the Kembles[3] and Mrs. Siddons[4]), writing to me about it, and saying it was "a most amazing and terrific thing," added, "but I am bound to tell you that I had an almost irresistible impulse upon me to *scream*, and that, if anyone had cried out, I am certain I should have followed." He had no idea that, on the night, Priestley,[5] the great ladies' doctor, had taken me aside and said: "My dear Dickens, you may rely upon it that if only one woman cries out when you murder the girl, there will be a contagion of hysteria all over this place." It is impossible to soften it without spoiling it, and you may suppose that I am rather anxious to discover how it goes on the Fifth of January!!! We are afraid to announce it elsewhere, without knowing, except that I have thought it pretty safe to put it up once in Dublin. I asked Mrs. Keeley,[6] the famous actress, who was at the experiment: "What do *you* say? Do it or not?" "Why, of course, do it," she replied. "Having got at such an effect as that, if must be done. But," rolling her large black eyes very slowly, and speaking very distinctly, "the public have been looking out for a sensation these last fifty years or so, and by Heaven they have got it!" With which words, and a long breath and a long stare, she became speechless. Again, you may supposed that I am a little anxious! [. . .]

1. The special trial performance for invited guests on 14 Nov. in St. James's Hall.
2. Revd William Harness (1790–1869), editor of *The Dramatic Works of Shakespeare*, 8 vols, 1825.
3. Frances Anne 'Fanny' Kemble (1809–93), actress; Adelaide Kemble (1814–79), vocalist and author.
4. Mrs Sarah Siddons (1755–1831), actress.
5. Sir William Overend Priestley (1829–1900), lecturer on midwifery and professor of obstetric medicine.
6. Mrs Mary Ann Keeley (1805?–99), actress.

Twenty-Second April 1869

[John Forster] . . . Don't say anything about it, but the tremendously severe nature of this work is a little shaking me.[1] At Chester last Sunday I found myself extremely giddy, and extremely uncertain of my sense of touch, both in the left leg and the left hand and arms. I had been taking some slight medicine of Beard's; and immediately wrote to him describing exactly what I felt, and asking him whether those feelings *could be* referable to the medicine? He promptly replied: "There can be no mistaking them from your exact account. The medicine cannot possibly have caused them. I recognise indisputable symptoms of overwork, and I wish to take you in hand without any loss of time." They have greatly modified since, but he is coming down here this afternoon.[2] Tomorrow night at Warrington I shall have but 25 more nights to work through. If he can coach me up for them, I do not doubt that I shall get all right again—as I did when I became free in America. The foot has given me very little trouble. Yet it is remarkable that it is *the left foot too*; and that I told Henry Thompson[3] (before I saw his old master Syme[4]) that I had an inward conviction that whatever it was, it was not gout.[5] I also told Beard, a year after the Staplehurst accident, that I was certain that my heart had been fluttered, and wanted a little helping. This the stethoscope confirmed; and considering the immense exertion I am undergoing, and the constant jarring of express trains, the case seems to me quite intelligible. Don't say anything in the Gad's direction about my being a little out of sorts. I have broached the matter of course; but very lightly. Indeed there is no reason for broaching it otherwise. . . .

1. Dickens began his Farewell Tour on 6 Oct. 1868, planning a final series of 100 readings (N, III, 722).
2. F. C. Beard arrived in time to examine Dickens before he began his scheduled performance at 8.00 p.m. After seeing him, Beard told Dolby that if he insisted 'on Dickens taking the platform to-night, I will not guarantee but that he goes through life dragging a foot after him', whereupon Dolby cancelled that and all remaining readings (Dolby, p. 408). 'I have had symptoms that must not be disregarded,' Dickens told his eldest daughter, as he left Lancashire and proceeded home for rest (N, III, 722).
3. Sir Henry Thompson (1820–1904), surgeon and author of books on the urethra and urinary organs.
4. James S. Syme (1799–1870), Scottish surgeon, 1833, Crown professor of clinical surgery, Edinburgh University, and author of medical texts on the urethra, and diseases of the joints and the rectum.
5. Syme rejected Sir Henry Thompson's diagnosis of gout as the cause of

Dickens's trouble and attributed his symptoms to cold, 'due to getting wet feet in long walks in the snow in America, and again in England'. Fatigue also aggravated Dickens's condition, which Syme thought curable 'by perfect rest' (Dolby, pp 384–5).

OFFICE OF ALL THE YEAR ROUND
Monday, Third May, 1869

MY DEAR MR. CHAPPELL,—I am really touched by your letter. I can most truthfully assure you that your part in the inconvenience of this mishap has given me much more concern than my own; and that if I did not hope to have our London Farewells yet, I should be in a very gloomy condition on your account.

Pray do not suppose that *you* are to blame for my having done a little too much—a wild fancy indeed! The simple fact is, that the rapid railway travelling was stretched a hair's breadth too far, and that *I* ought to have foreseen it. For, on the night before the last night of our reading in America, when Dolby was cheering me with a review of the success, and the immediate prospect of the voyage home, I told him, to his astonishment: "I am too far gone, and too worn out to realise anything but my own exhaustion. Believe me, if I had to read but twice more, instead of once, I couldn't do it." We were then just beyond our recent number. And it was the travelling that I had felt throughout.

The sharp precautionary remedy of stopping instantly, was almost as instantly successful the other day. I told Dr. Watson[1] that he had never seen me knocked out of time, and that he had no idea of the rapidity with which I should come up again.

Just as three days' repose on the Atlantic steamer made me, in my altered appearance, the amazement of the captain, so this last week has set me up, thank God, in the most wonderful manner. The sense of exhaustion seems a dream already. Of course I shall train myself carefully, nevertheless, all through the summer and autumn.

I beg to send my kind regards to Mrs. Chappell, and I shall hope to see her and you at Teddington in the long bright days. It would disappoint me indeed if a lasting friendship did not come of our business relations.

In the spring I trust I shall be able to report to you that I am ready to take my Farewells in London.[2] Of this I am pretty certain: that I never will take them at all, unless with you on your own conditions.

With an affectionate regard for you and your brother, believe me always,—Very faithfully yours.

1. Sir Thomas Watson (1792–1882), physician.
2. The London Farewells, consisting of twelve readings, ran from 11 Jan. to 15 Mar. 1870.

Part II
Social and Political Letters

Introduction

The impact of Dickens's first visit to the United States provides a useful starting point for a brief consideration of the letters grouped in this section. Before Dickens set out to see America in January 1842, he took issue with the hostile accounts of life in the New World common among returning travellers. America's experiment with democracy, he believed, improved life for its citizens by extending the franchise and by resolving to avoid the sickening excesses he associated with courts and kings. Yet within two months of exposure to America's social aspects, Dickens recorded in letters home his thwarted hopes for the new republic, whose successes, he had previously told Forster, haunted him 'night and day'. 'This is not the Republic I came to see,' he concluded as early as March 1842. Similar reflections appear in subsequent letters and in *American Notes* (1842), an account of his day-to-day impressions conveying what he called his 'corrected and sobered judgment' of the country. Using such terms, Dickens spoke frankly of his disappointments when he drafted a prefatory chapter to the travel book.

Although Forster dissuaded Dickens from using these comments as an introduction to *American Notes*,[1] he agreed with their substance and later endorsed Dickens's analysis of his altered hopes for the United States. Writing of Dickens's American travels in his *Life*, Forster noted that Dickens returned home in 1842 with 'wider views' than when he started and with 'more maturity of mind'. In what respects, therefore, did the journey abroad change Dickens's intellectual outlook and affect his social and political opinions?

In retrospect, two developments seem particularly striking. First, Dickens set out across the Atlantic full of airy notions about the superiority of life in the United States. Because he approved of having no Established Church and admired American attempts to abolish class barriers and other forms of social privilege he expected to find a better society abroad than at home. The 'influences and tendencies' Dickens observed during his travels, however, shook his assumption that a society with fewer controls inevitably promoted civility and

179

progress. If traditional forms and manners often hindered an individual's attempts to overcome his humble origins and succeed by his own efforts, custom at least, Dickens concluded, provided some useful checks. Without the restraining influence of tradition, manners, and culture, he thought, one risked the free-wheeling forms of behaviour that prevailed in the United States. To ambitious Americans, money became the sole means of distinguishing one person from the next in a country where all were free to define their own sense of remarkableness.

The American episodes of *Martin Chuzzlewit* (1843–4) develop fully Dickens's fears of a society indifferent to manners and provide a forceful but exaggerated view of early nineteenth-century America. Yet these criticisms in no way prepare us for the more positive conclusions he drew about America's ability to educate her people and care for the poor. In this respect, Dickens realized, the United States fulfilled its boasts and offered a model for the rest of the world. The achievements of Boston, in particular, proved especially impressive, a point Dickens stressed when he described the city's various Public Charities and Private Foundations in an affirmative passage in *American Notes*. Boston's institutions, Dickens noted, are 'emphatically the people's', whose government humanely recognized the poor and young as 'improvable creatures'. In England, by contrast, Dickens suggested that legislators took their responsibilities less seriously. In his experience, he found them slow to display 'any extraordinary regard for the great mass of the people', and contended that British politicians offered the poor very little shelter or relief 'beyond that which is to be found in the workhouse and the jail'. This attitude, Dickens concluded, inspired neither gratitude nor respect, but typified the British government, which he saw as a stern master, quick to correct and punish and apparently incapable of kindness and mercy. Here in Boston, he argued, the city's philanthropic institutions provided a superior model, one British leaders could emulate.[2]

The variety of Dickens's actions after returning suggest how profoundly these convictions affected him as he worked to alleviate some of the problems around him. On one occasion, he volunteered to serve as the editor of a liberal newspaper with the express intention of doing 'good service' (P, III, 236), while on others he stated a wish to turn his social knowledge to 'good practical account'. Dickens explained that he had in mind the possibility of serving as a police magistrate, commissioner, or inspector, positions of trust that would allow him to make known his interest in 'the Education of the People' and permit him to work on their behalf. 'I think I could do good service,' Dickens wrote, noting that he would enter into work of this kind with his 'whole heart' (P, III, 570; IV, 566–7).

Failure to obtain public employment in any one of the capacities he proposed did not deflect Dickens from exploring other ways to help the outcasts he frequently encountered in the streets of London. As the letters in this section reveal, Dickens found a satisfactory outlet for his philanthropic energy in his partnership with Angela Burdett Coutts, which developed shortly after he returned from the United States. By an informal arrangement, Dickens became her consultant, advising her about which charitable causes to support and investigating the numerous petitions for money her wealth inevitably attracted.[3] 'Trust me that I will be a faithful steward of your bounty;' Dickens assured Miss Coutts in July 1843, 'and that there is no charge in the Wide World I would accept with so much pride and happiness as any such from you.' (P, III, 533)

Their first co-operative venture in social work began in 1843 when the treasurer of the Ragged School in Field Lane applied personally to Miss Coutts for assistance (P, III, 561). Shortly afterwards Dickens visited the institution on Miss Coutts's behalf and then wrote to advise her that these free schools for slum children were 'an experiment most worthy' of her charitable support. Miss Coutts acted on Dickens's advice and thereafter contributed generously to the Field Lane school for several years. Through her munificence the building Dickens first inspected was transformed from 'a low-roofed den ... with all the deadly sins let loose' into a quiet and orderly loft, whose appearance he later described in an essay in *Household Words*.[4]

These united efforts on behalf of Ragged Schools led to a second, more ambitious undertaking: the establishment of a home for rehabilitating prostitutes. Miss Coutts apparently first mentioned her wish to do something about 'the Great Social Evil' to Dickens shortly before he left England for the Continent in 1846. Dickens promptly endorsed her proposal and promised his help. 'I have but one sincere and zealous wish to assist you, by any humble means in my power in carrying out your benevolent institution,' he wrote in May 1846 prior to his departure to Switzerland.

Dickens had much to offer as an ally, as his contributions to the project reveal. When he returned to London the following year, he engaged the support of two prison governors, acquiring in George Chesterton and Augustus Tracey experienced and reliable penologists. Dickens asked both to recruit suitable women from their respective prisons and persuaded Chesterton and Tracey to serve on a committee 'to administer Miss Coutts's proposed asylum as well. Dickens's knowledge of the work of another criminologist, Alexander Maconochie, also proved useful, allowing Dickens to modify Maconochie's Mark System and adapt it as the theoretical base of the Home's disciplinary system.[5] In addition, Dickens found time to inspect possible locations for the asylum before choosing one on the Acton Road, Shepherd's Bush. Further efforts by Dickens before the first inmates arrived in November 1847 included recruiting and interviewing staff, requisitioning furniture, choosing reading materials for the inmates, and drawing up a curriculum and daily regimen.

The sensible and practical measures he recommended were accompanied by a Dickensian admonition to avoid 'creeds and formulas'. Children in the Ragged Schools, Dickens urged Miss Coutts, should be amused and not wearied to death or driven away 'by long Pulpit discourses'. Similarly, he did not favour harsh and vindictive moralizing at Urania Cottage, as he named the house on Acton Road. By treating the inmates with affection, kindness and trust, Dickens argued, the home could tempt them to virtue. If the young women wore cheerful dresses, received their training in the rural atmosphere of Shepherd's Bush, and were encouraged to form habits of firmness and self-reliance, Dickens explained to Miss Coutts, the project would increase its chances of success. 'It is part of this system,' he continued, even to put money into the hands of the women, for unless they are used to some temptation within the walls, 'their capacity of resisting it without, cannot be considered as fairly tested.'

The years of Dickens's co-operation with Miss Coutts on behalf of slum children and prostitutes also reveal him working for a third objective: 'the total abolition of the Punishment of Death'. Dickens's advocacy of this goal, in fact, predates his philanthropic activities and extends back to the attacks he made on England's retributive penal code in his early fiction. *Oliver Twist* (1837–9) and *Barnaby Rudge* (1841) both reflect his opposition to the death penalty, as does his first pronouncement on the subject in *Sketches by Boz* (First Series, 1836). In 'A Visit to Newgate' Dickens pays tribute to the efforts of reformers at the turn of the century but laments the continuation of such customs as compelling the condemned felon to attend his own burial service on the Sunday before his execution and then terminating his career in a 'violent and shameful death'.

The five public letters Dickens wrote in 1846 state his unequivocable opposition to the death penalty and argue cogently against the practice of hanging offenders in public. As an experienced observer of these public spectacles, Dickens noted their failure to impress those whom they were supposed to deter. If anything, Dickens argued in the columns of *The Daily News*, the drama of the gallows incited more crime. The professional thief made the occasion 'a dry matter of business' by going there 'solely to pick pockets'. Other dissolute and ignorant people, he contended, expressed unwarranted sympathy 'always with the criminal, and never with the law'. Furthermore, such a repellent ceremony inevitably undermined respect for the judicial system by exhibiting it in a cruel and vicious role. Executing a murder also tempted 'a bad mind contemplating violence' to rationalize that the death of his victim could be excused by a plea. 'I took his life. I give up mine to pay for it.' Finally, Dickens argued that the ugly finger of the scaffold beckoned the murderer with a promise of notoriety by giving him an opportunity to play the protagonist in a brief but intense drama of his own making. 'Come, Tom, get your name up! Let it be a dashing murder that shall keep the wood-engravers at it for the next two months. You are the boy to go through with it, and interest the town!'

Three years later, Dickens modified his views when he realized that the state of 'the general mind' did not admit support for the total abolition of the death penalty. Adopting a more realistic position, he argued in two letters to the editor of *The Times* in 1849 that if society insisted on executions, at least the scaffold should be removed from public view. 'I do not believe that any community can prosper where such a scene of horror and demoralization as was enacted this morning outside Horsemonger Lane Gaol is presented at the very doors of good citizens, and is passed by, unknown or forgotten,' he warned readers of *The Times* on 14 November. Instead Dickens proposed summoning a jury of twenty-four to attend the execution, together with the governor of the gaol, the chaplain, the surgeon, and other officers, all of whom should sign 'a grave and solemn form of certificate' that the murderer had been hanged in their sight. Dickens also suggested closing all the shops and tolling all the bells to remind other inhabitants of the city or town 'of what was being done'.[6]

Dickens's desire to end these public spectacles, even at the expense of retaining the death penalty, later evolved into a third position. By 1864, he admitted that he had come to acknowledge society's need to rid itself of those who shed blood because he did not know what to do with 'the Savages of civilization' (N, III, 378). In this final phase of his thinking, a wish to see murderers punished replaces Dickens's former concern with the ethics of execution. Like his friend Carlyle, whose opinions about hardened criminals he shared, Dickens began by opposing the death penalty altogether and ended by accepting it as a necessity.[7]

The remaining letters in this section illustrate Dickens's characteristic assertion that progress towards England's general welfare and happiness must proceed on two fronts. On one hand, he held Parliament responsible for initiating reforms and addressing 'first necessities' such as 'the enormous black cloud of poverty' he saw hovering over cities. On the other, Dickens repeatedly urged individuals to take action, either by working collectively for specific political objectives or by attending personally to their own self-culture and happiness. In this respect, Dickens embraced opposing political principles by calling for government legislation *and* individual action as the best means of achieving social perfectability.

Dickens's tendency to combine solutions from both ends of the ideological spectrum represents an inherent weakness to those who fault his political philosophy for its lack of consistency. But to others, his disregard for a theoretical basis indicates a healthy flexibility and a laudable distrust of doctrinaire answers. Somewhere in the middle, we may identify another response. The emphasis Dickens placed on the individual's responsibility to improve himself, I suggest, typifies the outlook of someone who struggled successfully against poverty and misfortune in his early days. To a man with experiences of this kind behind him, a personal victory over economic and social forces could easily serve as the basis for an attractive social myth, especially for the novelist whose works repeatedly underscore each character's responsibility for his own fate.

Compassion and not complacency, however, characterize Dickens's fiction and no self-congratulatory egoism distorts his belief in free will. A similar spirit informs the social and political pronouncements we see in these letters, especially when Dickens tempers his conviction in the adult's freedom to corrupt or perfect himself with a Rousseauistic faith that the individual's inner core of goodness can prevail. As a moralist, Dickens shows no scruples in passing judgements. But even though he noisily banged the doors of hell on those who failed to repent, he offered a positive alternative. If his social and political views appear unsatisfactory because they lack theoretical prescriptions for improving society, they succeed in another respect. These letters, like his novels, remind us of his vision that individuals can become a little more humane and a little more civilized when they are encouraged to opt for good.

NOTES

1. For the text, 'Introductory, and Necessary to be Read', see Forster, III, viii, 264–6. Forster explains that he argued against publishing these remarks in 1842 because readers at that time might mistake Dickens's 'proper self-assertion' for 'an apprehension of hostile judgments'. In 1871 Forster reassessed the situation and concluded that the Preface could pose no danger to its author and therefore included it in his *Life*.
2. *AN*, ch. 3.
3. Angela Georgina Burdett (1814–1906), later Baroness Burdett-Coutts, inherited an estate worth about six million pounds with an annual income of about fifty thousand pounds from her maternal grandfather, Thomas Coutts, the banker. In 1837 she added her grandfather's name to her own on inheriting the fortune he left.
4. 'A Sleep to Startle Us', *HW*, 13 Mar. 1852. See also *MP*, I, 358–66. The transformation of the Ragged School Dickens describes in this essay appears to owe much to the generosity of Miss Coutts, presumably the anonymous lady referred to in the *Ragged School Union Magazine*, III (1851), 126 and 152, who 'in the various departments of Ragged School Labour, has expended upwards of £600 yearly'. Quoted by P. Collins, 'Dickens and the Ragged Schools', *The Dickensian*, 55 (May 1959), 104. For Dickens's other comments about Ragged Schools and essays about them by other writers he published in *HW*, see the note on p. 192.
5. For notes on Chesterton, Tracey, Maconochie, see pp 192 and 198.
6. This proposal possibly owed something to Henry Fielding's suggestion that adopting a quick, private, and solemn ceremony would remove the evils of public executions. See Fielding's *Inquiry into the Causes of the Late Increase of Robbers, etc. with Some Proposals for Remedying this Growing Evil*, section XI, vol. XIII of *Complete Works* (1751; repr. New York: Barnes and Noble, 1967), pp. 123–4.
7. In 'Model Prisons' Carlyle wrote: 'The scoundrel needs no protection. The scoundrel that *will* hasten to the gallows, why not rather clear the way for him! Better he reach *his* goal and outgate by the natural proclivity, than be so expensively damned-up and detained.' See *Latter-Day Pamphlets*, vol. XIX of Library Edition (1850; repr. London: Chapman and Hall, 1870), p. 80.

Ragged Schools

24th September 1843

[John Forster] . . . I sent Miss Coutts a sledge-hammer account of the Ragged schools;[1] and as I saw her name for two hundred pounds in the clergy education subscription-list, took pains to show her that religious mysteries and difficult creeds wouldn't do for such pupils.[2] I told her, too, that it was of immense importance they should be *washed*. She writes back to know what the rent of some large airy premises would be, and what the expense of erecting a regular bathing or purifying place; touching which points I am in correspondence with the authorities. I have no doubt she will do whatever I ask her in the matter. She is a most excellent creature, I protest to God, and I have a most perfect affection and respect for her. . . .

1. See To Miss Coutts, 16 Sep. 1843 (P, III, 562–4), where Dickens describes his first visit to the school in Field Lane on 14 Sep. 1843.
2. Dickens was anxious to persuade Miss Coutts to support practical measures for the children rather than religious schemes based exclusively on the teachings of the Established Church. Earlier, Miss Coutts contributed to the National Society for Promoting the Education of the Poor in the Principles of the Established Church. See P, III, 565n.

BROADSTAIRS, KENT
24th September, 1843

DEAR SIR,[1]—Allow me to ask you a few questions in reference to that most able undertaking in which you are engaged—with a view, I need scarcely say, to its advancement and extended usefulness. For the present, I wish it,[2] if you please, to be considered as put in confidence, but not to the exclusion of the gentlemen associated with you in the management of the Ragged School on Saffron Hill.[3]

It occurred to me, when I was there, as being of the most immense importance that, if practicable, the boys should have an opportunity of washing themselves before beginning their tasks.

Do you agree with me? If so, will you ascertain at about what cost a washing-place—a large trough or sink, for instance, with a good supply of running water, soap and towels—could be put up? In case you consider it necessary that some person should be engaged to mind it, and to see that the boys availed themselves of it in an orderly manner, please add the payment of such a person to the expense.

Have you seen any place, or do you know of any place, in that neighbourhood—any one or two good spacious lofts or rooms—which you would like to engage (if you could afford it), as being well suited for the school? If so, at what charge could it be hired, and how soon?[4]

In the event of my being able to procure you the funds for making these great improvements, would you see any objection to expressly limiting visitors (I mean visiting teachers—volunteers, whoever they may be), to confining their questions and instructions, as a point of honour, to the broad truths taught in the school by yourself and the gentlemen associated with you? I set great store by this question, because it seems to me of vital importance that no persons, however well intentioned, should perplex the minds of these unfortunate creatures with religious mysteries that young people, with the best advantages, can but imperfectly understand. I heard a lady visitor the night I was among you propounding questions in reference to the "Lamb of God," which I most unquestionably would not suffer anyone to put to my children, recollecting the immense absurdities that were suggested to my childhood by the like injudicious catechising.

I return to town on Monday, the 2nd of next month; if you write to me before then, please to address your letter here. If after that date, to my house in town.

With a cordial sympathy in your Great and Christian Labour,—I am, dear sir, faithfully yours.

1. Samuel R. Starey, treasurer of the Ragged School in Field Lane, Saffron Hill.
2. I could wish them (P, III, 573).
3. Revd P. Lorimer and W. D. Owen, whose names appeared with Starey's in an advertisement in *The Times* of 18 Feb. 1843 appealing for financial help.
4. In 'A Sleep to Startle Us', *HW*, 13 Mar. 1852, Dickens notes the improvements made to the Field Lane School since his first visit in 1843. Many of the changes evidently originated from Miss Coutts's donations. See my note on p. 185.

CRIME AND EDUCATION

To the Editors of *The Daily News.*   February 4, 1846

GENTLEMEN, I offer no apology for entreating the attention of the readers of *The Daily News* to an effort which has been making for some

three years and a half, and which is making now, to introduce among
the most miserable and neglected outcasts in London, some knowledge of the commonest principles of morality and religion; to
commence their recognition as immortal human creatures, before the
Jail Chaplain becomes their only schoolmaster; to suggest to Society
that its duty to this wretched throng, foredoomed to crime and
punishment, rightfully begins at some distance from the police-office;
and that the careless maintenance from year to year, in this the capital
city of the world, of a vast hopeless nursery of ignorance, misery, and
vice: a breeding place for the hulks and jails: is horrible to contemplate.

This attempt is being made, in certain of the most obscure and
squalid parts of the Metropolis; where rooms are opened, at night, for
the gratuitous instruction of all comers, children or adults, under the
title of RAGGED SCHOOLS.[1] The name implies the purpose. They who
are too ragged, wretched, filthy, and forlorn, to enter any other place:
who could gain admission into no charity-school, and who would be
driven from any church door: are invited to come in here, and find
some people not depraved, willing to teach them something, and show
them some sympathy, and stretch a hand out, which is not the iron
hand of Law, for their correction.

Before I describe a visit of my own to a Ragged School, and urge the
readers of this letter for God's sake to visit one themselves, and think
of it (which is my main object), let me say, that I know the prisons of
London, well. That I have visited the largest of them, more times than I
could count; and that the Children in them are enough to break the
heart and hope of any man. I have never taken a foreigner or a stranger
of any kind, to one of these establishments, but I have seen him so
moved at sight of the Child-offenders, and so affected by the
contemplation of their utter renouncement and desolation outside the
prison walls, that he has been as little able to disguise his emotion, as if
some great grief had suddenly burst upon him. Mr. Chesterton[2] and
Lieutenant Tracey[3] (than whom more intelligent and humane Governors of Prisons it would be hard, if not impossible, to find) know,
perfectly well, that these children pass and repass through the prisons
all their lies; that they are never taught; that the first distinctions
between right and wrong are, from their cradles, perfectly confounded
and perverted in their minds; that they come of untaught parents, and
will give birth to another untaught generation; that in exact proportion
to their natural abilities, is the extent and scope of their depravity; and
that there is no escape or chance for them in any ordinary revolution of

human affairs. Happily, there are schools in these prisons now. If any readers doubt how ignorant the children are, let them visit those schools and see them at their tasks, and hear how much they knew when they were sent there. If they would know the produce of this seed, let them see a class of men and boys together, at their books (as I have seen them in the House of Correction for this county of Middlesex), and mark how painfully the full grown felons toil at the very shape and form of letters: their ignorance being so confirmed and solid. The contrast of this labour in the men, with the less blunted quickness of the boys; the latent shame and sense of degradation struggling through their dull attempts at infant lessons; and the universal eagerness to learn; impress me, in this passing retrospect, more painfully than I can tell.

For the instruction, and as a first step in the reformation, of such unhappy beings, the Ragged Schools were founded. I was first attracted to the subject, and indeed was first made conscious of their existence, about two years ago, or more, by seeing an advertisement in the papers dated from West Street, Saffron Hill, stating "That a room had been opened and supported in that wretched neighbourhood for upwards of twelve months, where religious instruction had been imparted to the poor," and explaining in a few words what was meant by Ragged Schools as a generic term, including, then, four or five similar places of instruction.[4] I wrote to the masters of this particular school to make some further inquiries, and went myself soon afterwards.

It was a hot summer night;[5] and the air of Field Lane and Saffron Hill was not improved by such weather, nor were the people in those streets very sober or honest company. Being unacquainted with the exact locality of the school, I was fain to make some inquiries about it. These were very jocosely received in general; but everybody knew where it was, and gave the right direction to it. The prevailing idea among the loungers (the greater part of them the very sweepings of the streets and station houses) seemed to be, that the teachers were quixotic, and the school upon the whole "a lark." But there was certainly a kind of rough respect for the intention, and (as I have said) nobody denied the school or its whereabouts, or refused assistance in directing to it.

It consisted at that time of either two or three—I forget which—miserable rooms, upstairs in a miserable house. In the best of these, the pupils in the female school were being taught to read and write; and though there were among the number, many wretched creatures steeped in degradation to the lips, they were tolerably quiet, and listened with apparent earnestness and patience to their instructors. The appearance of this room was sad and melancholy, of course—how could it be otherwise!—but, on the whole, encouraging.

The close, low, chamber at the back, in which the boys were crowded, was so foul and stifling as to be, at first, almost insupportable. But its moral aspect was so far worse than its physical, that this was soon forgotten. Huddled together on a bench about the room, and shown out by some flaring candles stuck against the walls, were a crowd of boys, varying from mere infants to young men; sellers of fruit, herbs, lucifer-matches, flints; sleepers under the dry arches of bridges; young thieves and beggars—with nothing natural to youth about them: with nothing frank, ingenuous, or pleasant in their faces; low-browed, vicious, cunning, wicked; abandoned of all help but this; speeding downward to destruction; and UNUTTERABLY IGNORANT.

This, Reader, was one room as full as it could hold; but these were only grains in sample of a Multitude that are perpetually sifting through these schools; in sample of a Multitude who had within them once, and perhaps have now, the elements of men as good as you or I, and maybe infinitely better; in sample of a Multitude among whose doomed and sinful ranks (oh, think of this, and think of them!) the child of any man upon this earth, however lofty his degree, must, as by Destiny and Fate, be found, if, at its birth, it were consigned to such an infancy and nurture, as these fallen creatures had!

This was the Class I saw at the Ragged School. They could not be trusted with books; they could only be instructed orally; they were difficult of reduction to anything like attention, obedience, or decent behaviour; their benighted ignorance in reference to the Deity, or to any social duty (how could they guess at any social duty, being so discarded by all social teachers but the jailer and the hangman!) was terrible to see. Yet, even here, and among these, something had been done already. The Ragged School was of recent date and very poor;[6] but it had inculcated some association with the name of the Almighty, which was not an oath: and had taught them to look forward in a hymn (they sang it) to another life, which would correct the miseries and woes of this.

The new exposition I found in this Ragged School, of the frightful neglect by the State of those whom it punishes so constantly, and whom it might, as easily and less expensively, instruct and save; together with the sight I had seen there, in the heart of London; haunted me, and finally impelled me to an endeavour to bring these Institutions under the notice of the Government; with some faint hope that the vastness of the question would supersede the Theology of the schools, and that the Bench of Bishops might adjust the latter question, after some small grant had been conceded. I made the attempt: and have heard no more of the subject, from that hour.

The perusal of an advertisement in yesterday's paper, announcing a lecture on the Ragged Schools last night,[7] has led me into these remarks. I might easily have given them another form; but I address this letter to you, in the hope that some few readers in whom I have awakened an interest, as a writer of fiction, may be, by that means, attracted to the subject, who might otherwise, unintentionally, pass it over.

I have no desire to praise the system pursued in the Ragged Schools: which is necessarily very imperfect, if indeed there be one. So far as I have any means of judging of what is taught there, I should individually object to it, as not being sufficiently secular, and as presenting too many religious mysteries and difficulties, to minds not sufficiently prepared for their reception. But I should very imperfectly discharge in myself the duty I wish to urge and impress on others, if I allowed any such doubts of mine to interfere with my appreciation of the efforts of these teachers, or my true wish to promote them by any slight means in my power. Irritating topics, of all kinds, are equally far removed from my purpose and intention. But, I adjure those excellent persons who aid, munificiently, in the building of New Churches, to think of these Ragged Schools; to reflect whether some portion of their rich endowments might not be spared for such a purpose; to contemplate, calmly, the necessity of beginning at the beginning; to consider for themselves where the Christian Religion most needs and most suggests immediate help and illustration; and not to decide on any theory or hearsay, but to go themselves into the Prisons and the Ragged Schools, and form their own conclusions. They will be shocked, pained, and repelled, by much that they learn there; but nothing they can learn, will be one-thousandth part so shocking, painful, and repulsive, as the continuance for one year more of these things as they have been for too many years already.

Anticipating that some of the more prominent facts connected with the history of the Ragged Schools, may become known to the readers of *The Daily News* through your account of the lecture in question,[8] I abstain (though in possession of some such information) from pursuing the question further, at this time. But if I should see occasion, I will take leave to return to it.[9]

1. The *OED* defines *Ragged Schools* as free schools for the children of the poorest class and lists an advertisement in *The Times* on 18 Feb. 1843 (p. 1, col. 3) as the first recorded use of the term. The author of 'The Second Annual Report of the Ragged School Union' published in the *Quarterly Review*, 79 (Dec. 1846), 127–41, cannot date exactly the origin of these schools but associates their inception with the work of 'some excellent persons in humble life', who went forth 'not many years ago' into the streets and alleys to introduce reading and religious instruction to society's 'miserable outcasts'. By 1846, 26 schools were in existence in London, where 25 teachers supervised an average of about 2600 children. By this date the schools had extended their original focus on religious instruction and included industrial training. The schools also provided food, clothing and beds for those who attended regularly. On the origin of Ragged Schools, see also Forster, IV, 1, 281–2 and n.
2. G. L. Chesterton (d. 1868), Governor of Cold Bath Fields or Middlesex House of Correction.
3. Lieut. A. F. Tracey, RN (1798–1878), Governor of Westminster House of Correction, Tothill Fields.
4. For the full text of this advertisement in *The Times*, see P, III, 554n.
5. 14 Sep. 1843.
6. The School in Field Lane originated in the philanthropic work of the Earl of Shaftesbury and W. C. Bevan, who established the Field Lane Institution in 1842. This comprised the Ragged School, an Industrial School for maintaining and training 60 destitute boys under 14, a Home for Female Servants and girls training for domestic service, and Field Lane Night Refuge (1851), which provided food, fire, and lodging for 30 penniless men and a similar refuge for the same number of women. See Wheatley, II, 39.
7. A public lecture on Ragged Schools by the Revd Robert Ainslie on 3 Feb. 1846.
8. Ainslie's lecture was fully reported in the *DN* on 3 Feb.
9. Dickens's interest in the Ragged Schools continued. The following month he referred to a proposal to set up an experimental Ragged School free from 'Pulpit discourses' and committed to reforming boys by amusing and instructing them (P, IV, 527). No such model school was set up, but Dickens repeatedly stressed the importance of practical and secular training over religious indoctrination in his journalism. See 'Ignorance and Crime', *The Examiner*, 22 Apr. 1848 (repr. *MP*, I, 107–10), and 'Edinburgh Apprentice School Association', 30 Dec. 1848 (repr. *MP*, I, 146–7). For a critical view of Ragged Schools and the inadequacy of good intentions without sufficient emphasis on practical training, see the description of the school where Charley Hexam 'had first learned from a book' (*OMF*, II, ch. 1). Dickens's notes in the Numbers Plans (repr. in Ernest Boll, 'The Plotting of *Our Mututal Friend*', *Modern Philology*, 42 (Aug. 1944), 102–22), identify Hexam's as 'A ragged School'. See also the Selected Bibliography, pp 361–2.

Urania Cottage

DEVONSHIRE TERRACE
Twenty-Sixth May, 1846

[Miss Coutts] . . . In reference to the Asylum,[1] it seems to me very expedient that you should know, if possible, whether the Government would assist you to the extent of informing you from time to time into what distant parts of the World, women could be sent for marriage, with the greatest hope for their future families, and with the greatest service to the existing male population, whether expatriated from England or born there. If these poor women *could* be sent abroad with the distinct recognition and aid of the Government, it would be a service to the effort.[2] But I have (with reason) a doubt of all Governments in England considering such a question in the light in which men undertaking that immense responsibility, are bound, before God, to consider it. And therefore I would suggest this appeal to you, merely as something which you owe to yourself and to the experiment; the failure of which, does not at all affect the immeasurable goodness and happiness of the project itself.

I do not think it would be necessary, in the first instance at all events, to build a house for the Asylum. There are many houses, either in London or in the immediate neighbourhood, that could be altered for the purpose. It would be necessary to limit the number of inmates, but I would make the reception of them as easy as possible to themselves. I would put it in the power of any Governor of a London Prison to send an unhappy creature of this kind (by her own choice of course) straight from his prison, when her term expired, to the asylum. I would put it in the power of any penitent creature to knock at the door, and say For God's sake, take me in. But I would divide the interior into two portions; and into the first portion I would put all new-comers without exception, as a place of probation, whence they should pass, by their own good conduct and self-denial alone, into what I may call the Society of the house. I do not know of any plan, so well conceived, or so firmly grounded in a knowledge of human nature, or so judiciously addressed to it, for observance in this place, as what is called Captain

193

Maconnochie's Mark System,[3] which I will try very roughly and generally, to describe.

A woman or girl coming to the asylum, it is explained to her that she has come there for *useful* repentance and reform, and means[4] her past way of life has been dreadful in its nature and consequences, and full of affliction, misery, and despair to *herself*. Never mind society while she is at that pass. Society has used her ill and turned away from her, and she cannot be expected to take much heed of its rights or wrongs. It is destructive to herself, and there is no hope in it, or in her, as long as she pursues it. It is explained to her that she is degraded and fallen, but not lost, having this shelter; and that the means of Return to Happiness are now about to be put into her own hands, and trusted to her own keeping. That with this view, she is instead of being placed in this probationary class for a month, or two months, or three months, or any specified *time* whatever, required to earn there a certain number of *Marks* (they are mere scratches in a book) so that she may make her probation a very short one, or a very long one, according to her own conduct. For so much work, she has so many marks; for a day's good conduct, so many more. For every instance of ill-temper, disrespect, bad language, any outbreak of any sort or kind, so many—a very large number in proportion to her receipts—are deducted. A perfect Debtor and Creditor account is kept between her and the Superintendent, for every day; and the state of that account, it is in her own power and nobody else's, to adjust to her advantage. It is expressly pointed out to her, that before she can be considered qualified to return to any kind of society—even to the Society of the asylum—she must give proofs of her power of self-restraint and her sincerity, and her determination to try to shew that she deserves the confidence it is proposed to place in her. Her pride, emulation, her sense of shame, her heart, her reason, and her interest, are all appealed to at once, and if she pass through this trial, she *must* (I believe it to be in the eternal nature of things) rise somewhat in her own self-respect, and give the Managers a power of appeal to her, in future, which nothing else could invest them with. I would carry a modification of this mark system through the whole establishment; for it is its great philosophy and its chief excellence that it is not a mere form or course of training adapted to the life within the house, but is a preparation—which is a much higher consideration—for the right performance of duty outside, and for the formation of habits of firmness and self-restraint. And the more these unfortunate persons were educated in their duty towards Heaven and Earth, and the more they were tried on this plan, the more they would feel that to dream of returning to society, or of becoming virtuous wives, until they had earned a certain gross number of marks required of everyone without the least exception, would be to prove that they were not worthy of restoration to the place they had lost. It is a part of this system, even to put at last, some temptation within their reach, as enabling them to go out, putting them in possession of some money, and the like; for it is clear that unless they are used to some temptation and used to resist it, within the walls, their capacity of resisting it without, cannot be considered as fairly tested.

What they would be taught in the house, would be grounded in religion, most unquestionably. It must be the basis of the whole system. But it is very essential in dealing with this class of persons to have a system of training established, which while it is steady and firm, is cheerful and hopeful.[5] Order, punctuality, cleanliness, the whole routine of household duties, as washing, mending, cooking—the establishment itself would supply the means of teaching practically, to every one. But then I would have it understood by all—I would have it written up in every room—that they were not going through a monotonous round of occupation and self-denial which began and ended there, but which began, or was resumed, under that roof, and would end, by God's blessing, in happy homes of their own.

I have said that I would put it in the power of Governors of Prisons to recommend Inmates.[6] I think this most important, because such gentlemen as Mr. Chesterton of the Middlesex House of Correction and Lieutenant Tracey of Cold Bath Fields,[7] Bridewell (both of whom I know very well) are well acquainted with the good that is in the bottom of the hearts of many of these poor creatures, and with the whole history of their past lives, and frequently have deplored to me the not having any such place as the proposed establishment, to which to send them when they are set free from Prison. It is necessary to observe that very many of these unfortunate women are constantly in and out of the Prisons, for no other fault or crime than their original one of having fallen from virtue. Policemen can take them up, almost when they choose, for being of that class, and being in the streets; and the magistrates commit them to Jail for short terms. When they come out, they can but return to their old occupation, and so come in again. It is well known that many of them fee the Police to remain unmolested; and being too poor to pay the fee, or dissipating the money in some other way, are taken up again, forthwith. Very many of them are good, excellent, steady characters when under restraint—even without the advantage of systematic training, which they would have in this Institution—and are tender nurses to the sick, and are as kind and gentle as the best of women.

There is no doubt that many of them would go on well for some time, and would then be seized with a violent fit of the most extraordinary passion, apparently quite motiveless, and insist on going away. There seems to be something inherent in their course of life, which, engenders and awakens a sudden restlessness and recklessness which may be long suppressed, but breaks out like madness; and which all people who have had opportunities of observation in Penitentiaries and elsewhere, must have contemplated with astonishment and pity. I would have some rule to the effect that no request to be allowed to go away would be received for at least four and twenty hours,[8] and that in the interval the person should be kindly reasoned with, if possible, and implored to consider well what she was doing. This sudden dashing down of all the building up of months upon months, is, to my thinking, so distinctly a Disease with the persons under consideration that I would pay particular attention to it, and treat it with particular gentleness and anxiety; *and I would not make one, or two, or three, or four, or six departures from the establishment a binding reason against the re-admission of that person being again penitent*, but leave it to the Managers to decide upon the merits of the case: giving very great weight to general good conduct within the house.

I would begin with some comparatively small number—say thirty—and I would have it impressed upon them, from day to day, that the success of the experiment rested with them, and that on their conduct depended the rescue and salvation, of hundreds and thousands of women yet unborn. In what proportion this experiment would be successful, it is very difficult to predict;[9] but I think that if the Establishment were founded on a well-considered system, and were well managed, one half of the Inmates would be reclaimed from the very beginning, and that after a time the proportion would be much larger. I believe this estimate to be within very reasonable bounds.

The main question that arises is, if the co-operation of the Government—beginning at that point where they are supposed to be reclaimed—cannot be secured, how are they to be provided for, permanently? Supposing the Mark system and the training to be very successful, and gradually to acquire a great share of public confidence and respect, I think it not too sanguine to suppose that many good people would be glad to take them into situations. But the power of beginning life anew, in a world perfectly untried by them, would be so important in many cases, as an effectual detaching of them from old associates, and from the chances of recognition and challenge, that it is most desirable to be, some how or other, attained.

I do not know whether you would be disposed to entrust me with any share in the supervision and direction of the Institution. But I need not say that I should enter on such a task with my whole heart and soul; and that in this respect, as in all others, I have but one sincere and zealous wish to assist you, by any humble means in my power, in carrying out your benevolent institution.

And at all events it would be necessary for you to have, in the first instance, on paper, all the results of previous experience in this way, as regards scheme, plan, management, and expence. These I think I could procure, and render plain, as quietly and satisfactorily as any one. And I would suggest to you, this course of action.

That the School and Church proceeding—this Design remain in abeyance for the present. That when I go to Paris (whither I shall remove, please God, before Christmas)[10] I examine every Institution of this sort existing there, and gather together all the information I possibly can.[11] I believe more valuable knowledge is to be got there, on such a subject, than anywhere else; and this, combined with the results of our English experience, I would digest into the plainest and clearest form; so that you could see it, as if it were a Map. And in the meantime you would have these advantages.

1. That in the establishment of your school and Dispensary, you might find or make some Instruments that would be very important and useful in the working out of this school.[12]

2. That there will then have been matured, and probably tried, certain partial schemes going a very little way on this same road, which are now on foot in the City of London, and the success or failure of which will be alike instructive.

3. That there is a very great probability of the whole Transportation system being shortly brought under the consideration of the Legislature; and it is particularly worthy of consideration that the various preliminary reports on the subject, (which I have lately been reading) recognise the question of sending out women to the different settlements, as one of very great importance.

I have that deep sense, dear Miss Coutts, of the value of your confidence in such a matter, and of the pure, exalted, and generous motives by which you are impelled, that I feel a most earnest anxiety that such an effort as you contemplate in behalf of your Sex, should have every advantage in the outset it can possibly receive, and should, if undertaken at all, be undertaken to the lasting honor of your name and Country. In this feeling, I make the suggestion I think best calculated to promote that end. Trust me, if you agree in it, I will not lose sight of the subject, or grow cold to it, or fail to bestow upon it my best exertions and reflection. But, if there be any other course you would prefer to take, and you will tell me so; I shall be as devoted to you in that as in this, and as much honored by being asked to render you the least assistance. . . .

1. Dickens's first recorded reference to the plan to establish a Home for 'the reclamation and emigration' of two classes of young women: those who had already lost their characters 'and lapsed into guilt' and those who were in danger of falling into a similar condition. Dickens and Miss Coutts opened Urania Cottage, 'a detached house with a garden', on 13 Nov. 1847. The establishment housed thirteen inmates and two superintendents. The women, usually under the age of 26, came from a variety of backgrounds. Some were of good character but faced starvation, others were thieves, some girls with a history of violence, and others prostitutes, seduced domestic servants and attempted suicides. See Dickens, 'Home for Homeless Women', *HW*, 23 Apr. 1853. Also repr. in *MP*, I, 395–410.
2. Dickens stressed the importance of emigration for the women the Home reclaimed because he knew that England's social climate made it difficult for the inmates to start their lives again once they left the Home. Realising too the improbability of obtaining assistance from the Government to help the women emigrate led Dickens to advise Miss Coutts to try this experiment on a limited scale, since he knew that the Home itself would have to make all the necessary arrangements both for the support of the women and the provision of their passage abroad. Later Dickens did his best to publicize the work of Mrs Caroline Chisholm, founder of the Family Colonization Loan Society, and active champion of emigration schemes for the poor. For his and Mrs Chisholm's contributions to *HW* on this subject, see Lohrli, pp 226–8.
3. Capt. A. Maconochie, RN (1787–1860), penal reformer and originator of the Mark System, by which inmates earned points or marks for good work and so took some personal responsibility in their rehabilitation and release. The modified mark table at Urania Cottage was divided into nine heads; at the end of the day, each woman was assessed and marked for her conduct in every column. For every 1000 good marks, inmates earned 6s.6d., monies which were witheld in order to form a fund for each woman's subsistence on her disembarkation abroad. See 'Home for Homeless Women'. For an earlier explanation of the Mark Table, see App. F., P, v, 703–5. Dickens often misspelled Maconochie's name. P. Collins provides useful supplementary information about Maconochie and Dickens's indebtedness to his ideas in *Dickens and Crime*, ch. 7.
4. Because (P, IV, 553).
5. Scripture reading, morning and evening prayers, and attendance at church on Sunday constituted a regular part of the Home's regimen, but practical training in 'the whole routine of household duties' and 'book education' of a very plain kind also featured prominently.

6. Chesterton and Tracey served in this capacity; they also sat on the Home's administrative committee, which met monthly to audit the accounts, receive progress reports on each inmate from the principal superintendent, and interview each inmate separately to assess her progress month by month.

7. A slip; Dickens should have written Tothill Fields.

8. This principle was adopted. Anyone wishing to leave was locked in a room by herself to consider her wish until the following day; if she still persisted, she was formally discharged.

9. Writing in 1853, Dickens noted that of the 56 women admitted to that date, seven left of their own accord during their probation, ten were expelled for misconduct, seven ran away, three emigrated and relapsed on the passage out, and thirty settled in Australia and elsewhere, entering good service and acquiring good character. Of these, seven had married at the time Dickens published his account of the Home in *HW*. Giving these figures, Dickens makes an error either in the total number of women (57) admitted by 1853 or in the sub-totals of the various categories.

10. Dickens left England with his family on 31 May. After residing in Lausanne until mid Nov., they left for Paris, where they stayed until Feb. 1847.

11. The policies Dickens advocated in this letter differed sharply from those characterizing earlier institutions such as Bridewell (1553), Tothill Fields (1655) and other Houses of Correction, where emphasis on the harsh and vindictive punishment of offenders usually prevailed. One notes a shift in emphasis in the eighteenth century, with the opening of less punitive institutions such as Lock Hospital and Chapel (1747), the Lock Asylum (1787), Magdalen Hospital (1758) and the London Female Penitentiary (1807). See Wheatley, II, 412, 454, and 428.

12. Scheme (P, IV, 556).

ROSEMONT, LAUSANNE
Saturday Twenty-Fifth July, 1846

[Miss Coutts] . . . Your two objections to my sketch of a plan, I wish to offer half a dozen words upon.

1st As to Marriage. I do not propose to put that hope before them as the immediate end and object to be gained, but assuredly to keep it in view as the possible consequence of a sincere, true, practical repentance, and an altered life. A kind of penitence is bred in our prisons and purgatories just now, which is a very pretty penitence inside the walls, but fades into nothing when it comes into contact with worldly realities. In the generality of cases, it is almost impossible to produce a penitence which shall stand the wear and tear of this rough world, without Hope—worldly hope—the hope of at one time or other recovering something like the lost station. I would make this Hope, however faint and afar off it might be, exactly the one that out of the asylum and without its aid, seemed (and was) impossible of attainment.

2ndly With regard to Temptation. I would simply ask you to consider whether we do not, all of us, in our stations, tempt our fellow creatures at every turn. Whether there is a merchant in London who does not hourly expose his servants to strong temptation. Whether a night or morning ever comes when you do not tempt your butler with a hundred times the worth of his year's wages. Whether there are not at the Banking House in the Strand, many young men whose lives are one exposure to, and resistance of, temptation. And whether it is not a christian act to say to such unfortunate creatures as you purpose, by Gods' blessing, to reclaim, "Test for yourselves, the reality of your repentance and your power of resisting temptation, while you are *here*, and before you are in the world outside, to fall before it!"[1][. . .]

1. Precautions, nevertheless, proved necessary, as Dickens noted in his account of the Home in *HW*. 'Keys are never left about. The garden gate is always kept locked.'

DEVONSHIRE TERRACE
Thursday Night, Twenty-Eighth October, 1847
[Miss Coutts] . . . I am in a state of great anxiety to talk to you about your "Home" (that is the name I propose to give it) with which I have been very busy for some time, and which will be ready for the reception of its inmates, please God, on Saturday fortnight.[1]. . .

I have taken some pains to find out the dispositions and natures of any individual we take; and I think I know them pretty well, and may be able to give the Matron some useful foreknowledge of them, and to exercise some personal influence with them in case of need. A most extraordinary and mysterious study it is, but interesting and touching in the extreme.

I think it well to say to you that I have avoided Macconochie's ideas,[2] as they hardly seemed (or I fancied so) to meet with your full approval, and as they were perhaps unsuited to so small an establishment. The design is simply, as you and I agreed, to appeal to them by means of affectionate kindness and trustfulness—but firmly too. To improve them by education and example—establish habits of the most rigid order, punctuality, and neatness—but to make as great a variety in their daily lives as their daily lives will admit of—and to render them an innocently cheerful Family while they live together there. On the cheerfulness and kindness of all our hopes rest. . . .

1. 13 Nov. 1847. For the full text of this letter, see P, ɪᴠ, 177–9.
2. See p. 194.

DEVONSHIRE TERRACE
Wednesday, Third November, 1847

[Miss Coutts] . . . I have great faith in the soundness of your opinions in reference to the religious instruction; knowing you to be full of that enlarged consideration for the special circumstances under which it is to be administered in this case, without which nothing hopeful or useful can be done. I trust that those enlightenments to which you refer, are to be found in the *New* Testament? I am confident that harm is done to this class of minds by the injudicious use of the Old—and I am hardly less confident that I could shew you how, in talking the subject over.[1]

The expediency of explaining to them that the rules of the Establishment may alter, I greatly doubt. For this reason—If we did so, they would immediately conceive that we did not know what we were about, and that we were experimentalizing, which would desperately shake their trust in us. Such rules as we agree upon in the outset will be known only to the Superintendents and ourselves. They will not be told to the Inmates. There will be a certain daily routine which they will be called upon to observe. If we see fit to alter it, it will be altered as a matter of course, I should say—explaining to them beforehand the why and wherefore. But if the establishment worked well, I would strongly counsel you not to try experiments. My belief is that nothing would unsettle them so much, or render their staying with us so doubtful—recollect, that we address a peculiar and strangely-made character.

There is this objection to the address of the chaplain to each person individually. It would decidedly involve the risk of their refusing to come to us. The extraordinary monotony of the refuges and asylums now existing, and the almost insupportable extent to which they carry the words and forms of religion, is known to no order of people so well as to these women; and they have that exaggerated dread of it, and that preconceived sense of their inability to bear it, which the reports of those who have refused to stay in them have bred in their minds. I am afraid if they were thus taken to task, and especially by a clergyman, they would be alarmed—would say "it's the old story after all, and we have mistaken the sort of place. It's better to say at once that we are not fit for it"—and that so we should lose them. That they are sensible of the sinfulness and degradation of their lives—that nothing else but that, has been impressed upon them by society since they began those lives—is, to say the least, reasonably probable. And he must be a very remarkably discreet and gentle man indeed, who could execute this difficult task, without rendering them apprehensive of what was to follow.

That their past lives should never be referred to at the Home, there can be no doubt.[2] I should say that any such reference on the part of the Superintendent would be an instance of blind mistake that in itself would render her dismissal necessary.

The temptation that has occurred to you, in pursuance of Macconochie's idea, suggests this consideration—that it is one to which in all probability they will never be exposed abroad, and that it is a very severe one. If a girl goes out by herself, where is she to go? Every one she knows now is, to a greater or less extent, an infamous associate; and suffering her to go out by herself would be to expose her to the arts and temptations and recognitions of fifty such—even supposing that her old habits and her new freedom didn't lead her among them, it is likely some of them would come in her way; and her very decency might give them the advantage, as by inducing her to go away with them in the first instance, rather than be jeered and mocked in the open streets. I propose that, in the country, about the house, they shall constantly go out in two or threes with Mrs. Holdsworth.[3] I would, as they advanced in their training and shewed decided improvement, trust them with keys, and with many little offices within-doors that would test their self denial. . . .

One great point that I try to bear in mind continually, and which I hope the clergyman[4] will steadily remember, is, that these unfortunate creatures are to be *Tempted* to virtue. They cannot be dragged, driven, or frightened. You originate this great work for the salvation of the women who come into that Home; and I hold it to be the sacred duty of every one who assists you in it, first *to consider how best to get them there, and how best to keep them there*. Every other consideration should fade before these two, because every other consideration follows upon them, and is included in them, and is impracticable without them. It is for this vital reason that a knowledge of human nature as it shews itself in these tarnished and battered images of God—and a patient consideration for it—and a determined putting of the question to one's self, not only whether this or that piece of instruction or correction be in itself good and true, but how it can be best adapted to the state in which we find these people, and the necessity we are under of dealing gently with them, lest they should run headlong back on their own destruction—are the great, merciful, Christian thoughts for such an enterprize, and form the only spirit in which it can be successfully undertaken. Do you not feel with me that this must be kept steadily in view, and that a chaplain imbued with this feeling in the outset, is the only minister for the place?[5]. . .

I most entirely agree with you that it is right they should feel perfectly free before going abroad. If this system hold (and I have a faith in its doing so, simply because it is the system of Christianity, and nothing more or less) I believe they *will* feel perfectly free, when that time comes. But we can examine into this, and devise for it, leisurely. It has occurred to me that it would be an admirable means of promoting friendly and affectionate feelings among them, to give them to understand that no one should ever be sent abroad alone.[6] It would be a beautiful thing, and would give us a wonderful power over them, if they would form strong attachments among themselves. To say nothing of the encouragement and support they would be to one another in a foreign country.

My dear Miss Coutts, you will attribute my earnestness to the true cause—the unspeakable interest I have in a design fraught with such great consequences, and the knowledge I have (if I have any knowledge at all) of these sad aspects of humanity, and their workings—when I again refer to that indispensable necessity of remembering the formed character that is to be addressed, and of considering everything that is addressed to it, not with reference to itself alone, but in connexion with its adaptability to the nature, sufferings, and whole experience of the objects of your benevolence. In proportion as the details of any one of these young lives would be strange and difficult to a good man who had kept away from such knowledge, so the best man in the world could never make his way to the truth of these people, unless he were content to win it very slowly, and with the nicest perception always present to him, of the results engendered in them by what they have gone through. Wrongly addressed, they are certain to deceive. The greatest anxiety I feel in connexion with this scheme—it is a greater one than any that arises out of my sense of responsibility to you, though that is not slight—is, that the clergyman with whom I hope I am to act as one confiding in him and perfectly confided in, should be not only a well-intentioned man, as I believe most clergymen would be, but one of the kindest, most considerate, most judicious, and least exacting of his order. . . .

1. Dickens always placed great importance on the New Testament as a source for inspiring good conduct and repentance. Cf. E. B. L. Dickens, pp 167–8.
2. After each inmate had settled in the House, her history was taken down and entered into a book. This information, however, was kept confidential.

Nothing was said to the two superintendents and the inmates were admonished not to communicate details of their past to their associates.
3. The matron in charge until Feb. 1849. When the women attended church on Sundays, Dickens notes that they were 'invariably accompanied by one of the Superintendents'. See *HW* essay.
4. Revd E. Illingworth, Chesterton's chaplain, appointed to attend the Home.
5. Comments about possible inmates follow, together with a detailed summary of preparations Dickens had made in readiness for opening the Home. As with all his plans for this project, their comprehensiveness and mastery of the minutest detail compel respect. See P, IV, 183–7 for the passages omitted from N, II, 56–9.
6. Dickens writes in his *HW* essay that they usually went abroad 'three or four together'.

[AN APPEAL TO FALLEN WOMEN][1]

You will see, on beginning to read this letter, that it is not addressed to you by name. But I address it to a woman—a very young woman still—who was born to be happy and has lived miserably; who has no prospect before her but sorrow, or behind her but a wasted youth; who, if she has ever been a mother, has felt shame instead of pride in her own unhappy child.

You are such a person, or this letter would not be put into your hands. If you have ever wished (I know you must have done so some time) for a chance of rising out of your sad life, and having friends, a quiet home, means of being useful to yourself and others, peace of mind, self-respect, everything you have lost, pray read it attentively and reflect upon it aftwards.

I am going to offer you, not the chance but the *certainty* of all these blessings, if you will exert yourself to deserve them. And do not think that I write to you as if I felt myself very much above you, or wished to hurt your feelings by reminding you of the situation in which you are placed. God forbid! I mean nothing but kindness to you, and I write as if you were my sister.

Think for a moment what your present situation is. Think how impossible it is that it ever can be better if you continue to live as you have lived, and how certain it is that it must be worse. You know what the streets are; you know how cruel the companions that you find there are; you know the vices practised there, and to what wretched consequences they bring you, even while you are young. Shunned by decent people, marked out from all other kinds of women as you walk along, avoided by the very children, hunted by the police, imprisoned, and only set free to be imprisoned over and over again—reading this very letter in a common jail you have already dismal experience of the truth.

But to grow old in such a way of life, and among such company—to escape an early death from terrible disease, or your own maddened hand, and arrive at old age in such a course—will be an aggravation of every misery that you know now, which words cannot describe. Imagine for yourself the bed on which you, then an object terrible to look at, will lie down to die. Imagine all the long, long years of shame, want, crime, and ruin that will arise before you. And by that dreadful day, and by the judgment that will follow it, and by the recollection that you are certain to have then, when it is too late, of the offer that is made to you now, when it is NOT too late, I implore you think of it and weigh it well.

There is a lady in this town who from the window of her house has seen such as you going past at night,[2] and has felt her heart bleed at the sight. She is what is called a great lady, but she has looked after you with compassion as being of her own sex and nature, and the thought of such fallen women has troubled her in her bed.

She has resolved to open at her own expense a place of refuge near London for a small number of females, who without such help are lost for ever, and to make a HOME for them. In this home they will be taught all household work that would be useful to them in a home of their own and enable them to make it comfortable and happy. In this home, which stands in a pleasant country lane and where each may have her little flower-garden if she pleases, they will be treated with the greatest kindness: will lead an active, cheerful, healthy life: will learn many things it is profitable and good to know, and being entirely removed from all who have any knowledge of their past career will begin life afresh and be able to win a good name and character.

And because it is not the lady's wish that these young women should be shut out from the world after they have repented and learned to do their duty there, and because it is her wish and object that they may be restored to society—a comfort to themselves and it—they will be supplied with every means, when some time shall have elapsed and their conduct shall have fully proved their earnestness and reformation, to go abroad, where in a distant country they may become the faithful wives of honest men, and live and die in peace.

I have been told that those who see you daily in this place believe that there are virtuous inclinations lingering within you, and that you may be reclaimed. I offer the Home I have described in these few words, to you.

But, consider well before you accept it. As you are to pass from the gate of this Prison to a perfectly new life, where all the means of happiness, from which you are now shut out, are opened brightly to you, so remember on the other hand that you must have the strength to leave behind you all old habits. You must resolve to set a watch upon yourself; to be gentle, patient, persevering, and good-tempered. Above all things, to be truthful in every word you speak. Do this, and all the rest is easy. But you must solemnly remember that if you enter this Home without such constant resolutions, you will occupy, unworthily and uselessly, the place of some other unhappy girl, now wandering and lost; and that her ruin, no less than your own, will be upon your head, before Almighty God, who knows the secrets of our breasts; and Christ, who died upon the Cross to save us.

In case there should be anything you wish to know, or any question you would like to ask about this Home, you have only to say so, and every information shall be given to you. Whether you accept or reject it, think of it. If you awake in the silence and solitude of the night, think of it then. If any remembrance ever comes into your mind of any time when you were innocent and very different, think of it then. If you should be softened by a moment's recollection of any tenderness or affection you have ever felt, or that has ever been shown to you, or of any kind word that has ever been spoken to you, think of it then. If ever your poor heart is moved to feel truly, what you might have been, and what you are, oh think of it then, and consider what you may yet become.

Believe me that I am indeed,

Your Friend.

1. Dickens wrote 'An Appeal to Fallen Women' in 1847. This anonymous four-page leaflet was given to prostitutes when they were arrested by the police; copies were also distributed by hand in the streets. A copy of the Appeal turned up in the US, where it was later reprinted by the Boston Bibliophile Society for private circulation among members. See Edward F. Payne and Henry H. Harper, *The Charity of Charles Dickens* (Boston: Bibliophile Society, 1929). J. W. T. Ley reprinted the *Appeal* in the *Western Mail*, and then in *The Dickensian*, 26 (1930), 198–200.
2. Miss Coutts, whose house at No. 1 Stratton Street, Piccadilly, overlooked one of London's main thoroughfares.

DEVONSHIRE TERRACE
Sunday Twelfth December 1847
My Dear Hullah,[1]—I am actively engaged, for Miss Coutts, in the management of a private establishment (called her Home) for the

reclamation of certain young women, and for the training of them for colonization.

We want them to learn to sing in parts, on your system.[2] The class is now six or seven strong, and will never be more than thirteen. The place is at Shepherd's Bush, accessible by Acton omnibus from Oxford Street. If you will empower any one of your masters whom you may think best adapted to such a purpose, to communicate with me, and will beg him to call upon me any morning between half past ten and two—armed with your card, which will be his passport—I will settle with him such questions as whether one attendance in a week will be often enough, and will conclude the engagement on the spot. I am very anxious for the instruction beginning without delay, as I attach immense importance to its refining influence.—Ever yours cordially.

BROADSTAIRS, KENT
Nineteenth September 1848

MY DEAR HULLAH,—Miss Coutts thinks that your young ladies have made sufficient advancement in that scientific kind of instruction which Mr. Banister[3] communicates—which is better adapted, she holds, to the wants of a superior class of pupils who have not so much work to attend to—and therefore she would desire to terminate engagement at the expiration of the current quarter, or at any other reasonable notice you think right, and to substitute some female teacher of lower qualifications who could come on Saturday evenings, and sing hymns and so forth, with them. Her wish is, that they should now use what they have learnt in this wise, socially, and turn it to account in their devotion and relaxation, rather than they should learn more, as an abstract study or accomplishment.

I state her views, of course, without any admixture of my own.—Faithfully yours always.

1. J. P. Hullah (1812–84), musical composer and teacher; met Dickens in 1835. Dickens wrote the words for Hullah's opera 'The Village Coquettes'.
2. Hullah taught music and singing to groups of people and originated a movement, which began in Battersea in 1840, to provide teachers with an elementary musical education.
3. H. C. Banister (1831–97), composer and teacher, selected by Hullah in response to Dickens's previous letter.

TAVISTOCK HOUSE
Saturday, Fifteenth November, 1856

[Miss Coutts] . . . I return Derry.[1] I have no doubt it's a capital article, but it's a mortal dull color. Color these people always want, and color (as altered to fancy), I would always give them. In these cast-iron and mechanical days, I think even such a garnish to the dish of their monotonous and hard lives, of unspeakable importance. One color, and that of the earth earthy, is too much with them early and late. Derry might just as well break out into a stripe, or put forth a bud, or even burst into a full blown flower. Who is Derry that he is to make quakers of us all, whether we will or no![2]. . .

1. Miss Coutts had sent a pattern of a drab cotton material called 'derry', which she thought suitable for overalls and other purposes in the Home (N, II, 812n).

    Disagreement about dress, writes P. Collins, marks one of the few differences between Dickens and Miss Coutts over the running of Urania Cottage. She was suspicious of brightness, which she thought was the cause of much female delinquency; he countered that girls should be offered the bait of eventual marriage as a reward, and that in the later stages of their training, all temptations should not be removed (*Dickens and Crime*, p. 100).

2. About two years after writing this letter Dickens withdrew from his active engagement with the Home when existing mores made difficult the continued partnership of a man separated from his wife with an unmarried woman of Miss Coutts's social prominence. The Home continued to run but faltered without his help. 'There were gratifying cases of redemption with new starts in life;' wrote Miss Coutts's secretary, 'and some successful efforts at emigration. But, on the whole, the work proved even more difficult than Dickens had foreseen; and after many discouragements and failures the scheme was given up.' See Charles C. Osborne, ed., *Letters of Charles Dickens to Baroness Burdett-Coutts* (New York: E. P. Dutton, 1932), p. 175. Between 1847 and 1858, Urania Cottage admitted over 100 women and cost about £1000 a year to run and administer. See K. J. Fielding, *The Dickensian*, 51 (Dec. 1954), 32n.

TAVISTOCK HOUSE
Sunday Eighteenth April 1852

[Miss Coutts] . . . It is a very good thing to try several descriptions of houses,[1] but I have no doubt myself (after long consideration of the subject) that the large houses are best. You never can, for the same money, offer anything like the same advantages in small houses. It is *not* desirable to encourage any small carpenter or builder who has a few pounds to invest, to run up small dwelling houses. If they had been discouraged long ago, London would be an immeasurably healthier place than it can be made in scores of years to come. If you go into any common outskirts of the town now and see the advancing army of brick and mortar laying waste the country fields and shutting out the air, you cannot fail to be struck by the consideration that if large buildings had been erected for the working people, instead of the absurd and expensive separate walnut shells in which they live, London would have been about a third of its present size, and every family would have had a country walk miles nearer to their own door. Besides this, men would have been nearer to their work—would not have had to dine at public houses—there would have been thicker walls of separation and better means of separation than you can ever give (except at a preposterous cost) in small tenements—and they would have had gas, water, drainage, and a variety of other humanizing things which you *can't* give them so well in little houses. Further, in little houses, you must keep them near the ground, and you cannot by any possibility afford such sound and wholesome foundations (remedying this objection) in little houses as in large ones. The example of large houses appears to me, in all respects, (always supposing their locality to be a great place like London) far better than any example you can set by small houses; and the compensation you give for any overgrown shadow they may cast upon a street at certain hours of the day is out of all proportion to that drawback.

I know everybody at Manchester, and in most of those places. But I think the people for the suggestion-paper are people connected with Railways passing through remote Yorkshire Moors, where they have had to frame schools and churches, and establish an orderly system of society out of the strangest disorder—as in one case in Yorkshire, now, where a Tunnel has been making for some years. Also large ironmasters—of whom there are some notable cases—who have proceeded on the self-supporting principle, and have done wonders with their workpeople. Also other manufacturers in isolated places who have awakened to find themselves in the midst of a mass of workpeople going headlong to destruction, and have stopped the current, and quite turned it by establishing decent houses, paying schools, saving banks, little libraries, etc. Several of these instances come into my mind as I write this and I have no doubt we could get the results of such experience by merely asking for them. . . .

1. In addition to supporting Urania Cottage and the help she gave to the Ragged School in Field Lane, Miss Coutts also initiated two massive projects: St. Stephen's model parish, Westminster, which was begun in 1847 and completed in 1849, and Columbia Square, to which this letter refers. In it, Dickens suggested some of the principles which guided her work. Miss Coutts bought Nova Scotia Gardens, Bethnal Green, in 1852 for £8700; after the site was cleared of its unhealthy tenements, work began in 1859 and was finished in 1862. For £45 000 she provided four blocks of

wholesome, comfortable and low-cost model dwellings, a market-house and a church. Later (1866–9), Miss Coutts provided an additional £200 000 for Columbia Market, which consisted of a quadrangle for open-air business, a clock-tower, a market-hall and a Gothic Hall. See Wheatley, II, 606; I, 446–7. See also 'Hail Columbia——Square!' *AYR*, 7 June 1862, and K. J. Fielding, 'Dickens's Work with Miss Coutts', *The Dickensian*, 61 (May 1965), 112–9; (Sep. 1965), 155–60.

TAVISTOCK HOUSE
Wednesday Second May, 1855

[Miss Coutts] . . . I looked carefully at the Highgate piece of ground the other day, and I think it on the whole very eligible for presentation as an open space.

These are my reasons,

1. It abuts immediately on the lane as you go up to the Cemetery, and consequently never could be diminished or built in upon that margin.

2. If the field opposite to it and below your large summer-house belongs to you, that West side of the ground is wonderfully free.

3. The ground itself is so shaped that it seems scarcely possible to build anything outside the top wall but one or two villas on the top of the rise, with lawns or gardens sloping downward to the piece of ground, which would not at all detract from its beauty, and would not too closely hem it in.

4. The plan of building now carrying out at the East or Small Pox Hospital side, suggests that in that direction also, the piece of ground will have gardens turned towards it.

Lastly the ground itself is of a wonderfully appropriate shape for an open space, and is so high in the most ornamental part that the view must always remain. The bottom would make an admirable children's playground, and the upper part with a few seats and a few more trees would be a beautiful little Park in itself.[1] . . .

1. Miss Coutts did not carry out her suggestion of presenting a piece of ground in Swaim's Lane, Highgate, as an open space; but as an alternative she provided a site for the schools of St. Anne's Church, Highgate (N, II, 657n).

Capital Punishment

1 DEVONSHIRE TERRACE, YORK GATE, REGENTS PARK

Twenty-Eighth July 1845

MY DEAR SIR,[1]—As my note is to bear reference to business, I will make it as short and plain as I can. You want me to write a paper for you. I think I could write you a pretty good and a well-timed article on the Punishment of Death, and sympathy with great criminals: instancing the gross and depraved curiosity that exists in reference to them, by some of the outrageous things that were written, done, and said in recent cases. But as I am not sure that my views would be yours; and as their statement would be quite inseparable from such a paper; I will briefly set down their purpose, that you may decide for yourself.[2]

Society having arrived at that state, in which it spared bodily torture to the worst criminals: and having agreed, if criminals be put to Death at all, to kill them in the speediest way: I consider the question with reference to society, and not at all with reference to the criminal.[3] Holding that in a case of cruel and deliberate murder, he is already mercifully and sparingly treated.

But, as a question for the deliberate consideration of all reflective persons, I put this view of the case.—With such very repulsive and odious details before us, may it not be well to inquire whether the Punishment of Death be beneficial to society. I believe it to have a horrible fascination for many of those persons who render themselves liable to it, impelling them onward to the acquisition of a frightful notoriety; and (setting aside the strong confirmation of this idea afforded in individual instances) I presume this to be the case in very badly regulated minds, when I observe the strange fascination which everything connected with this punishment or the object of it, possesses for tens of thousands of decent, virtuous, well-conducted people, who are quite unable to resist the published portraits, letters, anecdotes, smilings, snuff-takings &c &c &c of the bloodiest and most unnatural scoundrel with the gallows before him. I observe that this strange interest does not prevail to anything like the same degree, where Death is not the penalty. Therefore I connect it with the Dread

211

and Mystery surrounding Death in any shape, but especially in this avenging form; and am disposed to come to the conclusion that it produces crime in the criminally disposed, and engenders a diseased sympathy—morbid and bad, but natural and often irresistible—among the well-conducted and gentle.

Regarding it as doing harm to both these classes, it may even then be right to enquire, whether it has any salutary influence on those small knots and specks of people, mere bubbles in the living ocean, who actually behold its infliction with their proper eyes. On this head, it is scarcely possible to entertain a doubt; for we know that robbery and obscenity and callous indifference are of no commoner occurrence anywhere than at the foot of the scaffold. Furthermore, we know that all exhibitions of agony and Death have a tendency to brutalise and harden the feelings of men, and have always been the most rife, among the fiercest people. Again, it is a great question whether ignorant and dissolute persons (ever the great body of spectators, as few others will attend), seeing *that* murder done, and not having seen the other, will not, almost of necessity sympathise with the man who dies before them; especially as he is shown, a martyr to their fancy—tied and bound—alone among scores—with every kinds of odds against him.

I should take all these threads up at the end by a vivid little sketch of the origin and progress of such a crime as Hocker's[4]—stating a somewhat parallel case, but an imaginary one, pursuing its hero to his death, and showing what enormous harm he does, *after* the crime for which he suffers. I should state none of these positions in a positive sledge-hammer way, but tempt and lure the reader into the discussion of them in his own mind; and so we come to this at last—whether it be for the benefit of society to elevate even this crime to the awful dignity and notoriety of death; and whether it would not be much more to its advantage to substitute a mean and shameful punishment, degrading the deed and the committer of the deed, and leaving the general compassion to expend itself upon the only theme at present quite forgotten in the history, that is to say, the murdered person.

I do not give you this as an outline of the paper, which I think I could make attractive. It is merely an exposition of the inferences to which its whole philosophy must tend.—Believe me—Always faithfully yours.

1. Macvey Napier (1776–1847), editor of the *Edinburgh Review* 1829–47.
2. Dickens did not write this article for Napier because a 'maze of distractions' delayed its composition. Several months later, however, he returned to the ideas sketched here and used them as the basis of the letters he contributed to *The Daily News.*

3. By 1845, all aggravated forms of the death penalty had been abandoned in practice if not in law. The beheading of traitors (after hanging them) did not continue after the five Cato Street conspirators were publicly decapitated outside Newgate on 1 May 1820 (*DNB*, 19, p. 624). England's last gibbeting occurred in Leicester in Aug. 1832, and the practice was abolished in 1834. In 1832 Parliament repealed the statute which allowed surgeons to dissect the executed murderer before exposing the body to public view. The drop, which replaced the former method of hanging offenders from carts, was introduced in 1783. Though primitive and subject to subsequent improvement, this device eliminated some of the clumsy brutality that characterized the grim ceremonies at Tyburn. See Radzinowicz, I, 219–20; 220n; 202–3.

4. T. H. Hocker (1823–45), executed on 28 Apr. 1845 for the murder of J. Delarue, a professor of music, at Hampstead on 21 Feb. 1845. The Hampstead Murder, as journalists called the case, attracted great attention because Hocker exhibited 'a very extraordinary degree of audacity, and of misdirected talent' during his trial by attempting to impute false crimes to his victim and make the murder seem almost an act of justice. 'In short,' said the writer of *AR* in 1845, 'a greater compound of wickedness, falsehood, and conceit, never graced the annals of Newgate.' See, 'Chronicle', 28 Apr. 1845, p. 57. *AR* also provides a full account of Hocker's trial and a transcript of one of the two papers he read from the dock purporting to explain his actions. See pp. 378–91. Dickens comments on Hocker's behaviour and personality in the *DN* letter of 9 Mar. 1846. See pp 227–8.

[I]

To THE EDITORS OF THE DAILY NEWS.   February 23, 1846
GENTLEMEN. I choose this time for addressing to you, the first of two or three letters[1] on the subject of Capital Punishment, because it seems to me that the importance of the question is very strongly presented to the public mind just now, by a recent execution in Ireland:[2] and the recent acquittal, in England, of one of the most cruel murderers of whom we have any record.[3] And although there can be no doubt that such a theme, of all others, should be considered with the calmest reference to its own broad Right and Wrong, and not with a limited appeal to its illustration in this or that instance; still, I apprehend that cases like these resolve themselves so directly into the general question, as to have a legitimate and very powerful bearing on it; and that no better occasion can be seized for reviving its discussion, than when such circumstances are generally remembered.

I wish to be distinctly understood, in the outset, as writing in no spirit of sympathy *with the criminal*. It will be a part of my purpose to endeavour to show that the morbid and odious sentimentality which has been exhibited of late years, in favour of ruffians utterly unworthy of it, but drawing nigh to the gallows, is one of the evil concomitants of the Punishment of Death. And I desire to consider it, with a reference to the criminal, only in two points of view. To these, I will confine this introductory letter.

First. Whether one of the two great objects of all punishment (reserving the second for its proper place) be not to reform the offender. Secondly. Whether an irrevocable Doom—which nothing can recall, which no human power can set right if it be wrong, which may be wrongfully inflicted with the most just intention and which has been wrongfully inflicted with the most just intention, as we all know, more than once—should ever be pronounced by men of fallible and erring judgment, on their fellow-creatures.

It may be urged that, in the preparation of a criminal for death, and in his devout reception of religious comfort, and in his full confession and late repentance, his reformation is achieved and worked out. Reverend ordinaries, at Newgate and elsewhere, have said so. Hosts of angels have been imagined, in enthusiastic sermons, waiting to conduct the murderer to Heaven; and strange parallels have even been suggested, in such discourses, between the Scaffold and the Cross. GOD forbid that I should presume to measure, or doubt, the mercy in store for the worst criminal ever executed! But I do distinctly challenge and dispute this kind of reformation. Besides that the reformation brought about by legal punishment, should be, to be satisfactory, a living, lasting, growing one: working on, in degradation and humility, from day to day; and striving, in its chains, and labour, and long-distant Hope, to make some atonement always;—besides this, I doubt the possibility of a great change being wrought in any man's heart and nature, in the flush and fever of that flying interval between the Warrant and the Noose. I see the dreadful hurry of the time, expressed in every word and action that comes leaking through the prison-walls, to be caught up by the thirsty crowd outside. I see Hope living on, and know it must live on, in some faint shape, until the Bell begins to toll. I see the restless mind wandering away, miserably, from the main theme of the repentant letter, written in the cell; and while it tells of trust and steadfastness, having power to settle nowhere. I see the abject clinging on to life, which clutches at the hangman's hand, and blesses him beneath the beam. I see, in everything, the same wild, rapid, incoherent dream: of which I believe the penitence and preparation to be, at least, as unsettled and unsubstantial as any other part. And I believe this, because of the natural constitution of the human mind, and its ordinary workings at such a frightful pass.

"I can give you no hope of life," said a gentleman to a criminal in Newgate, on the night before the day appointed for his execution. "Unless I had solemnly given the promise elsewhere, that I would tell you so, I should not be here. But, by much entreaty, I have obtained a respite: that there may be time to inquire into what I have represented as a doubtful point. Can you bear the thought of living, only for another week?" "O God, sir!" cried the man, "a week is a long time to live!" And being smitten, as if he were only a week old then, he fell down, senseless, on the ground.[4]

Upon the second question, whether an irrevocable punishment be, on principle, justifiable; ordained, as it necessarily is, by men of fallible judgment, whose powers of arriving at the truth are limited, and in whom there is the capacity of mistake and false deduction; upon this question alone, I submit that a firm and efficient stand may be made against the punishment of Death. Better that hundreds of guilty persons should escape scot-free (which, supposing any other punishment to be substituted in its place, they never could or would), than that one innocent person should suffer. Better, I will even say, that hundreds of guilty persons should escape, than that the possibility of any innocent man or woman having been sacrificed, should present itself, with the least appearance or colour of reason, to the minds of any class of men!

Take the case of SEERY, the man just now executed in Ireland:[5] in that unhappy country, where it is considered most essential to assert the law, and make examples through its means. My impression of the case, so far as I know it from the public reports, is, that the man was guilty; but that is nothing to the purpose. There are these facts in it:

The prosecutor was shot at, by night; and identified the wretched man who has suffered, as the person who fired at him: against whom there was some other evidence, but all of a circumstantial and constructible nature. Before that miserable man went to his death, he set on record, a deliberate and solemn protest against the justice of his sentence, and called upon his Maker before whom he would so soon appear, with all his sins upon his head, to bear witness to his innocence. Since his death, the prosecutor (an honourable and credible witness, no doubt), has repeated his "positive and unalterable conviction," that he was not mistaken in his previous identification, and that SEERY was the man who fired at him.

Will anyone deny that there is, here, the Possibility of mistake? I entreat all who may chance to read this letter, to pause for an instant, and ask themselves whether they can remember any occasion, on which they have, in the broad day, and under circumstances the most favorable to recognition, mistaken one person for another: and believed that in a perfect stranger, they have seen, going away from them or coming towards them, a familiar friend. I beg them to consider whether such mistakes be not so common, in all men's experience, as to render it highly probable that every Irish peasant in whose remembrance this dying declaration lives and burns, can easily recal one such for himself. And then I put this question—Is such an execution calculated to assist the law: to diffuse a wholesome respect for it: to represss atrocious crimes against the person: to awaken any new sense of the sacredness of human life?

Contending, at present, against the Justifiability of the Punishment of Death, on this second ground which I have stated: I submit that Probability of mistake is not required. The barest Possibility of mistake is a sufficient reason against the taking of a life which nothing can restore; whereas, it would weigh but as a shred of gossamer against the infliction of any other punishment, within the power of man to repair.

With this, I leave the question of Capital Punishment in its reference to the convict sentenced, and shall beg leave, in another letter, to consider it in its bearings on Society and Crime. But, as a part of its effects upon Society, I would, in conclusion, entreat your readers to reflect, whether such a declaration as that made by Seery before his execution, would be likely to have awakened a general sympathy among the Irish people, or any strong conviction of his innocence (unless afterwards revived and borne out by newly discovered circumstances), but for its being surrounded by the awful dignity of Death.

1. This, the first of five public letters, was published on 23 Feb. 1846; the remaining letters appeared in *The Daily News* on 28 Feb. and 9, 13, and 16 Mar. Until P. Collins reprinted the letter of 28 Feb. in *The Law as Literature*, ed. L. Blom-Cooper (1961) and K. Tillotson the letter of 23 Feb. in the *TLS*, 12 Aug. 1965, p. 704, scholars believed Dickens contributed only three letters on this subject to the paper.
2. B. Seery, hanged at Mullingar, Westmeath, Ireland, on 13 Feb. 1846. This case, one of four investigated by a Special Commission to Westmeath, occasioned great interest in a county upset by several disturbances. At first the jury failed to agree; on Seery's second trial, he was found guilty of attempting to murder his landlord, Sir F. Hopkins on 18 Nov. 1845.
3. Capt. G. Johnstone of the *Tory*, who was arrested in Nov. 1845 and

charged with committing atrocities against members of his crew and murdering three of them. At his trial on 5 and 6 Feb. 1846 the jury initially found him guilty of murder and then reconsidered, finding him not guilty on the grounds of insanity.
4. Dickens here appended this note: In consequence of the new proof elicited by this new inquiry, the man was saved.
5. See note 2.

II

To the Editors of The Daily News   February 28, 1846
Gentlemen, In the very remarkable Report made to the State Assembly of New York, in 1841,[1] by a select committee of that body, who arrived at the conclusion, 'that the punishment of death, by law, ought to be forthwith and for ever abolished' in that part of America, there is the following suggestion:

'. . . Whether there sleep within the breast of man, certain dark and mysterious sympathies with the thought of that death, and that futurity which await his nature, tending to invest any act expressly forbidden by that penalty, with an unconscious and inexplicable fascination, that attracts his thoughts to it, in spite of their very shuddering dread; and bids his imagination brood over its idea, 'till out of those dark depths in his own nature, comes gradually forth a monstrous birth of Temptation.[2]. . .'

Strongly impressed by this passage when I first read the report; and believing that it shadowed out a metaphysical truth, which, however wild and appalling in its aspect, was a truth still; I was led to consider the cases of several murderers, both in deed, and in intent, with a reference to it; and certainly it gathered very strong and special confirmation in the course of that inquiry. But, as the bearing, here, is on capital punishment in its influences on the commission of crime; and as my present object is to make it the subject of one or two considerations in its other influences on society in general; I, for the present, defer any immediate pursuit of the idea, and merely quote it now, as introducing this lesser and yet great objection to the punishment of death:

That there is, about it, a horrible fascination, which, in the minds—not of evil-disposed persons, but of good and virtuous and well-conducted people, supersedes the horror legitimately attaching to crime itself, and causes every word and action of a criminal under sentence of death to be the subject of a morbid interest and curiosity.

Which is odious and painful, even to many of those who eagerly gratify it by every means they can compass; but which is, generally speaking, irresistible. The attraction of repulsion being as much a law of our moral nature, as gravitation is in the structure of the visible world, operates in no case (I believe) so powerfully, as in this case of the punishment of death; though it may occasionally diminish in its force, through strong reaction.

When the murderers HOCKER[3] and TAWELL[4] had awakened a vast amount of this depraved excitement, and it had attained to an unusually indecent and frenzied height, one of your contemporaries, deploring the necessity of ministering to such an appetite, laid the blame upon the caterers of such dainties for the Press, while some other newspapers, disputing which of them should bear the greater share of it, divided it variously. Can there be any doubt, on cool reflection, that the whole blame rested on, and was immediately and naturally referable to, the punishment of death?

Round what other punishment does the like interest gather? We read of the trials of persons who have rendered themselves liable to transportation for life, and we read of their sentences, and, in some few notorious instances, of their departure from this country, and arrival beyond sea; but *they* are never followed into their cells, and tracked from day to day, and night to night; *they* are never reproduced in their false letters, flippant conversations, theological disquisitions with visitors, lay and clerical: or served up in their whole biography and adventures—so many live romances with a bloody ending. Their portraits are not rife in the print-shops, nor are their autographs stuck up in shop-windows, nor are their snuff-boxes handed affably to gentlemen in court, nor do they inquire of other spectators with eye-glasses why they look at them so steadfastly, nor are their breakfasts, dinners, and luncheons, elaborately described, nor are their waxen images in Baker-Street[5] (*unless they were in immediate danger, at one time, of the gallows*), nor are high prices offered for their clothes at Newgate, nor do turnpike trusts grow rich upon the tolls that people going to see their houses, or the scenes of their offences, pay. They are tried, found guilty, punished; and there an end.

But a criminal under sentence of death, or in great peril of death upon the scaffold, becomes, immediately, the town talk; the great subject; the hero of the time. The demeanour in his latter moments, of SIR THOMAS MORE[6]—one of the wisest and most virtuous of men—was never the theme of more engrossing interest, than that of HOCKER, TAWELL, GREENACRE,[7] or COURVOISIER.[8] The smallest circumstance in the behaviour of these, or any similar wretches, is noted down and published as a precious fact. And read, too—extensively and generally read—even by hundreds and thousands of people who object to the publication of such details, and are disgusted by them. The horrible fascination surrounding the punishment, and everything connected with it, is too strong for resistance; and when an attempt is made in this or that gaol (as it has been sometimes made of late), to keep such circumstances from transpiring, by excluding every class of strangers, it is only a formal admission of the existence of this fascination, and of the impossibility of otherwise withstanding it.

Is it contended that the fascination may surround the crime, and not the punishment? Let us consider whether other crimes, which have now no sort of fascination for the general public, had or had not precisely the gross kind of interest which now attaches to Murder alone, when they were visited with the same penalty. Was Forgery interesting, when Forgers were hanged?[9] and is it less interesting now when they are transported for life? Compare the case of Dr Dodd,[10] or Fauntleroy,[11] or the Reverend Peter Fenn,[12] or Montgomery,[13] or Hunton,[14] or any other generally known, with that of the Exchequer-Bill forgery in later times, which: with every attendant circumstance but death, or danger of death, to give it a false attraction, soon dwindled down into a mere item in a Sessions' Calendar. Coining, when the coiner was dragged (as I have seen one) on a hurdle to the place of execution;[15] or Burglary, or Highway Robbery—did these crimes ever wear an aspect of adventure and mystery, and did the perpetrators of them ever become the town talk, when their offences were visited with death? Now, they are mean, degraded, miserable criminals; and nothing more.

That the publication of these Newgate court-circulars[16] to which I have alluded, is injurious to society, there can be no doubt. Apart from their inevitable association with revolting details, revived again and again, of bloodshed and murder (most objectionable as familiarizing people's minds with the contemplation of such horrors), it is manifest that anything which tends to awaken a false interest in great villains, and to invest their greatest villainies and lightest actions with a terrible attraction, must be vicious and bad, and cannot be wholesome reading. But it is neither just nor reasonable to charge their publication on the newspapers, or the gleaners for the newspapers. They are published because they are read and sought for. They are read and sought for: not because society has causelessly entered into a monstrous and unnatural league on this theme (which it would be absurd to suppose), but because it is in the secret nature of those of whom society is made up, to have a dark and dreadful interest in the punishment at issue.

Whether public executions produce any good impression on their habitual witnesses, or whether they are calculated to produce any good impression on the class of persons most likely to be attracted to them, is a question, by this time, pretty well decided. I was present, myself, at the execution of Courvoisier. I was, purposely, on the spot, from midnight of the night before; and was a near witness of the whole process of the building of the scaffold, the gathering of the crowd, the gradual swelling of the concourse with the coming-on of day, the hanging of the man, the cutting of the body down, and the removal of it into the prison. From the moment of my arrival, when there were but a few score boys in the street, and those all young thieves, and all clustered together behind the barrier nearest to the drop—down to the time when I saw the body with its dangling head, being carried on a wooden bier into the gaol—I did not see one token in all the immense crowd; at the windows, in the streets, on the house-tops, anywhere; of any one emotion suitable to the occasion. No sorrow, no salutary terror, no abhorrence, no seriousness; nothing but ribaldry, debauchery, levity, drunkenness, and flaunting vice in fifty other shapes. I should have deemed it impossible that I could have ever felt any large assemblage of my fellow-creatures to be so odious. I hoped, for an instant, that there was some sense of Death and Eternity in the cry of 'Hats off!' when the miserable wretch appeared; but I found, next moment, that they only raised it as they would at a Play—to see the Stage the better, in the final scene.

Of the effect upon a perfectly different class, I can speak with no less confidence. There were, with me, some gentlemen of education and distinction in imaginative pursuits, who had, as I had, a particular detestation of that murderer; not only for the cruel deed he had done, but for his slow and subtle treachery, and for his wicked defence. And yet, if any one among us could have saved the man (we said so, afterwards, with one accord), he would have done it. It was so loathsome, pitiful, and vile a sight, that the law appeared to be as bad as he, or worse; being very much the stronger, and shedding around it a far more dismal contagion.[17]

The last of the influences of this punishment on society, which I shall notice in the present letter, is, that through the prevalent and fast-increasing feeling of repugnance to it, great offenders escape with a very inadequate visitation. Only a few weeks have elapsed since the streets of London presented the obscene spectacle of a woman being brought out to be killed before such a crowd as I have described, and, while her young body was yet hanging in the brutal gaze, of portions of the concourse hurrying away, to be in time to see a man hanged elsewhere, by the same executioner.[18] A barbarous murderer is tried soon afterwards, and acquitted on a fiction of his being insane—as any one, cognizant of these two recent executions, might have easily foreseen.

I will not enter upon the question whether juries be justified or not justified in evading their oaths, rather than add to the list of such deeply degrading and demoralizing exhibitions, and sanction the infliction of a punishment which they conscientiously believe, and have so many reasons for believing, to be wrong. It is enough for me that juries do so; and I presume to think that the able writer of a powerful article on Johnstone's trial in *The Daily News*,[19] does not sufficiently consider that this is no new course in juries, but the natural result and working of a law to which the general feeling is opposed. MR ABERCROMBIE,[20] five-and-thirty years ago, stated it in the House of Commons to have become a common practice of juries, in cases of Forgery, to find verdicts 'contrary to the clearest and most indisputable evidence of facts'; and cited the case of a woman who was proved to have stolen a ten-pound note, which the jury, with the approbation of the judge, found to be worth only thirty-nine shillings. SIR SAMUEL ROMILLY, in the same debate, mentioned other cases of the same nature; and they were of frequent and constant occurrence at that time.

Besides—that juries have, within our own time, in another class of cases, arrived at the general practice of returning a verdict tacitly agreed upon beforehand, and of making it applicable to very different sets of facts, we know by the notable instance of Suicide. Within a few years, juries frequently found that a man dying by his own hand, was guilty of self-murder. But this verdict subjecting the body to a barbarous mode of burial, from which the better feeling of society revolted (as it is now revolting from the punishment of death), it was abrogated by common consent, and precisely the same evasion established, as is now, unfortunately, so often resorted to in cases of murder. That it is an evasion, and not a proceeding on a soundly-proved and established principle, that he who destroys his own life must necessarily be mad—the very exceptions from this usual course in themselves demonstrate.

So it is in cases of Murder. Juries, like society, are not stricken foolish or motiveless. They have, for the most part, an objection to the punishment of death: and they will, for the most part, assert such verdicts. As jurymen, in the Forgery cases, would probably reconcile their verdict to their consciences, by calling to mind that the intrinsic value of a bank note was almost nothing, so jurymen in cases of Murder probably argue that grave doctors have said all men are more or less mad, and therefore they believe the prisoner mad. This is a great wrong to society; but it arises out of the punishment of death.

And the question will always suggest itself in jurors' minds—however earnestly the learned judge presiding, may discharge his duty—'which is the greater wrong to society? To give this man the benefit of the possibility of his being mad, or to have another public execution, with all its depraving and hardening influences?' Imagining myself a juror, in a case of life or death: and supposing that the evidence had forced me from every other ground of opposition to this punishment in the particular case, as a possibility of irremediable mistake, or otherwise: I would go over it again on this ground; and if I could, by any reasonable special pleading with myself, find him mad rather than hang him—I think I would.

1. J. L. O'Sullivan's *Report in Favor of the Abolition of the Punishment of Death by Law, Made to the Legislature of the State of New York, April 14, 1841* (New York: J. & H. G. Langley, 1841).
2. The phrase should read: 'a monstrous Frankenstein birth of Temptation'. See Sullivan, *Report* (repr. New York: Arno Press, 1974), p. 69.
3. Hocker, see note on p. 213.
4. J. Tawell, Quaker. Executed at Aylesbury on 28 Mar. 1845 for the murder of S. Hart, his mistress. Earlier, Tawell had been transported to Australia for forgery; after prospering abroad, he returned home, where, beneath his respectable appearance as a Quaker, 'sedate demeanour, and outward benevolence', he continued to live a life of 'total deficiency of morality and principle'. See *AR*, 1845, 'Chronicle', p. 43.
5. The permanent headquarters Marie Tussaud (1760–1850) established for her exhibition of waxwork figures. Tussaud's first opened in London in 1802; in 1884 it was moved to a building in Marylebone Road, the exhibition's present site.
6. Executed by Henry VIII in 1535 for refusing to recognize his monarch's marriage to Queen Anne and for not renouncing the Pope's spiritual authority.
7. J. Greenacre (1785–1837; *DNB*), executed 2 May 1837 before an estimated 20 000 spectators. Greenacre was found guilty of murdering Hannah Brown, to whom he proposed marriage but killed and dismembered the day before the wedding was scheduled.
8. F. B. Courvoisier (1817–40), the Swiss valet found guilty of murdering his master, Lord W. Russell, on 6 May 1840 and publicly executed on 6 July 1840. Dickens hired a room facing the gallows and watched Courvoisier's hanging. D. Maclise and H. Burnett accompanied him. See Burnett's

reminiscences, quoted in Kitton, *Charles Dickens by Pen and Pencil*, II, 142–3. For Dickens's account of the execution, see his description later in the letter.

9. Forgery was made a capital offence in 1634; thereafter over 400 statutes containing provisions against the offence were passed and remained in effect until 1832, when an act (2&3 Will. IV c. 123) abolished the death penalty for forgery. Of the forgers listed by Dickens, Dodd and Fauntleroy were the two most notable offenders to suffer execution.

10. W. Dodd (1729–77; *DNB*). Executed 27 June 1777 for forging a bond and selling it to a stockbroker.

11. H. Fauntleroy (1785–1824; *DNB*). Executed 30 Nov. 1824 before a crowd estimated at 10 000. Fauntleroy, a banker and partner in his father's bank of Marsh, Sibbald, & Co., was convicted of fraudulently selling stock and forging the signatures of the bank's trustees.

12. Revd P. Fenn, schoolmaster, sentenced to death on 11 Sep. 1828 for uttering forged bills of exchange. According to the 'Chronicle' in the AR (1828), p. 118, Fenn was not executed.

13. W. Montgomery, convicted of issuing forged notes and sentenced to death. On 4 July 1828 Montgomery foiled the hangman by committing suicide in his cell in Newgate the night before his execution had been scheduled.

14. J. Hunton, a wealthy Quaker, convicted of a series of forgeries and executed on 8 Dec. 1828.

15. Coinage offences, like those of forgery, were the subject of numerous capital statutes. The first was passed in 1350; in 1832 Parliament abolished the death penalty for all coinage offences. Between 1820 and 1830, 73 offenders were sentenced to death under the old statutes, ten of whom were hanged. The last execution for coining was in 1829. See Radzinowicz, I, 652–4. I have been unable to ascertain which execution for coining Dickens attended.

16. Series such as *The Newgate Calendar, or The Malefactors' Bloody Register* (began 1774) describing notorious criminals and their feats. Other accounts appeared in chap-books, ballads, and broadsides, many of which were published by the notorious Catnach Press.

17. Thackeray was also present and wrote of his disgust in 'Going to See a Man Hanged', *Fraser's Magazine*, 22 (Aug. 1840), 150–8.

18. Martha Browning (see also p. 224 and note), executed outside Newgate on 5 Jan. 1846 and S. Quennell, hanged on the same day outside Horsemonger Lane Gaol.

19. For Johnstone, see note on pp 216–7.

20. J. Abercromby (1776–1858; *DNB*), speaking on 29 Mar. 1811 cited official figures to show how juries often declined to prosecute those charged with stealing when the statutory penalty specified hanging. In 1810 Sir S. Romilly (1757–1811) introduced a bill to abolish the death penalty in cases of shoplifting, stealing in dwelling houses and stealing on navigable rivers. Romilly's bill was defeated in the Commons in 1810; he reintroduced it a year later, when the bill passed the Commons but was defeated in the Lords on 24 May 1811. For the passage Dickens cites from Abercromby's speech, see the Dwelling House Robbery Bill, *Hansard*, vol. 19, 652–4.

III

To THE EDITORS OF *The Daily News*.   March 9, 1846
GENTLEMEN, I will take for the subject of this letter, the effect of
Capital Punishment on the commission of crime, or rather of murder;
the only crime with one exception (and that a rare one) to which it is
now applied.[1] Its effect in preventing crime, I will reserve for another
letter: and a few of the more striking illustrations of each aspect of the
subject, for a concluding one.

THE EFFECT OF CAPITAL PUNISHMENT ON THE COMMISSION OF MURDER

Some murders are committed in hot blood and furious rage; some, in
deliberate revenge; some, in terrible despair; some (but not many) for
mere gain; some, for the removal of an object dangerous to the
murderer's peace or good name; some, to win a monstrous notoriety.

On murders committed in rage, in the despair of strong affection (as
when a starving child is murdered by its parent) or for gain, I believe
the Punishment of Death to have no effect in the least. In the two first
cases, the impulse is a blind and wild one, infinitely beyond the reach of
any reference to the punishment. In the last, there is little calculation
beyond the absorbing greed of the money to be got. Courvoisier, for
example, might have robbed his master with greater safety and with
fewer chances of detection, if he had not murdered him. But, his
calculations going to the gain and not to the loss, he had no balance for
the consequences of what he did. So, it would have been more safe and
prudent in the woman who was hanged a few weeks since,[2] for the
murder in Westminster, to have simply robbed her old companion in
an unguarded moment, as in her sleep. But, her calculation going to the
gain of what she took to be a Bank note; and the poor old woman living
between her and the gain; she murdered her.

On murders committed in deliberate revenge, or to remove a
stumbling block in the murderer's path, or in an insatiate craving for
notoriety, is there reason to suppose that the Punishment of Death has
the direct effect of an incentive and an impulse?

A murder is committed in deliberate revenge. The murderer is at no
trouble to prepare his train of circumstances, takes little or no pains to
escape, is quite cool and collected, perfectly content to deliver himself
up to the Police, makes no secret of his guilt, but boldly says "I killed
him. I'm glad of it. I meant to do it. I am ready to die." There was such a
case the other day.[3] There was such another case not long ago. There

are such cases frequently. It is the commonest first exclamation on being seized. Now, what is this but a false arguing of the question, announcing a foregone conclusion, expressly leading to the crime, and inseparably arising out of the Punishment of Death? "I took his life. I give up mine to pay for it. Life for life; blood for blood. I have done the crime. I am ready with the atonement. I know all about it; it's a fair bargain between me and the law. Here am I to execute my part of it; and what more is to be said or done?" It is the very essence of the maintenance of this punishment for murder, that it *does* set life against life. It is in the essence of a stupid, weak, or otherwise ill-regulated mind (of such a murderer's mind, in short), to recognise in this set off, a something that diminishes the base and coward character of murder. In a pitched battle, I, a common man, may kill my adversary, but he may kill me. In a duel, a gentleman may shoot his opponent through the head, but the opponent may shoot him too, and this makes it fair. Very well. I take this man's life for a reason I have, or choose to think I have, and the law takes mine. The law says, and the clergyman says, there must be blood for blood and life for life. Here it is. I pay the penalty.

A mind capable, or confounded in its perceptions—and you must argue with reference to such a mind, or you could not have such a murder—may not only establish on these grounds an idea of strict justice and fair reparation, but a stubborn and dogged fortitude and foresight that satisfy it hugely. Whether the fact be really so, or not, is a question I would be content to rest, alone, on the number of cases of revengeful murder in which this is well known, without dispute, to have been the prevailing demeanour of the criminal: and in which such speeches and such absurd reasoning have been constantly uppermost with him. "Blood for blood," and "life for life," and such balanced jingles, have passed current in people's mouths, from legislators downwards, until they have been corrupted into "tit for tat," and acted on.

Next, come the murders done to sweep out of the way a dreaded or detested object. At the bottom of this class of crimes, there is a slow, corroding, growing hate. Violent quarrels are commonly found to have taken place between the murdered person and the murderer: usually of opposite sexes. There are witnesses to old scenes of reproach and recrimination, in which they were the actors; and the murderer has been heard to say, in this or that coarse phrase, "that he wouldn't mind killing her, though he should be hanged for it"—in these cases, the commonest avowal.

It seems to me, that in this well-known scrap of evidence, there is a deeper meaning than is usually attached to it. I do not know, but it may be—I have a strong suspicion that it is—a clue to the slow growth of the crime, and its gradual development in the mind. More than this; a clue to the mental connexion of the deed, with the punishment to which the doer of that deed is liable, until the two, conjoined, give birth to monstrous and mis-shapen Murder.

The idea of murder, in such a case, like that of self-destruction in the great majority of instances, is not a new one. It may have presented itself to the disturbed mind in a dim shape and afar off; but it has been there. After a quarrel, or with some strong sense upon him of irritation or discomfort arising out of the continuance of this life in his path, the man has brooded over the unformed desire to take it. "Though he should be hanged for it." With the entrance of the Punishment into his thoughts, the shadow of the fatal beam begins to attend—not on himself, but on the object of his hate. At every new temptation, it is there, stronger and blacker yet, trying to terrify him. When she defies or threatens him, the scaffold seems to be her strength and "vantage ground." Let her not be too sure of that; "though he should be hanged for it."

Thus, he begins to raise up, in the contemplation of this death by hanging, a new and violent enemy to brave. The prospect of a slow and solitary expiation would have no congeniality with his wicked thoughts, but this throttling and strangling has. There is always before him, an ugly, bloody, scarecrow phantom, that champions her, as it were, and yet shows him, in a ghastly way, the example of murder. Is she very weak, or very trustful in him, or infirm, or old? It gives a hideous courage to what would be mere slaughter otherwise; for there it is, a presence always about her, darkly menacing him with that penalty whose murky secret has a fascination for all secret and unwholesome thoughts. And when he struggles with his victim at the last, "though he should be hanged for it," it is a merciless wrestle, not with one weak life only, but with that ever-haunting, ever-beckoning shadow of the gallows too; and with a fierce defiance to it, after their long survey of each other, to come and do its worst.

Present this black idea of violence to a bad mind contemplating violence; hold up before a man remotely compassing the death of another person, the spectacle of his own ghastly and untimely death by man's hands; and out of the depths of his own nature you shall assuredly raise up that which lures and tempts him on. The laws which regulate those mysteries have not been studied or cared for, by the maintainers of this law; but they are paramount and will always assert their power.

Out of one hundred and sixty-seven persons under sentence of Death in England, questioned at different times, in the course of years, by an English clergyman in the performance of his duty, there were only three who had not been spectators of executions.

We come, now, to the consideration of those murders which are committed, or attempted, with no other object than the attainment of an infamous notoriety. That this class of crimes has its origin in the Punishment of Death, we cannot question; because (as we have already seen, and shall presently establish by another proof) great notoriety and interest attach, and are generally understood to attach, only to those criminals who are in danger of being executed.

One of the most remarkable instances of murder originating in mad self-conceit; and of the murderer's part in the repulsive drama, in which the law appears at such great disadvantage to itself and to society, being acted almost to the last with a self-complacency that would be horribly ludicrous if it were not utterly revolting; is presented in the case of Hocker.[4]

Here is an insolent, flippant, dissolute youth: aping the man of intrigue and levity: over-dressed, over-confidence, inordinately vain of his personal appearance: distinguished as to his hair, cane, snuff-box, and singing-voice: and unhappily the son of a working shoemaker. Bent on loftier flights than such a poor house-swallow as a teacher in a Sunday-school can take; and having no truth, industry, perseverance or other dull work-a-day quality, to plume his wings withal; he casts about him, in his jaunty way, for some mode of distinguishing himself—some means of getting that head of hair into the print-shops; of having something like justice done to his singing-voice and fine intellect; of making the life and adventures of Thomas Hocker remarkable; and of getting up some excitement in connexion with that slighted piece of biography. The Stage? No. Not feasible. There has always been a conspiracy against the Thomas Hockers, in that kind of effort. It has been the same with Authorship in prose and poetry. Is there nothing else? A Murder, now, would make a noise in the papers! There is the gallows to be sure; but without that, it would be nothing. Short of that, it wouldn't be fame. Well! We must all die at one time or other; and to die game, and have it in print, is just the thing for a man of spirit. They always die game at the Minor Theatres and the Saloons, and the people like it very much. Thurtell,[5] too, died very game, and made a capital speech when he was tried. There's all about it in a book at the cigar-shop now. Come, Tom, get your name up! Let it be a dashing murder that shall keep the wood-engravers at it for the next two months. You are the boy to go through with it, and interest the town!

The miserable wretch, inflated by this lunatic conceit, arranges his whole plan for publication and effect. It is quite an epitome of his experience of the domestic melodrama or penny novel. There is the Victim Friend; the mysterious letter of the injured Female to the Victim Friend; the romantic spot for the Death-Struggle by night; the unexpected appearance of Thomas Hocker to the Policeman; the parlour of the Public House, with Thomas Hocker reading the paper to a strange gentleman; the Family Apartment, with a song by Thomas Hocker; the Inquest Room, with Thomas Hocker boldly looking on; the interior of the Marylebone Theatre, with Thomas Hocker taken into custody; the Police Office with Thomas Hocker "affable" to the spectators; the interior of Newgate, with Thomas Hocker preparing his defence; the Court, where Thomas Hocker, with his dancing-master airs, is put upon his trial, and complimented by the Judge; the Prosecution, the Defence, the Verdict, the Black Cap, the Sentence—each of them a line in any Playbill, and how bold a line in Thomas Hocker's life!

It is worthy of remark, that the nearer he approaches to the gallows—the great last scene to which the whole of these effects have been working up—the more the overweening conceit of the poor wretch shows itself; the more he feels that he is the hero of the hour; the more audaciously and recklessly he lies, in supporting the character. In public—at the condemned sermon—he deports himself as becomes the man whose autographs are precious, whose portraits are innumerable; in memory of whom, whole fences and gates have been borne away, in splinters, from the scene of murder. He knows that the eyes of Europe are upon him; but he is not proud—only graceful. He bows, like the first gentleman in Europe, to the turnkey who brings him a glass of water; and composes his clothes and hassock, as carefully as good Madame Blaize[6] could do. In private—within the walls of the condemned cell—every word and action of his waning life, is a lie. His whole time is divided between telling lies and writing them. If he ever have another thought, it is for his genteel appearance on the scaffold; as when he begs the barber "not to cut his hair too short, or they won't know him when he comes out." His last proceeding but one is to write two romantic love-letters to women who have no existence. His last proceeding of all (but less characteristic, though the only true one) is to swoon away, miserably, in the arms of the attendants, and be hanged up like a craven dog.

Is not such a history, from first to last, a most revolting and disgraceful one; and can the student of it bring himself to believe that it ever could have place in any record of facts, or that the miserable chief-actor in it could have ever had a motive for his arrogant wickedness, but for the comment and the explanation which the Punishment of Death supplies!

It is not a solitary case, nor is it a prodigy, but a mere specimen of a class. The case of Oxford,[7] who fired at Her Majesty in the Park, will be found, on examination, to resemble it very nearly, in the essential feature. There is no proved pretence whatever for regarding him as mad; other than that he was like this malefactor, brimful of conceit, and a desire to become, even at the cost of the gallows (the only cost within his reach) the talk of the town. He had less invention than Hocker, and perhaps was not so deliberately bad; but his attempt was a branch of the same tree, and it has its root in the ground where the scaffold is erected.

Oxford had his imitators. Let it never be forgotten in the consideration of this part of the subject, how they were stopped. So long as their attempts invested them with the distinction of being in danger of death at the hangman's hands, so long did they spring up. When the penalty of death was removed, and a mean and humiliating punishment substituted in its place, the race was at an end, and ceased to be.

1. In 1846, high treason, arson in Royal Naval dockyards and arson of dwelling houses with persons therein, piracy with violence, robbery attended with wounds, and sodomy remained capital crimes. In practice only murderers were executed and by no means all of them. See Radzinowicz, IV, 330.
2. Martha Browning was executed at Newgate on 5 Jan. 1846 for the murder of E. Mundell, an elderly woman living in Westminster, who gave shelter to her murderer. Mrs Mundell was found dead on 30 Nov. 1845 with a cord tied tightly around her neck; the coroner returned a verdict of suicide, until a relative of the deceased identified a sham note of the 'Bank of Elegance', known to belong to the victim, in the hands of Browning. The latter believed the note genuine and tried to cash it; when charged with the murder, she confessed. See *AR*, 'Chronicle', 3 Dec. 1845, pp 179–82.
3. Probably Thomas Wicks (see also p. 247), who, after murdering his master early in the morning returned to the scene of the crime, where police arrested him. At his trial Wicks was said to have exhibited 'a very brutal insensibility to his guilt', acting as if he were fully justified in murdering his employer (*AR*, 1846, p. 33).

4. T. H. Hocker, see note p. 213.
5. J. Thurtell (1794–1824), murderer of W. Weare in 1823. Thurtell was hanged after his accomplices, Probert and J. Hunt, turned King's evidence. For an account of the trial and Thurtell's peroration asserting his innocence, see *AR*, 1824, App., pp 1–27.
6. Madame Blaize, the subject of Goldsmith's burlesque elegy, 'An Elegy on That Glory of her Sex Mrs. Mary Blaize', *The Bee*, 4 (27 Oct. 1759).
7. Edward Oxford, an eighteen-year old pot-boy who attempted to assassinate Queen Victoria on 10 June 1840 as she returned to Buckingham Palace from an outing in Hyde Park. Oxford was tried for high treason, found guilty but insane, and confined at Bethlehem Royal Hospital, where he died.

IV

To the Editors of *The Daily News*   March 13, 1846

We come, now, to consider the effect of Capital Punishment in the prevention of crime.

Does it prevent crime in those who attend executions?

There never is (and there never was) an execution at the Old Bailey[1] in London, but the spectators include two large classes of thieves—one class who go there as they would go to a dog-fight, or any other brutal sport, for the attraction and excitement of the spectacle; the other who make it a dry matter of business, and mix with the crowd, solely to pick pockets. Add to these, the dissolute, the drunken, the most idle, profligate, and abandoned of both sexes—some moody ill-conditioned minds, drawn thither by a fearful interest—and some impelled by curiosity; of whom the greater part of an age and temperament rendering the gratification of that curiosity highly dangerous to themselves and to society—and the great elements of the concourse are stated.

Nor is this assemblage peculiar to London. It is the same in country towns, allowing for the different statistics of the population. It is the same in America. I was present at an execution in Rome, for a most treacherous and wicked murder, and not only saw the same kind of assemblage there, but, wearing what is called a shooting-coat, with a great many pockets in it, felt innumerable hands busy in every one of them, close to the scaffold.[2]

I have already mentioned that out of one hundred and sixty-seven convicts under sentence of death, questioned at different times in the performance of his duty by an English clergyman, there were only three who had not been spectators of executions. Mr. Wakefield,[3] in his *Facts relating to the Punishment of Death*, goes into the working, as it were, of this sum. His testimony is extremely valuable, because it is the evidence of an educated and observing man, who, before having personal knowledge of the subject and of Newgate, was quite satisfied that the Punishment of Death should continue, but who, when he gained that experience, exerted himself to the utmost for its abolition, even at the pain of constant public reference in his own person to his own imprisonment. "It cannot be egotism," he reasonably observed, "that prompts a man to speak of himself in connexion with Newgate."

"Whoever will undergo the pain," says Mr. Wakefield, "of witnessing the public destruction of a fellow creature's life, in London, must be perfectly satisfied that in the great mass of spectators, the effect of the punishment is to excite sympathy for the criminal and hatred of the law. . . . I am inclined to believe that the criminals of London, spoken of as a class and allowing for exceptions, take the same sort of delight in witnessing executions, as the sportsman and soldier find in the dangers of hunting and war. . . . I am confident that few Old Bailey Sessions pass without the trial of a boy, whose first thought of crime occurred whilst he was witnessing an execution. . . . And one grown man, of great mental powers and superior education, who was acquitted of a charge of forgery, assured me that the first idea of committing a forgery occurred to him at the moment when he was accidentally witnessing the execution of Fauntleroy.[4] To which it may be added, that Fauntleroy is said to have made precisely the same declaration in reference to the origin of his own criminality."

But one convict "who was within an ace of being hanged," among the many with whom Mr. Wakefield conversed, seems to me to have unconsciously put a question which the advocates of Capital Punishment would find it very difficult indeed to answer. "Have you often seen an execution?" asked Mr. Wakefield. "Yes, often." "Did it not frighten you?" "No. *Why should it?*"

It is very easy and very natural to turn from this ruffian, shocked by the hardened retort; but answer his question, why should it? Should he be frightened by the sight of a dead man? We are born to die, he says, with a careless triumph. We are not born to the treadmill, or to servitude and slavery, or to banishment; but the executioner has done no more for that criminal than nature may do to-morrow for the judge, and will certainly do, in her own good time, for judge and jury, counsel and witnesses, turnkeys, hangmen, and all. Should he be frightened by the manner of the death? It is horrible, truly, so horrible, that the law, afraid or ashamed of its own deed, hides the face of the struggling wretch it slays; but does this fact naturally awaken in such a man, terror—or defiance? Let the same man speak. "What did you think then?" asked Mr. Wakefield. "Think? Why, I thought it was a—shame."

Disgust and indignation, or recklessness and indifference, or a morbid tendency to brood over the sight until temptation is engendered by it, are the inevitable consequences of the spectacle, according to the difference of habit and disposition in those who behold it. Why should it frighten or deter? We know it does not. We know it from the police reports, and from the testimony of those who have experience of prisons and prisoners, and we may know it, on the occasion of an execution, by the evidence of our own senses; if we will be at the misery of using them for such a purpose. But why should it? Who would send his child or his apprentice, or what tutor would send his scholars, or what master would send his servants, to be deterred from vice by the spectacle of an execution? If it be an example to criminals, and to criminals only, why are not the prisoners in Newgate brought out to see the show before the debtor's door? Why, while they are made parties to the condemned sermon, are they rigidly excluded from the improving postscript of the gallows? Because an execution is well known to be an utterly useless, barbarous, and brutalising sight, and because the sympathy of all beholders, who have any sympathy at all, is certain to be always with the criminal, and never with the law.

I learn from the newspaper accounts of every execution, how Mr. So-and-so, and Mr. Somebody else, and Mr. So-forth shook hands with the culprit, but I never find them shaking hands with the hangman. All kinds of attention and consideration are lavished on the one; but the other is universally avoided, like a pestilence. I want to know why so much sympathy is expended on the man who kills another in the vehemence of his own bad passions, and why the man who kills him in the name of the law is shunned and fled from? Is it because the murderer is going to die? Then by no means put him to death. Is it because the hangman executes a law, which, when they once come near it face to face, all men instinctively revolt from? Then by all means change it. There is, there can be, no prevention in such a law.

It may be urged that Public Executions are not intended for the benefit of those dregs of society who habitually attend them. This is an absurdity, to which the obvious answer is, So much the worse. If they be not considered with reference to that class of persons, comprehending a great host of criminals in various stages of development, they ought to be, and must be. To lose sight of that consideration is to be irrational, unjust, and cruel. All other punishments are especially devised, with a reference to the rooted habits, propensities, and antipathies of criminals. And shall it be said, out of Bedlam,[5] that this last punishment of all, is alone to be made an exception from the rule, even where it is shown to be a means of propagating vice and crime?

But there may be people who do not attend executions, to whom the general fame and rumour of such scenes is an example, and a means of deterring from crime.

Who are they? We have seen, that around Capital Punishment there lingers a fascination, urging weak and bad people towards it, and imparting an interest to details connected with it, and with malefactors awaiting it or suffering it, which even good and well disposed people cannot withstand. We know that last dying speeches, and Newgate calendars, are the favourite literature of very low intellects. The gallows is not appealed to, as an example in the instruction of youth (unless they are training for it); nor are there condensed accounts of celebrated executions for the use of national schools. There is a story in an old spelling-book, of a certain Don't Care, who was hanged at last, but it is not understood to have had any remarkable effect on crimes or executions in the generation to which it belonged, and with which it has passed away. Hogarth's idle apprentice is hanged; but the whole scene—with the unmistakeable stout lady, drunk and pious, in the cast; the quarrelling, blasphemy, lewdness, and uproar; Tiddy Doll vending his gingerbread, and the boys picking his pocket[6]—is a bitter satire on the great example; as efficient then, as now.

It is efficient to prevent crime? The parliamentary returns demonstrate that it is not. I was engaged in making some extracts from these documents, when I found them so well abstracted in one of the papers published by the committee on this subject established at Aylesbury last year, by the humane exertions of Lord Nugent,[7] that I am glad to quote the general results from its pages:

"In 1843, a return was laid on the table of the House of the commitments and executions for murder in England and Wales, during the 30 years ending with December 1842; divided into five periods of six years each. It shows that in the last six years, from 1836 to 1842, during which there were only 50 executions, the commitments for murder were fewer by 61 than in the six years preceding with 74 executions; fewer by 63 than in the six years ending 1830 with 75 executions; fewer by 56 than in the six years ending 1824 with 94 executions; and fewer by 93 than in the six years ending 1818, when there was no less a number of executions than 122. But it may be said, perhaps, that, in the inference we draw from this return, we are substituting cause for effect, and that, in each successive cycle, the number of murders decreased in consequence of the example of public executions in the cycle immediately preceding, and that it was for that reason there were fewer commitments. This might be said with some colour of truth, if the example had been taken from *two* successive cycles *only*. But when the comparative examples adduced are of no less than *five* successive cycles, and the result gradually and constantly progressive in the same direction, the relation of facts to each other is determined beyond all ground for dispute, namely, that the number of these crimes has diminished in consequence of the diminution of the number of executions. More especially when it is also remembered that it was *immediately after* the first of these cycles of five years, when there had been the greatest number of executions and the greatest number of murders, that the greatest number of persons were suddenly cast loose upon the country, without employ, by the reduction of the Army and Navy; that then came periods of great distress and great disturbance in the agricultural and manufacturing districts; and *above all*, that it was during the subsequent cycles that the most important mitigations were effected in the law, and that the Punishment of Death was taken away not only for crimes of stealth, such as cattle and horse stealing, and forgery, of which crimes corresponding statistics show likewise a corresponding decrease, but for the crimes of violence too, *tending to murder*, such as are many of the incendiary offences, and such as are highway robbery and burglary. But another return, laid before the House at the same time, bears upon our argument, if possible, still more conclusively. In table 11, we have *only* the years which have occurred since 1810, in which *all* persons convicted of murder suffered death; and, compared with these an *equal* number of years in which the *smallest* proportion of persons convicted were executed. In the first case there were 66 persons convicted, *all* of whom underwent the penalty of death; in the second 83 were convicted, of whom 31 only were executed. Now see how these two very different methods of dealing with the crime of murder affected the commission of it *in the years immediately following*. The number of commitments for murder, in the four years immediately following those in which all persons convicted were executed, was 270.

"In the four years immediately following those in which little more than one-third of the persons convicted were executed, there were but 222, being 48 less. If we compare the commitments in the following years with those in the first years, we shall find that, immediately after the examples of unsparing execution, the crime *increased nearly 13 per cent.*, and that after commutation was the practice and capital punishment the exception, it *decreased 17 per cent.*

"In the same parliamentary return is an account of the commitments and executions in London and Middlesex, *spread over a space of 32 years*, ending in 1842, divided into two cycles of 16 years each. In the first of these, 34 persons were *convicted* of murder, *all of whom were executed*. In the second, 27 were *convicted*, and only 17 executed. The *commitments* for murder during the latter *long* period, with 17 executions, were *more than one half* fewer than they had been in the former *long* period with *exactly double the number of executions*. This appears to us to be as conclusive upon our argument as any statistical illustration can be upon any argument professing to place successive events in the relation of cause and effect to each other. How justly then is it said in that able and useful periodical work, now in the course of publication at Glasgow, under the name of the *Magazine of Popular Information on Capital and Secondary Punishment*; 'the greater the number of executions, the greater the number of murders; the smaller the number of executions, the smaller the number of murders. The lives of her Majesty's subjects are less safe with a hundred executions a year than with fifty; less safe with fifty than with twenty-five.' "

Similar results have followed from rendering public executions more and more infrequent, in Tuscany, in Prussia, in France, in Belgium.[8] Wherever Capital Punishments are diminished in their number, there, crimes diminish in their number too.

But the very same advocates of the Punishment of Death who contend, in the teeth of all facts and figures, that it does prevent crime, contend in the same breath against its abolition because it does not! "There are so many bad murders," say they, "and they follow in such quick succession, that the Punishment must not be repealed." Why, is not this a reason, among others, *for* repealing it? Does it not go to show that it is ineffective as an example; that it fails to prevent crime; and that it is wholly inefficient to stay that imitation, or contagion, call it what you please, which brings one murder on the heels of another?

One forgery came crowding on another's heels in the same way, when the same punishment attached to that crime. Since it has been removed, forgeries had diminished in a most remarkable degree.[9] Yet within five and thirty years, Lord Eldon,[10] with tearful solemnity, imagined in the House of Lords as a possibility for their Lordships to shudder at, that the time might come when some visionary and morbid person might even propose the abolition of the Punishment of Death for forgery. And when it *was* proposed, Lords Lyndhurst,[11] Wynford,[12] Tenterden,[13] and Eldon—all Law Lords—opposed it.

The same Lord Tenterden manfully said, on another occasion and another question, that he was glad the subject of the amendment of the laws had been taken up by Mr. Peel, "who had not been bred to the law; for those who were, were rendered dull, by habit, to many of its defects!" I would respectfully submit, in extension of this text, that a criminal judge is an excellent witness against the Punishment of Death, but a bad witness in its favour; and I will reserve this point for a few remarks in the next, concluding, Letter.

1. Old Bailey, a narrow street running between Ludgate Hill and Newgate Street, London. At the Newgate end stood the prison, where public executions took place until their abolition in 1868. Also on the street is the Old Bailey Sessions House, London's Central Criminal Court, where regicides and other notorious criminals were tried.
2. For Dickens's description of the beheading he witnessed in Rome on 8 Mar. 1845, see *Pictures from Italy*, ed. D. Paroissien (London: André Deutsch, 1973), pp 189–94.
3. E. G. Wakefield (1796–1862), colonial statesman and author of *Facts Relating to the Punishment of Death in the Metropolis*, London, 1831. Wakefield, who served three years in Newgate on the charge of fraudulent marriage, wrote of his prison experiences and argued that punishment worked as a deterrent according to its certainty not according to its severity.
4. H. Fauntleroy, (see p. 223, n. 11).
5. Bethlehem Royal Hospital (Bedlam), Lambeth Road, St. George's Fields. A hospital for insane people founded in 1246, originally as a priory in Bishopsgate Without, but converted into a hospital for lunatics in 1547. By the seventeenth century visiting Bedlam had become a popular pastime. A new hospital was completed in 1815 on a more open site in St. George's Fields.
6. William Hogarth's series of engravings, *Industry and Idleness* (1747), ends with no. xii, 'The Idle 'Prentice Executed at Tyburn'. In the foreground, Tiddy Dolly, a celebrated vender of gingerbread, offers his wares, while one of two boys picks his pockets, thus initiating a cycle of crime that in all probability will lead back to Tyburn and end the same way.
7. G. N. Grenville, Baron Nugent (1788–1850), MP for Aylesbury, 1812–32, 47–8; well-known advocate of the abolition of the death penalty and author of *On the Punishment of Death by law. An Argument in the way of dialogue*. London, 1840. On 23 Apr. 1845 about 400 people attended a public meeting in the County Hall, Aylesbury, to discuss the subject of the punishment of death. Lord Nugent introduced a resolution to abolish the death penalty and received unanimous support. According to Nugent, the public meeting at Aylesbury was the first of its kind in England. See *The Bucks Herald*, 26 Apr. 1845. Later Nugent supported the bill for the total

abolition of the death penalty introduced into the Commons on 14 Mar. 1847 by W. Ewart; it was defeated by 56 votes. A report on capital punishment was made in the Commons on 7 Mar. 1843 and in the Lords on 20 Mar. 1843, but no debates followed. See *Hansard*, vol. 67, pp 350 and 1095.

8. Opponents of the death penalty frequently alluded to the fact that a decrease in the frequency of executions in several European countries was attended with no increase in crime. In 1765 Tuscany substituted imprisonment at hard labour for execution; in Prussia, only murderers were punished by death, and figures for convictions and executions there showed an average well below that of England. France made similar penal reforms in the nineteenth century; in Belgium the death penalty was practically set aside after 1830 and all capital offences were reduced to hard labour. Holland, Denmark and Russia provided further evidence that fewer executions did not lead to a rise in crime. As a student of crime, Dickens appears to have been conversant with such evidence, which he could have drawn from several contemporary documents. A likely source of information in this letter and one acknowledged in his *DN* letter of 28 Feb. is J. L. O'Sullivan's *Report in Favor of the Abolition of the Punishment of Death by Law, Made to the Legislature of the State of New York*, Apr. 14, 1841 (1841; repr. New York: Arno Press, 1974), pp 110–10. Possibly Dickens obtained a copy of this report arguing for 'the total abolition of the punishment of death by law' during his American Tour of 1842.

9. Forgery was first made a statutory offence in English law in 1562; it became a capital offence in 1634, and subsequently forgery statutes increased to the extent that in the words of Sir William Blackstone, 'there was not a forgery which could be practised . . . for which a law did not exist which made the crime a capital offence'. Quoted by Sir Robert Peel (1788–1850), Home Secretary, on 1 Apr. 1830, *Hansard*, vol. 23, p. 1178. Peel therefore proposed to repeal all the Acts which made forgery a capital offence, except for forgery of everything which represented money. His Bill met opposition from those in the Commons who wanted to remove the death penalty for all offences, except forgery in the case of wills. An amendment to Peel's Bill passed but was defeated in the House of Lords. The Commons passed Peel's original Bill on its return rather than lose the opportunity to effect some reform.

   Although the Act of 1830 still upheld capital punishment for 42 kinds of forgery, after that date no offender was put to death in England for the offence. From 1820–9, 64 offenders were executed for forgery of a total of 733 sentenced to death (Radzinowicz, I, 594 and n.).

10. J. Scott (1751–1838), first Earl of Eldon, and Lord Chancellor.

11. J. S. Copley (1772–1863), Baron Lyndhurst.

12. W. D. Best (1767–1845), Baron Wynford.

13. C. Abbot (1762–1832), Baron Tenterden, and Lord Chief Justice.

V

To THE EDITORS OF *The Daily News*   March 16, 1846
The last English Judge, I believe, who gave expression to a public and
judicial opinion in favour of the Punishment of Death, is Mr. Justice
Coleridge,[1] who, in charging the Grand Jury at Hertford last year, took
occasion to lament the presence of serious crimes in the calendar, and
to say that he feared that they were referable to the comparative
infrequency of Capital Punishment.

It is not incompatible with the utmost deference and respect for an
authority so eminent, to say that, in this, Mr. Justice Colerdige was not
supported by facts, but quite the reverse. He went out of his way to
found a general assumption on certain very limited and partial
grounds, and even on those grounds was wrong. For among the few
crimes which he instanced, murder stood prominently forth. Now
persons found guilty of murder are more certainly and unsparingly
hanged at this time, as the Parliamentary Returns demonstrate, than
such criminals ever were. So how can the decline of public executions
affect that class of crimes? As to persons committing murder, and yet
not found guilty of it by juries, they escape solely because there *are*
many public executions—not because there are none or few.

But when I submit that a criminal judge is an excellent witness
against Capital Punishment, but a bad witness in its favour, I do so on
more broad and general grounds than apply to this error in fact and
deduction (so I presume to consider it) on the part of the distinguished
judge in question. And they are grounds which do not apply
offensively to judges, as a class; than whom there are no authorities in
England so deserving of general respect and confidence, or so
possessed of it; but which apply alike to all men in their several degrees
and pursuits.

It is certain that men contract a general liking for those things which
they have studied at great cost of time and intellect, and their
proficiency in which has led to their becoming distinguished and
successful. It is certain that out of this feeling arises, not only that
passive blindness to their defects of which the example given by my
Lord Tenterden was quoted in the last letter, but an active disposition
to advocate and defend them. If it were otherwise; if it were not for this
spirit of interest and partisanship; no single pursuit could have that
attraction for its votaries which most pursuits in course of time
establish. Thus legal authorities are usually jealous of innovations on
legal principles. Thus it is described of the lawyer in the Introductory

Discourse to the Description of Utopia, that he said of a proposal against Capital Punishment, " 'this could never be so established in England but that it must needs bring the weal-public into great jeopardy and hazard,'[2] and as he was thus saying, he shaked his head, and made a wry mouth, and so he held his peace." Thus the Recorder of London,[3] in 1811, objected to "the capital part being taken off" from the offence of picking pockets. Thus the Lord Chancellor, in 1813,[4] objected to the removal of the Penalty of Death from the offence of stealing to the amount of five shillings from a shop. Thus, Lord Ellenborough, in 1820,[5] anticipated the worst effects from there being no Punishment of Death for stealing five shillings' worth of wet linen from a bleaching ground. Thus the Solicitor General, in 1830,[6] advocated the Punishment of Death for forgery, and "the satisfaction of thinking" in the teeth of mountains of evidence from bankers and other injured parties (one thousand bankers alone!) "that he was deterring persons from the commission of crime, by the severity of the law." Thus, Mr. Justice Coleridge delivered his charge at Hertford in 1845. Thus there were in the criminal code of England, in 1790, one hundred and sixty crimes punishable with death. Thus the lawyer has said, again and again, in his generation, that any change in such a state of things "must needs bring the weal-public into jeopardy and hazard." And thus he has, all through the dismal history, "shaked his head, and made a wry mouth, and held his peace." Except—a glorious exception!—when such lawyers as Bacon,[7] More,[8] Blackstone,[9] Romilly,[10] and—let us ever gratefully remember—in later times, Mr. Basil Montagu,[11] have striven, each in his day, within the utmost limits of the endurance of the mistaken feeling of the people or the legislature of the time, to champion and maintain the truth.

There is another and a stronger reason still, why a criminal judge is a bad witness in favour of the Punishment of Death. He is a chief actor in the terrible drama of a trial, where the life or death of a fellow creature is at issue. No one who has seen such a trial can fail to know, or can ever forget, its intense interest. I care not how painful this interest is, to the good, wise judge upon the bench. I admit its painful nature, and the judge's goodness and wisdom to the fullest extent—but I submit that his prominent share in the excitement of such a trial, and the dread mystery involved, has a tendency to bewilder and confuse the judge upon the general subject of that penalty. I know the solemn pause before the verdict, the hush and stilling of the fever in the court, the solitary figure brought back to the bar, and standing there, observed of all the outstretched heads and gleaming eyes, to be, next minute, stricken dead, as one may say, among them. I know the thrill that goes round when the black cap is put on, and how there will be shrieks among the women, and a taking out of some one in a swoon; and, when the judge's faltering voice delivers sentence, how awfully the prisoner and he confront each other; two mere men, destined one day, however far removed from one another at this time, to stand alike as suppliants at the bar of God.[12] I know all this; I can imagine what the office of the judge costs, in this execution of it; but I say that in these strong sensations he is lost, and is unable to abstract the penalty as a preventive or example, from an experience of it, and from associations surrounding it, which are and can be, only his, and his alone.

Not to contend that there is no amount of wig or ermine that can change the nature of the man inside; not to say that the nature of a judge may be, like the dyer's hand, subdued to what it works in, and may become too used to this Punishment of Death, to consider it quite dispassionately; not to say that it may possibly be inconsistent to have, deciding as calm authorities in favour of death, judges who have been constantly sentencing to death;—I contend that for the reasons I have stated, alone, a judge, and especially a criminal judge, is a bad witness for the punishment but an excellent witness against it, inasmuch as in the latter case his conviction of its inutility has been so strong and paramount as utterly to beat down and conquer these adverse incidents. I have no scruple in stating this position, because, for anything I know, the majority of excellent judges now on the bench may have overcome them, and may be opposed to the Punishment of Death under any circumstances.

I mentioned that I would devote a portion of this letter to a few prominent illustrations of each head of objection to the Punishment of Death. Those on record are so very numerous that selection is extremely difficult; but in reference to the possibility of mistake, and the impossibility of reparation, one case is as good (I should rather say as bad) as a hundred; and if there were none but Eliza Fenning's,[13] that would be sufficient. Nay, if there were none at all, it would be enough to sustain this objection, that men of finite and limited judgment do inflict, on testimony which admits of doubt, an infinite and irreparable punishment. But there are on record numerous instances of mistake; many of them very generally known and immediately recognisable in the following summary, which I copy from the New York Report already referred to.[14]

"There have been cases in which groans have been heard in the apartment of the crime, which have attracted the steps of those on whose testimony the case has turned—when, on proceeding to the spot, they have found a man bending over the murdered body, a lantern in the left hand, and the knife yet dripping with the warm current in the blood-stained right, with horror-stricken countenance, and lips which, in the presence of the dead, seem to refuse to deny the crime in the very act of which he is thus surprised—and yet the man has been, many years after, when his memory alone could be benefited by the discovery, ascertained *not* to have been the real murderer! There have been cases in which, in a house in which were two persons alone, a murder has been committed on one of them—when many additional circumstances have fastened the imputation upon the other—and when, all apparent modes of access from without, being closed inward, the demonstration has seemed complete of the guilt for which that other has suffered the doom of the law—yet suffered *innocently*! There have been cases in which a father has been found murdered in an outhouse, the only person at home being a son, sworn by a sister to have been dissolute and undutiful, and anxious for the death of the father, and succession to the family property—when the track of his shoes in the snow is found from the house to the spot of the murder, and the hammer with which it was committed, (known as his own) found, on a search, in the corner of one of his private drawers, with the bloody evidence of the deed only imperfectly effaced from it—and yet the son has been innocent!—the sister, years after, on her deathbed, confessing herself the fratricide as well as the parricide. There have been cases in which men have been hung on the most positive testimony to identity (aided by many suspicious circumstances), by persons familiar with their appearance, which have afterwards proved grievous mistakes, growing out of remarkable personal resemblance. There have been cases in which two men have been seen fighting in a field—an old enmity existing between them—the one found dead, killed by a stab from a pitch-fork, known as belonging to the other, and which that other had been carrying, the pitch-fork lying by the side of the murdered man—and yet its owner has been afterwards found not to have been the author of the murder of which it had been the instrument, the true murderer sitting on the jury that tried him. There have been cases in which an innkeeper has been charged by one of his servants with the murder of a traveller, the servant deposing to having seen his master on the stranger's bed, strangling him, and afterwards rifling his pockets—another servant deposing that she saw him come down at that time at a very early hour in the morning, steal into the garden, take gold from his pocket, and carefully wrapping it up bury it in a designated spot—on the search of which the ground is found loose and freshly dug, and a sum of thirty pounds in gold found buried according to the description—the master, who confessed the burying of the money, with many evidences of guilt in his hesitation and confusion, has been hung of course, and proved innocent only too late. There have been cases in which a traveller has been robbed on the highway, of twenty guineas which he had taken the precaution to *mark*—one of these is found to have been paid away or changed by one of the servants of the inn which the traveller reaches the same evening—the servant is about the height of the robber, who had been cloaked and disguised—his master deposes to his having been recently unaccountably extravagant and flush of gold—and on his trunk being searched the other nineteen marked guineas and the traveller's purse are found there, the servant being asleep at the time, half-drunk—he is of course convicted and hung, for the crime of which his master was the author! There have been cases in which a father and daughter have been overhead in violent dispute—the words *'barbarity,'* *'cruelty'*, and *'death'* being heard frequently to proceed from the latter—the former goes out, locking the door behind him—groans are overhead, and the words, *'cruel father, thou art the cause of my death!'*—on the room being opened, she is found on the point of death from a wound in her side, and near her the knife with which it had been inflicted—and on being questioned as to her owing her death to her father, her last motion, before expiring, is an expression of assent—the father, on returning to the room, exhibits the usual evidences of guilt—he, too, is of course hung—and it is not till nearly a year afterwards that, on the discovery of conclusive evidence that it was a suicide, the vain reparation is made to his memory by the public authorities, of—waving a pair of colours over his grave in token of the recognition of his innocence."

More than a hundred such cases are known, it is said in this Report, in English criminal jurisprudence. The same Report contains three striking cases of supposed criminals being unjustly hanged in America; and also five more in which people whose innocence was not afterwards established were put to death on evidence as purely circumstantial and as doubtful, to say the least of it, as any that was held to be sufficient in this general summary of legal murders. Mr. O'Connell defended, in Ireland, within five-and-twenty years, three brothers who were hanged for a murder of which they were afterwards shown to have been innocent.[15] I cannot find the reference at this moment, But I have seen it stated on good authority, that but for the exertions, I think of the present Lord Chief Baron,[16] six or seven innocent men would certainly have been hanged. Such are the instances of wrong judgment which are known to us. How many more there may be, in which the real murderers never disclosed their guilt, or were never discovered, and where the odium of great crimes still rests on guiltless people long since resolved to dust in their untimely graves, no human power can tell.

The effect of public executions on those who witness them, requires no better illustration, and can have none, than the scene which any execution in itself presents, and the general Police-office knowledge of the offences arising out of them. I have stated my belief that the study of rude scenes leads to the disregard of human life, and to murder.[17] Referring since that expression of opinion to the very last trial for murder in London, I have made inquiry, and am assured that the youth now under sentence of death in Newgate for the murder of his master in Drury Lane,[18] was a vigilant spectator of the three last public executions in this City.[19] What effects a daily increasing familiarity with the scaffold, and with death upon it, wrought in France in the Great Revolution, everybody knows. In reference to this very question of Capital Punishment, Robespierre[20] himself, before he was "in blood stept in so far,"[21] warned the National Assembly that in taking human life, and in displaying before the eyes of the people scenes of cruelty and the bodies of murdered men, the law awakened ferocious prejudices, which gave birth to a long and growing train of their own kind. With how much reason this was said, let his own detestable name bear witness! If we would know how callous and hardened society, even in a peaceful and settled state, becomes to public executions when they are frequent, let us recollect how few they were who made the last attempt to stay the dreadful Monday-morning spectacles of men and women strung up in a row for crimes as different in their degree as our whole social scheme is different in its component parts, which, within some fifteen years or so, made human shambles of the Old Bailey.

There is no better way of testing the effect of public executions on those who do not actually behold them, but who read of them and know of them, than by inquiring into their efficiency in preventing crime. In this respect they have always, and in all countries, failed. According to all facts and figures, failed. In Russia, in Spain, in France, in Italy, in Belgium, in Sweden, in England, there has been one result. In Bombay, during the Recordership of Sir James Mackintosh,[22] there were fewer crimes in seven years without one execution, than in the preceding seven years with forty-seven executions; notwithstanding that in the seven years without Capital Punishment, the population had greatly increased, and there had been a large accession to the numbers of the ignorant and licentious soldiery, with whom the more violent offences originated. During the four wickedest years of the Bank of England (from 1814 to 1817, inclusive), when the one-pound note capital prosecutions were most numerous and shocking, the number of forged one-pound notes discovered by the Bank steadily increased, from the gross amount in the last of £28,412. But in every branch of this part of the subject—the inefficiency of Capital Punishment to prevent crime, and its efficiency to produce it—the body of evidence (if there were space to quote or analyse it here) is overpowering and resistless.

I have purposely deferred until now any reference to one objection which is urged against the abolition of Capital Punishment: I mean that objection which claims to rest on Scriptural authority.

It was excellently well said by Lord Melbourne,[23] that no class of persons can be shown to be very miserable and oppressed, but some supporters of things as they are will immediately rise up and assert—not that those persons are moderately well to do, or that their lot in life has a reasonably bright side—but that they are, of all sorts and conditions of men, the happiest. In like manner, when a certain proceeding or institution is shown to be very wrong indeed, there is a class of people who rush to the fountainhead at once, and will have no less an authority for it than the Bible, on any terms.

So, we have the Bible appealed to in behalf of Capital Punishment. So, we have the Bible, produced as a distinct authority for Slavery. So, American representatives find the title of their country to the Oregon territory distinctly laid down in the Book of Genesis. So, in course of time, we shall find Repudiation, perhaps, expressly commanded in the Sacred Writings.

It is enough for me to be satisfied, on calm inquiry and with reason, that an Institution or Custom is wrong and bad; and thence to feel assured that IT CANNOT BE a part of the law laid down by the Divinity who walked the earth. Though every other man who wields a pen, should turn himself into a commentator on the Scriptures—not all their united efforts, pursued through our united lives, could ever persuade me that Slavery is a Christian law; nor, with one of these objections to an execution in my certain knowledge, that Executions are a Christian law, my will is not concerned. I could not, in my veneration for the life and lessons of Our Lord, believe it. If any text appeared to justify the claim, I would reject that limited appeal, and rest upon the character of the Redeemer, and the great scheme of His Religion, where, in its broad spirit, made so plain—and not this or that disputed letter—we all put our trust. But, happily, such doubts do not exist. The case is far too plain. The Rev. Henry Christmas,[24] in a recent pamphlet on this subject, shows clearly that in five important versions of the Old Testament (to say nothing of versions of less note) the words, "by man," in the often-quoted text, "Whoso sheddeth man's blood, by man shall his blood be shed,"[25] do not appear at all. We know that the law of Moses was delivered to certain wandering tribes, in a peculiar and perfectly different social condition from that which prevails among us at this time. We know that the Christian Dispensation did distinctly repeal and annul certain portions of that law. We know that the doctrine of retributive justice or vengeance, was plainly disavowed by the Saviour, We know that on the only occasion of an offender, liable by the law to death, being brought before Him for His judgment, it was *not* death. We know that He said, "Thou shalt not kill." And if we are still to inflict Capital Punishment because of the Mosaic law (under which it was not the consequence of a legal proceeding, but an act of vengeance from the next of kin, which would surely be discouraged by our later laws if it were revived among the Jews just now), it would be equally reasonable to establish the lawfulness of a plurality of wives on the same authority.

Here I will leave this aspect of the question. I should not have treated of it at all, in the columns of a newspaper, but for the possibility of being unjustly supposed to have given it no consideration in my own mind.

In bringing to a close these letters on a subject, in connexion with which there is happily very little that is new to be said or written, I beg to be understood as advocating the total abolition of the Punishment of Death, as a general principle, for the advantage of society, for the prevention of crime, and without the least reference to, or tenderness for any individual malefactor whomsoever. Indeed, in most cases of murder, my feeling towards the culprit is very strongly and violently the reverse. I am the more desirous to be so understood, after reading a speech made by Mr. Macaulay in the House of Commons last Tuesday night,[26] in which that accomplished gentlemen hardly seemed to recognise the possibility of anybody entertaining an honest conviction of the inutility and bad effects of Capital Punishment in the abstract, founded on inquiry and reflection, without being the victim of "a kind of effeminate feeling." Without staying to inquire what there may be that is especially manly and heroic in the advocacy of the gallows, or to express my admiration of Mr. Calcraft, the hangman,[27] as doubtless one of the most manly specimens now in existence, I would simply hint a doubt, in all good humour, whether this be the true Macaulay way of meeting a great question? One of the instances of effeminacy of feeling quoted by Mr. Macaulay, I have reason to think was not quite fairly stated. I allude to the petition in Tawell's case. I had neither hand nor part in it myself; but, unless I am greatly mistaken, it did pretty clearly set forth that Tawell was a most abhorred villain, and that the House might conclude how strongly the petitioners were opposed to the Punishment of Death, when they prayed for its non-infliction even in such a case.

1. Sir John T. Coleridge (1790–1876), judge. Justice Coleridge's remarks on capital punishment and his charge to the Grand Jury at the Hertfordshire Summer Assizes held on 10 July 1845 may be found verbatim in the *Hertford Mercury*, 12 July 1845.
2. Spoken by the lawyer in response to Raphael Hythloday's arguments against the injustice of capital punishment. See Sir Thomas More, 'The First Booke', *Utopia*, in *Three Renaissance Classics* (1516; repr. New York: Charles Scribner's, 1953), p. 134.
3. Recorder of London, a magistrate or judge having criminal and civil jurisdiction in the city.
4. Lord Chancellor, 1813, Lord Eldon.
5. E. Law (1790–1871), first Earl of Ellenborough.
6. Solicitor General, 1830, Sir Edward B. Sugden (1781–1875).
7. Sir James Bacon (1798–1895), judge.
8. Sir Thomas More (1478–1535), Lord Chancellor, and author.
9. Sir William Blackstone (1723–80), judge, and author of *Commentaries on the Laws of England*, 4 vols 1765–9.
10. John Romilly (1802–74), lawyer.
11. B. Montagu (1770–1851), legal and miscellaneous writer.
12. Dickens returned to this point in the trial scene in *GE*, ch. 56, in which Pip recounts in a memorable passage how he saw 'two-and-thirty men and women put before the Judge' to receive the Sentence of Death.
13. E. Fenning (1791–1815), a domestic servant and cook charged with feloniously administering arsenic to the Turner family. Fenning asseverated her innocence during the trial but the jury found her guilty. Efforts to obtain a remission of sentence failed and she was executed on 26 June 1815. The public widely believed in her innocence; see also Dickens's letter to W. Thornbury of 5 Oct. 1867, in which he expresses his conviction that the arsenic was administered by the family's apprentice and not by Miss Fenning (N, III, 558).
14. O'Sullivan's *Report* (1841). See p. 222 n.1.
15. D. O'Connell (1775–1847), barrister and Irish politician. O'Sullivan states in his *Report* (see above), that in a speech at Exeter Hall in 1832 O'Connell mentioned five cases within his own knowledge of innocent people being hanged. Three of them were three brothers charged with the

murder of T. Franks, his wife, and their son on 9 Sep. 1823. O'Connell unsuccessfully defended Patrick, Maurice, and John Cremin, who were convicted on 10 Apr. 1824 and executed two days later. The brothers died protesting their innocence to the last moment. See *The Correspondence of Daniel O'Connell*, ed. M. R. O'Connell (Dublin: Irish Univ. Press, 1974), III, 65n.

16. Lord Chief Baron, Sir Jonathan F. Pollock.
17. See Dickens's letter of 28 Feb. 1846, pp 230–3.
18. T. Wicks, the apprentice of J. Bostock, a brass and gun-metal founder in Pitt's Place, Drury Lane, murdered his master on 16 Feb. 1846. Wicks was tried on 26 Feb. and executed on 30 Mar. 1846.
19. M. Browning, executed at Newgate on 5 Jan. 1846, S. Quennell at Horsemonger Lane Gaol the same day, and J. Connor, hanged outside Newgate on 2 June 1845.
20. F. Robespierre (1758–94), one of the leaders of the French Revolution.
21. *Macbeth*, III, iv, 136–7.
22. Sir James Mackintosh (1765–1832), philosopher; barrister; Recorder of Bombay, 1804–11; and MP.
23. W. Lamb, Viscount Melbourne (1779–1848). Statesman. Source not identified.
24. Revd H. Christmas (1811–68), author of *Capital Punishments Unsanctioned by the Gospel and Unnecessary in a Christian State. A Letter to The Revd Sir J. P. Wood*. London: Charles Gilpin, 1845.
25. Genesis, 9:16.
26. On 10 Mar. 1846 Thomas Babington Macaulay (1800–59), historian and MP for Edinburgh, spoke against a motion in the Commons by T. S. Duncombe to ask the Queen to pardon J. Frost, Z. Williams, and W. Jones. Frost and his companions had led a large body of armed Chartists into Newport, South Wales, on 4 Nov. 1839. Soldiers and special constables repulsed the attack; the leaders were taken, tried, and sentenced on 16 Jan. 1840 to be hung, drawn, and quartered for High Treason. Later the capital sentence was commuted to transportation for life.

   Duncombe's motion in Mar. was the first of several attempts to obtain a pardon for Frost and his associates. (None succeeded until a conditional pardon in 1854 was obtained, followed by a free pardon in 1856. See Frost, *DNB*). Macaulay opposed the motion because, he argued, if successful, the Commons would invite similar appeals in every other case where capital punishment was awarded. In making his point, Macaulay alluded to recent efforts to procure the release of 'a most infamous hypocrite' (Tawell) and those on behalf of a woman, said to be irreproachable throughout her life, whose only offence was 'the little one of having mixed some arsenic in her father's drink'. In his speech upholding the principle of capital punishment, Macaulay admitted that pardons originated as a 'natural reaction against England's former barbarous penal code', but he warned that as a result of recent reforms 'there was now such a sort of effeminate feeling in the country, that there was hardly a case of atrocity with respect to which they [the Commons] would not have thousands of persons petitioning for mercy', if the House encouraged the practice of asking the Crown to grant mercy. See *The Times*, 11 Mar. 1846, p. 3, col. 3. The phrase 'effeminate feeling' does not occur in Hansard's report of Macaulay's speech (vol. 84, pp 891–2).

27. W. Calcraft (1800–79), England's public hangman from 1828 to 26 May 1868; conducted the first private hanging on 3 Aug. 1868. Pensioned by the government in 1874.

To the Editor of *The Times*   November 14, 1849

Sir,

I was a witness of the execution at Horsemonger-lane this morning.[1] I went there with the intention of observing the crowd gathered to behold it, and I had excellent opportunities of doing so, at intervals all through the night, and continuously from daybreak until after the spectacle was over.

I do not address you on the subject with any intention of discussing the abstract question of capital punishment, or any of the arguments of its opponents or advocates. I simply wish to turn this dreadful experience to some account for the general good, by taking the readiest and most public means of adverting to an intimation given by Sir G. Grey[2] in the last session of Parliament, that the Government might be induced to give its support to a measure making the infliction of capital punishment a private solemnity within the prison walls (with such guarantees for the last sentence of the law being inexorably and surely administered as should be satisfactory to the public at large), and of most earnestly beseeching Sir G. Grey, as a solemn duty which he owes to society, and a responsibility which he cannot for ever put away, to originate such a legislative change himself.

I believe that a sight so inconceivably awful as the wickedness and levity of the immense crowd collected at that execution this morning could be imagined by no man, and could be presented in no heathen land under the sun. The horrors of the gibbet and of the crime which brought the wretched murderers to it, faded in my mind before the atrocious bearing, looks and language, of the assembled spectators. When I came upon the scene at midnight, the *shrillness* of the cries and howls that were raised from time to time, denoting that they came from a concourse of boys and girls already assembled in the best places, made my blood run cold. As the night went on, screeching, and laughing, and yelling in strong chorus of parodies on Negro melodies, with substitutions of "Mrs. Manning" for "Susannah," and the like, were added to these. When the day dawned, thieves, low prostitutes, ruffians and vagabonds of every kind, flocked on to the ground, with every variety of offensive and foul behaviour. Fightings, faintings, whistlings, imitations of Punch, brutal jokes, tumultuous demonstrations of indecent delight when swooning women were dragged out of the crowd by the police with their dresses disordered, gave a new zest to the general entertainment. When the sun rose brightly—as it did—it gilded thousands upon thousands of upturned faces, so inexpressibly odious in their brutal mirth or callousness, that a man had cause to feel ashamed of the shape he wore, and to shrink from himself, as fashioned in the image of the Devil. When the two miserable creatures who attracted all this ghastly sight about them were turned quivering into the air, there was no more emotion, no more pity, no more thought that two immortal souls had gone to judgment, no more restraint in any of the previous obscenities, than if the name of Christ had never been heard in this world, and there were no belief among men but that they perished like the beasts.[3]

I have seen, habitually, some of the worst sources of general contamination and corruption in this country, and I think there are not many phases of London life that could surprise me. I am solemnly convinced that nothing that ingenuity could devise to be done in this city, in the same compass of time, could work such ruin as one public execution, and I stand astounded and appalled by the wickedness it exhibits. I do not believe that any community can prosper where such a scene of horror and demoralization as was enacted this morning outside Horsemonger-lane Gaol is presented at the very doors of good citizens, and is passed by, unknown or forgotten. And when, in our prayers and thanksgivings for the season, we are humbly expressing before God our desire to remove the moral evils of the land, I would ask your readers to consider whether it is not a time to think of this one, and to root it out.[4]

I am, Sir, your faithful servant,

---

1. On 13 Nov. F. G. Manning (1821–49; *DNB*) and his Swiss wife, Maria (1821–49; *DNB*), were executed together, the first husband and wife to be hanged since 1700. The Mannings were convicted of murdering Maria's lover, P. O'Connor. Dickens refers to the Mannings in his 'Pet Prisoners', *HW*, 27 Apr. 1850 and in his 'Demeanour of Murderers', *HW*, 14 June 1856. Critics cite Maria Manning as a possible source for Mlle Hortense in *BH*. The case occasioned a flood of comment in newspapers of the time; for a recent study of the crime, see A. Borowitz, *The Woman Who Murdered Black Satin: The Bermondsey Horror* (1981).
2. Grey, the Home Secretary, opposed a bill to abolish hanging but spoke on 1 May 1849 against executing criminals in public as an evil which should be checked. Public hangings, he argued, were not necessary to the maintenance of capital punishment. See *Hansard*, vol. 104 (1849), p. 1072.

Public executions were not abolished until 1868, despite the recommenda-tion of a Select Committee of the House of Lords, appointed in 1856, that executions should be carried out within the precincts of a prison. A Report by a later Royal Commission (1855–6) led to the Capital Punishment Amendment Act in 1868, by which the hangman performed his work in private. See Radzinowicz, IV, 350–2.

3. J. Leech, who went with Dickens to the hanging, expressed similar repugnance in his cartoon, 'The Great Moral Lesson at Horsemonger Lane Gaol, Nov. 13', *Punch*, 17 (24 Nov. 1849), p. 210. Forster was also present. For his account of the scene, see J. A. Davies, 'John Forster at the Mannings' Execution', *The Dickensian*, 67 (1971), 12–15.

4. Commenting on Dickens's letter in its editorial of 14 Nov., *The Times* acknowledged the novelist's powerful language but expressed its inability to accept Dickens's point that executions should occur in private. 'Were it otherwise,' *The Times* argued, 'the mass of the people would never be sure that great offenders were really executed, or that the humbler class of criminals were not executed in greater numbers than the State chose to confess.' Acts of 'national homicide', the paper concluded, should there-fore be 'publicly as well as solemnly done.'

DEVONSHIRE TERRACE
Thursday evening, Fifteenth November 1849

DEAR MR. GILPIN,[1]—In reply to your letter of yesterday (which other engagements have prevented my sooner answering) I regret that I cannot attend the meeting on Monday next, because I think, and have thought for some time past, that the general mind is not in that state in which the total abolition of capital punishment can be advantageously advocated by Public meetings.

I believe that the enormous crimes which have been committed within the last year or two, and are fresh, unhappily, in the public memory, have indisposed many good people to share in the responsi-bility of abandoning the last punishment of the Law. And I know that there are many such who would lend their utmost aid to an effort for the suppression of *public* executions for evermore, though they cannot conscientiously abrogate capital punishment in extreme cases.

Now, it seems to me, when we know what a fearful and brutalising sight a public execution is, and when we know that we must do a great national service by bringing it to pass that such a sight shall never take place again, that the right course is to enlist this help (otherwise rejected) in behalf of the great reform of causing capital punishment to be privately and solemnly inflicted. I have not the least faith in the power of any amount of public meetings that can be held, to advance the abolition of capital punishment one jot, for a long time to come. But I feel convinced that the other vast improvement could be compassed in a very short time, and that it would save a prodigious amount of harm, indecency, and horror.[2]

Therefore I have resolved to limit my endeavours to the bringing about of that improvement as one greatly to be desired, certain to be supported by a very general concurrence, and irresistible (as I think) if temperately urged, by any Government. I wish I could learn that such a meeting as that which you propose to hold on Monday night,[3] had resolved to do so too.—Faithfully Yours.

1. C. Gilpin (1815–74), Quaker politician, philanthropist, and founder of the Society for the Abolition of Capital Punishment.
2. Dickens's compromise on capital punishment in 1849 made him unpopular among the abolitionists, including his friend D. Jerrold, who vigorously opposed his suggestion of executing criminals behind walls. The 'genius of English Society', argued Jerrold in a letter read to the Abolition Society meeting on 19 Nov. 1849, in Southwark, 'would never permit private hanging: the brutality of the mob was even preferable to the darkness of secrecy' (*Illustrated London News*, 24 Nov. 1849), p. 346. J. Bright and R. Cobden expressed similar views. 'Private hanging,' the latter wrote to Gilpin 'was simply assassination.'
3. See *The Times*, 20 Nov. 1849 for a report on the meeting at the Bridge House Hotel, Southwark. Responding the next day in an editorial, *The Times* took Bright and Cobden to task for stating that the advocates of private executions were dictated by a mere longing to put someone to death.

ROCKINGHAM CASTLE, NORTHAMPTONSHIRE
Twenty-Seventh November, 1849

[Miss Joll] Mr. Charles Dickens presents his compliments to Miss Joll.[1] He is, on principle, opposed to capital punishment, but believing that many earnest and sincere people who are favourable to its retention in extreme cases would unite in any temperate effort to abolish the evils of public executions, and that the consequences of public executions are disgraceful and horrible, he has taken the course with which Miss Joll is acquainted as the most hopeful, and as one undoubtedly calculated to benefit society at large.

1. Harriet Joll, wife of a Plymouth Bookseller (P, IV, 540n).

TO THE EDITOR OF *The Times*   November 19, 1849
SIR,

When I wrote to you on Tuesday last I had no intention of troubling you again; but as one of your correspondents has to-day expressed a reasonable desire that I would explain myself more clearly,[1] and as I hope I may do no injury to the cause I would serve by stating my views upon it a little more in detail, I shall be glad to do so, if you will allow me the opportunity.

My positions in reference to the demoralizing nature of public executions are—.

First, that they chiefly attract as spectators the lowest, the most depraved, the most abandoned of mankind; in whom they inspire no wholesome emotions whatever.

Secondly, that the public infliction of a violent death is not a salutary spectacle for any class of people; but that it is in the nature of things that on the class by whom it is generally witnessed it should have a debasing and hardening influence.

On the first head I must appeal again to my own experience of the execution of last Tuesday morning; to all the evidence that has ever been taken on the subject, showing that executions have been the favourite sight of convicts of all descriptions; to the knowledge possessed by the magistracy and police of the general character of such crowds; to the police reports that are sure to follow their assemblage; to the unvarying description of them given in the newspapers; to the indisputable fact that no decent father is willing that his son, and no decent master is willing that his apprentices or servants, should mingle in them; to the indisputable fact that all society, its dregs excepted, recoil from them as masses of abomination and brutality. (That there were not more robberies committed at this last execution was not the fault of the assembled thieves, whose numbers on the occasion the Home Secretary may easily learn from the Commissioners in Scotland-yard, but the merit of the police, whose vigilance was beyond all praise.)[2]

On the second head, after a passing allusion to the hardening influence which familiarity even with natural death produces on coarse minds, I must again refer to my own experience. Nothing would have been a greater comfort to me—nothing would have so much relieved in my mind the unspeakable terrors of the scene, as to have been enabled to believe that any portion of the immense crowd—that any grains of sand in the vast moral desert stretching away on every side—were moved to any sentiments of fear, repentance, pity, or natural horror by what they saw upon the drop. It was impossible to look around and rest in any such belief. With every consideration and respect for your suggestion that the concourse may have been belying their mental struggles by frantic exaggerations, I am confident that if you had been there beside me, seeing what I saw, and hearing what I heard, you could never have admitted the thought. Such a state of mind has its signs and tokens equally with any other, and no such signs and tokens were there. The mirth was not hysterical, the shoutings and fightings were not the efforts of a strained excitement seeking to vent itself in any relief. The whole was unmistakably callous and bad. As the ferocious woman who was charged on the same day with threatening to murder another in the midst of the multitude, proclaiming that she had a knife about her, and would have her heart's blood, and be hanged on the same gibbet with her namesake, Mrs. Manning, whose death she had come to see—as she had her evil passions excited to the utmost by the scene, so had all the crowd. I believe this was the whole and sole effect of what they had come to see, and I hold that no human being, not being the better for such a sight, could go away without being the worse for it.

To prevent such frightful spectacles in a Christian country, and all the incalculable evils they engender, I would have the last sentence of the law executed with comparative privacy within the prison walls. Before I state how, let me strengthen this proposal with some words of Fielding on this subject, to whose profound knowledge of human nature you, I know, will render full justice:—.

"The execution should be in some degree private. And here the poets will again assist us. Foreigners have found fault with the cruelty of the English drama, in representing frequent murders upon the stage. In fact, this is not only cruel, but highly injudicious: a murder behind the scenes, if the poet knows how to manage it, will affect the audience with greater terror than if it was acted before their eyes. Of this we have an instance in the murder of the King in *Macbeth*. Terror hath, I believe, been carried higher by this single instance than by all the blood which hath been spilt upon the stage. To the poets I may add the priests, whose politics have never been doubted. Those of Egypt in particular, where the sacred mysteries were first devised, well knew the use of hiding from the eyes of the vulgar what they intended should inspire them with the greatest awe and dread. The mind of man is so much more capable of magnifying than his eye, that I question whether every object is not lessened by being looked upon, and this more especially when the passions are concerned; for those are ever apt to fancy much more satisfaction in those objects which they affect, and much more of mischief in those which they abhor, than are really to be found in either. If executions, therefore, were so contrived that few could be present at them, they would be much more shocking and terrible to the crowd without doors than at present, as well as much more dreadful to the criminals themselves."[3]

From the moment of a murderer's being sentenced to death, I would dismiss him to the dread obscurity to which the wisest judge upon the bench consigned the murderer Rush.[4] I would allow no curious visitors to hold any communication with him; I would place every obstacle in the way of his sayings and doings being served up in print on Sunday mornings for the perusal of families. His execution within the walls of the prison should be conducted with every terrible solemnity that careful consideration could devise. Mr. Calcraft,[5] the hangman (of whom I have some information in reference to this last occasion), should be restrained in his unseemly briskness, in his jokes, his oaths, and his brandy. To attend the execution I would summon a jury of 24, to be called the Witness Jury, eight to be summoned on a low qualification, eight on a higher, eight on a higher still; so that it might fairly represent all classes of society. There should be present, likewise, the governor of the gaol, the chaplain, the surgeon, and other officers, the sheriffs of the county or city, and two inspectors of prisons. All these should sign a grave and solemn form of certificate (the same in every case) that on such a day, at such an hour, in such a gaol, for such a crime, such a murderer was hanged in their sight. There should be another certificate from the officers of the prison that the person hanged was that person, and no other; a third, that that person was buried. These should be posted on the prison-gate for 21 days, printed in the *Gazette*, and exhibited in other public places; and during the hour of the body's hanging I would have the bells of all the churches in that town or city tolled, and all the shops shut up, that all might be reminded of what was being done.

I submit to you that, with the law so changed, the public would (as is right) know much more of the infliction of this tremendous punishment than they know of the infliction of any other. There are not many common subjects, I think, of which they know less than transportation; and yet they never doubt that when a man is ordered to be sent abroad he goes abroad. The details of the commonest prison in London are unknown to the public at large, but they are quite satisfied that prisoners said to be in this or that gaol are really there and really undergo its discipline. The "mystery" of private executions is objected to; but has not mystery been the character of every improvement in convict treatment and prison discipline effected within the last 20 years? From the police van to Norfolk Island, are not all the changes changes that make the treatment of the prisoner mysterious. His seclusion in his conveyance hither and thither from the public sight, instead of his being walked through the streets, strung with 20 more to a chain, like the galley-slaves in *Don Quixotte*[6] (as I remember to have seen in my school-days), makes a mystery of him. His being known by a number instead of by a name, and his being under the rigorous discipline of the associated silent system—to say nothing of the solitary, which I regard as a mistake—is all mysterious. I cannot understand that the mystery of such an execution as I propose would be other than a fitting climax to all these wise regulations, or why, if there be anything in this objection, we should not return to the days when ladies paid visits to highwaymen, drinking their punch in the condemned cells of Newgate, or Ned Ward,[7] the London spy, went upon a certain regular day of the week to Bridewell to see the women whipped.

Another class of objector I know there are, who, desiring the total abolition of capital punishment, will have nothing less; and who, not doubting the fearful influence of public executions, would have it protracted for an indefinite term, rather than spare the demoralization they do not dispute, at the risk of losing sight for a while of their final end. But of these I say nothing, considering them, however good and pure in intention, unreasonable, and not to be argued with.

With many thanks to you for your courtesy, and begging most earnestly to assure you that I write in a deep conviction that I incurred a duty when I became a witness of the execution on Tuesday last, from which nothing ought to move me, and which every hour's reflection strengthens,

I am, Sir, your faithful servant,

1. One letter writer took issue with Dickens's assertion that public executions were 'the leading cause of the depravity' he described. In fact, the correspondent countered, 'they only afford exhibitions of it'. See *The Times*, 17 Nov. 1849, p. 4, col. 6.
2. *The Times* reported on 14 Nov. that 500 police kept order over a crowd estimated at 30 000.
3. H. Fielding's *Inquiry into the Causes of the Late Increase of Robbers* (1750).
4. J. B. Rush (?1800–49; *DNB*), hanged on 21 Apr. 1849 for the murder of I. Jermy, the owner of Stanfield Hall, Norwich, and Jermy's son.
5. W. Calcraft. See note on p. 248.
6. *Don Quixote*, bk. III, ch. 8.
7. E. Ward ('Ned') (1767–1831), tavern-keeper and author of *The London Spy* (1698–1709), a series of sketches of London life told by a country resident who meets a cockney acquaintance and goes about the city recording what he sees. In Part VI, Ward describes a visit to Bridewell, a House of Correction, where women were whipped. Public whipping of

women continued until 1817; thereafter it was done privately until the punishment was completely abolished for women in 1820. See Radzinow-icz, I, 578n.

GAD'S HILL

Thursday Night, Twenty-Fifth August, 1859

MY DEAR FORSTER,—heartily glad to get your letter this morning.

I cannot easily tell you how much interested I am by what you tell me of our brave and excellent friend the Chief Baron,[1] in connection with that ruffian.[2] I followed the case with so much interest, and have followed the miserable knaves and asses who have perverted it since, with so much indignation, that I have often had more than half a mind to write and thank the upright judge who tried him. I declare to God that I believe such a service one of the greatest that a man of intellect and courage can render to society. Of course I saw the beast of a prisoner (with my mind's eye) delivering his cut-and-dried speech, and read in every word of it that no one but the murderer could have delivered or conceived it. Of course I have been driving the girls out of their wits here, by incessantly proclaiming that there needed no medical evidence either way,[3] and that the case was plain without it. Lastly, of course (though a merciful man—because a merciful man I mean), I would hang any Home Secretary (Whig, Tory, Radical, or otherwise) who should step in between that black scoundrel and the gallows.[4] I cannot believe—and my belief in all wrong as to public matters is enormous—that such a thing will be done.[5]

1. Sir Jonathan F. Pollock, the Lord Chief Baron of the Exchequer, 1844–66, a reputedly strict judge and one of Dickens's several legal friends.
2. Dr T. Smethurst, a surgeon accused of poisoning his pregnant mistress, Isabella Bankes, whom be bigamously married on 9 Dec. 1858.
3. At Smethurst's trial (15–20 Aug. 1859) medical authorities testified that Miss Bankes had been poisoned by arsenic but offered no convincing proof. The jurors took only 40 minutes to reach their verdict of guilty; before passing the sentence of death, Pollock commented that he thought it would have been impossible to have come to any other conclusion.
4. Criticism of the legal proceedings after the trial led to a shift in opinion, especially after the publication of a letter signed by 30 London doctors, which argued that the Crown had failed to establish as a fact Bankes's death from arsenic poisoning. Receiving further protests, the Home Secretary, Sir George C. Lewes, felt compelled to act and submitted the evidence against Smethurst to Sir Benjamin Brodie, a well-known surgeon, for an opinion as to the justice of the verdict. When Brodie reported that he found no 'absolute and complete evidence of guilt', Lewes pardoned Smethurst on 15 Nov. 1859, in spite of vigorous protests from Pollock. The pardon,

however, did not include the crime of bigamy, with which Smethurst was charged upon his release. Under fresh proceedings, he was tried, convicted, and sentenced to hard labour for one year. For further reference to Smethurst, see the Selected Bibliography.
5. This letter, as P. Collins notes, provides an 'unambiguous indication' that Dickens had withdrawn his opposition to hanging (*Dickens and Crime*, p. 246). Dickens's championship of the judge and the faith he expresses in his own fallible judgment contrast sharply with the reservations he noted in his letter to *The Daily News* on 23 Feb. 1846. Cf. his comments on 25 Oct. 1864 about the first railway killer, F. Müller, a young German tailor who robbed and murdered T. Briggs on 9 July in a train compartment: 'I hope that gentleman will be hanged, and have hardly a doubt of it, though croakers contrariwise are not wanting. It is difficult to conceive any other line of defence than that the circumstances proved, taken separately, are slight. But a sound judge will immediately charge the jury that the strength of the circumstances lies in their being put together, and will thread them together on a fatal rope.' (N, iii, 402)

GAD'S HILL PLACE, HIGHAM BY ROCHESTER, KENT
Twenty-First January, 1864

DEAR SIR,[1]—In reply to your question, I beg to inform you that the descriptions in Oliver Twist and Barnaby Rudge are ideal, but are founded on close observation and reflection.[2] The Lewes Fair description is built on actual facts, but not by me.[3] From any file of the Times for the year to which I have no clue at hand when the Mannings were executed, you will find a letter from me with my name attached describing the horrors of public execution in London, and the unimpressible and degraded crowd that it attracts.[4] Distinguish if you please in quoting me between Public Executions and Capital Punishment. I should be glad to abolish both, if I knew what to do with the Savages of civilization. As I do not, I would rid Society of them, when they shed blood, in a very solemn manner but would bar out the present audience.—Faithfully yours.

1. J. Fayle, a Quaker schoolmaster.
2. Dickens refers to his description of the condemned cell in *OT* (ch. 52) and the public execution in *BR* (ch. 77).
3. G. A. Sala in 'Open-Air Entertainments', *HW*, 8 May 1852, comments on a public execution at Lewes, Sussex, and the rowdy behaviour of the crowd.
4. The Mannings were executed on 13 Nov. 1849. For the text of Dickens's letter to *The Times* referring to this event, see pp 251–5.

[December][1] 1867
[Bulwer Lytton][2] . . . Being in Cambridge, [Mass.], I thought I would go over the Medical School, and see the exact localities where

Professor Webster[3] did that amazing murder, and worked so hard to rid himself of the body of the murdered man. (I find there is of course no rational doubt that the Professor was always a secretly cruel man.) They were horribly grim, private, cold, and quiet; the identical furnace smelling fearfully (some anatomical broth in it I suppose) as if the body were still there; jars of pieces of sour mortality standing about, like the forty robbers in Ali Baba after being scalded to death; and bodies near us ready to be carried in to next morning's lecture. At the house where I afterwards dined I heard an amazing and fearful story;[4] told by one who had been at a dinner-party of ten or a dozen, at Webster's, less than a year before the murder. They began rather uncomfortably, in consequence of one of the guests (the victim of an instinctive antipathy) starting up with the sweat pouring down his face, and crying out, "O Heaven! There's a cat somewhere in the room!" The cat was found and ejected, but they didn't get on very well. Left with their wine, they were getting on a little better; when Webster suddenly told the servants to turn the gas off and bring in that bowl of burning minerals which he had prepared, in order that the company might see how ghastly they looked by its weird light. All this was done, and every man was looking, horror-stricken, at his neighbour; when Webster was seen bending over the bowl with a rope round his neck, holding up the end of the rope, with his head on one side and his tongue lolled out, to represent a hanged man! . . .

1. Forster's conjectural date for this letter appears to be incorrect. Dickens arrived in Boston on 4 Jan. 1868, where he stayed with the Fields after reading in New York and preparatory to reading in Boston on 6 and 7 Jan. On 5 Jan. Mrs Fields noted that Dickens went with Oliver Wendell Holmes to 'see the ground of the Parkman murder'. At dinner that evening talk reverted to Webster, whereupon Longfellow told his story, which Dickens recounts. See M. A. DeWolfe Howe, *Memories of a Hostess . . . Drawn Chiefly from the Diaries of Mrs. James T. Fields* (Boston: Atlantic Monthly Press, 1922), pp 150–3.
2. Sir Edward Bulwer Lytton (1803–73), first Baron Lytton. Author and close friend of Dickens.
3. J. W. Webster (1793–1850), taught at Harvard, 1824–49; professor of chemistry and minerology; also lecturer at Massachusetts Medical College, Grove Street, Boston. Webster murdered Dr G. Parkman, a noted Boston physician, to whom he owed a considerable sum of money, on 23 Nov. 1849. Parkman was last seen alive that day entering Webster's laboratory after the last lecture was over.
   After felling Parkman with a sledge-hammer, Webster spent the weekend attempting to dispose of his victim's corpse by incinerating, dissolving, and dumping parts of the body into a vault beneath the anatomy

room where he lectured. Public concern for the missing Parkman alerted the college janitor to Webster's curious behaviour during the long weekend, which he had spent unsuccessfully attempting to remove all traces of his crime. Driven by his suspicions, the janitor tunnelled into the vault, where he found the mangled loins and pelvis of a fresh corpse. He reported his discovery to the police, who searched the laboratory and promptly arrested Webster, charging him with Parkman's murder. The identity of the body was established by Parkman's false teeth, which were found in Webster's furnace, undestroyed by fire. Webster was tried (18 Mar.–1 Apr.), and sentenced to death. Subsequently he confessed to the murder after stout protestations of innocence, pleading for mercy because the deed was not premeditated. The Governor of Massachusetts denied the appeal; Webster was hanged on 30 Aug. 1850.

4. This anecdote of Webster's prank was recounted at the dinner party by Longfellow. See N, iii, 599 and *Memoirs of a Hostess*, p. 153. Dickens was aware of the main facts of this case before his visit, telling Wills in Oct. 1867 to expect from Sir James E. Tennent a narrative of Webster's crime based on 'official documents' (N, iii, 563). Tennent's account subsequently appeared in *AYR* on 14 Dec. 1867 as 'The Killing of Dr. Parkman'. J. Garner argues that the Parkman murder provided an important source for *ED*. See 'Harvard's Clue to the Mystery of Edwin Drood', *Harvard Magazine* (Jan.–Feb. 1983), pp 44–8.

Parliament and Self-help

1 DEVONSHIRE TERRACE, YORK GATE, REGENT'S PARK
Monday Evening, Thirty-First May, 1841
SIR,[1]—I am obliged and flattered by the receipt of your letter, which I should have answered immediately on its arrival but for my absence from home at the moment.

My principles and inclinations would lead me to aspire to the distinction you invite me to seek, if there were any reasonable chance of success, and I hope I should do no discredit to such an honour if I won and wore it. But I am bound to add, and I have no hesitation in saying plainly, that I cannot afford the expense of a contested election. If I could, I would act on your suggestion instantly. I am not the less indebted to you and the friends to whom the thought occurred, for your good opinion and approval. I beg you to understand that I am restrained solely (and much against my will) by the consideration I have mentioned, and thank both you and them most warmly.—Yours faithfully.

DEVONSHIRE TERRACE
Tenth June, 1841
DEAR SIR,—I am favoured with your note of yesterday's date, and lose no time in replying to it.

The sum you mention,[2] though small I am aware in the abstract, is greater than I could afford for such a purpose; as the mere sitting in the House and attending to my duties, if I were a member, would oblige me to make many pecuniary sacrifices, consequent upon the very nature of my pursuits.

The course you suggest did occur to me when I received your first letter, and I have very little doubt indeed that the Government would support me—perhaps to the whole extent. But I cannot satisfy myself that to enter Parliament under such circumstances would enable me to pursue that honourable independence without which I could neither preserve my own respect nor that of my constituents. I confess therefore (it may be from not having considered the points sufficiently, or in the right light) that I cannot bring myself to propound the subject to any member of the administration whom I know. I am truly obliged to you nevertheless, and am,—Dear Sir,—Faithfully yours.

1. G. Lovejoy, local Liberal agent from Reading, who invited Dickens to run for election there.
2. Lovejoy had written on 9 June, assuring Dickens that his election expenses would not likely exceed £1000. See P, II, 300n.

DEVONSHIRE TERRACE
Third May, 1843

MY DEAR JERROLD,[1] [. . .]—Oh Heaven, if you could have been with me at a hospital dinner last Monday! There were men there—your City aristocracy—who made such speeches and expressed such sentiments as any moderately intelligent dustman would have blushed through his cindery bloom to have thought of. Sleek, slobbering, bow-paunched, over-fed, apoplectic, snorting cattle, and the auditory leaping up in their delight! I never saw such an illustration of the power of purse, or felt so degraded and debased by its contemplation, since I have had eyes and ears. The absurdity of the thing was too horrible to laugh at. It was perfectly overwhelming. But if I could have partaken it with anybody who would have felt it as you would have done, it would have had quite another aspect; or would at least, like a "classical mask" (oh damn that word!) have had one funny side to relieve its dismal features.

Supposing fifty families were to emigrate into the wilds of North America yours, mine, and forty-eight others—picked for their concurrence of opinion on all important subjects and for their resolution to found a colony of common-sense. How soon would that devil, Cant, present itself among them in one shape or other? The day they landed do you say, or the day after? [. . .]—My Dear Jerrold—Faithfully your Friend.

1. D. W. Jerrold (1803–57), author.
2. Anniversary dinner of the Charterhouse Square Infirmary, 1 May 1843.

HOTEL DE L'ECU, GENEVA
20th October 1846

[John Forster . . .] You never would suppose from the look of this town that there had been anything revolutionary going on.[1] Over the window of my old bedroom there is a great hole made by a cannon-ball in the house-front; and two of the bridges are under repair. But these are small tokens which anything else might have brought about as well. The people are all at work. The little streets are rife with every sight and sound of industry; the place is as quiet by ten o'clock as Lincoln's-inn-fields; and the only outward and visible sign of public interest in political events is a little group at every street corner, reading a public announcement from the new Government of the forthcoming election of state-officers, in which the people are reminded of their importance as a republican institution, and desired to bear in mind their dignity in all their proceedings. Nothing very violent or bad could go on with a community so well educated as this. It is the best antidote to American experiences, conceivable. As to the nonsense "the gentlemanly interest" talk about, their opposition to property and so forth, there never was such mortal absurdity. One of the principal leaders in the late movement has a stock of watches and jewellery here of immense value—and had, during the distur-bance—perfectly unprotected. James Fazy[2] has a rich house and a valuable collection of pictures; and, I will be bound to say, twice as much to lose as half the conservative declaimers put together. This house, the liberal one, is one of the most richly furnished and luxurious hotels on the continent. And if I were a Swiss with a hundred thousand pounds, I would be as steady against the Catholic cantons and the propagation of Jesuitism as any radical among 'em: believing the dissemination of Catholicity to be the most horrible means of political and social degradation left in the world. Which these people, thoroughly well educated, know perfectly. . . . The boys of Geneva were very useful in bringing materials for the construction of the barricades on the bridges; and the enclosed song may amuse you. They sing it to a tune that dates from the great French revolution—a very good one. . . .

1. Forster explains the revolution Dickens refers to as the action of Swiss Protestants in Geneva. When the Roman Catholic cantons rose to object to a decree from the Federal Diet expelling Catholics, the Protestants deposed Geneva's grand council, established a provisional government, and dissolved the Catholic league. Forster, v, vi, 429.
2. James Fazy, new President of Geneva and head of the Radical party. See P, IV, 632n.

TAVISTOCK HOUSE
Twenty-Sixth October 1854

[Miss Coutts] . . . I am very sorry you are in a maze about the article to Working Men[1]—which was written by a friend of yours. Its meaning is, that they never will save their children from the dreadful and unnatural mortality now prevalent among them (almost too murderous to be thought of), or save themselves from untimely sickness and death, until they have cheap pure water in unlimited quantity, wholesome air, constraint upon little landlords like our Westminster friends to keep their property decent under the heaviest penalties, efficient drainage and such alterations in building acts as shall preserve open spaces in the closest regions, and make them where they are not now. That a worthless Government which is afraid of every little interest and trembles before the vote of every dust contractor, will never do these things for them or pay the least sincere attention to them, until they are made election questions and the working-people unite to express their determination to have them, or to keep out of Parliament by every means in their power, every man who turns his back upon these first necessities. It is more than ever necessary to keep their need of social Reforms before them at this time, for I clearly see that the war will be made an administration excuse for all sorts of shortcomings,[2] and that nothing will have been done when the cholera comes again. Let it come twice again, severely,—the people advancing all the while in the knowledge that humanly speaking, it is, like Typhus Fever in the mass, a preventible disease—and you will see such a shake in this country as never was seen on Earth since Samson pulled the Temple down upon his head.[3] [. . .]

1. Dickens's own essay, 'To Working Men', *HW*, 7 Oct. 1854, in which he argued that members of the working class owed it to themselves to insist on sanitary reforms. Let the people take the initiative, Dickens predicted, and 'The whole powerful middle-class' and the press would join them. 'It is only through a government so acted upon and so forced to acquit itself of its first responsibility,' he continued, 'that the intolerable ills arising from the present nature of the dwellings of the poor can be remedied.' See also *MP*, I, 484–7.
2. Dickens feared that concern over Britain's military setbacks during the Crimean War (1854–6) would divert attention from much needed social reform.
3. Outbreaks of cholera in London in Aug. and Sep. 1854 account in part for Dickens's sense of urgency.

TAVISTOCK HOUSE
Thirtieth January, 1855

MY DEAR KNIGHT,[1]—[. . .]
    My satire is against those who see figures and averages, and nothing else—the representatives of the wickedest and most enormous vice of

this time—the men who, through long years to come, will do more to damage the real useful truths of political economy than I could do (if I tried) in my whole life; the addled heads who would take the average of cold in the Crimea during twelve months as a reason for clothing a soldier in nankeens on a night when he would be frozen to death in fur, and who would comfort the labourer in travelling twelve miles a day to and from his work, by telling him that the average distance of one inhabited place from another in the whole area of England, is not more than four miles. Bah! What have you to do with these? [. . .]

1. C. Knight (1791–1873), author and publisher.
2. Dickens refers to *HT* (published as a weekly serial in *HW*, 1 Apr. to 12 Aug. 1854), where he attacked the current tendency of politicians to 'go in for statistics' and sift for hard facts among the mountains of accumulating rubbish 'in the national dustyard', as he referred to Parliament. Such activities, Dickens warned in the novel, left the honourable gentlemen deaf, dumb, blind, lame, and dead 'to every other consideration' than facts, tables, and measures. See *HT*, bk II, ch. 14.

3rd February 1855

[John Forster] . . . I am hourly strengthened in my old belief that our political aristocracy and our tuft-hunting are the death of England. In all this business I don't see a gleam of hope. As to the popular spirit, it has come to be so entirely separated from the Parliament and Government, and so perfectly apathetic about them both, that I seriously think it a most portentous sign. . . . I have rather a bright idea, I think, for Household Words this morning: a fine little bit of satire: an account of an Arabic MS, lately discovered very like the Arabian Nights—called the Thousand and One Humbugs.[1] With new versions of the best known stories. . . .

1. Subsequently published in *HW* as 'The Thousand and One Humbugs', pt i (21 Apr. 1855), pt ii (28 Apr.), and pt iii (5 May). In these amusing satires, Dickens makes fun of the Howsa Kummauns, the Grand Vizier Parmarstoon, and various manifestations of Parliamentary greed, stupidity, and incompetence. See also *MP*, II, 28–48.

TAVISTOCK HOUSE
Tuesday, Tenth April, 1855

My DEAR LAYARD,—I shall of course observe the strictest silence, at present, in reference to your resolutions.[1] It will be a most acceptable occupation to me to go over them with you, and I have not a doubt of their producing a strong effect out of doors.

There is nothing in the present time at once so galling and so alarming to me as the alienation of the people from their own public affairs. I have no difficulty in understanding it. They have had so little to do with the game through all these years of Parliamentary Reform, that they have sullenly laid down their cards, and taken to looking on. The players who are left at the table do not see beyond it, conceive that the gain and loss and all the interest of the play are in their hands, and will never be wiser until they and the table and the lights and the money are all overturned together. And I believe the discontent to be so much the worse for smouldering, instead of blazing openly, that it is extremely like the general mind of France before the breaking out of the first Revolution, and is in danger of being turned by any one of a thousand accidents—a bad harvest—the last strain too much of aristocratic insolence or incapacity—a defeat abroad—a mere chance at home—into such a devil of a conflagration as never has been beheld since.

Meanwhile, all our English tuft-hunting, toad-eating, and other manifestations of accursed gentitlity—to say nothing of Delmaston's,[2] Latham's,[3] Wood's,[4] Sidney Herbert's[5] and the Lord knows who's defiances of the proven truth before six hundred and fifty men—ARE expressing themselves every day. So, every day, the disgusted millions with this unnatural gloom and calm upon them are confirmed and hardened in the very worst of moods. Finally, round all this is an atmosphere of poverty, hunger, and ignorant desperation, of the mere existence of which, perhaps not one man in a thousand of those not actually enveloped in it, through the whole extent of this country, has the least idea.

It seems to me an absolute impossibility to direct the spirit of the people at this pass, until it shows itself. If they would begin to bestir themselves in the vigorous national manner—if they would appear in political reunion—array themselves peacefully, but in vast numbers against a system, that they know to be rotten altogether—make themselves heard like the Sea all round this Island—I for one should be in such a movement, heart and soul, and should think it a duty of the plainest kind to go along with it (and try to guide it), by all possible means. But you can no more help a people who do not help themselves, than you can help a man who does not help himself. And until the people can be got up from the lethargy which is an awful symptom of the advanced state of their disease, I know of nothing that can be done beyond keeping their wrongs continually before them.

I shall hope to see you soon after you come back. Your speeches at

Aberdeen are most admirable, manful, and earnest. I would have such speeches at every Market Cross, and in every town hall, and among all sorts and conditions of men—up in the very balloons, and down in the very diving-bells.—Ever Cordially Yours.

1. Presumably the motion Layard (see p. 117 n.2) introduced into the Commons on 15 June 1855 during the debate on Administrative Reform. Layard's resolutions censured the Government for sacrificing merit and efficiency in public appointments in preference to party and family influences and for threatening to discredit 'the national character' by its inept policies and 'great misfortunes'. See *Hansard*, vol. 138, pp 2040–1. For Dickens's contributions to *HW* expressing a similar degree of exasperation with the means by which men were selected for public service, see Selective Bibliography, p. 364.
2. Unidentified.
3. Unidentified.
4. Sir Charles Wood, MP, President of the Board of Control 1852–5; transferred to the Admiralty, 1855.
5. Sidney Herbert (1810–561; *DNB*), MP, War Secretary under Aberdeen, 1852–5, and member of Palmerston's ministry, from which he resigned in Feb. 1855.

27th April 1855

[John Forster] . . . A country which is discovered to be in this tremendous condition as to its war affairs; with an enormous black cloud of poverty in every town which is spreading and deepening every hour, and not one man in two thousand knowing anything about, or even believing in, its existence; with a non-working aristocracy, and a silent parliament, and everybody for himself and nobody for the rest; this is the prospect, and I think it a very deplorable one. . . . O what a fine aspect of political economy it is, that the noble professors of science on the adulteration committee should have tried to make Adulteration[1] a question of Supply and Demand! We shall never get to the Millennium, sir, by the rounds of that ladder; and I, for one, won't hold by the skirts of that Great Mogul of impostors, Master M'Culloch![2] . . .

FOLKESTONE
30th September 1855

[John Forster] . . . I really am serious in thinking—and I have given as painful consideration to the subject as a man with children to live and suffer after him can honestly give to it—that representative government is become altogether a failure with us, that the English gentilities and subserviences render the people unfit for it, and that the whole thing has broken down since that great seventeenth-century time, and has no hope in it. . . .

1. Earlier attempts to supervise the sale of coffee and prevent merchants adulterating it with chicory failed when MPs defeated a proposal to initiate legislation in 1851. Continued public concern brought the issue back to Parliament; on 26 June 1855 members agreed to W. Scholefield's motion calling for a Select Committee to inquire into the adulteration of food, drink and drugs.
2. J. R. McCulloch (1789–1864), statistician and former professor of political economy whose popular books on economics summed up the theories of A. Smith and other adherents of *laissez-faire* economics. Dickens caricatured McCulloch's ideas in *HT*, especially in some of Mr Bounderby's speeches.

TAVISTOCK HOUSE
Saturday, Thirtieth June, 1855

MY VERY DEAR MACREADY,—I write shortly, after a day's work at my desk, rather than lose a post in answering your enthusiastic, earnest, and young—how young, in all the best side of youth—letter.

To tell you the truth, I confidently expected to hear from you. I knew that if there were a man in the world who would be interested in, and who would approve of, my giving utterance to whatever was in me at this time, it would be you. I was as sure of you as of the sun this morning.

The subject is surrounded by difficulties; the Association[1] is sorely in want of able men; and the resistance of all the phalanx, who have an interest in corruption and mismanagement, is the resistance of a struggle against death. But the great, first, strong necessity is to rouse the people up, to keep them stirring and vigilant, to carry the war dead into the tent of such creatures as——, and ring into their souls (or what stands for them) that the time for dandy insolence is gone for ever. It may be necessary to come to that law of primogeniture (I have no love for it), or to come to even greater things; but this is the first service to be done, and unless it is done, there is not a chance. For this, and to encourage timid people to come in, I went to Drury Lane[2] the other night; and I wish you had been there and had seen and heard the people.

The Association will be proud to have your name and gift. When we sat down on the stage the other night, and were waiting a minute or two to begin, I said to Morley,[3] the chairman (a thoroughly fine earnest fellow), "this reminds me so of one of my dearest friends, with a melancholy so curious, that I don't know whether the place feels familiar to me or strange." He was full of interest directly, and we went on talking of you until the moment of his getting up to open the business.

They are going to print my speech in a tract form,[4] and send it all over the country. I corrected it for the purpose last night. We are all well. Charley in the City; all the boys at home for the holidays; three prizes brought home triumphantly (one from the Boulogne waters and one from Wimbledon); I taking dives into a new book,[5] and runs at leap-frog over Household Words; and Anne[6] going to be married—which is the only bad news.

Ever, my dearest Macready, with unalterable affection and attachment.—Your faithful Friend.

1. The Administrative Reform Association, a middle-class organization which first met on 5 May 1855 to call for an extensive reorganization of Britain's military and civil service and raise issues similar to those Layard brought up in Parliament. See p. 266 n.1. Dickens enrolled as a member.
2. To address members of the Association on 27 June 1855 at Drury Lane theatre. See Fielding, *Speeches*, pp 199–208 for the text of Dickens's statement. His involvement with the Association lasted for only a short period, as did the group itself, which lost its direction when Morley, the chairman, resigned in June 1856.
3. Samuel Morley (1809–96), Liberal MP.
4. Printed as a pamphlet in London by M. S. Rickerby in 1855.
5. *LD*, whose attacks on the Circulocution Office and Government inefficiency owe something to Dickens's interest in the campaign for Administrative Reform.
6. Catherine's maid.

Thursday, Fourth October, 1855

MY DEAREST MACREADY, I have been hammering away in that strenuous manner at my book,[1] that I have had leisure for scarcely any letters but such as I have been obliged to write; having a horrible temptation when I lay down my book-pen to run out on the breezy downs here, tear up the hills, slide down the same, and conduct myself in a frenzied manner, for the relief that only exercise gives me. [. . .]

As to the suffrage, I have lost hope even in the ballot.[2] We appear to me to have proved the failure of representative institutions without an educated and advanced people to support them. What with teaching people to "keep in their stations," what with bringing up the soul and body of the land to be a good child, or to go to the beer-shop, to go a-poaching and go to the devil; what with having no such thing as a middle class (for though we are perpetually bragging of it as our safety, it is nothing but a poor fringe on the mantle of the upper); what with flunkyism, toadyism, letting the most contemptible lords come in for all manner of places, reading The Court Circular for the New Testament, I do reluctantly believe that the English people are habitually consenting parties to the miserable imbecility into which we have fallen, *and never will help themselves out of it.* Who is to do it, if anybody is, God knows. But at present we are on the down-hill road to being conquered, and the people WILL be content to bear it, sing "Rule Britannia," and WILL NOT be saved.

In No. 3 of my new book[3] I have been blowing off a little of indignant steam which would otherwise blow me up, and with God's leave I shall walk in the same all the days of my life; but I have no present political faith or hope—not a grain. [. . .]

1. *LD*.
2. Agitation for further Parliamentary reform continued after 1832 but attempts to enfranchise urban working men and agricultural labourers did not succeed until 1867 and 1884. Women were excluded from the ballot until 1918.
3. See *LD*, bk I, ch. 10, 'Containing the Whole Science of Government', in which Dickens attacks nepotism, privilege and all the other ills he associated with the Government and its various departments.

NEWCASTLE ON TYNE
21st November 1861

DEAR SIR,[1]—Being here[2] for a day or two, I have observed, in your paper of yesterday, an account of a meeting of Finsbury electors, in which it was discussed whether I should be invited to become a candidate for the borough.[3] It may save some trouble if you will kindly confirm a sensible gentleman, who doubted at that meeting whether I was quite the sort of man for Finsbury. I am not at all the sort of man, for I believe nothing would induce me to offer myself as a Parliamentary representative of that place, or any other under the sun.—Yours faithfully.

1. Editor of *The Daily News.*
2. Dickens was in Newcastle for the second series of public readings given in the provinces between 28 Oct. 1861 and 30 Jan. 1862.
3. Following the death of T. S. Dumcombe (MP for Finsbury) on 13 Nov. 1861, a self-appointed group of Finsbury electors made overtures to several prominent figures in an attempt to find a suitable candidate for a seat the Liberals had held almost uninterruptedly since Finsbury became a Parliamentary borough in 1832.

DEVONSHIRE TERRACE, YORK GATE, REGENT'S PARK

28th March, 1844

GENTLEMEN,[1]—I beg to assure you that it gives me great satisfaction to have the honour of enrolling my name among the Vice-Presidents of your association.

My engagements will not permit, I regret to say, of my attending your Meeting at the Hanover Square Rooms, on Monday Evening. But, though absent in the body, I am with you in the spirit there and always. I believe that the objects you have in view, are not of greater importance to yourselves than to the welfare and happiness of society—in general; to whom the comfort, happiness, and intelligence of that large class of industrious persons whose claims you advocate, is, if rightly understood, a matter of the highest moment and loftiest concern.

I understand the late-hour system to be a means of depriving very many young men of all reasonable opportunities of self-culture and improvement, and of making their labour irksome, weary, and oppressive. I understand the early-hour system to be a means of lightening their labour without disadvantage to any body or any thing, and of enabling them to improve themselves, as all rational creatures are intended to do, and have a right to do; and therefore I hold there is no more room for choice or doubt between the two, than there is between good and bad, right and wrong.—I am, Gentlemen,—Your faithful Servant.

1. The Committee of the Metropolitan Drapers' Association, established in 1842. From 1843, when Dickens first addressed members of the Athenaeum, Manchester, he committed himself to frequent speaking engagements and other efforts to support institutions, groups of people, and societies acting on the principle of enlightened self-help and self-improvement. Dickens's speeches to artists, printers, actors, law clerks, governesses, etc. testify to his continued help.

OFFICE OF ALL THE YEAR ROUND

March, 1864

[Edmund Ollier][1] . . . I want the article on Working Men's Clubs[2] to refer back to The Poor Man and his Beer[3] in No. 1, and to maintain the principle involved in that effort.

Also, emphatically, to show that trustfulness is at the bottom of all social institutions, and that to trust a man, as one of a body of men, is to place him under a wholesome restraint of social opinion, and is a very much better thing than to make a baby of him.

Also, to point out that the rejection of beer in this club, tobacco in that club, dancing or what-not in another club, are instances that such clubs are founded on mere whims, and therefore cannot successfully address human nature in general, and hope to last.

Also, again to urge that patronage is the curse and blight of all such endeavours, and to impress upon the working men that they must originate and manage for themselves. And to ask them the question, can they possibly show their detestation of drunkenness better, or better strive to get rid of it from among them, than to make it a hopeless disqualification in all their clubs, and a reason for expulsion.

Also, to encourage them to declare to themselves and their fellow working men that they want social rest and social recreation for themselves and their families; and that these clubs are intended for that laudable and necessary purpose, and do not need educational pretences or flourishes. Do not let them be afraid or ashamed of wanting to be amused and pleased. . . .

1. E. Ollier (1827–86) journalist and poet.
2. 'Working Men's Clubs', *AYR*, 26 Mar. 1864.
3. Dickens's 'The Poor Man and his Beer', *AYR*, 30 Apr. 1859, in which he refers to a club set up so agricultural labourers could have their beer and pipes independently of a public house and manage their own recreational drinking.

DEVONSHIRE TERRACE, LONDON
First February, 1850

MY DEAR YOUNG FRIEND,[1]—You know that my replies to your letters will as usual be brief—not because I ever fail to take a real and strong interest in yours, but because I generally have so many to write every day.

The state of mind which you describe to me is not a wholesome one, I am afraid, and not a natural one. The remedy for it, however, is easy, and we all have it at hand—action, usefulness—and the determination to be of service, even in little things, to those about you, and to be doing something.

In every human existence, however quiet or monotonous, there is range enough for active sympathy and cheerful usefulness. It is through such means I humbly believe that God must be approached, and hope and peace of mind be won. The world is not a dream, but a reality, of which we are the chief part, and in which we must be up and doing something. A morbid occupation, as your mind with books—even with good books—and sad meditation is not its purpose.

There should be its beliefs and rewards. Come out into the world abou you, be it either wide or limited. Sympathize, not in thought only, bu in action, with all about you. Make yourself known and felt fo something that would be loved and missed, in twenty thousand littl ways, if you were to die, then your life will be a happy one, believe me.

Be resolute in this, I ask you. Let me have the great gratification o believing, one day, that the correspondence you have opened with m has done some good, and made a lighter and more cheeful heart than i found in you when it started.

Be earnest—earnest—in life's reality and do not let your life, whicl has a purpose in it—every life upon the earth has—fly by while you are brooding over mysteries.

The mystery is not here, but far beyond the sky. The preparation fo it, is in doing duty. Our Saviour did not sit down in this world and muse but labored and did good. In your small domestic sphere, you may de as much good as an Emperor can do in his.—Always faithfully yours.

1. Miss Emmely Gotschalk, identified in N, II, 203 as a young Danisl correspondent.

BROADSTAIRS, KENT
Wednesday, 16th July 1851

DEAR MISS GOTSCHALK,—Being in London for a few hours yester- day—for I am passing the summer on the sea beach here—I sent you a copy of David Copperfield, dated on the eighth of last month. I wrote your name in the book; I hope you will receive it safely and that it may express to you, though it has no voice, some of the good wishes for you and interest in you with which I give it.

My fair young friend, I do not know how to answer your inquiry, what I may think on a subject so difficult, which has baffled and divided the wisest men of all times. I may want to be enlightened thereupon, as much as you. If I took upon myself presumptuously to settle it for you, I could not settle it in my own breast, and could not rid myself of the consciousness that I am but a rash poor leader who do not see myself, the way I profess to others.

My advice to you, for your own peace and happiness, is to dismiss such speculations as you have and do right. It matters little what we call evil things, if we know them. Why should it concern you to embody or disembody evil? The great commandments of our Saviour are distinct and plain, and comprise as he said all the laws and rules. Your way in life is sufficiently clear and straight when you admit of your trying with a cheerful heart and with no discouragement to regulate your life's conduct by them. I think this is enough for your youth and innocence to do. And in so doing, it will make you more merciful and gentle to consider and forgive those who in the midst of a wilderness of adverse circumstances, lose their way and claim your pity.

The day will come to all of us when the meaning of life will be plain. Meanwhile the only certain light that shines upon us, shines along our path of duty. That is not hidden from you, I am sure. Whoever treads that path, my dear, induces someone else to tread it. It offers you, I think, not a hard journey—but I hope—a long and bright one. You sit down too soon to brood on all these matters by the way. Perhaps they will be clearer farther down the road. Take courage and try.—Your faithful friend.

Part III

Professional Letters

Introduction

Generally critics have conceded Dickens's enduring popularity as one of Britain's most widely read novelists, but many refused to grant him the status of a serious writer of fiction until recently. The period between 1939 and Dickens's Centenary saw a major reappraisal of his contribution to the novel and the growth of a new critical orthodoxy. Dickens is now ranked foremost among the Victorian novelists and included among the great figures of English literature.[1]

Critical reassessment of Dickens's achievement might have come more quickly had he left a body of critical writing. Something comparable, say, to Henry James's Prefaces or Notebooks, or a private record of creative labours, similar to the chronicle Flaubert left describing his attempts to perfect *Madame Bovary*, might have saved Dickens from those who saw art and popularity as mutually exclusive activities. A man who writes to explain his writing, however, 'makes a weak case', Dickens believed, because a work 'should explain itself; rest manfully and calmly on its knowledge of itself; and express whatever intention and purpose' are in the author (N, II, 385). Holding such views, Dickens wrote very brief prefaces and made few public statements about his art, one result of which was to foster the view of him as a brilliant but undisciplined autodidact. This misconception of Dickens remained unchallenged until the publication of The Nonesuch Letters in 1938 and important essays by Edmund Wilson and George Orwell.[2] These landmarks, recent writers agree, represent the turn of the critical tide and the beginning of the modern practice of taking Dickens seriously as a writer whose world view merits attention and whose contribution to the art of fiction commands respect.

The letters assembled in this third section serve several functions. The letters attest to Dickens's preoccupation with the novelist's craft, for example, and specific comments to young authors reveal some of his views about the purpose of character, the handling of plot, and the use of background and description. The letters also provide the raw material from which we can infer Dickens's opinion about literature's purpose and the gravity with which he saw his professional obligations.

The letters do not furnish a complete aesthetic credo, but taken together they illustrate the major principles that guided Dickens throughout his career as a novelist and journal editor.

As a young writer who quickly took his place in what he called 'the procession of Fame' (N, I, 279), Dickens frequently found himself called upon to dispense advice to others eager to follow the same path. This role was later reinforced when Dickens added to his achievements the successful editorship of *Household Words* and *All the Year Round*, where for a twenty-year period he exercised considerable influence upon the numerous contributors to both journals. Throughout his 'conductorship' and stretching back to his early days, Dickens gave writers consistent advice: master the form you choose, he told aspiring poets, dramatists, novelists, and all 'Voluntary Correspondents', who threw their thoughts upon paper, hoping vainly that their productions would merit publication in one of his journals (*Household Words*, 16 Apr. 1853).[3] Do not rush to print, Dickens advised, but hold yourself only to the most professional standards in self-appraisal. Most sobering to young writers was Dickens's plain-speaking about the personal sacrifice writing demanded. If time was spent 'at the cost of any bitterness of heart', the novice was wrong to make writing his vocation; if he did his duty cheerfully, and made 'these toils a relaxation and solace', he did right. One also needed the strength to take rejection notices without falling into 'vexation and disappointment'. But if failure made the writer wretched and if he pursued a career in literature with neither the talent nor the calling, Dickens did not spare the aspirant the necessary truth: 'lock up your papers, burn your pen, and thank Heaven you are not obliged to live by it' (N, I, 280).

The patient and informative letters Dickens wrote to those submitting stories to *Household Words* and *All the Year Round* make more specific points about the nature of fiction and are of interest for that reason. Turning to Dickens's letter to Wilkie Collins about the 1867 Christmas Story, *No Thoroughfare*, we see him stating succinctly the importance of generating narrative interest and the means by which the author provides 'a very Avalanche of power' to engage the reader. A flight and a pursuit, horrors and dangers, 'Ghostly interest, picturesque interest, breathless interest of time and circumstance' – all are basic ingredients used by Dickens to force the design, irrespective of length, to a powerful climax (N, III, 542).

By contrast, other letters concern those aspects of the craft of fiction about which earlier critics pronounced Dickens ignorant. Dickens frequently reminded less experienced writers of the importance of not intruding upon the narrator in their own persons, and of showing characters working out their purpose through dialogue and dramatic action in the manner of the novelist, who should not tell about his characters or talk of them discursively, in the manner of the essayist (N, III, 138). Do not cry, 'Lo here! Lo there! See where it comes!' Dickens told Constance Cross. Rather, try to present characters unaffectedly, with the art of seeming to leave them to present themselves (N, III, 774). To help readers see people or places, much could be done through the addition of 'little subtle touches of description' to give an 'attendant atmosphere of truth' and 'an air of reality'. Without that, Dickens thought, passionate characters ran the danger of glaring, wheeling, and hissing like great fireworks, which went out and lighted nothing (N, II, 850).

Other letters forcefully demonstrate the inaccuracy of the clichés about the supposed ease of serial composition, which enabled the writer to toss off his weekly or monthly quota to an undiscerning audience. Writing in 'detached portions' required a particular and exacting skill, one calling for an eye to be kept on the novel as a whole while attending to the serial parts. You cannot take a story and cut it up into the instalments into which it would have to be divided for a month's supply, Dickens wrote to Mrs Brookfield, without discovering the impossibility of such a procedure. Rather 'that specially trying mode of publication' by the week or by the month required 'a special design', in which the scheme of the chapters, the manner of introducing the people, and the plotting of the story's progress and principal scenes were all completely integrated into the serial's double focus of the instalment and the whole (N, III, 461).

Dickens is equally perceptive about the basic choices facing a novelist in the use of form. If the writer chooses to anatomize 'the souls of the actors', slowness, care, and 'a longer space of time' are necessary (N, II, 840). Otherwise, if restricted to a more limited compass, the novelist must limit himself to whatever can be accomplished within the bounds of length. And at all times, the writer must face the crucial question: what truly belongs to this ideal character under these particular imagined circumstances? 'When one is impelled to write this or that, one still has to consider,' Dickens wrote to Emily Jolly, ' "How much of it is my own wild emotion and superfluous energy," ' and how much of the subject matter is dictated by the intellectual logic of the fiction itself? Not surprisingly, Dickens offers no simple formula by which to judge the extent personal experience should or should not manifest itself in any work. Instead, he emphasized the importance of the writer's adjusting his original experience of persons, places and emotions to the new imaginative context of the fiction. 'It is in the laborious struggle to make this distinction, and in the determination to try for it, that the road to the correction of faults lies' (N, II, 850).

As Dickens admitted to Emily Jolly in support of the sincerity of his advice, his own tendency towards impatience and impulsiveness when writing made him all the more aware of the need for the control he urged upon others. '[I]t has been for many years the constant effort of my life to practise at my desk what I preach to you,' he explained to this talented contributor to *Household Words* (N, II, 850). Indeed, Dickens's injunction to self-discipline, seriousness and the need to master one's craft, represents the distillation of experience and the expression of the iron professional will that won him so outstanding a position among his contemporaries. When he fell hard at work on a book, Dickens usually put in a full day, routinely writing from nine to two in the afternoon through the period of the book's composition. Although Dickens was no word-counter like Trollope, who imprisoned himself at his desk and mercilessly produced '250 words every quarter of an hour',[4] he found that the demands of serial fiction superseded almost every aspect of his attention, including even emotional upsets and turmoil. 'Every Artist, be he writer, painter, musician, or actor, must bear his private sorrows as he best can, and must separate them from the exercise of his public pursuit,' Dickens wrote in an obituary notice for Clarkson Stanfield in *AYR*.[5] On this occasion the 'private loss of a dear friend' also represented 'a loss on the part of the whole community', which justified Dickens's stepping forth 'to lay his little wreath' for the painter he affectionately called 'Stanny'. Only once in Dickens's career did private sorrow become so overwhelming as to interrupt his work. As a young man, grief over Mary Hogarth's death on 7 May 1837, compelled him to break off the overlapping serial instalments of *The Pickwick Papers* and *Oliver Twist* for a month.

Although Dickens appears to have taken the view that literary creation owed more to perspiration than inspiration, he recognized the importance of getting excited and having the afflatus upon him, as William Godwin characterized his state of mind while writing *Things As They Are*; or, *The Adventures of Caleb Williams*.[6] 'You know that I have frequently told you that my composition is peculiar;' Dickens wrote to Catherine Hogarth, breaking an appointment to spend an evening with her during their courtship. 'I never can write with effect—especially in the serious way—until I have got my steam up, or in other words until I have become so excited with my subject that I cannot leave off' (P, I, 97).

Perhaps getting started on a book caused Dickens more anxiety than the actual composition, which, once the initial agonies of plotting and contriving were over, usually went along with the minimum of 'frowning horribly' at 'a blank quire of paper' (P, v, 419; N, II, 235). Some sense of the relish with which Dickens went about writing scenes is conveyed by his description of himself during the final stages of *Barnaby Rudge*. September 1841 found him burning into Newgate gaol, tearing 'the prisoners out by the hair of their heads', and showing the convicts playing 'the very devil' as they sacked Lord Mansfield's house. 'I feel quite smoky when I am at work,' he reported to Forster (N, I, 349; 353). On an earlier occasion, an eye-witness described Dickens intently at work on *Oliver Twist*, his facial muscles playing, his mouth set, and his tongue tightly pressed against closed lips as the feather of his pen moved rapidly across the paper.[7] Later, when Dickens was writing *David Copperfield*, his daughter Mamie saw another idiosyncracy. Watching her father at work from the couch in his study, where she lay convalescing from a serious illness, Mamie noted how he would write quietly for a period, and then jump up and rush to a mirror. Peering into it, he would pull a variety of faces, study each intently, and then return excitedly to his writing table, where he would resume the narrative.[8]

Although on one occasion Dickens told Forster that 'Invention, thank God, seems the easiest thing in the world' (N, I, 782), he could not get on 'FAST' or sustain a rapid pace of composition without the presence of streets and numbers of figures. London – that 'magic lantern' – was indispensable both to his imagination and to his physical need to walk extensively while working on a novel. Without streets and crowds, as he discovered in Italy in 1844, his ideas 'seemed disposed to stagnate', after a day spent toiling at his desk when no prospect of theatres, crowds, and accessible streets beckoned. Neither Genoa nor Lausanne substituted adequately for London, but when Dickens and his family moved to Paris in November 1847, he found that city – 'wicked and detestable' – a 'wonderfully attractive' stimulus to his work on *Dombey and Son* (N, I, 812).

After Dickens bought Gad's Hill and established himself there in the 1860s, France and Paris became increasingly important to him as outlets for his restlessness. Once separated from his wife in 1859 and after selling their family home, Tavistock House, Dickens turned away from London as a source of excitement, preferring to avoid the city, except for weekly visits to the office of *All the Year Round*, and went abroad for recreation and a change. 'My being on the Dover line, and my being very fond of France, occasion me to cross the Channel perpetually,' he wrote his friend W. J. Cerjat in 1864 of his new life after settling into Gad's Hill. 'Whenever I feel that I have worked too much, or am on the eve of overdoing it, and want a change, away I go by the mail-train, and turn up in Paris or anywhere else that suits my humour, next morning. So I come back as fresh as a daisy.' (N, III, 403)

*　　　*　　　*

When Dickens urged upon his fellow writers the seriousness and dignity of the profession of letters and exhorted them to enter authorship alert to the public responsibilities writing involved, he spoke with conviction. Primarily, Dickens believed that literature should enlarge the mind and improve the understanding by portraying the different varieties and shades of the human character and by showing, as his first protagonist learns, that there is more to life than business and the pursuit of wealth. Since Mr Pickwick could afford to retire comfortably and gracefully 'to some quiet pretty neighbourhood in the vicinity of London', his decision was obviously one born of privilege. At the same time, his retirement illustrates a more general truth in that he chooses to devote his remaining years to something other than commerce by voluntarily holding himself accountable to a moral code of decency and humility that does not presuppose financial success. 'If I have done but little good,' Mr Pickwick exclaims as he surveys his recent travels, 'I trust I have done less harm.' (*The Pickwick Papers*, ch. 57)

The significance of Mr Pickwick's resolution at the novel's opening to go in search of adventures that would provide him with amusing and pleasant recollections in his 'decline of life' is further reinforced by the narrator. Taking leave of 'our old friend', he reminds readers that there are ever some experiences 'to cheer our transitory existence hero', provided that we look for them. Seeking them out, we learn, depends less on one's wealth than on one's outlook. There are 'dark shadows on the earth', but we need not act like bats or owls, the narrator reminds us, by preferring the night.[9] Rather we ought to shift our view at will and fill some of our solitary hours with a sense of 'the brief sunshine of the world' conveyed by the novel.

Dickens took seriously the need to counterbalance darkness with sunshine, and he consistently stressed throughout his career the importance of uniting 'notices of all bad [things]' with 'all good [ones]'. Cheerful views, he thought, should combine with the 'sharp anatomization of humbug', and writers should ennoble human life, not denigrate it (N, I, 684). To do so, authors need not deny 'the darkest side of the picture'; rather, in treating evil, they should also treat good and do their best, as Dickens outlined his programme for *Household Words* in 1850, to encourage people to persevere individually, to retain their faith 'in the progress of mankind', and to inspire thankfulness 'for the privilege of living in the summer-dawn of time' ('A Preliminary Word', *Household Words*, 30 Mar. 1850).

In a significant but neglected essay published in *The Examiner* in 1848, Dickens spoke authoritatively of the artist's role in similar terms. 'The Rising Generation', a series of twelve drawings by John Leech prompted his remarks, which were broad enough to apply to literature as well as to art. Praising Leech as the first English caricaturist 'who has considered beauty as being perfectly compatible with his art', Dickens elaborated on the aesthetic implications of introducing beautiful faces and agreeable forms. What impressed Dickens was Leech's refusal to make his pictures wearisome by introducing 'a vast amount of personal ugliness'. A satirical point about a character could be made, Dickens wrote, without making the individual unappealing, a strategy Dickens defended not because he objected in principle to the portrayal of ugliness but because he saw no artistic reason for producing an unnecessarily disagreeable result. To the contrary, he argued, the audience is more likely to respond and to take an interest in a pleasant object than an unpleasant one. Besides, Dickens added, with reference to 'the old caricature' of the farmer's daughter 'squalling at the harpsichord', the satire on the manner of the girl's education 'would be just as good if she were pretty'. Furthermore, he contended, 'The average of farmers' daughters in England are [*sic*] not impossible lumps of fat. One is quite as likely to find a pretty girl in a farmhouse as to find an ugly one.'[10]

No one can justly question Dickens's willingness in his novels to admit that life's sombre hues exist, or infer from his comments on Leech's drawings that he recommended turning one's back upon the world's harsh realities. Treating unpleasant subjects, however, called for tact and for the 'becoming sense of responsibility and self-restraint' of the kind shown by Leech. His good nature, Dickens thought, was 'always improving' and Leech imparts 'some pleasant air of his own to things not pleasant in themselves'.[11] Leech, like Dickens's Uncommercial Traveller, was on the side of 'the great House of Human Interest

Brothers', whose business was served by trying to improve life and afford amusement by showing 'rather a large connection in the fancy goods way' ('His General Line of Business', *UT*).

The artist's role, in Dickens's view, is clearly linked with a conception of the nature and purpose of literature firmly rooted in a historical position similar to the Horatian formula that art should edify and combine instruction with pleasure. Amplifying Horace's *utile* and *dulce*, we might extend the terms along the lines suggested by Wellek and Warren, who include 'Useful' to mean not wasting time and deserving serious attention, while 'Sweet', they suggest, is equivalent to ' "not a bore", "not a duty", "its own reward" '.[12] If we narrow the context further, we can also see how such assumptions about literature's purpose merged with the reform tradition of the Victorian novel, in which novelists committed themselves to trying to improve nineteenth-century society. Regardless of how improvement could or should be implemented as a matter of social and political policy, the novelists agreed that fiction should provide a paradigm to show people how to behave more decently in the future and offer what Dickens called 'an occasional refuge to men busily engaged in the toils of life' (N, ii, 161).

The Victorian novelists' confidence in the educational role of letters and literature's ability to improve society was further reinforced by the optimism with which they saw the growth of literacy in nineteenth-century England. The 'educational metamorphosis',[13] in which the middle classes became more literary and the lower classes learned to read, was seen by both reformers and writers as the foundation for all political and social progress. Writing in *England and the English* in 1833, Bulwer Lytton perceptively recognized that with the demise of the British aristocracy signalled by the Reform Act of 1832, a new national effort must be made to create a better society. In Bulwer's opinion, writers were indispensible' to that goal. They bore the responsibility for renewing the country's energy and mobilizing a progressive and directive government because 'reformed legislation', he thought, was impossible without 'reformed opinion'. 'Now is the day for writers and advisers,' he declared; '*they* prepare the path for true lawgivers; they are the pioneers of good; no reform is final, save the reform of mind.'[14] By teaching the population to read and by providing people with morally improving books, his argument ran, social benefits would follow.

If the writer is committed to teaching and creating the '*new* moral standard of opinion' Bulwer called for, how do we distinguish the artist who approached life, in Orwell's phrase, 'always along the moral plane', from the propagandist?[15] Bulwer showed little interest in this issue in *England and the English*, but Dickens, less of a cultural historian than his friend, raised the question in *The Examiner* several months after the essay he published on Leech. On this occasion, Dickens wrote critically of 'The Drunkard's Children', a series of sketches by George Cruikshank which provoked from the novelist a 'gentle protest' about moral art that crossed the line between views expressed with sincerity and responsibility and those deliberately simplified and dogmatic. Cruikshank's design in 'The Drunkard's Children' was to provide a definitive statement about the dangers of alcohol, to which Dickens objected not because Cruikshank presumed to instruct but because 'teaching, to last, must be fairly conducted. It must not be all on one side.' A partisan commitment to temperance, Dickens understood, encouraged his former illustrator to reduce the problem of drunkenness to an inflexible proposition: it was either an inborn vice or the fault of the gin-shops. 'Drunkenness,' Dickens responded, cannot be confined to a single interpretation because it is 'the effect of many causes. Foul smells, disgusting habitations, bad workshops and workshop customs, want of light, air, and water, the absence of all means of decency and health, are the commonest among its common, everyday, physical causes.' And among its moral causes Dickens listed the mental weariness induced by unremitting labour, the lack of 'wholesome relaxation', ignorance and the need for 'reasonable, rational training'.[16] What the poor did not want was 'the mere parrot education' they were offered by the well-meaning but unimaginative philanthropists of the kind Dickens attacked in *Bleak House*.

Cruikshank's motives in 'The Drunkard's Children' and 'The Bottle', the first of his attacks on the evils of alcohol, Dickens granted, deserved the highest respect; but if the moralist is to strike at all, Dickens argued, he 'must strike deep and spare not'. By placing the blame solely upon those who indulged in the vice and by not bringing the deeper and more pervasive causes of drinking 'fairly and justly into the light', Cruikshank compromised the 'very serious and pressing truth' of the national origins of the problem. He also ran the danger, Dickens thought, of defeating the end the pictures were supposed to bring about. 'There is no class of society so certain to find out' the weakness of Cruikshank's argument 'as the class to which . . . [the pictures] are addressed.'[17] If art were to be affective, Dickens concluded, it must do more than propound a theorizer's doctrinaire solution. Rather the artist should be subversive in the sense that he should discourage complacency among his readers by moving them to look for explanations in the inadequacies of the status quo. Responsibly and imaginatively directed, good art could persuade readers or viewers to understand the implications of drunkeness by showing how it began 'in sorrow, or poverty, or ignorance—the three things in which, in its awful aspect, it *does* begin'. The design then, Dickens confided to Forster, would have been 'a double-handed sword' and 'too "radical" for good old George, I suppose' (N, II, 52).

* * *

Art's persuasiveness should not be limited to exploring the inadequacies of Victorian Britain and awakening readers to social and political injustice. A second assumption about literature's function to which Dickens subscribed with equal vigour was that fiction should supply readers with a satisfying emotional and imaginative experience. In this manner books had served Dickens during his impoverished childhood, so effectively keeping alive his fancy, as he wrote of the 'glorious host' of protagonists from eighteenth-century fiction, that the therapeutic influence of their company proved to him a lasting model of literature's ability to remedy unhappiness (*David Copperfield* ch. 4).[18] Fiction, Dickens always maintained, should provide a balm, confer happiness, and function as a counterweight to external gloom by creating romance from the realities of life. Indeed, Dickens's conviction that literature should furnish an antidote to 'facts' and soften everyday existence by transforming it with the imagination was one of his most characteristic attitudes.

Dickens's comments to Forster about the latter's biography of Goldsmith articulate similar views from a different perspective. A good biographer, Dickens thought, should always make the period to which his subject belonged as fresh and lively as if it were presented 'by the real actors come out of their graves on purpose'. At the same time, the biographer should choose someone whose life was worth the effort, an individual whom the reader could love and admire. On every page, Dickens wrote to Forster after reading his life of Goldsmith, he found reason to praise 'the sense, calmness, and moderation' with which Forster had achieved this end. As a result, the reader strengthened 'with his [Goldsmith's] strength—and weakness too, which is better still' (N, II, 82–3). Dickens did not suggest that Goldsmith's 'discouraging imprudences' should be avoided; in treating them, the responsible biographer took care not to make his subject's achievements any less impressive than they were. Following this formula, the biographer was free to acknowledge his subject's faults provided that he did not dwell on his failures, thereby reducing a great man's accomplishments and failing to present his character so as to elicit from others the goodness and courage evident in the life he records.

Dickens's contention that biographers should inspire is a variation of his position that fiction fulfilled its purpose by arousing cheerfulness and by burning with the bright light of fancy. Fancy, as critics have noted, is a variable term in Dickens's vocabulary, synonymous sometimes with the imagination and ranging at others to include an escape from the world of facts as well as the creative and contemplative power by which an artist transformed life. Yet for all its nuances, the notion of fancy as the imaginative re-creation of real life in romantic terms best illuminates Dickens's idea of the writer's function. The novelist should deal with 'real' life by looking on his mind as 'a sort of capitally prepared and highly sensitive plate' which received impressions of people and places from all walks of life, and then stored the information for later use. As Dickens described this process to W. H. Wills while on a reading tour in the north of England in 1858 his mind 'made . . . little fanciful photograph[s]' of everything that impressed him. Scenes from a walk – in this case through the squalid coal-mining villages of the Pit country between Durham and Sunderland – clearly provided glimpses of 'real' life, which would be useful, Dickens thought, when he returned home. In fact they might 'come well into *Household Words* one day', but only after the impressions taken on the spot had been modified by fancy (N, III, 58). As Dickens observed on another occasion, it was not enough 'to say of any description that it is the exact truth. The exact truth must be there,' he wrote to Forster in one of his most explicit comments about his practice, 'but the merit or art in the narrator, is the manner of stating the truth.' (Forster, IX, i, 279)

Dickens stuck tenaciously to his self-imposed injunction to dwell 'upon the romantic side of familiar things' (Preface, *Bleak House*) and not to be 'frightfully literal and catalogue-like' because he thought the very success of popular literature 'in a kind of popular dark age' depended on 'such fanciful treatment' (Forster, IX, i, 279). He also regarded his books as a personal communication, social acts between himself and his readers, which called for authorial delicacy and tact.[19] Care was particularly important in this relationship because, as he stated in the 1850 prospectus describing the editorial principles of

Household Words, he was ambitious to be admitted into many homes with affection and confidence'. Neither was guaranteed unless readers accepted Dickens's editorial presence, which they were unlikely to do without knowing what to expect. By 1850 Dickens had of course won a large measure of trust; but at the beginning of an experimental enterprise, he saw the importance of reaffirming the values he stood for. Old readers would be assured, he reasoned; and new ones might be attracted by the promise to portray 'many social wonders', provide knowledge of 'good and evil', and to treat life's hopes, triumphs, joys, and sorrows ('A Preliminary Word', *HW*, 30 Mar. 1850).

Dickens's regard for his audience and his resolve to avoid anything that might give offence by encouraging unproductive self-scrutiny and unhappiness among readers appear throughout his correspondence with contributors to the journals he ran between 1850 and 1870. In several letters he acknowledged his perception of the duties of the 'Editor of a periodical of large circulation' (N, III, 510), and discussed the conflicts that arose between an editor and an author. A work may well have artistic integrity, Dickens thought, and be the product of an accomplished writer who is a good man or woman, but it may nevertheless contain passages or scenes requiring cutting or modification, if the editor were to pass them as suitable to a mass of readers.

Modern readers will quickly equate Dickens's unwillingness to 'offend the ear', as he wrote in the 1841 Preface to *Oliver Twist*, with a nineteenth-century reticence about sex. In the case of Dickens's response to Charles Reade's *Griffith Gaunt*, (1866), they are correct. The novel depicted among other scenes Gaunt's going drunkenly to his wife's bed and fathering a child, as well as a passage where Kate, his wife, and Mary, his mistress, have Gaunt's 'illegitimate child upon their laps and look over its little points together'. On the basis of such incidents, Dickens wrote to Wilkie Collins, that if, hypothetically, he were under cross-examination and reminded that he was an editor, he would not pass them because they were capable of perversion 'by inferior minds' (N, III, 510).

Yet for all the predictability of Dickens's response, we over-simplify his reaction by portraying it solely in terms of Victorian prudery about sex. The more important observation in the letter to Collins is the weight Dickens placed on his responding as an editor. Were he free to speak as a writer or critic with a less specific family audience in mind, Dickens could express his appreciation of the novel's obvious artistic merits. *Griffith Gaunt*, Dickens thought, was the work of 'a highly accomplished writer and a good man'. This remark suggests that

Dickens recognized the complexity of the issue. A work by a serious author could legitimately include material that did not always coincide with his definition of editorial responsibility.

The letters Dickens wrote to Emily Jolly and Harriet Parr raise a similar problem. As a critic Dickens responded to stories by both writers with strong emotions and generous praise, admiring Emily Jolly's 'surprising knowledge of one dark phase of human nature' in her 'A Wife's Story' (N, II, 679), and marvelling at the power Harriet Parr displayed in *Gilbert Massenger* (1855). 'The novel moved me,' Dickens informed the author, 'more than I can express to you. . . . I felt the highest respect for the mind that produced it.' (N, II, 684) As an editor, however, Dickens had to consider how such fiction would affect a large audience. There was no point in causing unnecessary pain, he wrote to Miss Jolly, whose story closed with 'so tremendous a piece of severity' that Dickens judged the ending would defeat her purpose. The catastrophe, as it stands, Dickens objected, 'will throw off numbers of persons who would otherwise read it, and who . . . will be deterred by hearsay from doing so' (N, II, 679). Similarly, while moved and impressed by *Gilbert Massenger*, Dickens told Harriet Parr that he was not sure 'whether I could have prevailed upon myself to present to a large audience the terrible consideration of hereditary madness, when it was reasonably probable that there must be many—or some—among them whom it would awfully, because personally address.' With a palpable sigh of relief, Dickens ducked further discussion about publication by telling the author that the length of her story rendered it 'unavailable for *Household Words*' (N, II, 684).

Censorship or silences of the kind Dickens advocated are thought intolerable today. Perhaps sharing Virginia Woolf's observation that 'If you do not tell the truth about yourself you cannot tell it about other people', a contemporary editor or publisher would endorse her contention that Victorian writers crippled themselves, diminished their nature, and falsified their object. 'What books Dickens could have written had he been permitted! Think of Thackeray as unfettered as Flaubert or Balzac!' wrote Virginia Woolf, sympathetically quoting R. L. Stevenson's lament that writers in the late nineteenth century were condemned to avoid 'half the life' that passed them by.[20]

These remarks deserve comment because they are misleading without some qualification. First, Victorian standards of the acceptable were perhaps less uniform and more flexible than a modern writer like Woolf might assume. Even in the case of Dickens, who readily agreed to write novels and edit journals suitable for 'family fare', the most cursory glance at his work reveals a catalogue of illegitimate children, prostitutes, seducers, and individuals with perverse sexual appetites, to mention the topics most likely to bring a blush to the cheek of 'the young person'. Secondly, as this list suggests, the issue was perhaps less a matter of avoiding the forbidden and more one of the manner in which controversial subjects were treated. Moreover, the rationale for the kind of revisions Dickens frequently recommended rested upon aesthetic principles rather than a simple-minded commitment to bowdlerizing. When advising Emily Jolly to alter the ending of 'A Wife's Story' by sparing the life of the husband and one of the children, Dickens justified the change in this way: 'So [with the revisions he suggested] will you soften the reader whom you now as it were harden, and so you will bring tears from many eyes, which can only have their spring in affectionately and gently touched hearts. I am perfectly certain,' he added, curiously foreshadowing the argument Bulwer Lytton later used to persuade Dickens to alter the ending of *Great Expectations*, 'that with this change, all the previous part of your tale will tell for twenty times as much as it can in its present condition' (N, II, 680).

The 'good reasons' Bulwer urged upon Dickens to alter the original ending of *Great Expectations*, in which Pip and Estella are kept definitely apart by her remarrying 'a Shropshire doctor', do not exist in Bulwer's words. We can, however, infer from the essays Bulwer wrote about the aesthetics of narrative art, and from Dickens's general practice, that Bulwer's argument rested on a definition of the novel that certainly included the need for credible human beings but did not advocate a total commitment to realism or naturalism. Dickens and Bulwer both saw the novel more in terms of a Romance, in which the writer typically claimed 'a certain latitude', if we paraphrase Hawthorne's Preface to *The House of The Seven Gables*, to deviate from 'a very minute fidelity' not merely to 'the possible, but to the probable and ordinary course of man's experience'.[21] Rather than concern themselves with propositional truth about a character or situation, Dickens and Bulwer preferred to deal with truth to human nature. In the former, *truth about* presents assertions capable of verification; in the latter, *truth to*[22] is something in which the reader becomes persuaded when the writer convinces by making the reader willingly substitute his belief in the probable for a possible 'marvellous truthfulness' arising from the situation depicted. 'Those critics who . . . have the most thoughtfully analysed laws of aesthetic beauty,' wrote Bulwer in 1863 'concur in maintaining that the real truthfulness of all works of imagination—sculpture, painting, written fiction—is so purely in the imagination, *that the artist never seeks to represent the positive truth, but the idealized image of a truth*. As HEGEL well observes, "That which exists in nature is a something purely individual and particular. Art, on the contrary, is essentially destined to manifest the general." '23

We might consider Bulwer's argument for revising the end of *Great Expectations* as an illustration of this theoretical point. In less abstract language, the possibility of Pip's coming across Estella eleven years after he last saw her is not the real critical issue as Bulwer and Dickens perceived it. Accepting without question the appropriateness of their meeting – the convincing atmosphere and medium of the narrative cleverly discourage our calculating the probability of their coming across each other that particular evening in December – we are moved in our hearts by Pip's obvious happiness and by the inference we draw from his final words. His seeing no shadow of another parting suggests that indeed one does not fall. Admittedly the text allows a different semantic interpretation – because Pip cannot see the shadow of Estella's departure does not preclude her going away again – but since Dickens made Estella a widow in the revised version, presumably so she was elligible to marry Pip, her rejecting him is possible though hardly likely if Dickens wanted to affect our hearts and feelings. There is therefore considerable latitude for an author despite the requirement that he or she idealize truth in the manner favoured by Dickens and Bulwer. As Dickens emphasized to Emily Jolly, on a similar matter of revising one of her stories, the changes he suggested were concerned solely with the manner in which positive attitudes should be conveyed. 'I would leave her new and altered life to be inferred,' Dickens said of the heroine in 'A Wife's Story'. 'It does not appear to me either necessary or practicable (within such limits) to do more than that.' (N, II, 681)

*   *   *

While the novelist legitimately concerned himself with an idealized truth about human experience and with the thoughts and feelings that arose from the world of the author's imagination, he should not neglect the everyday reality to which his readers belonged. Dickens took as self-evident the view that art had four reference points – the universe, the work, the author, and the audience – and that the novelist wrote not to test the reader's interpretive ingenuity in the way that, say,

Robbe-Grillet does, but to be understood. While the text allowed a certain degree of interpretive freedom, it was designed to have a core of fixed or clearly defined meanings accessible to any competent reader familiar with the language and form employed by the author. Communication between the author and his readers therefore meant that the novelist passed along his knowledge of the world – religious, social, political, and psychological – and that he tried to ensure that his readers understood the correspondence between the text and external reality.

Any view of art based upon these assumptions also recognizes the need of the writer to operate within what Fielding called 'the Bounds of Possibility'. We must believe in the characters as people resembling those in life; the events that unfold around them must be credible; and the places characters visit and the homes they live in must be based on actuality. Dickens shared Fielding's call for 'Possibility', and both his theorizing about fiction and his practice confirm how he strove to create characters, scenes, and plots that fell within his interpretation of Fielding's definition of 'the Compass of human Agency'.[24]

One way to ensure a sense of authenticity and verisimilitude, as several letters attest, was to draw on the manners, speech, and appearance of individuals known to the author. As the letters make clear, Dickens went to considerable length to observe people in action and gather the details which imparted a convincing air to his fiction. Requiring a magistrate 'whose harshness and insolence' would render him a fit subject for satirical presentation in *Oliver Twist*, Dickens arranged to be smuggled into London's Hatton Garden police court to watch the notoriously severe Mr Laing at work (N, I, 110–1). He undertook an arduous winter journey to north Yorkshire, falsely presenting himself as the agent of a widow anxious to place her boys at a Yorkshire school in order to observe a local master whose infamy had spread as far as London (N, I, 185–6). Similarly, Dickens spent a morning in July 1840 wandering about Bevis Marks 'to look at a house for Sampson Brass' (N, I, 263). He directed his illustrator to study the face of a particular City merchant, whom Dickens thought resembled Mr Dombey 'to a T', when Phiz was making sketches for the protagonist of the novel (N, I, 768), and he included among his other works fictional versions of real people so accurately observed as to cause pain to those who found the portraits unflattering.

Upon one occasion, Dickens's artistic process even worked the other way. Instead of his going to real people for corroborative details and the specifics which conferred a palpable reality, someone so compellingly fascinating presented himself that Dickens added a new character to a work already carefully plotted and under way. Mr Venus in *Our Mutual Friend* – 'Preserver of Animals and Birds' and 'Articulator of human bones' – was 'discovered' by Marcus Stone, the illustrator, after the first two monthly numbers of the manuscript had been written (N, III, 380). Regardless of the sequence of events governing the creative process, however, Dickens's commitment to mimetic art – the representation of real life in a recognizable form – remained a paramount assumption throughout his career. Making the reader see the 'awful reality' of people and things around was one of the artist's major functions and the indispensable component of any masterpiece. Even Cruikshank's dogmatic moralizing in 'The Drunkard's Children', Dickens thought, compelled respect because of its mimetic achievement. The power of the closing scene, he wrote, 'is extraordinary', conveying the reality of a death-bed scene in the hulks and the presence of the surrounding figures with a fidelity 'worthy of the greatest painter'. The Old Bailey Trial scene also impressed Dickens because the eye could 'wander round the court, and observe everything that is a part of the place'. The very light, atmosphere, and reality, he believed, were reproduced with 'astonishing truth'. 'So in the gin-shop and the beer-shop; no fragment of the fact is indicated and slurred over, but every shred of it is honestly made out.'[25]

Yet portraying 'reality' was not without problems, as Dickens quickly learned, especially for the writer interested in 'these melancholy shades of life' where poverty and misery dwelt.[26] Anyone seriously concerned with the portrayal of those who skulked uneasily through the 'great black world of Crime and Shame'[27] ran the danger of pushing *de facto* limits governing the treatment of low life to their extreme. No publisher or public censor ruled that thieves, housebreakers, or prostitutes were forbidden subjects; but reviewers of *Oliver Twist* raised objections, especially to Nancy and her love for Bill Sikes.[28] In an aggressive Preface written in 1841 to counter his critics, Dickens assumed a rhetorical posture later adopted by Zola, similarly harassed, in his volume of essays entitled *Le Roman expérimental* of 1880. Why waste time, both argued, railing at novelists for presenting things that really happened? 'It is useless to discuss whether the conduct and character of the girl seems [*sic*] natural or unnatural, probable or improbable, right or wrong,' Dickens asserted in 1841. 'IT IS TRUE.' Thirty-nine years later, Zola claimed much greater licence with the same principle for the Rougon-Macquart series, invoking the truth as a justification for writing freely about sexuality, the laws of heredity, and 'the overflow of appetite'.[29] Dickens of course was unwilling to pursue the argument as far as Zola, but he did not shy from following truth through 'profligate and noisome ways' to the 'bottom of the weed-choked well'. The novelist must be free, he believed, to look at 'the best and worst shades of our nature', including its 'ugliest hues'. Where Dickens differed from Zola was in his manner of stating the truth: one could treat the lives of licentious wretches without overstepping commonly held definitions of decency and acceptability.

Perhaps one of the best illustrations of how truthful but disturbing material can be introduced in a non-offensive way is John Peerybingle's fireside nightmare in *The Cricket on the Hearth* (1845). Designed as a Christmas story with a seasonal song of comfort, the narrative also shows that shadows can fall upon even the most domestic and blissful of hearths. The cloud in this instance is a wife's supposed infidelity, which the protagonist and the reader are manipulated into temporarily believing when Dot Peerybingle is portrayed as the apparent accomplice of the mysterious stranger whom her husband unexpectedly brought home one day. Dot's affectionate behaviour and her complicity in the stranger's disguise are grossly misinterpreted by Tackleton, the story's merchant-villain, as he asks the carrier to look through the window of his warehouse. Sitting alone that evening by his own hearth, 'now cold and dark', John Peerybingle broods over the spectacle of Dot whispering and joking with the stranger, whose transformation from the deaf, old, white-haired man he befriended to the young gallant he had recently witnessed from Tackleton's counting house. Back in his disguise, the stranger now lies asleep beneath Peerybingle's 'outraged roof', happy in the knowledge, the carrier imagines, that he has won the heart that '*he* had never touched'. Grief-stricken, the carrier sits alone until 'fiercer thoughts' arise in his usually generous and warm breast. A loaded gun on the wall inspires a dark, ill-timed thought, which dilates in his mind like 'a monstrous demon', and takes complete possession of him: 'it was just to shoot this man like a Wild Beast.' But just as love is turning into hate and gentleness into blind ferocity, the moralist in the form of the chirping Cricket steps in with his supernatural aids. The fairies of destruction are banished and pain and doubt are exorcised and transformed by the suggestion of a more noble response. In a paradigm of behaviour obviously offered to the reader for emulation, John remembers the happiness he and his wife have formerly enjoyed. In turn, these memories awaken his better nature, under whose influence he proposes a rather extraordinary solution for a Victorian husband. He will make his wife the best reparation in his power and do her the greatest possible kindness by releasing her 'from the daily pain of an unequal marriage, and the struggle to conceal it. She shall be as free as I can render her.'[30]

Nineteenth-century readers likely to question the heterodoxy of the carrier's proposal are quickly reassured by later events. The deaf old man was not Dot's lover in disguise but her friend May Fielding's fiancé, who had come back dressed unlike himself in order to observe May and to judge whether or not she still loved him after he had heard that May was to bestow herself upon another and a richer man. Thus what John Peerybingle saw from the counting-house was not his wife's plotting with the stranger to supplant him but Dot's spontaneous joy upon learning that the arranged marriage between Tackleton and Mrs Fielding's daughter could be averted by the timely appearance of May's true lover, who also turns out to be Caleb Plummer's long-lost son.

As a summary of the plot suggests, the predominant mood is one of romance and festivity, and the darker side of life's problems – present in the delicate hint of the difficulties surrounding matrimony – is resolved by the narrator's clearing up the misunderstandings among the characters and unravelling the mysteries. Such authorial manipulation was perfectly legitimate according to Dickens, who saw no objection to comforting people with a moving tale of happiness and generosity, especially at Christmas. No time was more singularly appropriate to remind readers of the importance of not making coffins of their hearts and sealing up forever their best affections.

This same Christmas story also includes Caleb Plummer, whose work as a toymaker can serve as a useful metaphor for the artist intent on providing delight by making artefacts which are drawn from life. Stories, like the toys and dolls' houses crafted by Caleb and his blind daughter, Bertha, are designed for pleasure; they also, like the playthings, represent 'all stations in life'. Just as there were 'Suburban tenements for Dolls of moderate means; kitchens and single apartments for Dolls of the lower classes; [and] capital town residences for Dolls of high estate,' so stories, we can infer, should be based upon a similar fidelity to life. But in denoting social degrees and in confining dolls to their respective stations, the makers of the toys, like the writers, were nevertheless free to improve on Nature, who 'is often froward and perverse'. The narrator makes this point lightly, joking that Caleb and Bertha substitute 'wax limbs of perfect symmetry' for the 'Doll-lady of Distinction' and her compeers, but the comment contains a serious assumption. Nature – whether in the form of people, houses, or dogs, whose tails Caleb attempts to pinch because he wants 'To go as close to Natur' ' as he can to fill the order he has received for barking dogs – provides the subject matter to be transformed by the artist's 'bold poetical licence'.[31]

The importance of transforming reality becomes clearer if we look at Caleb's activities on a domestic level too. To his own life and his blind daughter's he brings the same kind of magic or art that he imparts to the toys. The cracked and ugly ceiling, the four bare walls of the room they share, Caleb's sack-cloth coat, and their cold, harsh, and exacting employer Tackleton are all appropriately altered. Respectively, the 'blotched' and peeling walls become 'an enchanted home of Caleb's furnishing, where scarcity and shabbiness were not', the coat a 'beautiful new great-coat' and Tackleton 'an eccentric humourist who loved to have his jest with them'. Bertha of course cannot see what is really there; what she 'sees' nevertheless is true in the sense that hers is a trancendental vision of how things could be. And that such a change is possible is dramatised by the events of the narrative: Caleb's son returns rich from South America and Tackleton is converted into a compassionate and generous human being. The blind girl therefore was right because she trusted the eyes given to her by the artist. Caleb, the narrator reminds us, is no sorcerer, but he has mastered the only magic that remains to us: 'the magic of devoted, deathless love: Nature has been the mistress of his study; and from her teaching, all the wonder came'.[32]

*   *   *

Dickens's view of literature's 'eternal duties'[33] is closely integrated with his social and political beliefs. As one who walked London's shelterless midnight streets and prowled the city's 'foul and frowsy dens',[34] he did not shy from presenting what he knew of vice and hunger or from using every fictional resource he commanded to persuade readers to sympathize with society's outcasts. Among those most crucially in need of help were the young children, who grew up, as Jaggers puts the case in *Great Expectations*, 'as so much spawn', to be 'imprisoned, whipped, transported, neglected, cast out, [and] qualified in all ways for the hangman' (ch. 51). The catalogue is a long one, but Dickens knew perhaps more intimately than most of his contemporaries just how extensive the threat was to all who existed beyond the pale of middle-class life.

The picture of nineteenth-century society one can construct from Dickens's later novels is a bleak one, showing little hope for the children Jaggers described as living in 'an atmosphere of evil' and only limited opportunities for adult happiness in an urban environment where hostile forces appeared to prevail. But such an interpretation, I think, requires qualification, particularly in view of the novels' implicit optimism and Dickens's equally unshaken faith in the moral authority of the artist to encourage hope. The novelist, Dickens believed, had a duty to present his readers with valid models of human behaviour and to provide a vision of life capable of urging people to virtue and goodness. As John Gardner argues in his essay on 'Moral Fiction', societies are created or destroyed by the myths or fiction to which they subscribe because art affects society. 'To put it another way, mankind has always lived by myth, religious or poetic. By myth we shape our understanding of ourselves, and lay the foundation of the future. By bad myths . . . [portraying man as innately evil, doomed, irrational, and depraved] we plant the future in land mines.'[35]

If the best fiction is to humanize, what are the implications for the novelist? Essentially this view, as Gardner suggests, commits the writer to portraying protagonists who are useful models of human behaviour, characters whose struggle against confusion, error and evil gives support to our own battle with similar problems. Such an obligation does not preclude the importance of delight – the sense that in Sleary's words, 'People mutht be amuthed'. Nor does it mean that the writer should sacrifice his concern with form. At the same time, aesthetic scrupulousness cannot suffice for any novelist holding the view that fiction should focus upon the importance of finding honourable responses to contemporary problems and encouraging in readers a love of life as an end in itself.

Dickens's confidence in the ability of art to affect people positively by providing models of good behaviour drew strength from his Christian vision of life and his faith that somewhere in the world order and intelligibility exist. Although his characters might not fully perceive this, there is a fundamentally Christian sense emanating from the novels, especially in the belief that repentance is genuinely possible for all except those who will their destruction by refusing to change their hearts. Even in the later novels, where Dickens is most obviously pessimistic, the works nevertheless provide a counter to the sense of a universe devoid of moral absolutes and inured to misery and destruction. Painful though Esther Summerson's reconstruction of an authentic self is, she does manage to attain a degree of confidence and stability to make her a mature individual; bewildering though readers find Victorian London, Bucket's rational (and, at times, humane) intelligence shows us how the fragments of urban life can be put together. Arthur Clennam, a male version of Esther, goes from moral and mental stasis to an eventually modest and fulfilled life. And even in *Our Mutual Friend*, the nadir of Dickens's despair for many critics, such middle-class values as belief in the past and the future, the capacity to sublimate one's own needs to those of others or to values outside the self, and the conception of love as self-sacrifice instead of self-fulfillment miraculously survive in the daughter of a Thames water-rat, a bad idle dog called Wrayburn, the spoilt, mercenary Bella, John Harmon, a lonely orphan, and in the misshapen but beautiful Jenny Wren. Lack of personal esteem, profound dissatisfaction, intense ennui – certainly each of the characters, in varying degrees, is subject to these torments; but their dilemmas are neither permanent nor incapable of resolution.

Change for the better in these novels is of course limited to individuals and not to the whole of society. But that is an important distinction to a writer like Dickens, who was steeped in the Protestant tradition with its emphasis on the conversion of the inner man or woman as the precondition of change in the world. The roots of this belief, as Eugene Goodheart suggests, are based not upon political ideology but upon a religious idea inspired by England's experience of Protestantism.[36] To improve society was a matter of individual responsibility and of exerting one's 'best self'. Any art, therefore, that tried to bring about a change in readers, and by extension the society they lived in, was exercising its highest moral authority. Such a view of literature's function, Goodheart contends, was abetted by the persistent strain of Pelagian belief in England – evident at its most secular in the Victorian idea of self-help – that accomplishing one's salvation was a personal responsibility. And people, Dickens believed in his broadly Unitarian way, had the means to perfect or corrupt themselves by the exercise of their free will.

The enduring theme in Dickens's fiction that it is never too late for penitence and atonement embodies this optimistic faith. Given the encouragement that moral fiction ought to provide, people can and will opt for good. The price of maintaining this essentially progressive view of history in the face of circumstances offering unsettling evidence to the contrary doubtless exacted its toll on Dickens's emotional and imaginative resources. Yet however conjectural any final assessment of his personality must remain, consensus on one issue is surely possible. Dickens's novels testify to his belief that literature could never be 'too faithful to the people' by advocating their happiness, advancement, and prosperity[37] just as certainly as his untiring dedication to amusing and delighting readers accounts for his pre-eminence and popularity today.

NOTES

1. See Ada Nisbet, 'Charles Dickens', *Victorian Fiction: A Guide to Research*, ed. Lionel Stevenson (Cambridge, Mass.: Harvard Univ. Press, 1966), pp. 44–153; 'Dickens & Fame 1870–1970: Essays on the Author's Reputation', *The Dickensian*, 66 (May 1970), 83–185; and Philip Collins, 'Charles Dickens', *Victorian Fiction: A Second Guide to Research*, ed. George H. Ford (New York: MLA, 1978), pp 34–113.
2. Edmund Wilson, 'Dickens: The Two Scrooges', *The Wound and the Bow* (Boston: Houghton Mifflin, 1941); George Orwell, 'Charles Dickens', *Inside the Whale* (London: Gollancz, 1940).
3. Dickens and H. Morley, 'H.W.', 16 Apr. 1853. Harry Stone includes this essay in his *Uncollected Writings* and speculates about the portions written by Dickens. See Stone, II, 467.
4. Anthony Trollope, *An Autobiography* (1838; repr. London: Oxford Univ. Press, 1923), ch. xv, p. 249.
5. 'The Late Mr. Stanfield', *AYR*, 1 June 1867 (also *MP*, II, 240).
6. William Godwin, Preface to the Standard Novels Edition of *Fleetwood* (1832) and App. II, *Caleb Williams*, ed. David McCracken (London: Oxford Univ. Press, 1970), p. 338.
7. Frederic G. Kitton, citing Henry Burnett's description of his visit one night to Doughty Street, in *The Novels of Charles Dickens* (London: E. Stock, 1897), p. 29.
8. Turning towards her, Dickens also 'began talking rapidly in a low voice' after his 'extraordinary facial contortions'. Mamie notes that she found the experience 'most curious' and did not fully appreciate its significance until she recognized the natural intensity with which Dickens threw himself into the characters he created. Mamie Dickens, *My Father as I Recall Him* (New York: E. P. Dutton, n.d.), pp 46–8.
9. *PP*, ch. 57. Cf. the narrator's observation in *OT*, ch. 34: 'Men who look on nature, and their fellow-men, and cry that all is dark and gloomy, are in the right; but the sombre colours are reflections from their own jaundiced eyes and hearts. The real hues are delicate, and need a clearer vision.' Dickens later spoke of his 'invincible repugnance to that mole-eyed philosophy which loves the darkness, and winks and scowls in the light' in Boston on 1 Feb. 1842 (*Speeches*, p. 19). And in *NN*, ch. 53, the narrator reflects: 'But youth is not prone to contemplate the darkest side of a picture it can shift at will.'

10. 'Leech's "The Rising Generation," ' *The Examiner*, 30 Dec. 1848 (also *MP*, I, 148).
11. *MP*, I, 150.
12. René Wellek and Austin Warren, *Theory of Literature* (1949; repr. Harmondsworth: Penguin, 1963), p. 30.
13. E. E. Kellet, 'The Press', *Early Victorian England 1830–1865*, ed. G. M. Young (London: Oxford Univ. Press, 1934), II, 3.
14. Edward Bulwer Lytton, *England and the English*, ed. Standish Meacham (1833; repr. Chicago, Univ. of Chicago Press, 1970), pp 381–2.
15. George Orwell, 'Charles Dickens', *The Collected Essays, Journalism and Letters of George Orwell*, ed. Sonia Orwell and Ian Angus (London: Secker & Warburg, 1968), I, 427.
16. 'Cruikshank's "The Drunkard's Children" ', *The Examiner*, 8 July 1848 (*MP*, I, 114). In his own essay 'The Drunkard's Death', *SB*, Second Series, Dickens writes not to show how the bottle leads to ruin but to present a study of an irrational state of mind in which drunkeness becomes equated with madness, not sin.
17. *MP*, I, 116.
18. Kathleen Tillotson comments perceptively on Dickens's habits: 'He is perhaps chiefly a re-reader – going back and back to that shelf of boyhood favourites lovingly enumerated in *David Copperfield*.' See, 'Writers and Readers in 1851', *Mid-Victorian Studies*, Geoffrey and Kathleen Tillotson (London: Athlone Press, 1965), p. 309.
19. See, for example, Dickens's 1841 Preface to the first book edition of *OCS* in which he quotes with approval from Henry Fielding's Preface to *Tom Jones*. An author should view himself, wrote Fielding, 'as one who keeps a public ordinary, at which all persons are welcome for their money'. And to prevent giving offence or disappointing his customers Fielding argued that the writer, like 'the honest and well-meaning host', should provide 'a bill of fare'. Later, Dickens wrote to a prospective contributor to the 1852 Christmas number of *HW* telling him how the issue should have 'some fireside name' and consist of stories supposed to be told 'by a family sitting round the fire' (N, II, 422).
20. Virginia Woolf, quoted by Tillie Olsen in her *Silences* (New York: Dell, 1978), pp 142–3. Readers should note that Dickens's acceptance of the restraints forced upon him by his large audience were not always freely given. Writing to Forster from Boulogne on 15 Aug. 1856, Dickens spoke strongly of his resentment at the moralistic expectations he was compelled to adopt in the interests of his readership. See N, II, 797.
21. Nathaniel Hawthorne, Preface, *The House of The Seven Gables*, 1851.
22. For a useful discussion of this distinction and comments on how artistic truth differs from propositional truth, see John Hospers, *Meaning and Truth in the Arts* (Chapel Hill: Univ. of North Carolina Press, 1946), chs V and VI.
23. Bulwer Lytton, 'On Certain Principles of Art in Works of Imagination', *Caxtonia: A Series of Essays on Life, Literature, and Manners* (1863; repr. New York: Harper and Row, 1864), p. 312.
24. Henry Fielding, *Tom Jones*, bk VIII, ch. i, 'Concerning the Marvellous' in fiction.

25. *MP*, i, 116.
26. 1841 Preface, *OT*.
27. Dickens to Miss Coutts, 4 Jan. 1854, *The Heart of Charles Dickens*, p. 252.
28. W. M. Thackeray made this point in 'Going to See a Man Hanged', *Fraser's Magazine*, 22 (Aug. 1840), 154–5; 'Horae Catnachiane', *Fraser's Magazine*, 19 (Apr. 1839), 408–9; and *Catherine: A Story* (1839–40), ch. 3 and the final paragraphs. For a list of other attacks on *OT*, see Kathleen Tillotson, *OT*, Clarendon Dickens, App. F, p. 399.
29. Emile Zola, Preface, *The Fortunes of the Rougon Family* (1871) in *Documents of Modern Literary Realism*, ed. George J. Becker (Princeton: Princeton Univ. Press, 1963), p. 161. Becker also provides the text of Zola's 'Experimental Novel' (1880), pp 162–96.
30. 'Chirp the Third', *CH* (1845).
31. 'Chirp the Second', and 'Chirp the First'.
32. 'Chirp the Second.'
33. See Dickens's letter to Macready, 14 Jan. 1853 p. 350.
34. 1841 Preface, *OT*.
35. John Gardner, 'Moral Fiction', *The Hudson Review*, 29 (Winter 1976–7), 497–8.
36. Eugene Goodheart, *The Failure of Criticism* (Cambridge, Mass.: Harvard University Press, 1978), p. 28. Ch. 2 of Goodheart's book, 'English Social Criticism and the Spirit of Reformation', provides a stimulating analysis of the moral basis of the criticism of Carlyle, Ruskin, and Arnold.
37. *Speeches*, p. 157.

Advice to Authors

BROADSTAIRS
September 27, 1839

DR SIR,[1]—I can have no objection to your stating to the Editor of Tait's Magazine[2] or of Blackwood's[3] the substance of what I wrote to you concerning your Songs, or (if you have the note by you) the exact terms in which I expressed myself.

I should have answered your letter before, but I have been out of town, in different places, for some months and did not receive it in due course,[4] this is the reason why I have not returned your play long ago. I shall be in town towards the end of next week and will send it to you.

Am sorry to say—and would not say, but that I know you wish me to speak plainly, and that I ought to do so—that of the play itself, I cannot speak favorably. The production is most honourable and creditable to you, but it would not benefit you, either in pocket or reputation, if it were printed,—and acted, I do not think it ever could be.

Not to mention that the verse contains most singular instances of inverted expressions (which I may describe more familiarly as putting the cart before the horse) and many words not to be found in the language—not to mention these faults which are easily susceptible of correction, there are some in the plot and characters, which seem to me incurable. The father is such a dolt, and the villain *such* a villain, the girl so exceptionally credulous and the means used to deceive them so very slight and transparent, that the reader *cannot* sympathize with their distresses. Action too is terribly wanting, and the characters not being strongly marked (except in impossibilities) the Dialogues grow tedious and wearisome. I read it with great care, and not long ago, either, but I don't remember at this moment any difference in the mode or matter of their speech which enabled me to distinguish, in recollection, one character from the other—except the maiden lady and the villain, of whom the former is very good, and the latter but an average villain who speaks in dashes and interjections and constantly interrupts himself.

I think so highly of the exertions you have made and the difficulties against which you have struggled, that I am unwilling you should suppose you had no mart for worthy labour, and were *kept down* by obstacles against which you could not contend. I firmly believe that if this play had been written by Sheridan Knowles⁵ or Sir Edward Bulwer, it would not have been acted. I am *sure* it would not, from what I know of the proceedings of both these gentlemen and the friendly criticism and judgment to which they have several times submitted. Remember how very difficult it is to produce a good play, how very few men can do it, and how many fail and how few try or if they do try ever permit their trials to see the light.

Calling these things to mind, you will not (I am sure) be discouraged or hurt by what I tell you—remembering too, that I communicate but my individual opinion, and that I am as likely to commit an error in judgment as anybody else.—Yours truly.

1. John A. Overs (1808–44), a London cabinet-maker whom Dickens helped with his writing. Dickens liked Overs's 'Songs of the Seasons' and 'would gladly have published them' when he received them in Jan. 1839, had he continued to edit *Bentley's Miscellany*. See the Preface he later wrote for Overs's *Evenings of a Working Man*, 1844, in which he described his relationship with him (*MP*, I, 16–9).
2. *Tait's Edinburgh Magazine* (1832–61), ed. W. Tait, published the 'Songs' between Jan. and Dec. 1842.
3. *Blackwood's Edinburgh Magazine*, a monthly periodical founded in 1817 by W. Blackwood.
4. Course. This (P, I, 587).
5. James Sheridan Knowles (1784–1862), dramatist.

1 DEVONSHIRE TERRACE, YORK GATE, REGENT'S PARK
Twenty-Fifth November 1840

SIR,¹—I have read the little poems you sent me (and which I now return), and in compliance with your request, have to give you my opinion of them. I am by no means satisfied, nor do I wish you to be, that my conclusions are infallible; and I scarcely expect, and certainly do not desire, that you should attach any weight to them, whatever.

First, as the more grateful task, let me say what I have to say of praise. You are a very young man, you tell me, with other occupations to employ your time; and you can only cultivate these thoughts and aspirations by stealth. A love of the good and beautiful, and a desire to illustrate it in one so circumstanced is always a thing to be commended—to be very highly commended. It should increase your own happiness whether it adds to the happiness and entertainment of mankind or no, and from pursuits so worthy and humanising, I would not turn you aside by one discouraging word. The pursuit of excellence in any path which has the light of Truth upon it, is, in the abstract, a noble employment, and like the search for the Philosopher's stone will reward you with a hundred incidental discoveries though you fall short of the one great object of your desire.

Beyond this, I think that you have many good thoughts—occasionally a power of expressing them, very simply and well—a love of nature and all creation—and, of course, (for these are its necessary companions) deep feeling and strong sympathy.

On the other hand, you have very much to learn. Your versification is often harsh and irregular, your conceits strained and unnatural, your images fraught with more sound than sense. The first fault is one which only time and reading can remove; a few instances of the other two, I have marked as they have struck me in the perusal. To spell a tiger from all thoughts of harm—to clasp blood springs with tendril fingers (which appears difficult, to say the least)—to make the sun unfurl his bannered robe—to engrave words *with* fire—to describe the birds as couching with gasping pants of bliss—to tear a man to pieces with links—to fold love's banner o'er a lady's brow—are so near being absurdities that I hardly know what else to call them. You may find, I know, startling and monstrous conceits in the writings of our greatest Poets; but you must remember that *they* were great, not because of these blots, but in despite of them, having for every one a crowd of beautiful and grand thoughts which bore down all before them. Never imitate the eccentricities of genius, but toil after it in its truer flights. They are not so easy to follow, but they lead to higher regions.

You have too much about faëry land, and faëry things—by far too much mention of nerves and heart strings—more agonies of despondency than suit my taste—mysterious promptings too in your own breast which are much better there, than anywhere else. It is not the province of a Poet to harp upon his own discontents, or to teach other people that they ought to be discontented. Leave Byron to his gloomy greatness, and do you

> Find tongues in trees, books in the running brooks,
> Sermons in stones, and good in everything.[2]

The young painter's last dream pleased me very much in its opening; the change of time and coming on of morning are very beautifully described, and the aspect of his room and the familiar things about it I really think *highly* of. But surely in the close of this piece you have quite perverted its proper object and intention. To make that face his comfort and trust—to fill him with the assurance of meeting it one day in Heaven—to make him dying, attended, as it were, by an angel of his own creation—to inspire him with gentle visions of the reality sitting by his bedside and shedding a light even on the dark parth of Death—and so to let him gently pass away, whispering of it and seeking the hand to clasp in his—would be to complete a very affecting and moving picture. But, to have him struggling with Death in all its horrors, yelling about foul fiends and bats' wings, with staring eyes and rattles in his throat, is a ghastly, sickening, hideous end, with no beauty, no moral, nothing in it but a repulsive and most painful idea. If he had been the hero of an epic in seventy books and had out-Lucifered Lucifer in every line of them, you could scarcely have punished him at last in a more revolting manner. I do hope that you will write this piece again with some such alteration. If you ever do so, I shall be glad to see it.

"Withered Leaves" opens, I think, very prettily—But it is not so well sustained and treads rather closely at last (in the idea; not in the manner of expressing it) upon a song of Mr. Lover's,[3] founded on an Irish superstition. It is called, if I remember right, the Four Leaved Shamrock. The ode to the moon, very good. These are the only *data* I have, by which to form an opinion of your powers.

The advice I have to give you, is given in a very few words. I don't think you would ever find a publisher for a volume of such compositions unless at your own expence; and if you could, and have anything in you, the time would very soon come, when you would most heartily regret the having rushed into print. There are a great many people who write as well—many who write better. If you are to pass them or are to take any place in the procession of Fame, you will do so none the later for keeping these effusions in your desk. At the same time, I see no objection to your sending some piece of moderate length—the painter for instance, but not in its present form—to such a magazine as Blackwood's; and no improbability—no unusual improbability I mean—in the way of its acceptance and insertion. If you do this, give yourself the advantage of plain penmanship and a sheet of paper large enough to hold the lines, or it will never be read. And don't write to the Editor to tell him who you are or what you are, for he will care very little about that, and the public will care less.

It is impossible for me to say on such means as you have given me, whether I think you ever will be a great man, or whether you have God's gifts, to become one. Some men would consider it their bounden duty to warn you off the dangerous ground of Poetry, but that I will not do,—firstly because I know you would still trespass there as boldly as ever, and secondly because for aught I know the land may be yours by right. Therefore, I make such remarks upon your writings as occur to me in reading them, and point out to you the course you would do best to take—the course I took myself when I was about one and twenty—and the course most writers have adopted when unknown and untried.

It is impossible that being unknown and untried, I could introduce you to a publisher with any beneficial result. I could not say that I thought your book would *pay* (that would be his first question); I could not even tell him that it was likely to attract public attention. I know but a dozen leaves of it, and if I said of those leaves to him, what I have said to you, he would be perfectly satisfied; and with the utmost deference and respect, and with the sincerest possible thanks, would decline the honor I proposed to confer upon him, and express the deepest gratitude for the preference.

You wish to know whether you do right in sacrificing so much time to what may fail at last. If you do so at the cost of any bitterness of heart, or any disgust with the employment in which you are engaged, you certainly do *wrong*. If you have strength of mind to do your duty cheerfully, and to make these toils a relaxation and solace of which nobody can deprive you, you do *right*. This is a question which none but yourself can determine. It is settled easily. When you have finished something carefully and to please yourself, make the trial I have suggested. If it fail in one quarter, try it again in another. If it fail in half a dozen, and each failure bring with it vexation and disappointment, lock up your papers, burn your pen, and thank Heaven you are not obliged to live by it.—Faithfully Yours.

1. S. Harford, a young solicitor's clerk at Exeter who later went to Australia for his health and died there. His real name was Robert Sydney Horrell (N, I, 275n).
2. *As You Like It*, I, ii, 16–7.
3. Samuel Lover (1797–1868), Irish novelist and song-writer. 'The Four-Leaved Shamrock', *Songs of the Superstitions of Ireland*.

1 DEVONSHIRE TERRACE
Fifteenth January 1841

SIR,[1]—I cannot forbear saying a very few words in reply to your letter of the ninth. As my time is short, I must say them briefly.

I did not expect you to defer to my opinion *now*. I should say that in three years time you will be more disposed to entertain it, and that in five—at the longest—we shall have come to think alike.

Are you quite sure that you do not confound my means of estimating your genius, with your own? Pray consider that I am ignorant of the feelings which you admit, yourself, you express inadequately—that I have not been the companion of your thoughts—that I have seen but a very few lines of your writing—and that you would be a very extraordinary man, indeed, if on so short an acquaintance I could pronounce you in my own mind—a Poet.

You seem to desire that I should expressly say whether you would do best to pursue this bent, or to abandon it for ever. I am not in a condition to do so. I have not sufficient knowledge of your abilities. It is impossible for me to acquire it from the data you have given me. And I am confident that if you laid those same pieces before any man who considered the responsibility you imposed upon him, he would say in so many words what I now tell you.

In answer to some of the objections I ventured to suggest to you, you plead the absence of needful revision and correction. Now, I must say you are foolish and wrong in this. The question you wish me to decide, has reference, not only to what you think, but to your power of expressing what you think. How can I judge of that, upon your mere assurance that you have the power of writing regular verse, but have not taken the trouble to exert it? For aught I know, a great many men may *think* poetry—I dare say they do—but the matter between us, is, whether you can write it or no.

Do not suppose that the entertaining a distaste for such extremely light labour as reading and revising your own writings, is a part of the true poetical temperament. Whatever Genius does, it does well; and the man who is constantly beginning things and never finishing them is no true Genius, take my word for it.

I do not remember to have ever had, within the last four or five years, any composition sent me by a young man (and I have had a great number) who did not give me to understand that it was the worst he had ever written, and that he had much better ones at home.

I tell you candidly that I am interested in you—that I should be glad if you would do justice both to yourself and me, and give me the means of knowing what you really can do—and that I should be delighted to cheer and encourage you if I found I could. I should like to see the Young Painter's Dream with its altered (that is, with its original) conclusion; and if I should not receive them from you by any other mode, I shall certainly if I visit Exeter next summer—as I think I shall—hope to take the two poetical tales from your own hand.

I hope you will not misunderstand me in anything I have said to you, either in this, or in my former letter. If I seem cruel it is only to be kind, believe me. You do not know, and can form no conception of the misery (often untold to any other ears) which I see everyday of my life in young men who mistook their vocation when they were younger, and have become the very beggars of Literature. It is because I know the bitterness and anguish of such mistakes, and looking along the path you wish to tread, see these dismal scarecrows in it, that I must know well what your qualification is, before I encourage you in your perilous desire.

If my last letter to you were unsatisfactory, it was so because the specimens you sent me were unsatisfactory too, and insufficient. What I have seen of yours, I should have read with pleasure if it had caught my eye by chance. I cannot say more, unless I repeat that I see every day, writing which is to my mind quite as good. You say you can write better. I wish to be enabled to say so too.

I regret very much to hear that you have been unwell, and sincerely hope your health is now improving. Assuring you that your confidence needs no apology or excuse.—I am,—Faithfully Yours.

1. S. Harford.

GAD'S HILL PLACE, HIGHAM BY ROCHESTER, KENT
Thursday, Twenty-Seventh December, 1866
DEAR MADAM,[1]—You make an absurd, though common mistake, in supposing that any human creature can help you to be an authoress, if you cannot become one in virtue of your own powers. I know nothing about "impenetrable barriers," "outsiders," and "charmed circles." I know that anyone who can write what is suitable to the requirements of my own journal—for instance—is a person I am heartily glad to discover, and do not very often find.[2] And I believe this to be no rare case in periodical literature. I cannot undertake to advise you in the abstract, as I number my unknown correspondents by the hundred. But if you offer anything to me for insertion in All the Year Round, you may be sure that it will be honestly read, and that it will be judged by no test but its own merits and adaptability to those pages.

But I am bound to add that I do not regard successful fiction as a thing to be achieved in "leisure moments."—Faithfully yours.

1. Unidentified.
2. As editor of *HW* and *AYR*, Dickens was constantly beset by requests from unknown writers to read unsolicited contributions to the journals. My correspondents, he joked with Lady Devonshire on 26 Sep. 1866, 'are of two classes. One class wants print; the other wants money.' (N, III, 468).
   Dickens characterized the 'voluntary Correspondent' as one who viewed

literature as 'the easiest amusement in the world', 'throws his thoughts' on paper in leisure hours, dispenses with orthography, and ignores the principles of composition. 'It would amaze his incredulity beyond all measure, to be told that such elements as patience, study, punctuality, determination, self-denial, training of mind and body, hours of application and seclusion to produce what he reads in seconds, enter into such a career.' See Dickens and H. Morley, 'H.W.', *HW*, 16 Apr. 1853.

He exercised the same editorial vigilance even with his friends. See the letter to Percy Fitzgerald below.

OFFICE OF ALL THE YEAR ROUND
Tuesday, Fifth February, 1867

DEAR SIR,[1]—I have looked at the larger half of the first volume of your novel, and have pursued the more difficult points of the story through the other two volumes.

You will, of course, receive my opinion as that of an individual writer and student of art, who by no means claims to be infallible.

I think you are too ambitious, and that you have not sufficient knowledge of life or character to venture on so comprehensive an attempt. Evidences of inexperience in every way, and of your power being far below the situations that you imagine, present themselves to me in almost every page I have read. It would greatly surprise me if you found a publisher for this story, on trying your fortune in that line, or derived anything from it but weariness and bitterness of spirit.

On the evidence thus put before me, I cannot even entirely satisfy myself that you have the faculty of authorship latent within you. If you have not, and yet pursue a vocation towards which you have no call, you cannot choose but be a wretched man. Let me counsel you to have the patience to form yourself carefully, and the courage to renounce the endeavour if you cannot establish your case on a very much smaller scale. You see around you every day, how many outlets there are for short pieces of fiction in all kinds. Try if you can achieve any success within these modest limits (I have practised in my time what I preach to you), and in the meantime put your three volumes away.—Faithfully yours.

1. Unidentified.

OFFICE OF ALL THE YEAR ROUND
Wednesday, Ninth March 1870

MY DEAR FITZGERALD,[1]—You make me very uneasy on the subject of your new long story here,[2] by sowing your name broadcast in so many fields at once, and undertaking such an impossible amount of fiction at one time. Just as you are coming on with us,[3] you have another story in progress in The Gentleman's Magazine,[4] and another announced in Once a Week.[5] And so far as I know the art we both profess, it cannot be reasonably pursued in this way. I think the short story you are now finishing in these pages obviously marked by traces of great haste and small consideration; and a long story similarly blemished would really do the publication irreparable harm.

These considerations are so much upon my mind that I cannot forbear representing them to you, in the hope that they may induce you to take a little more into account the necessity of care and preparation, and some self-denial in the quantity done. I am quite sure that I write fully as much in your interest as in that of All the Year Round. —Believe me, always faithfully yours.

1. Percy Hetherington Fitzgerald (1834–1925), novelist and prolific miscellaneous writer, whose hasty and slipshod productions cost Dickens much editorial labour. On 18 Nov. 1869, Dickens had written: 'For my sake—if not for Heaven's—do, *I entreat you*, look over your manuscript before sending it to the printer. Its condition involves us all in hopeless confusion, and really occasions a great unnecessary cost' (N, III, 751).
2. *The Doctor's Mixture*, published weekly in *AYR* between 4 June 1870 and 28 Jan. 1871. Later republished in 3 vols by Hurst and Blacket (1871) as *Two Fair Daughters*.
3. *Bridge of Sighs: A Yachting Story*, published in *AYR* (1 Jan. to 26 Mar. 1870).
4. *Will He Escape?* published in *The Gentleman's Magazine* (Sep. 1869 to June 1870).
5. *The Sword of Damocles*, which appeared in *Once a Week* between 9 Apr. and 9 July 1870.

TAVISTOCK HOUSE, TAVISTOCK SQUARE, LONDON, W.C.

Saturday Night, Seventh January, 1860

MY DEAR WILKIE,—I have read this book[1] with great care and attention. There cannot be a doubt that it is a very great advance on all your former writing, and most especially in respect of tenderness. In character it is excellent. Mr. Fairlie as good as the lawyer, and the lawyer as good as he. Mr. Vesey and Miss Halcombe, in their different ways, equally meritorious. Sir Percival, also, is most skilfully shown, though I doubt (you see what small points I come to) whether any man ever showed uneasiness by hand or foot without being forced by nature to show it in his face too. The story is very interesting, and the writing of it admirable.

I seem to have noticed, here and there, that the great pains you take express themselves a trifle too much, and you know that I always contest your disposition to give an audience credit for nothing, which necessarily involves the forcing of points on their attention, and which I have always observed them to resent when they find it out—as they always will and do. But on turning to the book again, I find it difficult to take out an instance of this. It rather belongs to your habit of thought and manner of going about the work. Perhaps I express my meaning best when I say that the three people who write the narrative[2] in these proofs have a DISSECTIVE property in common, which is essentially not theirs but yours; and that my own effort would be to strike more of what is got *that way* out of them by collision with one another, and by the working of the story.

You know what an interest I have felt in your powers from the beginning of our friendship,[3] and how very high I rate them? *I* know that this is an admirable book, and that it grips the difficulties of the weekly portion and throws them in a masterly style. No one else could do it half so well. I have stopped in every chapter to notice some instance of ingenuity, or some happy turn of writing; and I am absolutely certain that you never did half so well yourself.

So go on and prosper, and let me see some more, when you have enough (for your own satisfaction) to show me. I think of coming in to back you up if I can get an idea for my series of gossiping papers.[4] One of these days, please God, we may do a story together; I have very odd half-formed notions, in a mist, of something that might be done that way.—Ever affectionately.

1. *The Woman in White*, followed *TTC* in *AYR* and ran in 40 weekly parts from 26 Nov. 1859 to 25 Aug. 1860.
2. The three principal 'Epochs' of the story are narrated by two major characters; several other figures contribute to each of the three sections as well.
3. Collins met Dickens in 1851; their interest in fiction, theatricals, and *HW* drew them together, and Collins became, writes Forster, 'for all the rest of the life of Dickens, one of his dearest and most valued friends' (Forster, VI, v, 73). The two had already collaborated on several enterprises: 'The Wreck of the Golden Mary', Christmas number of *HW* 1856; 'The Lazy Tour of Two Idle Apprentices', for *HW*, 3–31 Oct. 1857; 'The Perils of Certain English Prisoners', Christmas number of *HW* 1857; and 'A Message from the Sea', Christmas number of *AYR* 1860.
4. Dickens's 'gossiping papers' appeared as the *UT* series, which began in *AYR* on 28 Jan. 1860.

TAVISTOCK HOUSE, TAVISTOCK SQUARE, LONDON, W.C.
Nineteenth November, 1859

My dear Charles Collins,[1]—In retaining the Story (though I am afraid not for the Christmas No)[2] I feel that I ought to say a word or two to you about it, because I doubt it. And I am so afraid of your else going wrong in your book, and disappointing yourself, that I feel the responsibility I am under of telling you the truth.

Rely upon it, the story is altogether in want of touches of relief, and life, and truth. It is greatly too much in the manner of the stories of about the time of the Essayists; it does not hang well together; it is not easy; and there is too much of the narrator in it—the narrator not being an actor. The result is, that I can *not* see the people, or the place, or believe in the fiction. I am absolutely certain—mind!—that this is no peculiarity of mine. If you were to show it to Wilkie[3] without a word of comment, he must see the same defects in it. If you were to read it yourself after trying something else, you would see them quite as plainly.

You have such an excellent humour—of your own—and such a correct and delicate observation—that it is a great pity not to give the quality more play in such a narrative. As, for instance, by making the sister who writes to the Sailor, some recognisable type of woman. A wolfish kind of thing like the Italian, requires a Red Riding Hood, or a Grandmother. I feel after reading the story, exactly as if it had been told me by somebody who couldn't tell it; and as if I had to fill in all the things to make it life-like, myself.

Don't let the Eye Witness[4] drop. It will certainly do you good; It's a capital name for you; if you went on with it, I think it would be the best name you could put upon the Title page of your book; it is your own idea, and one that you may stand by for years.—Ever faithfully.

1. Charles Allston Collins (1828–73), painter, writer, contributor to *HW* and *AYR*. Married Katey Dickens in 1860.
2. 'The Haunted House' (1859), contained nothing by C. Collins, but he contributed stories to four subsequent Christmas numbers.
3. Collins's brother.
4. Collins's 'Eye-Witness' series began in *AYR* on 25 June 1859 and appeared intermittently until 28 July 1860. Collins later collected his 24 sketches and republished them as *The Eye-Witness, and His Evidence About Many Wonderful Things* (London: S. Low, 1860).

GAD'S HILL PLACE, HIGHAM BY ROCHESTER, KENT
Friday, Twenty-Third August, 1867

MY DEAR WILKIE,—I have done the overture,[1] but I don't write to make *that* feeble report.

I have a general idea which I hope will supply the kind of interest we want. Let us arrange to culminate in a wintry flight and pursuit across the Alps, under lonely circumstances, and against warnings. Let us get into all the horrors and dangers of such an adventure under the most terrific circumstances, either escaping from or trying to overtake (the latter, the latter, I think) some one, on escaping from or overtaking whom the love, prosperity, and Nemesis of the story depend. There we can get Ghostly interest, picturesque interest, breathless interest of time and circumstance, and force the design up to any powerful climax we please. If you will keep this in your mind as I will in mine, urging the story towards it as we go along, we shall get a very Avalanche of power out of it, and thunder it down on the readers' heads.—Ever affecly.

1. 'The Overture', Dickens's introductory chapter to *No Thoroughfare*, the story he and W. Collins wrote for the 1867 Christmas number of *AYR*. The letter refers to Act III, Dickens's other contribution, in which Jules Obenreizer, the villain, attempts to murder George Vendale (alias Walter Wilding) while they cross the Simplon Pass in a raging winter storm. Marguerite Obenreizer, the neice of the villain, follows the two without their knowledge because she suspects her uncle's intentions towards Vendale, whom she loves. Collins wrote the whole of Act II and contributed to I and IV.

TAVISTOCK HOUSE
Friday Evening, Ninth February, 1855

MY DEAR MISS KING,[1]—I wish to get over the disagreeable part of my letter in the beginning. I have great doubts of the possibility of publishing your story in portions.

But I think it possesses *very great merit*. My doubts arise partly from the nature of the interest which I fear requires presentation as a whole, and partly on your manner of relating the tale. The people do not sufficiently work out their own purposes in dialogue and dramatic action. You are too much their exponent; what you do for them, they ought to do for themselves. With reference to publication in detached portions (or, indeed, with a reference to the force of the story in any form), that long stoppage and going back to possess the reader with the antecedents of the clergyman's biography, are rather crippling. I may mention that I think the boy (the child of the second marriage) a little too "slangy." I know the kind of boyish slang which belongs to such a character in these times; but, considering his part in the story, I regard it as the author's function to elevate such a characteristic, and soften it into something more expressive of the ardour and flush of youth, and its romance. It seems to me, too, that the dialogues between the lady and the Italian maid are conventional but not natural. This observation I regard as particularly applying to the maid, and to the scene preceding the murder. Supposing the main objection surmountable, I would venture then to suggest to you the means of improvement in this respect.

The paper is so full of good touches of character, passion, and natural emotion, that I very much wish for a little time to reconsider it, and to try whether condensation here and there would enable us to get it say into four parts.[2] I am not sanguine of this, for I observed the difficulties as I read it the night before last; but I am very unwilling, I assure you, to decline what has so much merit.

I am going to Paris on Sunday morning for ten days or so. I purpose being back again within a fortnight. If you will let me think of this matter in the meanwhile, I shall at least have done all I can to satisfy my own appreciation of your work.

But if, in the meantime, you should desire to have it back with any prospect of publishing it through other means, a letter—the shortest in the world—from you to Mr. Wills at the Household Words office will immediately produce it. I repeat with perfect sincerity that I am much impressed by its merits, and that if I had read it as the production of an entire stranger,[3] I think it would have made exactly this effect upon me.—My dear Miss King,—Very faithfully yours.

1. Louisa King. Not identified.
2. 'Mother and Step-Mother', the story to which Dickens refers here, was revised according to his suggestions and published in *HW* in three parts on 12, 19, and 26 May 1855.
3. Earlier, King had contributed 'Why My Uncle Was a Bachelor' [story] to *HW* (11 Feb. 1854).

TAVISTOCK HOUSE
Saturday Morning, Thirtieth May, 1857

DEAR MADAM,[1]—I read your story, with all possible attention, last night. I cannot tell you with what reluctance I write to you respecting it, for my opinion of it is not favourable, although I perceive your heart in it, and great strength.

Pray understand that I claim no infallibility. I merely express my honest opinion, formed against my earnest desire. I do not lay it down as law for others, though, of course, I believe that many others would come to the same conclusion. It appears to me that the story is one that cannot possibly be told within the compass to which you have limited yourself. The three principal people are, every one of them, in the wrong with the reader, and you cannot put any of them right, without making the story extend over a longer space of time, and without anatomising the souls of the actors more slowly and carefully. Nothing would justify the departure of Alice, but her having some strong reason to believe that in taking that step, *she saved her lover*. In your intentions as to that lover's transfer of his affections to Eleanor, I descry a striking truth; but I think it confusedly wrought out, and all but certain to fail in expressing itself. Eleanor, I regard as forced and overstrained. The natural result is, that she carries a train of anti-climax after her. I particularly notice this at the point when she thinks she is going to be drowned.

The whole idea of the story is sufficiently difficult to require the most exact truth and the greatest knowledge and skill in the colouring throughout. In this respect I have no doubt of its being extremely defective. The people do not talk as such people would; and the little subtle touches of description which, by making the country house and the general scene real, would give an air of reality to the people (much to be desired) are altogether wanting. The more you set yourself to the illustration of your heroine's passionate nature, the more indispensable this attendant atmosphere of truth becomes. It would, in a manner, oblige the reader to believe in her. Whereas, for ever exploding like a great firework without any background, she glares and wheels and hisses, and goes out, and has lighted nothing.

Lastly, I fear she is too convulsive from beginning to end. Pray reconsider, from this point of view, her brow, and her eyes, and her drawing herself up to her full height, and her being a perfumed presence, and her floating into rooms, also her asking people how they dare, and the like, on small provocation. When she hears her music being played, I think she is particularly objectionable.

I have a strong belief that if you keep this story by you three or four years, you will form an opinion of it not greatly differing from mine. There is so much good in it, so much reflection, so much passion and earnestness, that, if my judgment be right, I feel sure you will come over to it. On the other hand, I do not think that its publication, as it stands, would do you service, or be agreeable to you hereafter.

I have no means of knowing whether you are patient in the pursuit of this art; but I am inclined to think that you are not, and that you do not discipline yourself enough. When one is impelled to write this or that, one has still to consider: "How much of this will tell for what I mean? How much of it is my own wild emotion and superfluous energy—how much remains that is truly belonging to this ideal character and these ideal circumstances?" It is in the laborious struggle to make this distinction, and in the determination to try for it, that the road to the correction of faults lies. (Perhaps I may remark, in support of the sincerity with which I write this, that I am an impatient and impulsive person myself, but that it has been for many years the constant effort of my life to practise at my desk what I preach to you.)

I should not have written so much, or so plainly, but for your last letter to me. It seems to demand that I should be strictly true with you, and I am so in this letter, without any reservation either way.—Very faithfully yours.

1. Emily Jolly, novelist. Dickens rejected this and two other stories Miss Jolly sent to *HW* (Lohrli, p. 329), but he did publish 'A Wife's Story' in 1855. (See pp 352–5.) Later, he accepted 'An Experience' for *AYR* with 'more than readiness'. 'I think so VERY highly of it,' he later told the author on 22 July 1869, 'that I will have special attention called to it in a separate advertisement.' (N, III, 731) The story appeared in *AYR* on 14 and 21 Aug. 1869.

OFFICE OF HOUSEHOLD WORDS
Monday, First June, 1857

MY DEAR STONE,[1]—I know that what I am going to say will not be agreeable; but I rely on the authoress's good sense; and say it, knowing it to be the truth.

These Notes are destroyed by too much smartness. It gives the appearance of perpetual effort, stabs to the heart the nature that is in them, and wearies by the manner and not by the matter. It is the commonest fault in the world (as I have constant occasion to observe here), but it is a very great one. Just as you couldn't bear to have an épergne or a candlestick on your table, supported by a light figure always on tiptoe and evidently in an impossible attitude for the sustainment of its weight, so all readers would be more or less oppressed and worried by this presentation of everything in one smart point of view, when they know it must have other, and weightier, and more solid properties. Airiness and good spirits are always delightful, and are inseparable from notes of a cheerful trip; but they should sympathise with many things as well as see them in a lively way. It is but a word or a touch that expresses this humanity, but without that little embellishment of good nature there is no such thing as humour. In this little MS. everything is too much patronised and condescended to, whereas the slightest touch of feeling for the rustic who is of the earth earthy, or of sisterhood with the homely servant who has made her face shine in her desire to please, would make a difference that the writer can scarcely imagine without trying it. The only relief in the twenty-one slips is the little bit about the chimes. It *is* a relief, simply because it is an indication of some kind of sentiment. You don't want any sentiment laboriously made out in such a thing. You don't want any maudlin show of it. But you do want a pervading suggestion that it is there. It makes all the difference between being playful and being cruel. Again I must say, above all things—especially to young people writing: For the love of God don't condescend! Don't assume the attitude of saying, "See how clever I am, and what fun everybody else is!" Take any shape but that.

I observe an excellent quality of observation throughout, and think the boy at the shop, and all about him, particularly good. I have no doubt whatever that the rest of the journal will be much better if the writer chooses to make it so. If she considers for a moment within herself, she will know that she derived pleasure from everything she saw, because she saw it with innumerable lights and shades upon it, and bound to humanity by innumerable fine links; she cannot possibly communicate anything of that pleasure to another by showing it from one little limited point only, and that point, observe, the one from which it is impossible to detach the exponent as the patroness of a whole universe of inferior souls. This is what everybody would mean in objecting to these notes (supposing them to be published), that they are too smart and too flippant.

As I understand this matter to be altogether between us three, and as I think your confidence, and hers, imposes a duty of friendship on me, I discharge it to the best of my ability. Perhaps I make more of it than you may have meant or expected; if so, it is because I am interested and wish to express it. If there had been anything in my objection not perfectly easy of removal, I might, after all, have hesitated to state it; but that is not the case. A very little indeed would make all this gaiety as sound and wholesome and good-natured in the reader's mind as it is in the writer's.—Affectionately always.

1. Frank Stone, see p. 84, n.4.

Tuesday, Twentieth February, 1866

MY DEAR MRS. BROOKFIELD,[1]—Having gone through your MS. (which I should have done sooner, but that I have not been very well), I write these few following words about it. Firstly, with a limited reference to its unsuitability to these pages. Secondly, with a more enlarged reference to the merits of the story itself.

If you will take a part of it and cut it up (in fancy) into the small portions into which it would have to be divided here for only a month's supply, you will (I think) at once discover the impossibility of publishing it in weekly parts. The scheme of the chapters, the manner of introducing the people, the progress of the interest, the places in which the principal places fall, are all hopelessly against it. It would seem as though the story were never coming, and hardly ever moving. There must be a special design to overcome that specially trying mode of publication, and I cannot better express the difficulty and labour of it than by asking you to turn over any two weekly numbers of A Tale of Two Cities, or Great Expectations, or Bulwer's story, or Wilkie Collins', or Reade's, or At the Bar,[2] and notice how patiently and expressly the thing has to be planned for presentation in these fragments, and yet for afterwards fusing together as an uninterrupted whole.

Of the story itself I honestly say that I think highly. The style is particularly easy and agreeable, infinitely above ordinary writing, and sometimes reminds me of Mrs. Inchbald[3] at her best. The characters are remarkably well observed, and with a rare mixture of delicacy and truthfulness. I observe this particularly in the brother and sister, and in Mrs. Neville. But it strikes me that you constantly hurry your narrative (and yet without getting on) *by telling it, in a sort of impetuous breathless way, in your own person, when the people should tell it and act it for themselves*. My notion always is, that when I have made the people to play out the play, it is, as it were, their business to do it, and not mine. Then, unless you really have led up to a great situation like Basil's death, you are bound in art to make more of it. Such a scene should form a chapter of itself. Impressed upon the reader's memory, it would go far to make the fortune of the book. Suppose yourself telling that affecting incident in a letter to a friend. Wouldn't you describe how you went through the life and stir of the streets and roads to the sick-room? Wouldn't you say what kind of room it was, what time of day it was, whether it was sunlight, starlight, or moonlight? Wouldn't you have a strong impression on your mind of how you were received, when you first met the look of the dying man, what strange contrasts were about you and struck you? I don't want you, in a novel, to present *yourself* to tell such things, but I want the things to be there. You make no more of the situation than the index might, or a descriptive playbill might in giving a summary of the tragedy under representation.

As a mere piece of mechanical workmanship, I think all your chapters should be shorter; that is to say, that they should be subdivided. Also, when you change from narrative to dialogue, or *vice versa*, you should make the transition more carefully. Also, taking the pains to sit down and recall the principal landmarks in your story, you should then make them far more elaborate and conspicuous than the rest. Even with these changes I do not believe that the story would attract the attention due to it, if it were published even in such monthly portions as the space of "Fraser"[4] would admit of. Even so brightened, it would not, to the best of my judgment, express itself piecemeal. It seems to me to be so constituted as to require to be read "off the reel." As a book in two volumes I think it would have good claims to success, and good chances of obtaining success. But I suppose the polishing I have hinted at (not a meretricious adornment, but positively necessary to good work and good art) to have been first thoroughly administered.

Now, don't hate me, if you can help it. I can afford to be hated by some people, but I am not rich enough to put you in possession of that luxury.—Ever faithfully yours.

1. Mrs Jane Octavia (Elton) Brookfield (1821–96), novelist. Dickens refers to the MS of *Only George: A Story*, which was published in 2 vols by Chapman and Hall in 1866. The story centres around young Amy Neville and her three suitors. Amy loves George Evelyn, a talented but poor physician, ignores Basil Maitland, an artist, and marries haughty Lord Chilworth because she is ill-advised by her parents. Chilworth subsequently dies; the book ends with the death of Maitland and Amy's happy remarriage to George Evelyn.
2. *TTC* was followed in *AYR* by W. Collins's, *The Woman in White* (26 Nov. 1859 to 25 Aug. 1860), *GE* (1 Dec. 1860 to 3 Aug. 1861), Bulwer Lytton's, *A Strange Story* (10 Aug. 1861 to 8 Mar. 1862), W. Collins's, *No Name* (15 Mar. 1862 to 17 Jan. 1863), Charles Reade's, *Very Hard Cash* (28 Mar. to 26 Dec. 1863), and C. A. Collins's, *At the Bar* (23 Sep. 1865 to 6 Jan. 1866).
3. Mrs Elizabeth Inchbald (1756–1821), actress, dramatist, and author of *A Simple Story* (1791) and *Nature and Art* (1796), two novels widely praised for their realism.
4. *Fraser's Magazine*, founded in 1830 by M. Maginn and H. Fraser.

Thursday Evening [Fifteenth] June 1854

MY DEAR MRS GASKELL,[1]—I have read the MS[2] you have had the kindness to send me, with all possible attention and care. I have shut myself up for the purpose, and allowed nothing to divide my thoughts. It opens an admirable story, is full of character and power, has a strong suspended interest in it (the end of which, I don't in the least foresee), and has the very best marks of your hand upon it. If I had had more to read, I certainly could not have stopped, but must have read on.

Now, addressing myself to the consideration of its being published in weekly portions, let me endeavour to shew you as distinctly as I can, the divisions into which it must fall.[3] According to the best of my judgment and experience, if it were divided in any other way—reference being always had to the weekly space available for the purpose in Household Words—it would be mortally injured.

I would end No. 1—With the announcement of Mr Lennox at the parsonage.

I would end No. 2—With Mr. Hale's announcement to Margaret, that Milton-Northern is the place they are going to. This No. therefore would contain Lennox's proposal, and the father's communication to his daughter of his leaving the church.

I would end No. 3—With their fixing on the watering-place as their temporary sojourn.

I would end No. 4—With Margaret's sitting down at night in their new house, to read Edith's letter. This No. therefore, would contain the account of Milton, and the new house, and the Mill Owner's first visit.

I would end No. 5—With the Mill-Owner's leaving the house after the tea-visit. This No. therefore would contain the introduction of his mother, and also of the working father and daughter—the Higgins family.

I would end No. 6—With Margaret leaving their dwelling, after the interview with Bessy when she is lying down.

These Nos. would sometimes require to be again divided into two chapters, and would sometimes want a word or two of conclusion. If you could be content to leave this to me, I could make those arrangements of the text without much difficulty. The only place where I do not see my way, and where the story—always with a special eye to this form of publication—seems to me to flag unmanageably, without an amount of excision that I dare scarcely hint at, is between Nos. 2 and

3, where the dialogue is long—is on a difficult and dangerous subject—and where, to bring the murder out at once, I think there is a necessity for fusing two Nos. into one.[4] This is the only difficult place in the whole 114 sides of foolscap.

As nearly as I can calculate, *about* 18 sides of your writing would make a weekly No. On *about* this calculation, the MS I have, would divide at the good points I have mentioned, and pretty equally. I do not apologize to you for laying so much stress on the necessity of its dividing well, because I am bound to put before you my perfect conviction that if it did not, the story would be wasted—would miss its effect as it went on—*and would not recover it when published complete*. The last consideration is strong with me, because it is based on my long comparison of the advantages and disadvantages of the periodical form of appearance.

I hope these remarks will not confuse you, but will come out tolerably clear after a second reading, and will convey to you the means of looking at your whole story from the weekly point of view. It cannot, I repeat, be disregarded with injury to the book. All the MS that I have—with the exception I have mentioned and allowing a very reasonable margin indeed for a little compression here and there—might have been expressly written to meet the exigencies of the case.

Saturday Seventeenth June

That my calculations might be accurate, I thought it well to stop my note and send eighteen of your sides to the Printer's (I took them out at random) to be calculated. Their estimate exactly accords with mine. I have therefore no doubt of its correctness.[5]

Is there anything else that I can tell you, or anything else you want to ask me? Pray do not entertain the idea that you can give me any trouble I shall not be delighted to encounter.

My address is,

Villa du Camp de droite
Boulogne-sur-Mer.[6]

—where I shall be anxious to hear from you that you comprehend this long dull story of mine.[7] That you may the more easily do so, I will make it no longer.

Have you thought of a name? I cannot suggest one without knowing more of the story. Then perhaps I might hit upon a good title if you did not.—Ever My Dear Mrs Gaskell—Faithfully Yours.

P.S.—I have never thanked you for Mr Gaskell's lectures,[8] which I have read with uncommon pleasure. They are so sagacious and unaffected and tell so much that is interesting.

VILLA DU CAMP DE DROITE, BOULOGNE
Wednesday Twenty-Sixth July, 1854

MY DEAR MRS GASKELL,—Having finished my story and got to London a week earlier than I had expected,[9] I brought back the continuation of your MS to read here. Confining myself as in my last note, strictly to the business of the subject (that I may be the better understood). I proceed, first, to say how I would divide it.

I would make five weekly parts of it. The first to close with the end of the strike conversation held by Margaret and her father with Mr Thornton. The second to close with the receipt of the dinner Invitation. The third to close with Margaret's leaving Higgins's house after Boucher has charged his miseries upon Higgins and the Union. The fourth to close with her being admitted into the Mill on the day of the Riot, and the porter's shutting the gate. The fifth to close with the end of the Thornton declaration scene, and the end of the MS I have.

This fifth part would be a long one, but the interest and action are strong, and it would not be too long. It appears to me that the conversation in the first part is unnecessarily lengthy, and I think that portion—not only as a portion, but as a part of the book—could be very materially improved if you would not object to make some curtailment in the printed proof.

North and South appears to me to be a better name than Margaret Hale.[10] It implies more, and is expressive of the opposite people brought face to face by the story.

I should be happy to begin the publication at once, having so much MS in hand. I should advertise the tale as to be completed in about 20 weekly portions, and as being by the author of Mary Barton. These particulars, and its name, would be all that the announcement need state. By the expression "at once," I mean on Saturday the Second of September, nominally: but really on the preceding Wednesday—the No being always actually published on Wednesday, though dated Saturday.

I do not understand whether you permit me to divide the story with chapters. But I believe you are aware that it will at least be necessary to begin every weekly portion as a new chapter.

May I ask you to be so good as to reply to me, as soon as you can, whether you are content to have the story announced as I have proposed. It is very important that early advantage should be taken of all the usual channels of literary advertisement.[11] There is no time to spare.—My Dear Mrs Gaskell.—Faithfully Yours always.

VILLA DU CAMP DE DROITE, BOULOGNE
Sunday Twentieth August 1854

MY DEAR MRS GASKELL,—I have just received from Wills, in proof, our No for the 9th of September containing the Second Part of North and South, as it originally stood, and *unaltered by you*.[12]

This is the place where we agreed that there should be a great condensation, and a considerable compression, where Mr Hale states his doubts to Margaret. The mechanical necessities of Household Words oblige us to get to press with this No *immediately*. In case you should not already have altered the proof and sent it to Wills (which very possibly you have: and in that case forgive my troubling you) will you be so kind as to do so at once. What I would recommend—and did recommend—is, to make the scene between Margaret and her father relative to his leaving the church and their destination being Milton-Northern, as short as you can find it in your heart to make it.

I have made a break at Lennox's going away, and begin a new chapter (*not* a new weekly part, you understand) with "He was gone." I've not a notion what he means. [. . .]—Always Very faithfully Yours.

1. Elizabeth Cleghorn Gaskell (1810–65), novelist.
2. *North and South*, which appeared serially in *HW* running from 2 Sep. 1854 to 27 Jan. 1855. After reading *Mary Barton* (1848), a novel that 'most profoundly affected and impressed' him, as he told her on 31 Jan. 1850, Dickens urged Mrs Gaskell to submit something to *HW* for publication. In response, she sent him 'Lizzie Leigh', whose publication in three parts (30 Mar., 6 and 13 Apr.) marked the beginning of her numerous fictional contributions to the journal.
3. After Mrs Gaskell accepted Dickens's offer to publish *North and South* as a weekly serial, he wrote to assure her not to worry about dividing the manuscript into instalments. Write it your own way, he advised. 'When we come to get a little of it into type, I have no doubt of being able to make such little suggestions as to breaks of chapters as will carry us over all that easily.' (N, II, 542) This letter, therefore, represents Dickens's first attempt to adapt Mrs Gaskell's manuscript to the form in which it was first to appear.
4. The divisions Dickens proposed correspond with the weekly numbers as they appeared in *HW*, but the absence of the manuscript of *North and South* makes impossible any full study of the extent to which Mrs Gaskell acted on his suggestions.
5. To Dickens's discomfort, he subsequently learned that the printer had

carelessly estimated his formula for converting Mrs Gaskell's handwritten pages to their equivalent in print. When he received proofs for the first number, the quantity of the text alarmed him because it exceeded his previous calculations. 'It is not objectionable for a beginning,' he wrote to Wills on 19 Aug. 1854, 'but would become so in the progress of a not compactly written and artfully devised story.' (N, II, 580) Later, Dickens complained to Wills, 'If I had known how it was to turn out, . . . I could not, in my senses, have accepted the story.' (N, II, 583) But having done so, Dickens faced a dilemma: either he had to devote a greater portion of *HW* to the story than he had done in the case of *HT* and so risk ruining the journal (N, II, 581), or cut Mrs Gaskell's proofs in order to accommodate the serial divisions he had originally approved.

6. The family residence from late June to mid Oct.
7. *HT*, Dickens's own industrial novel.
8. *Two Lectures on the Lancashire Dialect*, 1854, by William Gaskell, Mrs Gaskell's husband.
9. Dickens had just returned to London, bringing the manuscript of the final section of *HT*.
10. *North and South* was Dickens's suggestion for the title, one which Mrs Gaskell accepted, although she preferred 'Death and Variations'. 'There are 5 deaths, each beautifully suited to the character of the individual.' See Letter 220 in *The Letters of Mrs. Gaskell*, ed J. A. V. Chapple and Arthur Pollard (Manchester: Manchester Univ. Press, 1966), p. 324.
11. The first notice for *North and South* appeared in *HW* on 19 Aug. 1854.
12. Mrs Gaskell's slowness in returning proofs and her reluctance to cut her work in order to fit the requirements of weekly publication in *HW* caused Dickens much anxiety. Shortly after *North and South* began, Wills reported a drop in sales. Unsurprised, Dickens laid the blame on Mrs Gaskell's story, 'which so divided, is wearisome in the last degree', he replied (N, II, 598). There was, however, little Dickens could do; and when Mr Gaskell intervened with the suggestion that increasing the quantity of the instalments would help his wife's difficulties with the serialization, he concurred and told Wills on 29 Oct. to signal his assent. See A. B. Hopkins, *Elizabeth Gaskell: Her Life and Work* (1952), p. 148. As a result, the proportion of the novel to the rest of *HW* steadily increased. In Sep. *North and South* averaged 12 columns; by Dec., the average had risen to 16. *HT* never exceeded 11, except for the average of 16 in the last two numbers.

For Mrs Gaskell's allusions to her difficulties with the weekly serial numbers for *HW*, see her Preface to the first edition of *North and South* in 2 vols (1855). To remedy the obvious defect with which she was forced 'to hurry on events with an improbable rapidity towards the close', she explained, she expanded chs 44, 45, and 46 in *HW* (*North and South*, vol. II, chs 19, 22, and 26), and added 2 new chs (*North and South*, II, 20 and 21).

Literature and Life

48 DOUGHTY ST. MECKLENBURGH SQUARE
Saturday June 3rd 1837

MY DEAR SIR,[1]—Beard, our mutual friend,[2] was to have been the medium of an introduction between us, but as he has not seen you for some time, I venture to introduce myself as "Boz," and when I tell you why I have not had patience to wait for his intervention, I dare say you will feel highly gratified.

In my next number of Oliver Twist,[3] I must have a magistrate; and casting about for a magistrate whose harshness and insolence would render him a fit subject to be "shewn up" I have, as a necessary consequence, stumbled upon Mr. Laing[4] of Hatton Garden celebrity. I know the man's character perfectly well, but as it would be necessary to describe his appearance also, I ought to have seen him, which (fortunately or unfortunately as the case may be) I have never done.

In this dilemma it occurred to me that perhaps I might under your auspices be smuggled into the Hatton Garden Office for a few moments some morning. If you can further my object, I shall be really very greatly obliged to you.

I am staying at Hampstead at present, but if you will direct a line to my house in town, stating when I shall call on you, or you on me, I will be punctual. Whether you can render me the assistance I require, or not, I shall be happy to avail myself of that opportunity of becoming known to you.—Believe me—My Dear Sir—Faithfully yours.

1. Thomas Haines, reporter at the City Police Court, which was held in the basement of Mansion House, the residence of the Lord Mayor of London.
2. One of Dickens's rare solecisms, although such collocations, as the *OED* notes, are frequent. H. W. Fowler speculates that Dickens's later title, *Our Mutual Friend*, no doubt had 'much to do with the currency of *mutual friend*'. Its frequent usage, Fowler concludes, perhaps qualifies the phrase for admission to 'the STURDY INDEFENSIBLES'.
3. Number 5, which appeared in the July 1837 issue of *Bentley's Miscellany*, comprising chs 9–11.
4. Allan Stewart Laing (1788–1862), the notoriously severe police magistrate of Hatton Garden, provided a model for Mr Fang. See *OT*, ch. 11.

48 DOUGHTY STREET
Monday Evening [1837]

My dear Ross,[1]—Many thanks for your statistical Magazine,[2] which contains tables contemning[3] juvenile delinquency that I was particularly anxious to see in a well digested form. Reciprocating all your kind wishes most cordially.—Most Sincerely yours.

1. Charles Ross (1800–84), Parliamentary reporter.
2. The tables appeared in the *Statistical Journal and Record of Useful Knowledge*, 1 (Oct. 1837). 'Statistics of Crime' gave the number of juvenile delinquents in age groups for 1834–6. Dickens might have read this as background material for *OT*.
3. Concerning (P, I, 315).

DOUGHTY STREET, LONDON
Twelfth December, 1838

RESPECTED SIR,[1]—I have given Squeers one cut on the neck and two on the head, at which he appeared much surprised and began to cry, which, being a cowardly thing, is just what I should have expected from him—wouldn't you?

I have carefully done what you told me in your letter about the lamb and the two "sheeps" for the little boys. They have also had some good ale and porter, and some wine. I am sorry you didn't say *what* wine you would like them to have. I gave them some sherry, which they liked very much, except one boy, who was a little sick and choked a good deal. He was rather greedy, and that's the truth, and I believe it went the wrong way, which I say served him right, and I hope you will say so too.

Nicholas had his roast lamb, as you said he was to, but he could not eat it all, and says if you do not mind his doing so he should like to have the rest hashed to-morrow with some greens, which he is very fond of, and so am I. He said he did not like to have his porter hot, for he thought it spoilt the flavour, so I let him have it cold. You should have seen him drink it. I thought he never would have left off. I also gave him three pounds of money, all in sixpences, to make it seem more, and he said directly that he should give more than half to his mamma and sister, and divide the rest with poor Smike. And I say he is a good fellow for saying so; and if anybody says he isn't I am ready to fight him whenever they like—there!

Fanny Squeers shall be attended to, depend upon it. Your drawing of her is very like, except that I don't think the hair is quite curly enough. The nose is particularly like hers, and so are the legs. She is a nasty disagreeable thing, and I know it will make her very cross when she sees it; and what I say is that I hope it may. You will say the same I know—at least I think you will.

I meant to have written you a long letter, but I cannot write very fast when I like the person I am writing to, because that makes me think about them [*sic*], and I like you, and so I tell you. Besides, it is just eight o'clock at night, and I always go to bed at eight o'clock, except when it is my birthday, and then I sit up to supper. So I will not say anything more besides this—and that is my love to you and Neptune; and if you will drink my health every Christmas Day I will drink yours—come.—I am,—Respected Sir,—Your affectionate Friend.

P.S.—I don't write my name very plain, but you know what it is you know, so never mind.

1. William Hastings Hughes (1833–1907), younger brother of Thomas Hughes, author of *Tom Brown's Schooldays*. After his father told him the story of *NN* and showed young Hughes the illustrations, the boy expressed his disgust that Nicholas and his friends received no proper rewards and Squeers and his family no punishment. Hoping to persuade Dickens to alter the ending, Hughes dictated a letter to the novelist, to which the above is Dickens's fanciful reply.

DOUGHTY STREET
December 29th, 1838

MY DEAR MRS. HALL,[1]—I am exceedingly obliged to you for your kind note, and the interesting anecdote which you tell so well. I have laid it by in the MS of the first number of Nickleby, and shall keep it there in confirmation of the truth of my little picture.

Depend upon it that the rascalities of those Yorkshire schoolmasters *cannot* easily be exaggerated, and that I have kept down the strong truth and thrown as much comicality over it as I could, rather than disgust the reader with its fouler aspects. The identical scoundrel you speak of I saw—curiously enough. His name is Shaw,[2] the action was tried (I believe) eight or ten years since, and if I am not much mistaken another action was brought against him by the parents of a miserable child, a cancer in whose head he opened with an inky penknife, and so caused his death. The country for miles round was covered, when I was there, with deep snow. There is an old church near the school, and the first grave-stone I stumbled on that dreary winter afternoon was placed above the grave of a boy, eighteen long years old, who had died—suddenly, the inscription said;[3] I suppose his heart broke—the camel falls down "suddenly" when they heap the last load upon his back—died at that wretched place. I think his ghost put Smike into my head upon the spot.

I went down in an assumed name,[4] taking a plausible letter to an old Yorkshire attorney from another attorney in town, telling him how a friend had been left a widow and wanted to place her boys at a Yorkshire school, in hopes of thawing the frozen compassion of her relations. The man of business gave me an introduction to one or two schools, but at night he came down to the Inn where I was stopping, and after much hesitation and confusion—he was a large-headed, flat-nosed, red-faced, old fellow—said with a degree of feeling one would not have given him credit for, that the matter had been upon his mind all day—that they were sad places for mothers to send their orphan boys to—that he hoped I would not give up him as my adviser—but that she had better do anything with them—let them hold horses, run errands—fling them in any way upon the mercy of the World—rather than trust them there. This was an attorney, a well-fed man of business, and a rough Yorkshireman.

Mrs. Dickens and myself will be delighted to see the friend you speak of—we write in regards to yourself and Mr. Hall and I throw myself single-handed upon your good nature, and beseech you to forgive me this long story—which you ought to do, as you have been the means of drawing it from me.—Believe me, Dear Mrs. Hall,—Very faithfully yours.

1. Anna Maria Hall (1800–81), writer, and wife of S. C. Hall (1800–89), writer and journalist.
2. William Shaw (?1783–1850), owner of Bowes Academy, Yorkshire, since 1822, whom Dickens and Browne saw on 2 Feb. 1838 (Diary entry, P, I, 622). The description of Shaw in this letter draws on two unrelated incidents. The first refers to a case in 1823 when two parents recovered damages against Shaw for negligently causing blindness in their sons; the second Dickens heard as a boy from a Chatham friend who attended a school in Yorkshire called Bowes Hall. For a summary of the proceedings against Shaw, see *The Dickensian*, 11 (Oct. 1915), 260–3; for further details about the 'inky penknife', see the Preface to *NN*, First Cheap Ed., 1848. Years later, the boy who told Dickens the story owned that he himself, not his master, had used a penknife to cut a pimple off his own nose (P, I, 482 n.2).
3. Reference to the inscription on the gravestone in Bowes Churchyard of George Ashton Taylor, 'who died suddenly', at Shaw's Academy, and to a list of boys interred in unrecorded graves in the Churchyard, may be found in *The Dickensian*, 7 (Jan. 1911), 11, and *The Dickensian*, 35 (Mar. 1939), 107–8. For an account of life at a Yorkshire school written before *NN*, see

The Dickensian, 13 (Sep. 1917), 260–3; reference to the attorney whom Dickens visited in nearby Barnard Castle may be found in *The Dickensian*, 11 (Nov. 1915), 296–9.

4. See the 1848 Preface to *NN* for details of this 'pious fraud'.

July [1840][1]

[John Forster] . . . I intended calling on you this morning on my way back from Bevis-marks,[2] whither I went to look at a house for Sampson Brass. But I got mingled up in a kind of social paste with the Jews of Houndsditch, and roamed about among them till I came out in Moorfields, quite unexpectedly. So I got into a cab, and came home again, very tired, by way of the City Road. . . .

1. Written in the summer of 1840 (Forster, II, vii, 119), soon before Dickens began ch. 33 of *OCS* (no. 24, 12 Sep. 1840), which opens with a description of Sampson Brass's house.
2. Bevis Marks, a corruption of Burie's Markes, i.e. the boundary of land which belonged formerly to the abbots of Bury, Suffolk and extended from Duke Street, Aldgate, to St. Mary Axe. Nearby was the Spanish and Portuguese Jews' Synagogue; many Jewish merchants lived in the area. Dickens never explicitly identifies Brass as a Jew but the effect of this and other textual details seems to make Brass appear Jewish.

LAUSANNE
18th July 1846

[John Forster] . . . I think the general idea of Dombey is interesting and new, and has great material in it. But I don't like to discuss it with you till you have read number one, for fear I should spoil its effect. When done—about Wednesday or Thursday, please God—I will send it in two days' posts, seven letters each day. If you have it set up at once (I am afraid you couldn't read it, otherwise than in print) I know you will impress on B. & E.[1] the necessity of the closest secrecy. The very name getting out, would be ruinous. The points for illustration, and the enormous care required, make me excessively anxious. The man for Dombey, if Browne could see him, the class man to a T, is Sir A——E——, of D——s.[2] Great pains will be necessary with Miss Tox. The Toodle Family should not be too much caricatured, because of Polly. I should like Browne to think of Susan Nipper, who will not be wanted in the first number. After the second number, they will all be nine or ten years older; but this will not involve much change in the characters, except in the children and Miss Nipper. What a brilliant thing to be telling you all these names so familiarly, when you know nothing about 'em! I quite enjoy it. By the bye, I hope you may like the introduction of Solomon Gills. I think he lives in a good sort of house. [. . .]

1. Bradbury and Evans, Dickens's publishers.
2. Unidentified. Browne was unable to get a glimpse of the living person Dickens had in mind; Forster, therefore, sent Dickens a sheetful of heads drawn by the illustrator – actual and fanciful – from which he chose (Forster, VI, ii, 23–4). Only two characters in *DS*, Forster adds, had living originals: Mrs Pipchin, whose real prototype was Mrs Roylance, and Miss Blimber, who was based upon Louisa King, the daughter of the schoolmaster J. C. King, whose small school in St. John's Wood, London, Charley and Walter Dickens attended. See K. Tillotson, 'Louisa King and Cornelia Blimber', *The Dickensian*, 74 (May 1978), 91–5. As for Mr Dombey, his resemblance to 'the aimiable and excellent city-merchant', writes Forster, was no more than one of physical likeness (Forster, VI, ii, 35).

DEVONSHIRE TERRACE
Twenty-First December 1849

SIR,[1]—I received your letter late last night.[2]

Now that I learn from you that Mrs. Hill[3] and her friends consider that the alteration I offered (in my letter to her) to make in the character in question will tend to repair the uneasiness I have unintentionally caused her, I have not the least hesitation in pledging myself to make it.

But I must beg you to understand that it can only be made in the natural progress and current of the story. Even if the next number were not already in the Press, it would be impossible to be made there, because the character is not introduced, and the course of the tale is not at all in that direction.[4]—I am Sir—Your obedient Servant.

28th December 1849

[John Forster] . . . I have had the queerest adventure this morning, the receipt of the enclosed from Miss Mowcher! It is serio-comic, but there is no doubt one is wrong in being tempted to such a use of power.[5] . . .

1. Robert Rogers, solicitor.
2. Rogers had written to Dickens on behalf of his client Mrs Hill to support her earlier letter to Dickens (18 Dec.) complaining that he drew too freely on her personal deformities and occupation when he introduced Miss Mowcher in the Dec. number of *DC* (ch. 22). Rogers told Dickens that he was content with the novelist's pledge to remedy the discomfort he unwittingly caused Mrs Hill, but expressed his hope that he would receive further assurance from Dickens that reparation would be forthcoming in the next monthly number.
3. Mrs Jane Seymour Hill, a dwarf who worked as a professional chiropodist

and manicurist. For Dickens's apology to his near-neighbour, see P, IV, 674–5.

4. Dickens was unable to redeem his promise until the Mar. number, where in ch. 32 he reverses the insinuation in ch. 22 that Miss Mowcher would assist Steerforth in the seduction of Little Em'ly. In ch. 61, Miss Mowcher helps arrest Littimer and so further reinforces her honorable conduct, leaving 'nothing but an agreeable impression' (Forster, VI, vii, 99).

5. Dickens, despite his penitence, could not resist the temptation to caricature Leigh Hunt in his next novel. See the following letters to John Forster & Leigh Hunt, and notes.

TAVISTOCK HOUSE
7th March 1852

[John Forster . . .] . . . I am sorry to say that after all kinds of evasions, I am obliged to dine at Lansdowne House[1] to-morrow. But maybe the affair will come off to-night and give me an excuse! I enclose proofs of No. 2.[2] Browne has done Skimpole, and helped to make him singularly unlike the great original. Look it over, and say what occurs to you. . . . Don't you think Mrs. Gaskell charming?[3] With one ill-considered thing that looks like a want of natural perception, I think it masterly. . . .

17th March 1852

. . . You will see from the enclosed that Procter[4] is much of my mind. I will nevertheless go through the character again in the course of the afternoon, and soften down words here and there. . . .

18th March 1852

. . . I have again gone over every part of it very carefully, and I think I have made it much less like. I have also changed Leonard to Harold. I have no right to give Hunt pain, and I am so bent upon not doing it that I wish you would look at all the proof once more, and indicate any particular place in which you feel it particularly like. Whereupon I will alter that place. . . .

GAD'S HILL PLACE, HIGHAM BY ROCHESTER, KENT
Thursday Twenty-Third June 1859

MY DEAR LEIGH HUNT,—Believe me, I have not forgotten that matter; nor will I forget it. To alter the book itself, or to make any reference in the preface of the book itself, would be to revive a forgotten absurdity, and to establish the very association that is to be denied and discarded.[5]

In the matter of the smitten cheek, I hold you to be thoroughly right in principle. But be sure that you do not give importance to what is worthless and insignificant, or drag any obscure person or thing into your own light. That is always the risk when a man of your mark honours Grub Street with a look.—Affectionately yours.

1. Lansdowne House, Berkeley Square, London, home of the third Marquess of Lansdowne (1780–1863).
2. Ch. 6 of *BH* (no. 2, Apr. 1852), introduces Harold Skimpole, whom Dickens based on James Henry Leigh Hunt (1784–1859), poet and essayist. Hunt, a friend and admirer of Dickens, was deeply pained by the similarities between himself and the irresponsible parasite Skimpole. Dickens tried to exonerate himself in conversation with Hunt, by altering Leonard in the MS of *BH* to Harold, and by the revisions he refers to on 17 and 18 Mar. 1852. For the *BH* revisions, see the Textual Notes to chs 6 and 43 in *BH*, ed. Ford and Monod. He also tried to make amends by publishing an appreciative article in *HW* on Hunt's *Stories in Verse* ('By Rail to Parnasus', by H. Morley, 16 June 1855), and by apologizing in public after Hunt's death. See 'Leigh Hunt: A Remonstrance', *AYR*, 24 Dec. 1859.

   Dickens's delight in his accomplishment seems to undercut his professed concern for Hunt's feelings. On 25 Sep. 1853, he wrote to Mrs R. W. Watson: 'I suppose [Hunt] is the most exact portrait that was ever painted in words! I have very seldom, if ever, done such a thing. But the likeness is astonishing. I don't think it could possibly be more like himself. It is so awfully true that I make a bargain with myself 'never to do so any more.' There is not an atom of exaggeration or suppression. It is an absolute reproduction of a real man. Of course I have been careful to keep the outward figure away from the fact; but in all else it is the life itself.' See D. Welch, 'Dickens in Switzerland: Some Unpublished Letters and Reflections', *Harper's Monthly Magazine*, 112 (Apr. 1906), 718–9. For Forster's comments on Dickens's use of original figures, see Forster vi, vii, 98–109.
3. Dickens thought highly of Mrs Gaskell's eight 'Cranford' stories, which began in *HW* on 13 Dec. 1851 and ran until 21 May 1853.
4. Bryan Waller Procter (1784–1874), poet.
5. A response to Hunt's suggestion that Dickens make some conciliatory remarks denying the connection between Hunt and Skimpole in the forthcoming Library Edition of Dickens's works. *BH* appeared in 2 vols in June and July 1859.

TAVISTOCK HOUSE
Seventh February 1853

My dear Elliotson,[1]—I am very truly obliged to you for the loan of your remarkable and learned Lecture on Spontaneous Combustion; and I am not a little pleased to find myself fortified by such high authority.[2] Before writing that chapter of Bleak House, I had looked up all the more famous cases you quote (as I dare say you divined in reading the description); but three or four of those you incidentally mention—two of them in 1820–are new to me—and your explanation is so beautifully clear, that I could particularly desire to repeat it several times before I come to the last No. and the Preface.

May I keep it carefully by me until the summer? I can warrant myself most reliable in all matters connected with the preservation of papers, and should have it here under my hand at any time. Or shall I return it to you, first copying it?—which I do not like to do without your permission.

It is inconceivable to me how people can reject such evidence,[3] supported by so much familiar knowledge, and such reasonable analogy. But I suppose the long and short of it is, that they don't know, and don't want to know, anything about the matter.—Ever faithfully yours.

1. John Elliotson (1791–1868), MD, phrenologist, mesmerist, professor of the practice of medicine at University College, London, 1832–8, and friend of Dickens. Elliotson resigned from his professorship in 1838 because his colleagues disapproved of his belief in mesmerism; in 1849 Elliotson founded a mesmeric hospital.
2. According to G. S. Haight, the pamphlet Elliotson lent Dickens was never published. See 'Dickens and Lewes on Spontaneous Combustion', *Nineteenth-Century Fiction*, 10 (June 1955), 57. Dickens, however, drew on it during his debate with Lewes following the publication of ch. 32 of *BH*, 'The Appointed Time' in No. 10 (Dec. 1852), in which Dickens describes Krook's sudden fiery demise. Responding to the Dec. number, G. H. Lewes publically upbraided Dickens for 'overstepping the limits of Fiction, and giving currency to a vulgar error' which contradicted scientific truth and ran counter to 'all known laws of combustion'. See *The Leader*, 11 Dec. 1852, p. 1189. Dickens responded to Lewes's attack by mocking the proceedings of the 'men of science and philosophy' in *BH*, ch. 33 (No. 11, Jan. 1853), to which Lewes replied briefly in *The Leader* on 15 Jan. 1853. First, he denied the authority of those whom Dickens cited to support the validity of the phenomenon (p. 64); next, he published two letters to Dickens in the same journal (5 Feb., pp 137–8; 12 Feb., pp 161–3), with the object of showing that 'the highest scientific authorities of the day distinctly disavow the notion of spontaneous combustion'. Moreover, Lewes argued, the theories supporting it were absurd, and its occurrence was 'an impossibility' (5 Feb. 1853).
   Two days after Lewes's first letter, Dickens thanked Elliotson for the loan of his 'remarkable and learned Lecture'; later that month, he took issue with Lewes's charge that he had ignored his duty to readers and told Lewes in private: 'I looked into a number of books, with great care, expressly to learn what the truth was. I examined the subject as a Judge might have done and without laying down any law upon the case.' For the text of this previously unpublished letter, see Haight, pp 58–60. Lewes published part of Dickens's reply to him in *The Leader* of 26 Mar. 1853, p. 303, and then dropped the issue. Earlier, he had called on Dickens in *The*

Leader of 12 Feb. 1853 to at least provide a qualifying statement in the Preface to *BH* to the effect that even if he (Dickens) believed in spontaneous combustion 'the highest scientific authorities of the day' rejected it (p. 163). Dickens refused to make any such retraction in the 1853 Preface, asserting instead that he did not 'wilfully or negligently' mislead his readers. The public controversy between Dickens and Lewes ended on 5 Sep. 1853, when Lewes criticized his failure to treat the matter 'with the fullness and impartiality demanded by the case' and called upon him again to qualify his position (*The Leader*, p. 306).

3. Belief in the alleged occurrence of spontaneous combustion among persons addicted to the excessive use of alcohol was widespread in the late eighteenth century and throughout much of the nineteenth. See Selected Bibliography, p. 364.

BOULOGNE

Eighteenth September 1853

SIR,[1]—I observe two statements from a country paper, copied into your columns of Saturday last,[2] and therefore made important. They represent me as having availed myself of the experiences of that excellent police-officer, Mr. Inspector Field, in Bleak House, and also as having undertaken to write the said excellent officer's biography.

Allow me to assure you that amidst all the news in the Times, I found nothing more entirely and completely new to me than these two pieces of intelligence.— Your faithful Servant.

1. The Editor of *The Times*.
2. ' "A Detective in his Vocation" (from the *Bath Chronicle*),' in *The Times*, 17 Sep. 1853, p. 11, col. f. The article describes how Inspector Charles Frederick Field of the London Metropolitan Police tracked down a fictitious baronet, whose real name was Tom Provis. The report ends with the allegations Dickens denies in his letter about making use of Field's experiences for Inspector Bucket of *BH* and undertaking to write a life of Field.

Dickens's reply is disingenuous. While he never planned to write Field's biography, certain features of Inspector Bucket in *BH* are derived from his observations of Field in action. Dickens first wrote about the police for *HW*, where he introduced Field as Inspector 'Wield'. See 'A Detective Police Party', part i, 27 July 1850; part ii, 10 Aug. 1850. Subsequently Dickens wrote 'On Duty with Inspector Field', *HW*, 14 June 1851, and 'Down with the Tide', *HW*, 5 Feb. 1853. (See also *RP*, 1858).

Possibly Dickens recalled the name 'Provis' when he needed an alias for Magwitch; similarly, the account in *The Times* of criminal activities involving false identities, stealing, an old lady burdened with family troubles, and a ruined wife may have suggested aspects of Compeyson's history in *GE*.

BOSTON
4th April 1868
[Miss Palfrey][1] . . . Convey yourself back to London by the agency of that powerful Locomotive, your imagination, and walk through the centre avenue of Covent Garden Market from West to East:—that is to say, with your back towards the church, and your face towards Drury Lane Theatre. Keep straight on along the side of the Theatre, and about halfway down, on the left side of the way, behind the houses, is a closely hemmed-in grave yard—happily long disused and closed by the Law. I do not remember that the grave-yard is accessible from the street now, but when I was a boy it was to be got at by a low covered passage under a house, and was guarded by a rusty iron gate. In that churchyard I long afterwards buried the "Nemo" of Bleak House.[2]

This important piece of information is in redemption of a pledge I gave you in Halifax Harbour walking the deck of the Cuba one bright cold morning in last November. . . .

1. Miss Palfrey, an unidentified passenger on the Cuba, in which Dickens sailed to America in Nov. 1867.
2. The existence of two burial grounds in the Drury Lane district complicates the problem of determining which location Dickens had in mind when he described the obscene burial ground in *BH* (chs 11, 16, and 49). His instructions in the letter to Miss Palfrey, as W. L. Gadd notes, seem to indicate the cemetery of St. Martin-in-the-Fields, near the corner of Drury Lane and Russell Street. See 'The Topography of *Bleak House*: Some Uncertainties Examined', *The Dickensian*, 26 (Summer 1930), 210–2. But while the location of the former burial ground fits with Dickens's instructions, the appearance of the cemetery – open to Drury Lane and not hemmed in – contradicts the text. A more likely site for Nemo's interment appears to be the burial ground of St. Mary-le-Strand, which lay behind Russell Court, Covent Garden. It was small, hemmed-in, closely surrounded on all sides by squalid buildings, and only accessible by a low passage under a house and guarded by a gate at the foot of four or five steps. For an alternative hypothesis, see W[alter] [Dexter], who suggests in 'Poor Jo's Churchyard Identified', *The Dickensian*, 25 (Spring 1929), 143, that the burial ground on the corner of Drury Lane and Russell Street had a *second* entrance in Crown Court, which 'was probably the . . . passage that Dickens had in mind when describing Esther Summerson's discovery of her mother'.

Contemporary reports show that Dickens's description of 'a hemmed-in churchyard, pestiferous and obscene' does not exaggerate the horror of many London graveyards. At 'the loathsome and noxious graveyard' in Portugal Street, close to Forster's house in Lincoln's Inn Fields, observed one witness, 'the churchwardens caused a hole, thirty feet in depth, to be dug in one portion of the ground, and the skulls and human remains thrown up were occasionally so fresh that the medical students were in the habit of purchasing them – the price of 7s. 6d. having been lately offered for a head, the eyes and teeth of which were perfect'. (Quoted in *The Examiner*, 'Public Health and Nuisances', 1 Sep. 1849, p. 546).

The Board of Health closed the burial ground in Portugal Street soon afterwards, but many similar abuses came to public notice. Another witness at an inquest spoke of 3000 bodies being buried recently at Spafields graveyard, where pits were dug in the old ground to receive cholera victims. 'How space was made for newcomers,' he could not say, 'unless by the destruction of the bodies and coffins.' Commenting on this and other statements, the writer in *The Examiner* added: '[T]here is really no burial, as the body deposited in the earth one day is soon disturbed, dismembered, and thrown to the surface again to make room for other corpses . . . Is that burial? The proper name would be the putrid ground or the putrid yard of every parish.' See 'Intramural Interment,' *The Examiner*, 8 Sep. 1849, pp 561–2.

TAVISTOCK HOUSE
Monday Twentieth February 1854

MY DEAR MARK,[1]—Will you note down and send me any slang terms among the tumblers and circus-people, that you can call to mind? I have noted down some—I want them in my new story[2]—but it is very probable that you will recall several which I have not got.—Ever affectionately.

1. Mark Lemon (1809–70), playwright, journalist and co-founder of *Punch*, 1841.
2. *HT*.

TAVISTOCK HOUSE
Saturday Eleventh March 1854

MY DEAR CUNNINGHAM,[1]—Being down at Dover yesterday, I happened to see the Illustrated London News lying on the table, and there read a reference to my new book which I believe I am not mistaken in supposing to have been written by you.[2]

I don't know where you may have found your information, but I can assure you that it is altogether wrong. The title was many weeks old, and chapters of the story were written, before I went to Preston or thought about the present strike.

The mischief of such a statement is twofold.[3] First, it encourages the public to believe in the impossibility that books are produced in that very sudden and cavalier manner (as poor Newton used to feign that he produced the elaborate drawings he made in his madness,[4] by winking at his table); and secondly in this instance it has this bearing: it localizes (so far as your readers are concerned) a story which has a direct purpose in reference to the working people all over England, and it will cause, as I know by former experience, characters to be fitted on to individuals whom I never saw or heard of in my life.

I do not suppose that you can do anything to set this mis-statement right, being made; nor do I wish you to set it right. But if you will, at any future time, ask me what the fact is before you state it, I will tell you, as frankly and readily as it is possible for one friend to tell another, what the truth is and what it is not.—Always faithfully yours.

1. Peter Cunningham (1816–69), author and scholar.
2. Writing in 'Town and Table-Talk on Literature, Art', *The Illustrated London News*, 4 Mar. 1854, p. 194, Cunningham gave the title of Dickens's new novel as *Hard Times* and commented: 'His recent inquiry into the Preston strike ['On Strike', *HW*, 11 Feb. 1854] is said to have originated the title and, in some respects, suggested the turn of the story.'
3. One can understand Dickens's annoyance with Cunningham's remark because the genesis of some of the ideas that led to the composition of *HT* began well before he visited Preston on 29 Jan. 1854. Even before the completion of *BH* in Aug. 1853, Dickens expressed uneasiness with current utilitarian theories of education (N, II, 479); and when Cruikshank altered a collection of traditional fairy tales by inserting propaganda against alcohol and other social evils, Dickens protested. (See 'Frauds on the Fairies', *HW*, 1 Oct. 1853, where his championship of the imagination and fancy anticipates his satire against Gradgrind's educational views.) Later the same year, Dickens followed the reports of 'the unhappy strikes' and disturbances in Lancashire, which he alluded to when he spoke of the antagonism between classes at Birmingham on 30 Dec. On that occasion, he propounded his belief in the need to unite employers and employees and argued for their common interests in terms similar to those of the novel (*Speeches*, p. 167). Three weeks later, Dickens sent Forster a list of titles for the new *HW* story, one of which was 'Hard Times'; on 23 Jan. he told Miss Coutts that he had 'fallen to work again'. The main idea of the story, he explained, was one he had often spoken of with her, and he was going to write it now because his printers and co-partners in *HW* thought that a weekly story by him would improve the journal's circulation (N, II, 537).
4. Newton's ill health in 1692–3 led to exaggerated accounts of his distress, including stories of his temporary insanity.

7th May 1857

[John Forster] . . . Went to the Borough[1] yesterday morning before going to Gadshill, to see if I could find any ruins of the Marshalsea.[2] Found a great part of the orignal building—now "Marshalsea Place." Found the rooms that have been in my mind's eye in the story.[3] Found, nursing a very big boy, a very small boy, who, seeing me standing on the Marshalsea pavement, looking about, told me how it all used to be.

God knows how he learned it (for he was a world too young to know anything about it), but he was right enough. . . . There is a room there—still standing, to my amazement—that I think of taking! It is the room through which the ever-memorable signers of Captain Porter's petition[4] filed off in my boyhood. The spikes are gone, and the wall is lowered, and anybody can go out now who likes to go, and is not bedridden; and I said to the boy "Who lives there?" and he said, "Jack Pithick." "Who is Jack Pithick?" I asked him. And he said, "Joe Pithick's uncle." . . .

1. 'The Borough' was a short name for the Borough of Southwark, the 26th ward of London on the Surrey side of the Thames. It is also the name commonly given to part of the High Street, Southwark.
2. The Marshalsea was a fourteenth-century prison in the High Street attached to the King's House, and so called 'as pertaining to the Marshals of England'. The original structure, a little north of the building Dickens knew as a child, was destroyed in 1381 by the rebels of Kent. The prison was subsequently rebuilt, and two more prisons were established nearby: the White Lion prison, near St. George's Church which served as the County Gaol, and the adjoining King's Bench prison. The latter was moved in 1755–8 to a more open site further south; the White Lion prison was also improved, but by 1800 it was unfit for use. In 1811 a new prison was built on this site and the old Marshalsea, which for centuries had stood nearer to London Bridge, was transferred to this building. See W. Rendle, *Old Southwark and its People* (1878), quoted by G. F. Young, 'The Marshalsea Re-Visited', *The Dickensian*, 28 (Summer 1932), 221. It was in this building that John Dickens was imprisoned for debt from 20 Feb. to 24 May 1824. The Marshalsea Court and prison were abolished in 1849 (12 and 13 Vict., c. 101), and the new prison was shortly after taken down (Wheatley, III, 498; II, 475).
3. When Dickens wrote *LD* (1856–7), he returned to examine the locality to see what portions of the Marshalsea yet stood (see Preface to *LD*). The remains he found and described in *LD* as 'an oblong pile of barrack building' (Preface, and *LD*, I, ch. vi) were part of the former County Gaol, which had been altered to serve as a prison for the Marshal and the Admiralty, and not the fourteenth-century Marshalsea. See Ida Darlington, 'The Marshalsea', *LCC Survey of London*, 25 (1955), p. 15.
4. Captain Porter was the Marshalsea debtor who read a petition drawn up by John Dickens, and signed by the prisoners, asking for leave to drink the health of George IV on his birthday on 12 Aug. 1824. See Forster, I, ii 29–30.

GAD'S HILL

Sunday, Eighteenth October, 1857

MY DEAR MORLEY,—I particularly want a little piece of information, with a view to the construction of something for Household Words.[1] I have not the means of reference here, and I dare say you can supply them out of your own reading. It will oblige me very much, if you will consider and reply to the following question.

Whether, at any time within a hundred years or so, we were in such amicable relations with South America as would have rendered it reasonably *possible* for us to have made, either a public treaty, or a private bargain, with a South American Government, empowering a little English colony, established on the spot for the purpose, to work a Silver Mine (on purchase of the right), and whether in that supposititious case, it is reasonably *possible* that our English Government at home would have sent out a small force of a few marines or so, for that little colony's protection; or (which is the same thing) would have drafted them off from the nearest English military Station?[2]

Or can you suggest from your remembrance any more probable set of circumstances in which a few English people—gentlemen, ladies and children—and a few English soldiers, would find themselves alone in a strange wild place and liable to hostile attack? I wish to avoid India itself; but I want to shadow out, in what I do the bravery of our ladies in India.[3]—Very faithfully yours.

1. Henry Morley (1822–94), author and staff member of *HW* and *AYR*. See also p. 105 n.2. Possibly Dickens asked Morley because Morley had written about South America for *HW* and contributed a series of travel papers called 'Our Phantom Ship'. See especially 'Our Phantom Ship: Central America', *HW*, 22 Feb. 1851, which provides a description of the former British settlement of Belize.
2. Perhaps acting on Morley's response, Dickens set 'The Perils of Certain English Prisoners', in Belize, a British colony founded in 1640. Up to 1840, the name applied both to the capital city and to the colony as a whole, but little else about this Christmas Story, first published in *HW* in 1857, corresponds to its eighteenth-century context. Struggles against the Spanish not pirates dominate the early part of the settlement's history, and cutting and exporting logwood and mahogany rather than mining for silver formed the main staple of trade and the country's economic development. Reports of the alleged discovery of valuable mines did occur in the nineteenth century, however, and 'A general impression . . . prevailed . . . that precious metals abound in the Colony', wrote one official in 1849. See, *Archives of British Honduras, 1841 to 1884*, ed. Sir John A. Burdon (1935), III, 120.
3. Dickens's story tells of a small group of British colonists, mainly women and children, who are betrayed by a 'half-negro and half-Indian Sambo', kidnapped after a valiant but futile battle to defend themselves, and later led to freedom by a brave private in the Royal Marines. The treachery of many of the dark-skinned natives, government red-tape, and the hesitancy of British officials, the story suggests, jeopardize the efforts of England's brave colonists; but decisive action by officers and soldiers in the field can save the day.

Dickens's comments to Miss Coutts make clear his allegorical intention in the story. '. . . I have planned with great care,' Dickens wrote on 25 Nov. 1857, 'in the hope of commemorating, without any vulgar catchpenny connexion or application, some of the best qualities of the English character that have been shown in India. I hope it is very good and I think it will make a noise' (N, II, 894).

For an informative analysis of the extent to which 'The Perils' mirrors Victorian sentiment about the Indian Mutiny of 1857 and expresses a sense of 'the splendid qualities of courage, endurance, fidelity to duty, and unflinching fortitude under disaster . . . displayed by the Anglo-Saxon race . . . in the great Indian Mutiny' (*Annual Review*, 1857, 'History', p. 335), see W. Oddie, 'Dickens and the Indian Mutiny', *The Dickensian*, 68 (Jan. 1972), 3–15.

GAD'S HILL
Tuesday, Fifth June, 1860

MY DEAR BULWER LYTTON,—I am very much interested and gratified by your letter concerning A Tale of Two Cities. I do not quite agree with you on two points, but that is no deduction from my pleasure.

In the first place, although the surrender of the feudal privileges (on a motion seconded by a nobleman of great rank) was the occasion of a sentimental scene,[1] I see no reason to doubt, but on the contrary, many reasons to believe, that some of these privileges had been used to the frightful oppression of the peasant, quite as near to the time of the Revolution as the doctor's narrative,[2] which, you will remember, dates long before the Terror. And surely when the new philosophy was the talk of the salons and the slang of the hour, it is not unreasonable or unallowable to suppose a nobleman wedded to the old cruel ideas, and representing the time going out, as his nephew represents the time coming in,[3] [*sic*] as to the condition of the peasant in France generally at that day, I take it that if anything be certain on earth it is certain that it was intolerable. No *ex post facto* enquiries and provings by figures will hold water, surely, against the tremendous testimony of men living at the time.

There is a curious book printed at Amsterdam, written to make out no case whatever, and tiresome enough in its literal dictionary-like minuteness, scattered up and down the pages of which is full authority for my marquis. This is Mercier's Tableau de Paris.[4] Rousseau is the authority for the peasant's shutting up his house when he had a bit of meat.[5] The tax-table was the authority for the wretched creature's impoverishment.

I am not clear, and I never have been clear, respecting that canon of fiction which forbids the interposition of accident in such a case as Madame Defarge's death.[6] Where the accident is inseparable from the passion and emotion of the characters, where it is strictly consistent with the whole design, and arises out of some culminating proceeding on the part of the character which the whole story has led up to, it seems to me to become, as it were, an act of divine justice. And when I use Miss Pross (though this is quite another question) to bring about that catastrophe, I have the positive intention of making that half-comic intervention a part of the desperate woman's failure, and of opposing that mean death—instead of a desperate one in the streets, which she wouldn't have minded—to the dignity of Carton's wrong or right; this *was* the design, and seemed to be in the fitness of things. [. . .]—Ever affectionately and faithfully.

1. On the night of 4 Aug. 1789, members of the French nobility proposed the abolition of feudal privileges and formally renounced their own as an example before the National Assembly. Dickens's reference to the night as 'a sentimental scene' may owe something to Carlyle's account of the event in *The French Revolution*, vol. I, bk VI, ii.
2. Dickens sets Dr Manette's narrative (bk III, ch. 10) about the abused lives peasants led in 1767; the Reign of Terror began in 1793.
3. For the conflict between 'the old cruel ideas' and 'the new philosophy', see bk II, ch. 9.
4. Louis-Sébastien Mercier (1740–1814), dramatist, critic and author of *Tableau de Paris*, Nouvelle Edition, Corrigée and augmentée, 4 vols (Amsterdam, 1783). Mercier's *Tableau* was probably among the books Dickens received from Carlyle, who sent two cartloads in answer to the novelist's request for materials on the French Revolution. Mercier published the first two volumes in 1781; the work was subsequently completed in 1788 and published in twelve volumes. See *The Picture of Paris Before and After the Revolution*, trans. W. and E. Jackson (London: Routledge, 1929), pp. 3 and 9. Dickens's nobleman makes a dramatic appearance in bk II, ch. 7, when his coach, driven through Paris with 'inhuman abandonment', kills Gaspard's child. Reckless driving by the nobility threatened pedestrians to the extent that the gutters of the capital '[ran] with citizens' blood' (Mercier, ch. iii). Mercier, whom Dickens cites as his authority for the Marquis's behaviour, makes this point forcefully in his *Tableau*. Cf. E. Davis, *The Flint and the Flame: The Artistry of Charles Dickens* (Columbia: Univ. of Missouri Press, 1963), p. 243, who argues that Mercier provided Dickens with an instance of the notorious *droit du seigneur*, which he incorporated into Manette's narrative, and J. A. Falconer, 'The Sources of *A Tale of Two Cities*,' *Modern Language Notes*, 36 (Jan. 1921), 3–5, who suggests that Mercier's anecdote in ch. 238 about a released Bastille prisoner provided the prototype of Dr Manette.
5. Jean-Jacques Rousseau (1712–78), philosopher. Dr Manette records in his confession how the peasants suffered under the nobles. They were so pillaged, taxed, robbed and plundered, he learns from the dying brother of the young woman raped by the younger Evrémonde brother, 'that when we chanced to have a bit of meat, we ate it in fear, with the door barred and the

shutters closed, [so] that his people [the elder Evrémonde's] should not see it and take it from us' (bk III, ch. 10).
6. Madame Defarge accidentally shoots herself in her struggle with Lucie's servant, Miss Pross. Her death, Dickens argues, should be seen as part of the novel's design, whereby love and self-sacrifice prove stronger and far superior to hate and vengeance.

STATION HOTEL, NEWCASTLE
Friday Afternoon, Twenty-Fourth September, 1858
MY DEAR WILLS,—[. . .] So, we are working our way further North.[1] I walked from Durham to Sunderland, and made a little fanciful photograph in my mind of Pit Country, which will come well into H.W. one day. I couldn't help looking upon my mind as I was doing it, as a sort of capitally prepared and highly sensitive plate. And I said, without the least conceit (as Watkins[2] might have said of a plate of his) "it really is a pleasure to work with you, you receive the impression so nicely." [. . .]

1. On his first provincial reading tour (2 Aug. to 13 Nov.). Walking from Durham to Sunderland on this occasion, Dickens covered about 14 miles, many of which were through the coal-mining country of the northeast. He made no contribution to *HW* on this topic.
2. One of the Watkins brothers, London photographers, whose services Dickens commissioned.

BROADSTAIRS
Thursday, Sixteenth October, 1851
MY DEAR WILLS,—I sent the proof of The Child's History[1] by the cheap train.

I have been looking over the back Numbers. Wherever they fail, it is in wanting elegance of fancy. They lapse too much into a dreary, arithmetical, Cocker-cum-Walkingame dustyness that is powerfully depressing.[2]—Faithfully always.

1. Dickens's *Child's History of England*, published in *HW* between 25 Jan. 1851 and 10 Dec. 1853.
2. Edward Cocker (1631–75) and Francis Walkingame (fl. 1751–85), were, respectively, authors of *Cocker's Arithmetick* and *The Tutor's Assistant*. Dickens considered 'According to Cocker' as a possible title for *HT*. The reference signified in Dickens's vocabulary a disturbing trust in mechanical knowledge and unfeeling theorizing, to which 'Fancy' was the best corrective. Cf. Dickens's 'solemn and continual Conductorial Conjunction' to Wills from Rome on 17 Nov. 1853: 'KEEP HOUSEHOLD WORDS IMAGINATIVE!' (N. II, 518).
   In Dickens's view, the 'graces of the imagination' were never frivolous or

escapist; ideally, they should be fused with 'the realities of life'. (See 'All the Year Round' [Announcement], *HW*, 28 May 1859). When references to the latter were absent in *HW*, Dickens was equally upset. See the next letter.

BOULOGNE

Monday, Twenty-Fifth September, 1854

MY DEAR WILLS,—I really am quite shocked and ashamed on looking at the new No. to find nothing in it appropriate to the memorable time. I have written a little paper To Working Men, which I hope may do good, and I send it to you enclosed.

But I am so painfully impressed with a sense of our being frivolous that IF YOU HAVE NOT ALREADY GOT TO PRESS WITH No. 237, *I entreat you to unmake it and put this article first*.[1] Forster will correct it, if you give him the copy, quite accurately I am sure; therefore it would only involve a delay of a few hours. Even if but a few 237's were printed, it would be better to cancel them—stop—and get this paper in.

No. 238 and the parcel, I will send by tomorrow morning's boat.—In haste, ever faithfully.

1. Wills duly revised No. 237 (*HW*, 7 Oct. 1854), and Dickens's address 'To Working Men' appeared as the lead.

The Novelist and his Public Responsibility

DEVONSHIRE TERRACE
[June 1845]

[John Forster] . . . I really think I have an idea, and not a bad one, for the periodical.[1] I have turned it over, the last two days, very much in my mind: and think it positively good. I incline still to weekly; price three halfpence, if possible; partly original, partly select; notices of books, notices of theatres, notices of all good things, notices of all bad ones; Carol philosophy, cheerful views, sharp anatomization of humbug, jolly good temper; papers always in season, pat to the time of year; and a vein of glowing, hearty, generous, mirthful, beaming references in everything to Home, and Fireside. And I would call it, sir,—

THE CRICKET
A cheerful creature that chirrups on the Hearth.
Natural History.

Now, don't decide hastily till you've heard what I would do. I would come out, sir, with a prospectus on the subject of the Cricket that should put everybody in a good temper, and make such a dash at people's fenders and armchairs as hasn't been made for many a long day. I could approach them in a different mode under this name, and in a more winning and immediate way, than under any other. I would at once sit down upon their very hobs; and take a personal and confidential position with them which should separate me, instantly from all other periodicals periodically published, and supply a distinct and sufficient reason for my coming into existence. And I would chirp, chirp, chirp away in every number until I chirped it up to—well, you shall say how many hundred thousand![2] . . . Seriously, I feel a capacity in this name and notion which appears to give us a tangible starting-point, and a real, defined, strong, genial drift and purpose. I seem to feel that it is an aim and name[3] which people would readily and pleasantly connect with *me*; and that, for a good course and a clear one,

344

instead of making circles pigeon-like at starting, here we should be safe. I think the general recognition would be likely to leap at it; and of the helpful associations that could be clustered round the idea at starting, and the pleasant tone of which the working of it is susceptible, I have not the smallest doubt. . . . But you shall determine. What do you think? And what do you say? The chances are, that it will either strike you instantly, or not strike you at all. Which is it, my dear fellow? You know I am not bigoted to the first suggestions of my own fancy: but you know also exactly how I should use such a lever, and how much power I should find in it. Which is it? What do you say?—I have not myself said half enough. Indeed I have said next to nothing; but like the parrot in the negro-story, I "think a dam deal."

1. The idea of a miscellaneous weekly serial attracted Dickens as early as 1839, when he first sketched the outline of his plan for *MHC* in a letter to Forster (N, I, 218–20). Despite Dickens's failure to sustain that enterprise without contributing a novel of his own (*OCS*), he continued to express an interest in a cheap weekly publication of the kind outlined here. He began no such journal in 1845, but he revived 'The old notion of the Periodical' in 1849 (N, II, 174 and 178), successfully translating these principles, with some modifications, into *HW* and its successor, *AYR*. For the similarities between this prospectus and those describing the two later journals, see 'A Preliminary Word', *HW*, 30 Mar. 1850 and 'All the Year Round' [Announcement], *HW*, 28 May 1859 (repr. in *MP*, 1, 181–4).
2. Dickens's two weekly periodicals both sold well, with *HW* averaging 40 000 copies a week and *AYR* reaching 100 000 with the weekly publication of *TTC* and *GE*. For some of the Christmas numbers, the figures rose between 185 000 and nearly 300 000. See N, III, 378, 453, 504, and Forster, VIII, v, 230.
3. Dickens used *The Cricket* in the title of his third Christmas story that year but he sought similar cheerful associations when he considered possible titles for *HW* and *AYR*. See Forster, VI, iv, 65–6 and VIII, v, 227–8.

DEVONSHIRE TERRACE
Saturday, Twenty-Second April, 1848
MY DEAR FORSTER,—I finished Goldsmith[1] yesterday, after dinner, having read it from the first page to the last with the greatest care and attention.

As a picture of the time, I really think it impossible to give it too much praise. It seems to me to be the very essence of all about the time that I have ever seen in biography or fiction, presented in most wise and humane lights, and in a thousand new and just aspects. I have never liked Johnson[2] half so well. Nobody's contempt for Boswell[3] ought to be capable of increase, but I have never seen him in my mind's eye half so plainly. The introduction of him is quite a masterpiece. I should point to that, if I didn't know the author, as being done by somebody with a remarkably vivid conception of what he narrated, and a most admirable and fanciful power of communicating it to another. All about Reynolds[4] is charming; and the first account of the Literary Club[5] and of Beauclerc[6] as excellent a piece of description as ever I read in my life. But to read the book is to be in the time. It lives again in as fresh and lively a manner as if it were presented on an impossibly good stage by the very best actors that ever lived, or by the real actors come out of their graves on purpose.

And as to Goldsmith himself, and *his* life, and the tracing of it out in his own writings, and the manful and dignified assertion of him without any sobs, whines, or convulsions of any sort, it is throughout a noble achievement, of which, apart from any private and personal affection for you, I think (and really believe) I should feel proud, as one who had no indifferent perception of these books of his—to the best of my remembrance—when little more than a child. I was a little afraid in the beginning, when he committed those very discouraging imprudences, that you were going to champion him somewhat indiscriminately; but I very soon got over that fear, and found reason in every page to admire the sense, calmness, and moderation with which you make the love and admiration of the reader cluster about him from his youth, and strengthen with his strength—and weakness too, which is better still.

I don't quite agree with you in two small respects. First, I question very much whether it would have been a good thing for every great man to have had his Boswell, inasmuch that I think that two Boswells, or three at most, would have made great men extraordinarily false, and would have set them on always playing a part, and would have made distinguished people about them for ever restless and distrustful. I can imagine a succession of Boswells bringing about a tremendous state of falsehood in society, and playing the very devil with confidence and friendship. Secondly, I cannot help objecting to that practice (begun, I think, or greatly enlarged by Hunt[7] of italicising lines and words and whole passages in extracts, without some very special reason indeed. It does appear to be a kind of assertion of the editor over the reader—almost over the author himself—which grates upon me. The author might almost as well do it himself to my thinking, as a disagreeable thing; and it is such a strong contrast to the modest, quiet, tranquil beauty of The Deserted Village,[8] for instance, that I would almost as soon hear "the town crier" speak the lines. The practice always reminds me of a man seeing a beautiful view, and not thinking how beautiful it is half so much as what he shall say about it.

In that picture at the close of the third book (a most beautiful one) of Goldsmith sitting looking out of window at the Temple trees,[9] you speak of the "gray-eyed" rooks. As you sure they are "gray-eyed"? The raven's eye is a deep lustrous black, and so, I suspect, is the rook's, except when the light shines full into it.

I have reserved for a closing word—though I *don't* mean to be eloquent about it, being far too much in earnest—the admirable manner in which the case of the literary man is stated throughout this book. It is splendid. I don't believe that any book was ever written, or anything ever done or said, half so conducive to the dignity and honour of literature as The Life and Adventures of Oliver Goldsmith, by J. F., of the Inner Temple. The gratitude of every man who is content to rest his station and claims quietly on literature, and to make no feint of living by anything else, is your due for evermore. I have often said, here and there, when you have been at work upon the book, that I was sure it would be; and I shall insist on that debt being due to you (though there will be no need for insisting about it) as long as I have any tediousness and obstinacy to bestow on anybody. Lastly, I never will hear the biography compared with Boswell's except under vigorous protest. For I do say that it is mere folly to put into opposite scales a book, however amusing and curious, written by an unconscious coxcomb like that, and one which surveys and grandly understands the characters of all the illustrious company that move in it.

My dear Forster, I cannot sufficiently say how proud I am of what you have done, or how sensible I am of being so tenderly connected with it.[10] When I look over this note, I feel as if I had said no part of what I think; and yet if I were to write another I should say no more, for I can't get it out. I desire no better for my fame, when my personal dustiness shall be past the control of my love of order, than such a biographer and such a critic. And again I say, most solemnly, that literature in England has never had, and probably never will have, such a champion as you are,[11] in right of this book.—Ever affectionately.

1. John Forster, *The Life and Adventures of Oliver Goldsmith* (London: Bradbury & Evans, 1848). Forster later expanded his popular study and republished his original book as *The Life and Times of Oliver Goldsmith* in two vols in 1854. This work treated Goldsmith's contemporaries in greater detail. R. Vallance in 'Forster's *Goldsmith*', *The Dickensian*, 71 (Jan. 1975), 21–9 comments on Forster's work and examines some of the differences between the 1848 edition and the revised version of 1854.

2. Dr Samuel Johnson (1709–84), author and lexicographer.
3. James Boswell (1740–95), author and Johnson's biographer (1791).
4. Sir Joshua Reynolds (1723–92), painter.
5. The Literary Club (founded 1764), included these and other notable figures such as Edmund Burke, C. J. Fox, and David Garrick.
6. Topham Beauclerk (1739–80), was a friend of Johnson and another original member of the Club.
7. Leigh Hunt.
8. Goldsmith's poem, 'The Deserted Village', 1770, looks nostalgically at English country life before the industrial revolution.
9. Goldsmith took chambers in the Temple in 1776. He lived first in Garden Court, then King Bench Walk, and finally at 2 Brick Court, where he remained until his death in 1774. The Temple, so called from the Knights Templars, who took up residence there in 1184, is the district between Fleet Street and the Thames.
10. The work was dedicated to Dickens.
11. Dickens also stressed Forster's characteristic generosity and conscientiousness as a biographer when he reviewed his *Walter Savage Landor: A Biography* (1869) in *AYR*, 24 July 1869. He concluded that Forster had struck a balance in the book between the good and ill in Landor's Life and that Landor's genius would not be treasured the less, or less understood 'for the more perfect knowledge of his character'. (See also, *MP*, ii, 343–50).

57 GLO'STER PLACE, HYDE PARK GARDENS
Tuesday, Twenty-ninth March, 1864

MY DEAR FORSTER,—[. . .] Concerning Eliot,[1] I sat down, as I told you, and read the book through with the strangest interest and the highest admiration. I believe it to be as honest, spirited, patient, reliable, and gallant a piece of biography as ever was written, the care and pains of it astonishing, the completeness of it masterly; and what I particularly feel about it is that the dignity of the man, and the dignity of the book that tells about the man, always go together, and fit each other. This same quality has always impressed me as the great leading speciality of the Goldsmith, and enjoins sympathy with the subject, knowledge of it, and pursuit of it in its own spirit; but I think it even more remarkable here. I declare that apart from the interest of having been so put into the time, and enabled to understand it, I personally feel quite as much the credit and honour done to literature by such a book. It quite clears out of the remembrance a thousand pitiful things, and sets one up in heart again. I am not surprised in the least by Bulwer's enthusiasm. I was as confident about the effect of the book when I closed the first volume, as I was when I closed the second with a full heart. No man less in earnest than Eliot himself could have done it, and I make bold to add that it never could have been done by a man who was so distinctly born to do the work as Eliot was to do his. [. . .]

1. John Forster, *Sir John Eliot: A Biography, 1590–1632*, 2 vols (London: Longman, Green, Longman, Roberts & Green, 1864). Forster first published a life of Sir John Eliot (together with one of Thomas Wentworth, Earl of Strafford) in 1836. This vol., the first of five Forster contributed to the *Lives of Eminent British Statesmen* in Dionysius Lardner's *Lardner's Cabinet Cyclopaedia* (London, 1830–49), appeared with contributions by Sir James Mackintosh, J. Macdiarmid and T. P. Courtenay, all of which were originally published in London between 1831 and 1839. Forster's other contributions included: John Pym and John Hamden (1837), Sir Henry Vane and Henry Marten (1838) and a two volume life of Oliver Cromwell (1839).

Sir John Eliot was the parliamentary leader who in 1626 instituted impeachment proceedings against George Villiers, the first Duke of Buckingham and powerful favourite of James I and Charles I. Buckingham escaped trial when Charles I dissolved Parliament, but he was murdered in 1628. Eliot was imprisoned after further protests against the King's authority; he died in the Tower of London in 1632. Dickens alludes briefly to the proceedings against Buckingham in *A Child's History of England* (1851–3), ch. 33, but ignores Eliot.

BROADSTAIRS
Wednesday 11th July 1849

[The Editor, *The Daily News*] . . . I have no other interest in, or concern with, a most facetious article on last Saturday's dinner at the Mansion-house,[1] which appeared in your paper of yesterday, and found its way here to-day, than that it misrepresents me in what I said on the occasion. If you should not think it at all damaging to the wit of that satire to state what I did say, I shall be much obliged to you. It was this. . . . That I considered the compliment of a recognition of Literature by the citizens of London the more acceptable to us because it was unusual in that hall, and likely to be an advantage and benefit to them in proportion as it became in future less unusual. That, on behalf of the novelists, I accepted the tributes as an appropriate one; inasmuch as we had sometimes reason to hope that our imaginary worlds afforded an occasional refuge to men busily engaged in the toils of life, from which they came forth none the worse to a renewal of its strivings; and certainly that the chief magistrate of the greatest city in the world might be fitly regarded as the representative of that class of our readers. . . .

1. The banquet to Literature, Science and Art given by the Lord Mayor of London, Sir James Duke, on 7 July 1849. When the Lord Mayor proposed

as a toast 'Honour and Prosperity to those engaged in the Pursuits of Literature', Dickens replied, saying that one of the best tributes which could be paid to his brethren was to receive recognition 'at the hands of the Chief Magistrate of the City of London'. A frivolous editorial and report of the proceedings in the *Daily News* annoyed Dickens and prompted this reply. Forster suppressed the letter but provided its text in the *Life* (VI, vi, 87). See also *Speeches*, pp 98–100.

TAVISTOCK HOUSE
Friday Night, Fourteenth January, 1853

MY DEAREST MACREADY,—I have been much affected by the receipt of your kindest and best of letters; for I know out of the midst of what anxieties it comes to me, and I appreciate such remembrance from my heart. You and yours are always with us, however. It is no new thing for you to have a part in any scene of my life. It very rarely happens that a day passes without our thoughts and conversation travelling to Sherborne. We are so much there that I cannot tell you how plainly I see you as I write.

I know you would have been full of sympathy and approval if you had been present at Birmingham,[1] and that you would have concurred in the tone I tried to take about the eternal duties of the arts to the people. I took the liberty of putting the court and that kind of thing out of the question, and recognising nothing *but* the arts and the people. The more we see of life and its brevity, and the world and its varieties, the more we know that no exercise of our abilities in any art, but the addressing of it to the great ocean of humanity in which we are drops, and not to bye-ponds (very stagnant) here and there, ever can or ever will lay the foundations of an endurable retrospect. Is it not so? *You* should have as much practical information on this subject, now, my dear friend, as any man.

My dearest Macready, I cannot forbear this closing word. I still look forward to our meeting as we used to do in the happy times we have known together, so far as your old hopefulness and energy are concerned. And I think I never in my life have been more glad to receive a sign, than I have been to hail that which I find in your handwriting.

Some of your old friends at Birmingham are full of interest and enquiry. I am ever, and no matter where I am—am quite as much in a crowd as alone—my dearest Macready,—Your affectionate and most attached Friend.

1. On 6 Jan. 1853 Dickens accepted from the citizens of Birmingham a silver

ring and salver presented to him in recognition of his contribution to literature. Following the presentation and a dinner, the Archdeacon of Coventry toasted Dickens and praised him for having done 'more than any living man' to elevate the nation's lighter literature and enforce in his writings 'precepts which we might venerate as Christians' (*Speeches*, p. 156). Dickens responded by elaborating on the principles he alludes to in his letter to Macready. For the full text of his remarks at the presentation and his response to the toasts after the dinner, see *Speeches*, pp 154–60.

5 HYDE PARK PLACE, W.

Tuesday, Twenty-Ninth March, 1870

MY DEAR HARRY,[1]—Enclosed is a cheque for £25.

Your next Tuesday's subject is a very good one. I would not lose the point that narrow-minded fanatics, who decry the theatre and defame its artists, are absolutely the advocates of depraved and barbarous amusements. For wherever a good drama and a well-regulated theatre decline, some distorted form of theatrical entertainment will infallibly arise in their place. In one of the last chapters of Hard Times, Mr. Sleary says something to the effect: "People will be entertained thomehow, thquire. Make the betht of uth, and not the wortht."—Ever affectionately.

1. Henry Fielding Dickens.

TAVISTOCK HOUSE

Tuesday, Thirtieth May, 1854

MY DEAR WILLS,—I think Thomas's story[1] very good indeed. Close, original, vigorous, and graphic. It strikes me that I see better things in it than he has done yet.

An alteration occurs to me—easily made—which I think would greatly improve it, in respect of interest and quiet pathos, and a closing sentiment of pleasure to the reader. It should be delicately expressed that the man (admirably described) who comes a-courting Miss Furbey is the old lover who has always been faithful. I think Miss Furbey might have always had a miniature of him, hanging up, or in a pet drawer and sometimes brought out, taken when he was a young man; and that when the narrator begins to observe him and his visits, she should still see in the grey hair and the worn face something of that portrait.

I wish you would make the suggestion in my words. Beg him not to delay the story, for I don't like to keep anything of so much merit out of print. [. . .]—Ever faithfully. . . .

1. William Moy Thomas (1828–1910), journalist, scholar, and author of 'Miss Furbey', *HW*, 17 June 1854. Thomas altered the story to incorporate

Dickens's suggestion of making Miss Furbey's fiancé her old and faithful lover, whose miniature she keeps in a little casket locked in a chest of drawers.

TAVISTOCK HOUSE
Thursday, Twelfth July, 1855

MY DEAR WILLS,—There is no doubt whatever, that the Wife's Story is written by a very remarkable woman.[1] I am quite clear that there is a strong reason to believe that a great writer is coming up in this person, whoever it is.

The story is extremely difficult of adaptation to our purpose, but I think I see a way to doing it in four parts. It would require, however, to be condensed in the beginning, and I believe the catastrophe to be altogether wrong.[2] That part must be re-written if I accept it, and I should particularly like to see the writer on that subject.

If you have the means of communicating readily with the lady—I assume the writer to be a lady—I will see her at the office on Monday at 11, if that day and hour should suit her convenience. In the event of her living in the country, I suppose I must write; but I would prefer an interview. I think there is a surprising knowledge of one dark phase of human nature throughout this composition; and that it is expressed, generally, with the uncommon passion and power.

You may quote as much of this—part or all, as you like—in writing to this author, and I particularly wish you would add that the story only came under my perusal this morning.

I enclose another MS. which will be inquired for at the office. The lady's name and address I have marked in pencil upon it. I have written to her and declined it.—Faithfully ever. [. . .]

3 ALBION VILLAS, FOLKESTONE, KENT
Tuesday, Seventeenth July, 1855

DEAR MADAM,[3]—Your manuscript, entitled a Wife's Story, has come under my own perusal within these last three or four days. I recognise in it such great merit and unusual promise, and I think it displays so much power and knowledge of the human heart, that I feel a strong interest in you as its writer.

I have begged the gentleman, who is in my confidence as to the transaction of the business of Household Words, to return the MS. to you by the post, which (as I hope) will convey this note to you. My object is this: I particularly entreat you to consider the catastrophe.[4] You write to be read, of course. The close of the story is unnecessarily painful—will throw off numbers of persons who would otherwise read it, and who (as it stands) will be deterred by hearsay from so doing, and is so tremendous a piece of severity, that it will defeat your purpose. All my knowledge and experience, such as they are, lead me straight to the recommendation that you will do well to spare the life of the husband, and of one of the children. Let her suppose the former dead, from seeing him brought in wounded and insensible—lose nothing of the progress of her mental suffering afterwards when that doctor is in attendance upon her—but bring her round at last to the blessed surprise that her husband is still living, and that a repentance which can be worked out, *in the way of atonement for the misery she has occasioned to the man whom she so ill repaid for his love, and made so miserable*, lies before her. So will you soften the reader whom you now as it were harden, and so you will bring tears from many eyes, which can only have their spring in affectionately and gently touched hearts. I am perfectly certain that with this change, all the previous part of your tale will tell for twenty times as much as it can in its present condition. And it is because I believe you have a great fame before you if you do justice to the remarkable ability you possess, that I venture to offer you this advice in what I suppose to be the beginning of your career.

I observe some parts of the story which would be strengthened, even in their psychological interest, by condensation here and there. If you will leave that to me, I will perform the task as conscientiously and carefully as if it were my own. But the suggestion I offer for your acceptance, no one but yourself can act upon.

Let me conclude this hasty note with the plain assurance that I have never been so much surprised and struck by any manuscript I have read, as I have been by yours.—Your faithful Servant.

3 ALBION VILLAS, FOLKESTONE
Twenty-First July, 1855

DEAR MADAM,—I did not enter, in detail, on the spirit of the alteration I propose in your story; because I thought it right that you should think out that for yourself if you applied yourself to the change. I can now assure you that you describe it exactly as I had conceived it; and if I had wanted anything to confirm me in my conviction of its being right, our both seeing it so precisely from the same point of view, would be ample assurance to me.

I would leave her new and altered life to be inferred. It does not appear to me either necessary or practicable (within such limits) to do more than that. Do not be uneasy if you find the alteration demanding time. I shall quite understand that, and my interest will keep. *When* you finish the story, send it to Mr. Wills. Besides being in daily communication with him, I am at the office once a week; and I will go over it in print, before the proof is sent to you.—Very faithfully yours.

1. Emily Jolly, 'A Wife's Story', in four instalments, *HW*, 1, 8, 15, and 22 Sep. 1855. Evidently no interview took place. See the next letters.
2. This story narrates the experiences of an unhappy governess, who escapes her harsh employer and marries an eligible suitor. 'I want you to be happy,' says her husband, 'and leave everything to me.' To this end, he provides books, birds, pictures, flowers and music, but he expresses disapproval when his wife takes the piano seriously and composes brilliant but unsettling music. The birth of two children adds temporary joy to a deteriorating marriage, but the wife's continued battle for 'real and unreal rights' and refusal to submit to 'any imposed yoke' destroy the family. In the first version, she breaks down, the husband is killed in an accident, and the children die from the fever.
3. Emily Jolly.
4. Dickens argued that Jolly's original catastrophe was 'altogether wrong' because he thought that readers would find the close unnecessarily painful. In the revised version, the husband does not die, one child survives, and the protagonist learns to recognise 'the controlling power of a higher will'. After a period in which husband and wife recuperate, they come together and celebrate 'a second marriage'. While kneeling over the grave of their son, the wife admits that she had found her 'rightful place . . . at [her] husband's feet. I had learnt to reverence him, and so found rest on earth.'

These particulars, we should note, were the author's not Dickens's, who, although he entreated Jolly to alter the ending, did not specify its form. Furthermore, despite the changes, the story's protest against Victorian assumptions about marriage remains. We infer from the close that Annie Aston Warden becomes a better wife, in accordance with Victorian conventions, but not before Jolly has shown the destructive effects of enforced docility upon a wilful yet talented and creative woman compelled to subordinate her life to her well-meaning but unimaginative husband.

Angus Easson takes a more critical view of Dickens's intervention, arguing that his suggestion to save the husband and show the wife repenting constitutes an unwarranted 'piece of editorial dictation'. By making the heroine submit to her husband, he notes, Jolly falsifies her psychology and 'emasculate[s]' the artistic integrity of the original. See 'Dickens, *Household Words*, and a Double Standard', *The Dickensian*, 60 (May 1964), 107–14.

OFFICE OF ALL THE YEAR ROUND
Tuesday, Third August, 1869

MY DEAREST MAMIE,—I send you the second chapter of the remarkable story.[1] The printer is late with it, and I have not had time to read it, and as I altered it considerably here and there, I have no doubt there are some verbal mistakes in it. However, they will probably express themselves.

But I offer a prize of six pairs of gloves—between you, and your aunt,[2] and Ellen Stone,[3] as competitors—to whomsoever will tell me what idea in this second part is mine. I don't mean an idea in language, in the turning of a sentence, in any little description of an action, or a gesture, or what not in a small way, but an idea, distinctly affecting the whole story *as I found it*. You are all to assume that I found it in the main as you read it, with one exception. If I had written it, I should have made the woman love the man at last. And I should have shadowed that possibility out, by the child's bringing them a little more together on that holiday Sunday.

But I didn't write it. So, finding that it wanted something, I put that something in. What was it?—Your affectionate Father.

1. Emily Jolly, 'An Experience', in two chs, *AYR*, 14 and 21 Aug. 1869. This is a tale of medical hubris about a young physician who unwisely agrees to perform a dangerous experiment designed to cure the lame child of a beautiful and mysterious widow. The operation causes the child's death, and the doctor, mortified by his failure, suffers a prolonged mental breakdown. In the second chapter, the widow attends him, and he falls in love with her and proposes marriage, unaware that revenge prompts her devotion to him during his illness. When the child died, she resolved to entice the doctor to marry her, in return for which she planned to curse him as her child's butcher, grind down his heart, and finally murder him in bed.

   Jolly clearly intended the scheme to fail; the idea Dickens seems to have found wanting was the basis for the widow's change of heart. We can infer that originally the widow left unrevenged, perhaps after a brief explanation, never to see the doctor again. In the revised version, the two still separate, but before the widow goes, she explicitly renounces a desire for vengeance. The day before the wedding, Mrs Rosscar confesses to the doctor at her daughter's graveside: 'I cannot do it, I cannot do it! The mother in me will not let me. You were once kind to her. You made her happy for one bright blessed day' (that holiday Sunday to which Dickens refers). Later that evening she adds that she intended to marry for hate, but because love had arisen in her soul, she could not carry out her plan. The germ of the widow's repentance therefore appears in the story as Dickens found it; 'that something' he put in reaffirms his conviction in the salutary effects of penitance and sharpens the moral design.

2. Georgina Hogarth.
3. Ellen Stone, a genre painter active in London between 1874–7.

FOLKESTONE, KENT
Tuesday, Fourteenth August, 1855

DEAR MADAM,[1]—As I understand from Mr. Wills that you gave me leave to write to you, I beg to assure you that I read your tale with the strongest emotion—and with a very exalted admiration of the great power displayed in it.[2] Both in sincerity and tenderness I thought it masterly. It moved me, more than I can express to you. I wrote to Mr. Wills that it had completely unsettled me for the day: and that by whomsoever it was written, I felt the highest respect for the mind that had produced it.

It so happened that I had been for some days at work upon a character extremely like the Aunt.[3] And it was very strange to me indeed to observe how the two people seemed to be near to one another at first, and then hurried off upon their own ways so wide asunder.

I told Wills that I was not sure whether I could have prevailed upon myself to present to a large audience the terrible consideration of hereditary madness, when it was reasonably probable that there must be many—or some—among them whom it would awfully, because personally, address. But I was not obliged to ask myself the question, inasmuch as the length of the story rendered it unavailable for Household Words.[4] I speak of its length in reference to that publication only relatively to what is told in it. I need not spare a page of your manuscript.

Experience shows me that a story in four portions is best suited to the peculiar requirements of such a journal, and I assure you it will be an uncommon satisfaction to me if this correspondence should lead to your enrolment among its contributors.[5] But my strong and sincere conviction of the vigour and pathos of this beautiful tale, is quite apart from, and not to be influenced by any ulterior results. You had not existence, as to me when I read it. The actions and sufferings of the characters affected me by their own force and truth, and left a profound impression on me.—Dear Madam,—Very faithfully yours.

1. Harriet Parr (1828–1900), novelist. Pseudonym 'Holme Lee'.
2. *Gilbert Massenger*
3. Upon reading the novel, Dickens was struck with the resemblances between Parr's aunt, Gertrude Massenger, a pious unloving figure who brings up the novel's protagonist 'in the bonds of fear', and his own Mrs Clenam of *LD*, whose second number he began in mid-Aug. 1854 (N, II, 685). For a note on the two novels, see E. Showalter, *DSN*, 10 (June–Sep. 1979), 59–60.
4. Although Dickens cites length as the major obstacle to the publication of *Gilbert Massenger*, its subject appears to be a significant factor as well. By 1855, Dickens had already published two novels in *HW*, his own *HT* and Mrs Gaskell's *North and South*. Later that year, Smith and Elder published Parr's novel in a single volume.

5. Parr was already a contributor, under her pseudonym. See Lohrli, pp. 395–6.

OFFICE OF ALL THE YEAR ROUND
Tuesday, Twelfth February, 1867

MY DEAR WILKIE,—Coming back here yesterday I found your letter awaiting me.

Owing to my heavy engagements I have not read Charles Reade's last book,[1] but I will take it away with me to-morrow, and do so at once. If the trial should come off in this present month, however, I *cannot* be a witness; for I go to Scotland to-morrow, and come back for only one night at St. James's Hall before going to Ireland.[2] The public announcements are all made, and heavy expenses are incurred by Chappell, wherefore I must be producible, in common honour. But I hope the action may not be tried so soon.[3] I do not agree with the legal authorities, and I rather doubt Cockburn's[4] allowing such evidence to be given on the ground that the *onus probandi* lies with the reviewer, and that it is not disproof that is required—but this is beside the question. Say everything that is brotherly in art from me to Reade, and add that I will write to you again after having got through the story.

I am as fresh as can possibly be expected under the work of the Readings. But the railways shake me, as witness my present handwriting. Since the Staplehurst experience[5] I feel them very much.

This day fortnight I shall be at St. James's Hall in the evening, and perhaps we can then have a word together—unless you are in Paris by that time.—Ever affec'ly.

1. Charles Reade (1814–84), novelist. *Griffith Gaunt, or Jealousy* appeared simultaneously in the London and New York editions of the *Argosy* between Dec. 1865 and Nov. 1866. Ticknor and Fields of Boston also published serial instalments in the *Atlantic Monthly* and brought out a three volume edition in 1866. Chapman and Hall published the novel in London.
2. On 15 Jan. 1867 Dickens began his second Chappell season, a group of 52 readings arranged by his agents of Bond Street. He read at St. James's Hall, one of London's principal concert rooms, and in various towns throughout England, Scotland, and Ireland.
3. Reade initiated two separate suits against the critics of his novel who, upset by a study of adultery, bigamy and seduction, attacked the author with unusual vehemence. In America, Reade sought $25 000 damages against the editors of *The Round Table*, in whose columns several hostile attacks on the novel had appeared. See Selected Bibliography, pp 364–5. In Britain, he prepared similar charges against *The London Review* for reprinting some of the 'foreign dirt' spread by *The Round Table* but dropped the charges some time in 1867. As the journal reported on 15 June 1867

(p. 689), Reade learned, 'we know not from what source, a fact which has convinced him that we, like himself, were the victims of an inadvertence. On this, he has left the matter with us, instead of referring it to a jury.'
4. Sir Alexander J. E. Cockburn (1802–80), Lord Chief Justice of England, 1859–80.
5. For the details of the railway accident on 9 June 1865, see pp 150–2.

BRIDGE OF ALLAN, SCOTLAND
Wednesday, Twentieth February, 1867
MY DEAR WILKIE,—I have read Charles Reade's book, and here follows my state of mind—*as a witness*—respecting it.

I have read it with the strongest interest and admiration. I regard it as the work of a highly accomplished writer and a good man; a writer with a brilliant fancy and a graceful and tender imagination. I could name no other living writer who could, in my opinion, write such a story nearly so well. As regards a so-called critic who should decry such a book as Holywell Street literature,[1] and the like, I should have merely to say of him that I could desire no stronger proof of his incapacity in, and his unfitness for, the post to which he has elected himself.

Cross-examined, I should feel myself in danger of being put on unsafe ground, and should try to set my wits against the cross-examiner, to keep well off it. But if I were reminded (as I probably should be, supposing the evidence to be allowed at all) that I was the Editor of a periodical of large circulation in which the Plaintiff himself had written,[2] and if I had [*had*] read to me in court those passages about Gaunt's going up to his wife's bed drunk and that last child's being conceived, and was asked whether, as Editor, I would have passed those passages, whether written by the Plaintiff or anybody else, I should be obliged to reply No. Asked why? I should say that what was pure to an artist might be impurely suggestive to inferior minds (of which there must necessarily be many among a large mass of readers), and that I should have called the writer's attention to the likelihood of those passages being perverted in such quarters. Asked if I should have passed the passage where Kate and Mercy have the illegitimate child upon their laps and look over its little points together? I should be again obliged to reply No, for the same reason. Asked whether, as author or Editor, I should have passed Neville's marriage to Mercy, and should have placed those four people, Gaunt, his wife, Mercy, and Neville, in those relative situations towards one another, I should again be obliged to reply No. Hard pressed upon this point, I must infallibly say that I consider those relative situations extremely coarse and disagreeable.[3] [. . .]

1. Holywell Street. A narrow lane occupied chiefly by second-hand booksellers and pornographers. Formerly, the street ran parallel with the Strand from St. Clement's Danes to St. Mary-le-Strand.
2. *Hard Cash*, which Reade contributed to *AYR* in 1863.
3. Griffith Gaunt lives happily with his wife, Kate, at Castle Hernshaw for eight years until the ascendancy of a young priest in the household leads Gaunt to conclude that his wife's spiritual father is in fact her lover. After recriminations and bitter quarrels, the jealous and tormented husband leaves. He falls ill at an inn, where he is nursed by Mercy Vint, whom he bigamously marries. Their new life succeeds until the need for money drives Gaunt home. A reconciliation with his lawful wife follows; after dinner one evening and emboldened by wine, Gaunt goes to Kate's bedroom and a child is conceived (chs 32 and 40).

    Gaunt wants to resume his former life, but his concern for Mercy and her family, who need money, prompts him to go back to the inn. Reunited with Mercy and their newborn son, Gaunt finds himself unable to leave. Mercy, however, discovers his secret and compels Gaunt to return to Kate. Mercy later follows with her son when she learns that Kate is wrongly accused of murdering Gaunt, whom Mercy knows is alive. Willing to save Kate's life by exposing her own bigamous marriage, Mercy asks Kate for permission to stand as a witness in her defence. The two women reach an understanding; they also comprehend 'that to have been both of them wronged by one man was a bond of sympathy, not hate', as they lay the child of Mercy and Gaunt across their laps 'and weep over him together' (ch. 53).

    Mercy's appearance on the stand concludes a long trial scene, at which emerges proof that the body presumed to be the slain Gaunt's was that of his half-brother, who drowned in the mere because he was drunk not because he was shot. Subsequently Mercy marries Sir George Neville, a former suitor of Kate's, and Gaunt and his wife resolve their differences. The two couples forestall gossip by not meeting in society, but the wives correspond and help each other in charitable works.

Selected Bibliography

I have arranged these entries to correspond with the three principal divisions
of the book and the sub-sections within those divisions. Readers should also
note that I have listed only those sources I found more than casually useful.
Exceptions to this policy occur only for materials I judge of particular interest
for those seeking further information. Otherwise, other sources will be found
fully cited in the Notes.

Part I: BIOGRAPHY

Adrian, Arthur A., *Georgina Hogarth and the Dickens Circle* (London:
Oxford Univ. Press, 1957).
Allen, Michael, 'The Dickens Family at Portsmouth', *The Dickensian*, 77
(Autumn 1981), 131–43.
——, 'The Dickens Family at London and Sheerness, 1815–1817', *The
Dickensian*, 78 (Spring 1982), 2–7.
——, 'The Dickens Family at Chatham, 1817–1822', *The Dickensian*, 78
(Summer 1982), 66–88.
——, 'The Dickens Family in London 1822–24', *The Dickensian*, 78 (Autumn
1982), 130–51.
——, 'The Dickens Family in London, 1824–1827', *The Dickensian*, 79
(Spring 1983), 3–20.
Aylmer, Felix, *Dickens Incognito* (London: Rupert Hart-Davis, 1959).
Collins, Philip (ed.) *Charles Dickens The Public Readings* (Oxford: Claren-
don, 1975).
Dexter, Walter (ed.) *Mr. and Mrs. Charles Dickens: His Letters to Her*
(London: Constable, 1935).
—— (ed.) *The Letters of Charles Dickens*, The Nonesuch Dickens, 3 vols
(Bloomsbury: The Nonesuch Press, 1938).
Dickens, Sir Henry F., *Memories of My Father* (London: Gollancz, 1928).
——, *The Recollections of Sir Henry Dickens, K.C.* (London: Heinemann,
1934).
Dickens, Mary, *Charles Dickens by His Eldest Daughter* (London: Cassell,
1885), republished as *My Father as I Recall Him* (London: Roxburghe
Press, 1897).
Easson, Angus, ' "I, Elizabeth Dickens": Light on John Dickens's Legacy',
The Dickensian, 67 (Jan. 1971), 35–40.
——, 'John Dickens and the Navy Pay Office'. *The Dickensian*, 70 (Jan. 1974),
35–45.
Dolby, George, *Charles Dickens as I knew Him. The Story of the Reading*

Tours in Great Britain and America (1866–1870) (London: T. Fisher Unwin, 1885).

Fielding, K. J., 'Bradbury v. Dickens', *The Dickensian*, 50 (Mar. 1954), 73–82.

——, 'Charles Dickens and His Wife: Fact or Forgery?' *Etudes Anglaises*, 8 (1955), 212–22.

——, 'Dickens and the Hogarth Scandal', *Nineteenth-Century Fiction*, 10 (June 1955), 64–74.

——, *Charles Dickens: A Critical Introduction* (London: Longmans, Green, 1958), 2nd edn 1965.

——, *The Speeches of Charles Dickens* (Oxford: Clarendon, 1960).

Forster, John, *The Life of Charles Dickens* [1872–4] 2 vols (ed.) A. J. Hoppé (London: Dent, 1969).

House, Madeline, and Storey, Graham (eds) *The Letters of Charles Dickens*, Pilgrim Edition, 5 vols (Oxford: Clarendon, 1965–81).

Johnson, Edgar, *Charles Dickens, His Tragedy and Triumph*, 2 vols (New York: Simon and Shuster, 1952).

——, (ed.) *The Heart of Charles Dickens*. [Letters from Dickens to Miss Coutts, 1841–65] (New York: Duell, Sloan and Pierce, 1952).

Kent, Charles, 'Charles Dickens as a Journalist', *Time*, 5 (July 1881), 361–74.

Morley, Malcolm, 'The Theatrical Ternans', *The Dickensian*, 54 (Jan. 1958), 38–43; (May 1958), 95–106; (Sep. 1958), 155–63; 55 (Jan. 1959), 36–44; (May 1959), 109–17; (Sep. 1959), 159–68; 56 (Jan. 1960), 41–6; (May 1960), 76–83; (Sep. 1960), 153–7; 57 (Jan. 1961), 29–35.

Nisbet, Ada B., *Dickens and Ellen Ternan* (Berkeley: Univ. of California Press, 1952).

Parker, David and Slater, Michael, 'The Gladys Storey Papers', *The Dickensian*, 76 (Spring 1980), 3–16.

Storey, Gladys, *Dickens and Daughter* (London: Muller, 1939).

Part II: RAGGED SCHOOLS

Collins, Philip, *Dickens's Periodicals: Articles on Education* [Annotated bibliography]. Vaughan College Papers, No. 3 Leicester (1957).

——, 'Dickens and the Ragged Schools'. *The Dickensian*, 55 (May 1959), 94–109.

——, 'The Duty of the State', in his *Dickens and Education* (London: Macmillan, 1963).

Dickens, Charles, 'Ignorance and Crime', *The Examiner*, 22 Apr. 1848.

——, 'Edinburgh Apprentice School Association', *The Examiner*, 30 Dec. 1848.

Fielding, K. J., 'Dickens's Work with Miss Coutts', *The Dickensian*, 61 (May 1965), 112–9; (Sep. 1965), 155–60.

Household Words The following essays argue for the educational needs of poor children: CD, 'A Walk in a Workhouse', 25 May 1850; CD, 'A December Vision', 14 Dec. 1850; W. H. Wills and CD, 'Small Beginnings', 5 Apr. 1851; H. Morley and CD, 'Boys to Mend', 11 Sep. 1852. See also: A. Mackay, 'The Devil's Acre', 22 June 1850, W. H. Wills, 'The Power of Small Beginnings', 20 July 1850, and H. Morley, 'Tilling the Devil's Acre', 13 June 1857, all three of which refer to aspects of Miss Coutts's charitable work in the parish of Westminster. Taylor and W. H. Wills, 'A Day in a Pauper Palace', 13 July 1850; F. K. Hunt, 'London Pauper Children', 31 Aug. 1850; F. K. Hunt, 'What a London Curate Can Do If He Tries', 16 Nov. 1850; J. Hannay, 'Lambs to be Fed', 30 Aug. 1851; H. Morley, 'Little Red Working-Coat', 27 Dec. 1851; H. Morley, 'How Charity Begins at Home, near Hamburg', 17 Jan. 1852; W. B. Jerrold, 'Anybody's Child', 4 Feb. 1854; H. Morley and G. E. Jewsbury, 'Instructive Comparisons', 29 Sep. 1855; and Mrs Hill, 'Ragged Robin', 7 May 1856.

Mayhew, Henry, 'Ragged Schools', Letters 43–5, in *Voices of the Poor: Selections from the Morning Chronicle 'Labour and the Poor' (1849–1850)* (ed.) Anne Humphreys (London: Frank Cass, 1971).

'The Second Annual Report of the Ragged School Union, Established for the Support of Schools for the Destitute Poor, London, 9 June 1846', *Quarterly Review*, 79 (Dec. 1846), 127–41.

URANIA COTTAGE AND PROSTITUTION

Acton, William, *Prostitution* (ed.) Peter Fryer (1857) (repr. London: Mac-Gibbon and Kee, 1968).

Collins, Philip, 'The Marks System', in his *Dickens and Crime* (London: Macmillan, 1962).

Dickens, Charles, 'The Pawnbroker's Shop', *Sketches by Boz* 30 June 1835.

——, 'The Prisoners' Van', *Sketches by Boz* 29 Nov. 1835.

——, 'Home for Homeless Women', *Household Words*, 23 Apr. 1853.

Fielding, K. J., 'A Great Friendship (Miss Burdett Coutts)', *The Dickensian*, 49 (June 1953), 102–7.

——, 'Dickens's Novels and Miss Burdett-Coutts', *The Dickensian*, 51 (Dec. 1954), 30–4.

——, 'Dickens and Miss Burdett-Coutts: The Last Phase', *The Dickensian*, 57 (May 1961), 97–105.

Household Words For CD's support for the Family Loan Colonization Society, which Mrs Caroline Chisholm founded to help poor women and families leave England, see the following articles: CD and Mrs Chisholm, 'A Bundle of Emigrants' Letters', 30 Mar. 1850; Mrs Chisholm and R. H. Horne, 'Pictures of Life in Australia', 22 June 1850; S. Sidney, 'Family Colonisation Loan Society', 24 Aug. 1850; ——, 'Two Scenes in the Life of John Bodger', 15 Feb. 1851; ——, 'Three Colonial Epochs', 31 Jan. 1852; ——, 'Better Ties than Red Tape Ties', 28 Feb. 1852; ——, 'What to Take to Australia', 3 July 1852; 'W. H. Wills, 'Safety for Female Emigrants', 31 May 1851; ——, 'Official Emigration', 1 May 1852.

Kennedy, George E., 'Women Redeemed: Dickens's Fallen Women', *The Dickensian*, 74 (Jan. 1978), 42–7.

Orton, Diana, *Made of Gold: A Biography of Angela Burdett Coutts* (London: Hamish Hamilton, 1980).

Payne, Edward F., and Henry H. Harper, *The Charity of Charles Dickens* (Boston: Bibliophile Society, 1929).

Smith, Albert Richard, 'Rogues' Walk', *Household Words*, 12 Sep. 1857.

CAPITAL PUNISHMENT AND CRIME

All the Year Round CD contributed the following articles on crime and criminal justice: 'Five New Points of Criminal Law', 24 Sep. 1859, 'The Ruffian', 10 Oct. 1868, and 'On an Amateur Beat', 27 Feb. 1869. Other unsigned essays dealing with various aspects of crime in *AYR* include: 'Of Right Mind', 22 Sep. 1860; 'Incorrigible Rogues', 8 Feb. 1862; 'M.D. and M.A.D.', 22 Feb. 1862; 'Small-Beer Chronicles' [Transportation], 11 Oct. 1862; [Garotting], 6 Dec. 1862; [The Convict System], 10 Jan. 1863; 'Home-Office Inspiration', 24 Jan. 1863; 'Street Terrors', 14 Feb. 1863; 'Fat Convicts', 25 Mar. 1865; 'Rough Doings', 23 Nov. 1867; 'Now', 15 Aug. 1868; and 'Injured Innocents', 3 Apr. 1869.

Borowitz, Albert, *The Woman Who Murdered Black Satin: The Bermondsey Horror* (Columbus: Ohio State Univ. Press, 1981).

Brice, Alec W., and K. J. Fielding, 'On Murder and Detection – New Articles by Dickens', *Dickens Studies*, 5 (May 1969), 45–61.

Carlyle, Thomas, 'Model Prisons', in his *Latter-Day Pamphlets* (1850) (repr. London: Chapman and Hall, 1870).

Collins, Philip, *Dickens and Crime* (London: Macmillan, 1962).

Cooper, David, *The Lesson of the Scaffold: The Public Execution Controversy in Victorian England* (Athens: Ohio Univ. Press, 1974).

Davies, James Atterbury, 'John Forster at the Mannings' Execution', *The Dickensian*, 67 (Jan. 1971), 12–5.

Dickens, Charles, 'A Visit to Newgate', *Sketches by Boz* [1836].

Garner, Jim, 'Harvard's Clue to The Mystery of Edwin Drood', *Harvard Magazine*, Jan.–Feb. 1983, pp 44–8.

Household Words For CD's comments on the psychology of criminals and on prison discipline, see: 'Perfect Felicity. In a Bird's Eye View', 6 Apr. 1850; 'Pet Prisoners', 27 Apr. 1850; 'The Finishing Schoolmaster', 17 May 1851; 'The Demeanour of Murderers', 14 June 1856; 'The Murdered Person', 11 Oct. 1856; and 'Murderous Extremes', 3 Jan. 1857. Of related interest are CD's 'On Duty with Inspector Field', 14 June 1851; 'Down with the Tide', 5 Feb. 1853; and, with W. H. Wills, 'The Metropolitan Protectives', 26 Apr. 1851. See also in *HW*: W. H. Wills, 'The Great Penal Experiments', 8 June 1850; G. A. Sala, 'Open-Air Entertainments', 8 May 1852; and E. S. Dixon, 'To Hang or Not to Hang', 4 Aug. 1855.

Irving, H. B. (ed.) *Trial of Franz Müller* (Edinburgh: William Hodge, n.d.).

Parry, Leonard A. (ed.) *Trial of Dr. Smethurst* (Edinburgh: William Hodge, 1931).

Radzinowicz, Leon, *A History of English Criminal Law and its Administration from 1750*, vol. IV (London: Stevens, 1968).

[Thackeray, William Makepeace], 'Going to See a Man Hanged', *Fraser's Magazine*, 22 (Aug. 1840), 150–8.

Tillotson, Kathleen, 'A Letter from Dickens on Capital Punishment', *TLS*, 12 Aug. 1965, p. 704.

PARLIAMENT AND SELF-HELP

House, Humphry, *The Dickens World* (1941); (repr. London: Oxford Univ. Press, 1960).

Household Words The following essays by CD expose various aspects of Parliamentary inefficiency: 'Legal and Equitable Jokes', 23 Sep. 1854; 'Mr. Bull's Somnambulist', 25 Nov. 1854; 'That Other Public', 3 Feb. 1855; 'Supposing', 10 Feb. 1855; 'Prince Bull. A Fairy Tale', 17 Feb. 1855; 'Gone to the Dogs', 10 Mar. 1855; 'Fast and Loose', 24 Mar. 1855; 'The Thousand and One Humbugs' (i), 21 Apr. 1855; (ii), 29 Apr.; (iii), 5 May; 'The Toady Tree', 26 May 1855; 'Cheap Patriotism', 9 June 1855, 'Our Commission', 11 Aug. 1855; 'A Slight Depreciation of the Currency', 3 Nov. 1855; 'Proposals for a National Jest-Book', 3 May 1856; 'Nobody, Somebody, and Everybody', 30 Aug. 1856.

Kettle, Arnold, 'Dickens and the Popular Tradition', in *Marxists on Literature: An Anthology* (ed.) David Craig (Harmondsworth: Penguin, 1975).

Lohrli, Anne (comp.) *Household Words ... Table of Contents, List of Contributors and their Contributions* (Toronto: Univ. of Toronto Press, 1973).

Shelden, Michael, 'Dickens, *The Chimes*, and the Anti-Corn Law League', *Victorian Studies*, 25 (Spring 1982), 329–53.

[Stephen, James Fitzgerald.] 'Mr. Dickens as a Politician', *Saturday Review*, vol. III (3 Jan. 1857), 8–9.

Part III: THE PROFESSION

Blount, Trevor, 'Dickens and Mr. Krook's Spontaneous Combustion', *Dickens Studies Annual*, 1 (1970), 183–211.

Butt, John, and Kathleen Tillotson, *Dickens at Work* (1957); (repr. London: Methuen, 1968).

Collins, Philip (ed.) *Dickens: The Critical Heritage* (London: Routledge and Kegan Paul, 1971).

Fielding, K. J., and A. W. Brice, '*Bleak House* and the Graveyard', *Dickens The Craftsman: Strategies of Presentation* (ed.) Robert B. Partlow, Jr. (Carbondale: Southern Illinois Univ. Press, 1970).

Gardner, John, 'Moral Fiction', *The Hudson Review*, 29 (Winter 1976–7), 497–512.

Gaskell, E., 'More About Spontaneous Combustion', *The Dickensian*, 69 (Jan. 1973), 25–35.

McMaster, Rowland D., 'Dickens and the Horrific', *Dalhousie Review*, 38 (Spring 1958), 18–28.

Orwell, George, 'Charles Dickens', *Inside the Whale* (London: Gollancz, 1940).

Perkins, George, 'Death by Spontaneous Combustion in Marryat, Melville, Dickens, Zola and Others', *The Dickensian*, 60 (Jan. 1964), 57–63.

Reade, Charles, 'The Prurient Prude', *New York Times*, 6 Oct. 1866, p. 5.

——. For hostile reviews of *Griffith Gaunt*, see 'Library Table', *The Round Table*, 3, 9 June 1866, and 'An Indecent Publication', *The Round Table*, 3,

28 July 1866. See also further comments in *The Round Table* on 11 Aug. and 15 Oct. 1856.

——. For details of Reade's suit against the editors of *The Round Table*, see the *New York Times*, 16 Feb. 1867, p. 4; 27 Feb. 1869, p. 8; 2 Mar., p. 5; 3 Mar., p. 2; 4 Mar., p. 2, and 5 Mar. p. 4.

Wiley, Elizabeth, 'Four strange Cases', [Spontaneous combustion] *The Dickensian*, 58 (May 1962), 120–5.

Wilkinson, Ann Y., '*Bleak House*: From Faraday to Judgment Day', *English Literary History*, 34 (June 1967), 225–47.

Wilson, Edmund, 'Dickens: The Two Scrooges', *The Wound and the Bow: Seven Studies in Literature* (1941); (repr. London: Methuen, 1961).

Index of Correspondents

General Index

Dickens's works (novels, sketches, essays, etc.) are indexed under their titles.